WOMEN
as
WIDOWS

Widows

WOMEN
as
WIDOWS
Support Systems

HELENA ZNANIECKA LOPATA

Loyola University of Chicago

Elsevier · New York
NEW YORK · OXFORD

Exclusive Distribution
throughout the World by
Greenwood Press, Westport,
Ct. U.S.A.

ELSEVIER NORTH HOLLAND, INC.
52 Vanderbilt Avenue, New York, New York 10017

Distributors outside the United States and Canada:
THOMOND BOOKS
(A Division of Elsevier/North-Holland
Scientific Publishers, Ltd.)
P.O. Box 85
Limerick, Ireland

Library of Congress Cataloging in Publication Data

Lopata, Helena Znaniecki, 1925-
    Women as widows: support systems

    Bibliography: p.
    Includes index.
    1. Widows.   2. Widows—Illinois—Chicago—Case
studies.   I. Title.
HQ1058.L66   301.42'86   78-21255
ISBN 0-444-99053-4
LIST OF TABLES

Manufactured in the United States of America

Designed by Loretta Li

Dedicated to Richard

Contents

Preface

The purpose of this book is to present to the student, the professional and other interested readers the results of eight years of reading, research and writing about widows—in particular about women in the metropolitan Chicago area who became, many of whom still are, widows. The research began when the Administration on Aging funded my proposal to study a sample of 300 widows, 50 years of age or older, living in the Chicago Standard Metropolitan Statistical Area. I was then teaching at Roosevelt University in downtown Chicago and finishing a study of housewives with at least one pre-high-school child. The results of that research are summarized in *Occupation: Housewife* (Oxford University Press, 1971). It was that study which led me to an interest: What happens to women, whether working for pay outside of the home or full-time housewives, in the "shrinking circle" stage of their life course after the children have left home and the husband has died. The older widow study was built upon the concept of social role. The book which is a report of it, *Widowhood in an American City*, traces what happens with the role of wife, mother, sister, participant in the kinship network, friend, neighbor, worker and member of the community in widowhood. What does happen to these roles is a result not merely of changes introduced by the death of the husband and subsequent events, but also of voluntaristic decisions of the widow and of others in her social circles. The interview also contained a self-administered "relations-restricting attitude scale," based on the awareness that the attitudes of people toward their environment can restrict their relations with others.

On completion of the role-modification study of older widows, I was asked by the Social Security Administration whether I had sociologically and societally interesting questions about widowhood that remained unanswered or had surfaced as a result of the prior research. I doubt that there are many social scientists who would have answered in the negative, especially when the subject is as much "understudied" as this one. I thereupon embarked on a new project, with a contract from the Social Security Administration and the cooperation of Dr. Henry Brehm, Director of Research Grants and Contracts, and staff member of the Division of Retirement and Survivor Studies, Office of Research and Statistics. Other staff members who provided special assistance were Drs. Lenore Bixby and Lola Ireland. The theoretical framework of this study focuses upon the support systems of widows in urbanizing centers; the interview benefited from discussions with Drs. Adam Kurzynowski of the Szkola Glowna Planowania i Statystyki, Warsaw, Poland; Jerzy Piotrowski, then of the Instytut Gospodarstwa Spolecznego, Warsaw, Poland; and Dr. Nada Smolic Krkovic and her staff of the Institute of Social Work in Zagreb, Yugoslavia. Although it became impossible for the Polish and Yugoslav teams to undertake comparative research for a variety of reasons, Dr. Brehm and I had discussed the study with other researchers, which resulted in the use of its instruments as a basis for a study of widows in Tehran, Iran, by Dr. Jacqueline Touba, and in Cairo, Egypt, by Dr. Nawal Nadim. The support systems study focuses upon the societal, community and personal resources available to every woman who is or has been a widow and seeks to establish how she utilizes these resources in building her economic, service, social and emotional support systems.

Many people were involved in both studies of women as widows, either directly working with me or as contributors to my knowledge, formally or informally. Early in the research, while I was hesitating over approaching women with questions about the traumatic events connected with their being or becoming widows, psychiatrists Eric Lindemann and David Maddison, sociologists Robert Fulton and Robert Weiss and psychologist Phyllis Silverman reassured me that women do not hesitate to talk about their experiences; in fact, one of the problems of modern American life is that they do not get the opportunity, although they do need to review them to complete their "grief work." These scholars are part of a small handful of social scientists who have studied the process of grief work in a society which, until recent years, has not dealt with it, or with other death-related subjects. Jessie Gertman and Marvin Taves at the Administration on Aging provided encouragement and information. The various seminars of students and faculty connected with the Midwest Council for Social Research on Aging helped clarify my ideas and "listened" as I went through the painful and joyful stages of the research process. Colleagues at Loyola University of Chicago, where I was at this time, have discussed segments and aspects of the study, including Bill Bates (with whom I have long debates on the concept of sanctification), Tom Gannon, Bob McNamara, and Kathy Norr. Ethel Shanas, Bernice Neugarten and the late Robert Winch were very helpful consultants in the role-modification study. Many people have moved through the Center for the Comparative Study of Social Roles in a variety of capacities, and special thanks are due to Terry Baumer, Sister Gertrud Kim, Suzanne Meyering, Marlene Simon and Frank Steinhart. Monica Velasco, Deb Burdeno, Sue Dawson, Rob Dickerson, Caryl Kumbalek, Lucille McGill, Pam Rose and Mary Sherwood all helped prepare the reams of manuscript generated by the two studies. As usual, my family, including my mother, Eileen Markley Znaniecki, my mother-in-law, Helen Lopata-Scott-Burns, my husband Richard and my children, Stefan and Teddy deserve thanks for their assistance. Both mothers had personally experienced widowhood.

Special thanks go to Gloria Heinemann and the rest of the staff of the Survey Research Laboratory of the University of Illinois, who conducted the fieldwork and cooperated in other stages of the work.

List of Tables

I

WIDOWHOOD

O N E

Widowhood, Other Places, Other Times and in America

Theoretical Perspectives

This book examines the social integration and support systems involving one particular member of modern, urban American society; the woman who has become a widow. Widowhood generally disorganizes prior supports and social engagements of human beings and often necessitates the modification of old, even the forming of new, social relations and social roles, or a constriction of social life spaces. The forms of integration available to or forced on a woman who is widowed reflect the social structure and culture of the society and of the community in which she lives.

People are integrated into their community and the wider society through a complex of support systems, interactional sequences and social relations, which combine to form social roles (Goffman, 1967; Lopata, 1973a; Rosow, 1973; Znaniecki, 1965). They may be located geographically in specific dwellings, alone or with other people, at given distances from other units, on a farm, in a village or a neighborhood of a larger community. They may be located socially in the consciousness of others as they move through space and interact, fleetingly or over many years, with the social circles of their social roles and groups. They are able to maintain themselves in this envi-

3

ronment with the help of a variety of objects or actions which provide supports in daily life or unusual situations. A support is an action or object which the society generally defines as necessary or helpful in maintaining a style of life of a category of its members. A support system is a set of similar supportive actions or objects involved in social interaction. A support network encompasses the people with whom a person is involved in supportive interaction. Here we are focusing upon the support systems and networks of American metropolitan widows.

New members enter a society and a supportive network through birth, voluntary or involuntary migration, or the expansion of its political and social boundaries. All societies are so organized as to insure the flow of supports necessary for the survival of new members deemed worthy of survival until they are able to develop their own support systems. As children grow into adulthood and as foreign residents learn to function in the host culture and community, they are expected to develop, more or less voluntaristically, personal support systems, involving the exchange of objects or actions defined as necessary, or, at least, helpful in maintaining their style of life. Those unable to carry their share in the maintenance systems are either "cared for" by other people or fulfill other functions for the group. Support exchanges are not necessarily (in fact, they are not usually) expected to be symmetrical in either content or flow. People receive more of certain types of supports or more support from some of their associates than they give in return. Most adult children in America, for instance, do not contribute to the supports of their elderly parents as much as parents contributed to those of their children when the latter were establishing their households.

Since society and the person change their definitions of needs and resources to meet these needs, support systems must remain flexible. Crises are situations that the person and her or his associates define as requiring a heavy contribution

4

of supportive actions and objects. Social and individual problems develop when a person and her or his associates differ as to the support each needs and as to the best way of meeting these needs. Of course, conflict between expectations and reality can be a problem in all social interaction, but it becomes more acute in situations where a person sees them critical enough to warrant special attention. That is often the case with persons recovering from a shattering experience, such as the loss of a significant other. Problems with support systems can also arise when changes in outlook or disorganizing events in one's life make past supports and the way they are organized seem unsatisfactory or dysfunctional. Thus, a woman or a man who has lost a spouse must usually reorganize her or his former support system. Finally, problems with support exchanges can arise if the person is seen by associates as somehow different or unable to participate "normally" in conventional interaction. This is especially likely to occur in the case of divorced or widowed women or men in a society such as ours, which favors the marital state as the norm of all adults.

Support systems of any person at any stage of the life-span can be almost automatically engaging, embedded in a limited number of social roles. A person is born into a family and, if most of the institutionalized spheres of life—its educational, economic, political, religious and recreational activities—are performed within it, she or he can continue within the family until death. In most societies some members leave the family of orientation in which they were born to join the family of the chosen husband or wife—or else to create their own family of procreation, relatively independent of the families of orientation of either spouse. It is the thesis here that modern, urbanized and industrialized societies, especially America, have created a social system in which social engagement and support systems are decreasingly assigned at birth for life, decreasingly automatically guaranteed and increasingly dependent on voluntaristic individual action. We are aware of this need for voluntaristic analysis of personal needs, resources and plans of action on the part of young people choosing a school, a mate, a job, a residence. Sociologists are now becoming more interested in what happens when the social engagement and support systems of Americans become dramatically changed through retirement (Streib & Schneider, 1971; Atchley, 1975; Orbach and Friedman, 1974) and divorce (Goode, 1956; Kitson and Sussman, 1977). The consequences of the sudden break in past relations and the social life spaces available to, and engaged in by, women and men, who are widowed, are also gaining attention (Berardo, 1967, 1968; Marris, 1958; Glick, Weiss and Parkes, 1974; Lopata, 1973a).

There are several cogent reasons for limiting this book to women who are widows in urban America. In the first place, the position and social integration of different kinds of women who are widows reflect the social system within which they live. Variations and changes in the lives of these women are indicative of the structure and changes in the larger system. Most past societies were patriarchal, patrilineal and often patrilocal; but urbanization, industrialization, mobility and increased societal complexity have changed the basic family unit and the relation of each member to other members and to the community at large (Winch and Blumberg, 1968). This is particularly true of urban America because of the rapid expansion of the country, the fact that so many of its members come from migrant families, the strong emphasis on the economic institution, egalitarianism and mass education, plus many other features, making this a unique society. The life-styles of men, let alone women, have changed dramatically in recent decades and these changes are reflected in the social engagement and support systems of urban widows. In sociological terms, the changes in the macrosystem are evident in the microsystem of the social life space of different kinds of widows.

6

The support systems of men also undergo disorganization with the death of their wives, particularly in our "person-oriented" form of marriage and our focus upon the nuclear family in its own housing unit. In fact, several social scientists (Berardo, 1968, 1970; Bernard, 1973) find that widowers exhibit more severe symptoms of disorganization than do widows. They have higher rates of suicide, physical illness, mental illness requiring treatment, alcoholism, automobile and work-related accidents, etc. *U.S. News and World Report* documented these facts in 1974. However, because of my research on women (see *Occupation: Housewife*, 1971a, *Widowhood in an American City*, 1973a, and articles listed in the Bibliography), the study that forms the major base of this book focuses on the lives of widows and on the factors affecting diversity in these lives, rather than on a comparison between widows as a group and widowers. An incidental reason for studying widows is their greater number and their lesser tendency to remarry; thus, the greater ease to locate them. In addition, the dependence of women in America on a husband as bread-winner, father to their children and escort, which evolved since urbanization and industrialization, leads a researcher to the easy assumption that widows have more problems that need study than widowers, despite indications to the contrary. Americans tend to view widows as problem-ridden and the societies that gave birth to this view have tended to shy away from widowed women. This combination of reasons makes the focus of this book. It is our hope that members of this society and scientists interested in the family, in women, in the elderly, in adult socialization, in death and dying and in related subjects will also find the topic of women as widows of interest.

7

Wives and Widows: General Trends

A review of mainly anthropological literature on societal and family systems in a variety of societies points to four sets of factors that influence the social integration and support systems of widows.[1] The first of these is the society itself, its structure, composition and culture. Modern, complex cultures offer a variety of resources for social engagement in the form of personal relations, social groups and problem-solving agencies that any person can use to build a role cluster. The social life space within which the relations and roles of a person are located can be concentrated in one institution, as in the case of a priest or someone focused upon the family or it can be multidimensional, as in the case of a widowed mother who is also a worker, a member of a union, a friend, an active neighbor, a churchgoer and so forth. Different social classes make available or constrict the social roles available to wives or widows. Cultural prescriptions or proscriptions influence women in the actions and roles they deem appropriate, or worthy, at the different stages of the life course. The social system establishes status positions for men and women and for wives and widows, surrounding them with duties and rights that contribute to their supports or to a failure of potential resources. The population composition of a society often determines the availability of social roles; for example, making remarriage difficult for middle-aged and older widows if they outnumber men of their own age or older in a society where most men marry younger women.

The community within which women are located, whether Chicago or a town in North Dakota, also plays a role in delineating the status of the wife or widow. Not all aspects of the societal and cultural systems are available as resources in every community.

8

The society's most relevant cultural domain—the institution of the family, including mate selection, the nature of the marriage, parental roles, and the manner in which the marital unit is embedded in a larger kin network and in other social units—influences both wifehood and widowhood. The marriage contract varies considerably from one society to another. Inheritance rules, rights of women to property and to mobility strongly affect the ability of a wife and a widow to create their support systems.

Finally, the woman's personal resources affect the manner in which she utilizes societal resources within the constraints and the facilitating circumstances of her position in the larger system and in the family. Personal resources include people and groups with which she is associated, such as parents or children, as well as her abilities and personal stance vis-à-vis people, social groups, the community and the society at large. In modern urban America these abilities are usually developed early in life in a more or less urbanized home which is able to instill knowledge and skills, self-confidence, self-esteem and competence, a breadth of perspective and intellectual aptitude for abstract planning (Warshay, 1962). These abilities are expanded through a system of formal schooling, providing not only content but training in the solution of problems and the marshalling of resources for long-range planning. Experience in other societal systems, such as work organizations and adult socialization, is generally needed to broaden the framework in which new social roles and relations can be entered when past support systems are made dysfunctional by voluntary changes such as marriage, or by unplanned events such as the death of a spouse.

Other characteristics that affect the lives of widows include age at marriage, age at widowhood and the presence, affiliation, ages and role clusters of children. Circumstances surrounding the death of the spouse, income and other economic resources, housing and its location in the community, the prior role cluster and the needs for change in any component role or the content or structure of this cluster are also influential elements.

The factors bearing upon the social integration of wives and widows include the rights and duties they have or have had in relation not only to their husband, but also to everyone involved in their role of wife during the husband's life and after his death (Znaniecki, 1965). The tendency of human beings to make themselves and each other into social persons, that is, to interact on the basis of images and expectations developed during the socialization process and the experiences of "taking the role of the other," is evident in the influence that a deceased person continues to exert on the interaction of the survivors. Thus, relations of the widow in many, if not most, societies of the world are influenced by the fact that she had been the wife of a particular man who is now dead. His death affects not only her but many others: his parents, siblings and other kin members, his children and other heirs, his debtors and creditors and anyone else who was in any way involved in his social roles or to whose roles he contributed. To understand the support systems of widows in any particular social system, we must look at the common set of rights and duties of marital roles and of widowhood before illustrating these general trends in specific social systems.

All societies known to us through anthropological or historical research have clearly defined, albeit with numerous exceptions, the basic rights and duties of wives and husbands. Since the majority of these social systems throughout history have been patriarchal, patrilineal and patrilocal, it is not surprising that Paul Bohannan (1963) outlines only the rights of husbands (Murdock, 1949). The families in which these rights operate contain a male authority line headed by the eldest male unless he has retired and passed the responsibility on to his inheriting son. The family name and property are transmitted down the male line (Sussman, Cates and Smith, 1970). The strongest exercise of the rights of the husband is found in situations that are also patrilocal, in that the wife leaves her family at a given stage of the marriage ritual and joins the family of her husband, who then insists that she meet her obligations. The rights of a husband are not claimed uniformly in all of the world's patriarchal families, with consequent differences in the rights and freedom of the respective wives. The social structure of families, including patriarchal ones, obviously affects the rights, duties, exchanges and support systems. History has known few social roles and methods of self-maintenance of individual members outside of family groups.

Patriarchal, patrilineal and patrilocal families recruit wives for their sons through careful matchmaking, ensuring the best arrangement for the new unit, as well as for the families of both the future husband and wife. The man's relatives either provide him with the price to be paid to the bride's family to compensate for the loss of her services or childbearing potential—or else the woman's family provides a dowry to help set up housekeeping. The bride's status in her husband's family unit depends on the status of her family, the valued qualities she brings with her and the position of her husband. Bohannan (1963) finds that patriarchal societies grant certain rights to the husband "in the woman" on marriage. These include the right of sharing a domicile, whether a room in an extended or joint family household, a rented or owned home or any other dwelling. This unit is maintained with the help of an institutionalized division of labor. The right of sexual access to the wife is universal—in the past mainly due to the strong desire by the male line to continue it for future generations. The third clearly defined right in these kinds of families is that of *in genetricem* filiation to his line of all children to which the husband is social father. This means that the children do not legally or normatively belong to the wife and that she cannot take them away should she choose to leave her husband, even after his death. The final set of rights mentioned by Bohannan, which varies considerably from society to society, is that to economic goods that the bride brings, which she and her hus-

11

band produce together, or which she gains through independent efforts. Barbara Ward (1963) and William Goode (1963) point out that the status of women in a society is both reflected in, and a reflection of, their economic rights.

What Bohannan (1963) does not discuss, because of the predominance of patriarchal societies, although it is apparent from the above, are the rights acquired by women on marriage. In such societies, the wife has the right to a domicile provided by the man or his family. She has the right to have her husband carry out the duties that fall into his domain in the division of labor. Sexual access is a masculine concept, and many societies insist that women engage in sexual intercourse only for the sake of procreation (not for pleasure) and only with the "legitimate" father, but the wife does have the right to expect impregnation by her husband. This is particularly true of societies that demand that she become a mother and value her positively only after she has produced children, especially sons. Even in societies or class situations in which the mother does not actually rear her children, she is expected to supervise their care and socialization so that they may take their rightful place in the father's family. In this, she usually is given the help of that family. Thus, the wife has the universal right to have her husband acknowledge the children she bears as biologically or at least socially his, unless proven otherwise, and to perform the role of father with all its filiation duties. The filiation leads not only to the activation of many kinship roles— as grandchildren, nieces and nephews, grandparents, aunts and uncles, and so forth—but also to guarantees of the proper arrangements for marriage and for inheritance when so designated. The sons the woman bears for the family line may expect to have available to them a sequence of hierarchal steps up the authority ladder, the inheritance of both status and property as they come in line of inheritance. Many reports, historical and literary, tell of a mother's insistence on the benefits her children are entitled to because of their filiation to the father's line of descent. Finally, the wife can expect to be either part of a production and consumption unit, or economically supported if she is not allowed to contribute directly to her economic support. The economic rights extend to her children. If she is not to produce their necessities or contribute directly to the process, then she has the right to their economic support by her husband and/or his family.

The structure of the extended lineal group and its power over each nuclear unit strongly affect what happens to the survivors when a major member of the line dies. The social roles and relations available to the survivors depend on who they are and how they are integrated into the larger social unit. In the patriarchal past of most societies, the fate of the widower has not usually been as disorienting as that of the widow. Most of the literature on widowers deals with procedures for remarriage. The man remains with his family line, simply replacing his former partner with another woman. Often the marital relation is not seen as the primary consideration. Widows have chosen or been assigned many different life-styles, depending on the factors just discussed. Some of these are exemplified in the literature, describing marriage and widowhood in past times or in societies other than modern, urban America.

Comparative Perspectives

The roles and life-styles available to widows in the past, and in some cases even today, have largely depended on the main contribution their communities expected them to make after the death of the husband (Lopata, 1972). In certain societies the greatest service a woman could render was self-immolation on the funeral pyre of her husband so she could continue to attend him in afterlife (Dube, 1963; Sarasvati, 1888). "The practice was voluntary, but instances are cited which indicate that social pressures forced many women to follow it" (Ward, 1963, p. 187). Self-immolation was especially favored for the wives

13

of kings. "Junior queens had to have separate pyres, and rights of seniority helped panels decide who was burned where" (Thomas, 1964, p. 293). "Widows past child-bearing age, pregnant women and mothers with infants-in-arms were not permitted to die with their husbands" (p. 294). Self-immolation was generally not practiced by middle- and lower-caste Indian women, for these households could not afford the loss of two workers. However, many communities in this subcontinent forbade the remarriage of widows and treated them demeaningly, particularly the childless widow. In some districts her head was shaved and religious codes demanded that she be deprived of attractive clothing and ornaments, forced to lead a secluded, sheltered life (Felton, 1966).[2] In fact, many other groups have forced or encouraged widows to wear distinctive attire for the rest of their lives—clothing that stigmatized them or made them unattractive and stereotyped. Such physical restrictions are usually aimed at preventing them from becoming sexually attractive to men outside of the husband's family, averting the possible birth of offspring who could not be filiated with the family line.

However, many societies, interested in having their women bear children as long as biologically possible, have developed a variety of arrangements to safeguard this contribution to the male family line. The most frequent of these solutions that involve a widow of childbearing age are remarriage and the levirate system (Lopata, 1972, 1973a, 1977; Goode, 1963; Bohannan, 1963). In strongly patrilineal families allowing remarriage, the widow may be required to marry a male agnate— that is, a male relative of her late husband, or else her new husband must be a part of her former husband's family. The children born of this new union must, of course, be filiated with the line of the late husband if the woman and her children by the prior marriage continue as part of it. Such an arrangement is most frequently found in societies that allow polygyny—the marriage of a man to more than one wife. Thus, one of the brothers (usually a younger one) marries the widow as either his first or later wife (Goode, 1963; Thomas, 1964). An alternative to widow remarriage is the levirate system, by which a male agnate of the deceased "enters the hut" of the widow to "raise up the seed" of the late husband, who remains the social father of any children the widow bears after his death (Bohannan, 1963). Bohannan stresses the differences between widow remarriage in which the man undertakes all the duties and rights of a husband and the levirate relation in which only sexual and sometimes economic exchanges take place. Evans-Pritchard (1956, pp. 163 and 113) found other variations on the theme among the Nuer in Africa.

> Widows are neither remarried nor inherited but continue till death to be married to their dead husbands to whose names they continue to bear children begotten by their dead husbands' brothers, with whom they have in certain circumstances an obligation to live. . . . The custom of ghost-marriage further ensures that every man must have a son who will be called after him. . . . Leviratic marriage is very different from ghost-marriage. In a ghost-marriage the vicarious husband actually marries the wife in the sense that he pays the cattle and performs the rites of marriage, even though in the name of another. In leviratic marriage the legal husband has performed these actions himself and the brother merely enters as pro-husband of a family already in being. The widow is always referred to as the wife of the dead man and not as the pro-husband's wife, as she generally is in ghost-marriage.

Bohannan does not consider the relation just described as leviratic marriage *to be* a marriage.

Although foreign to American marriage customs, widow remarriage or levirate relations without choice are not unusual in societies in which the initial marriage was arranged. In addition, such arrangements benefit the woman, because to varying degrees they ensure her continued membership in the family unit with all of its support exchanges, as well as services. In addition, most women in many such societies want children, especially sons, because their presence guarantees care by the extended family and, when they are grown, by the

15

sons. In fact, in patrilineal families the women are often not allowed to inherit property, so that their maintenance, as well as that of any children who are not heirs, is dependent on close affiliation with the inheritance line. Of course, these, as well as the preceding comments, refer only to patriarchal, patrilineal and patrilocal families in which the women cannot maintain themselves economically outside a family group. The same is true of men in these kinds of societies in which subsistence was, or is, minimal and dependent on the efforts of more than one person.

An example of the complications of life connected with a strict male inheritance pattern is in traditional Albania (Durham, 1928). "In a country where the rate of death by violence reaches the level of 40 percent of all male deaths in some localities and where girls are married at 14 or 15, many are widowed" (p. 25a). The life style of the widow is dependent on her parental status. She may remain in the home and with the zadruga if she has sons. "Such a widow must be cared for by the men of her husband's family, since they have paid for her and she has joined their group" (p. 74). She can enter a levirate relation or marry as the second wife of an agnate of her late husband. "If she had a son who predeceased his father," she can negotiate her continued residence in her home. If it is small, she can usually remain; if it is large, she becomes a "member of the heir's household so long as she is unmarried" (p. 74). If she has a daughter but no sons, "she has the right to remain a hundred days in the home. Then, if the heirs order her to leave, she must go, but her daughter remains as part of the heir's household and he has the right to choose her husband and dispose of her." Finally, if she has no children, or if the heirs are willing, she may return to her father's home, but "the heir or heirs must supply her regularly with wool for spinning, bread, cheese, and other necessities so long as she remains unmarried" (p. 74).

Even when the widow is technically allowed to leave her husband's family and remarry, that unit may discourage her departure. Both Fortune (1935) and Mead (1930) describe the Manus attitude toward widow remarriage.

> Her husband's heir and financiers interested in her alone profess a moral horror at the idea of her remarriage, because meanwhile she works for them. And if she leaves them her children are left motherless with them. The children should stay with the patrilineal gens of their fathers. It's felt advisable that a widow should stay with her children and work for those who will be most intimately concerned with her children in the future (Fortune, 1935, p. 338).

The basic reason for the community's unwillingness to allow a widow to remarry is a religious one.

> Ghosts of former moral husbands are believed to punish remarriage of widows as drastically as Sir Ghosts punish sexual misconduct or non-payment of economic obligations. Unfortunately, for steadfast perpetual widowhood, ghosts are not believed to punish the remarriage of widowers equivalently (p. 338).

The woman who has met her obligation to her community and to her husband's family by giving birth to and mothering a son in a society interested in line descent frequently benefits enormously when the son matures and can return some of the supports. This pattern is in evidence in many societies but traditional China and India are ideal-typical examples. The older widow in traditional southeastern China wielded a great deal of power over her family (Freedman, 1965; Ross, 1961). In fact, she controlled the work of her daughter-in-law. The situation of a new bride, practically sold by her family to the husband's group was not easy, as evidenced by the suicide rate of women in that situation. However, as the women produced sons, grew older and became widows, their power increased. Widow inheritance and remarriage were discouraged, but the widowed women could control their sons and daughters-in-law, as well as their grandchildren. The same situation, with less formal power but greater affectionate ties, existed in traditional India.

> Mother-son relations were most often stressed as being of love and affection more than any other, including husband and wife which were seldom mentioned and, when they were, were spoken of as entailing dislike and hatred as well as affection (Ross, 1961, p. 97).

The mother is left in an advantageous position when her son takes over the management of the household after the father dies. At that time "his mother might retain the authority over the household, particularly if she was very close to her son or her daughter-in-law was not old enough or could not stand up for herself" (p. 57). In general, old age in traditional societies brings rewards in the form of increased status, less work, and fewer behavioral restrictions. One of the authors abstracted in the *Human Relations Area Files* states that, the position of a mother-in-law is often quite comfortable (Schram, 1954). In deference to their age, older widows, even if not managing a household, were given adequate supports as rewards for prior contributions (Cowgill and Holmes, 1972; Rosow, 1973). Once a widow reaches menopause and the worry of impregnation by "the wrong man" is removed, she, particularly if she has proved herself through the lives of her sons, is often allowed great freedom of movement, even in societies that restrict the sphere of younger women. Such, for example, is the case of the women who market their goods in western Africa (Huntington, 1975).

All in all, the degree of disorganization brought on by the death of a husband and the forms of reengagement of the widow, varied according to several factors. Each of these societies provided several alternatives that depended on the age and the motherhood status of the widow. These included: remaining with the late husband's family and remarriage to a male agnate of the deceased or acceptance of a levir or a quardian; remaining with the late husband's family, with a son taking over the management of the household; or returning to the home of her family to start again or to fulfill some other functions in that unit. It was not until societies commenced to develop larger settlements that social roles outside of familial ones were opened for women, enabling them to maintain themselves after the death of the husband. A major change also occurred in their lives with the breaking of the power of the male family line. Modern urban and industrialized societies have dramatically expanded the choices and alternatives of widowed women.

Historical Perspectives: Europe

We move now to the European societies that laid the foundation of modern American social structure and culture where we find many revolutionary changes since the 17th century, which had a great impact upon the lives of wives and widows. The legal position of women in continental Europe had been gradually deteriorating from the early Middle Ages. Herlihy (1976, p. 24) found "that the woman during the Middle Ages everywhere had always had some importance in the management of the household economy." The Crusades and other wars took men away from their property, leaving their wives in charge of the whole economy. (They had managed the "inner" economy even when the men were home.) In many cases widows could inherit. The Middle Ages allowed women a public life and an involvement not only in agriculture but in other occupations. "Women's membership in artisan guilds, which were on occasion exclusively filled with women, depended upon the social right to participate in public life" (Stuard, 1976, p. 5). Philippe Aries (1965, p. 355) emphasizes the same point. "We know too that from the end of the Middle Ages on, the power of the wife steadily diminishes. She loses the concept of joint ownership." He quotes the comment of a M. Petiot on this subject:

19

Starting in the fourteenth century, we see a slow and steady deterioration of the wife's position in the household. She loses the right to take the place of the husband in his absence or insanity. . . . Finally, in the sixteenth century, the married woman is placed under a disability so that any acts she performs without the authority of her husband or the law are null and void. This development strengthens the powers of the husband, who is finally established as a sort of domestic monarch (p. 356).

However, Ann Oakley (1975) found English town-women active in a variety of guilds and occupations as late as the 18th century. Wives helped their craftsmen husbands and took over the occupation and the business after their death and even had apprentices working under them (Laslett, 1973). This was true, even though, as Kate Millett (1970, p. 67) points out, British common law places "the married woman in the position both of minor and chattel throughout her life," adding that actually a widow was better off because she was more independent. Several trends in the family life helped to keep women's rights highly restricted. In addition, societal changes brought on by the growth of capitalism and industrialism actually contributed to the removal of the married woman from public life and her isolation in a small unit household. This development removed the family from complex social interaction to a more private life.

Although medieval Europe had cities (usually built around princely courts, trading or other congregating activities), most families still lived in villages or manor homes. As Aries (1965) concludes from the examination of pre-18th century art, life was quite public in all these locations, as well as in the towns. Much of life was carried on in the streets. People met on the way to shops or fields and conducted business, politics, family and friendship affairs in public. Leisure time was also spent this way, with contacts crossing age, sex and even class lines— as in game-playing, a favorite pastime. Men and women were surrounded by other people at all times—day and night, especially in pleasant weather. The same was true of the manor home, which usually contained many people, as many as 200, who took part in its life, eating, sleeping, conducting business, socializing as part of the "polite companionship" (Znaniecki, 1965) ritual and even gave birth and died in large central rooms. Beds and tables were portable and brought out as required. Both the manor lord and his wife were relatively well-educated, managing their complex households—having been trained in childhood by governesses and tutors.

For both the gentry and the villagers, marriage was not a romantic match but a practical matter—arranged by the families to ensure economic support and children. In neither type of household was the mother the *sole* rearer of children. In fact, after bearing and nursing them, she usually turned them over to other people, as she managed the household and bore *more* offspring. Child mortality until fairly recently was so high that people did not invest much affection in offspring until they had survived several years (Aries, 1965; Shorter, 1975). The apprenticeship system usually involved "the farming out" of young children, and the English ensured the strict socialization of children from the age of seven by sending them as "boys" and "maids," as servants to the homes of other people (Laslett, 1973; Shorter, 1975; Oakley, 1975). Upper-class women often did not even nurse their infants themselves but sent them out to wet-nurses in the village, seeing them occasionally. A major reform movement gained impetus in several countries that urged the mothers to at least bring the wet-nurses into their homes to ensure more frequent contact with their infants and a lower death rate than experienced at that time (Shorter, 1975).

All in all, the life of both women and men in pre-18th century Western Europe was spent in an extensive network of extended family and nonfamilial relations. These were not necessarily pleasant and supportive, but they provided resources for social integration. In societies in which women were not granted full political rights and lacked other than family-transmitted economic supports, widows as a rule could not main-

21

tain themselves on their own, even if they were allowed to, but their contributions to the economic sphere of life made them valuable members of the system. Because of the high death rate of women in childbirth and through disease, there was a scarcity of older widows; hence most of these societies permitted the remarriage of younger ones. One offspring was likely to remain in the parental home, so that the surviving older widows were usually guaranteed care and continued economic and service supports; and friendships, as well as street life, continued to provide social supports.

Aries (1965) attributes the privatization of the family in the late 17th century to the competition between the nuclear family and all other associations of its members for their attention and loyalty and to what he considers the victory of the family. The nuclear unit, consisting of the husband, wife and their pre-adult children, withdrew to homes that had changed in structure—the main hall becoming broken up into many private rooms, cutting off servants from employers, children from parents, and the household from unexpected visitors and other outsiders. Family life became a private affair with definite boundary-maintaining rituals.

The second development that changed the rights of wives and widows was the increasing emphasis on primogeniture, whereby the eldest male child succeeded to the fief (Walker, 1976, p. 160). The male heir, if under age (frequent in societies geared to war) was assigned a guardian other than the mother. The widow inherited her share of the husband's estate or dower. "Dower was usually a cumulative life interest in roughly a third of the husband's feudal estate" (p. 161). The land went to the heir "and the heirs were placed in the familial custody of a relative who could not inherit in the event of the child's death—a grim reminder that improper care of the child might hasten the inheritance" (p. 164). Walker estimates that "many, probably most, heirs were not raised by their widowed mothers." After the heir or heiress (daughters sometimes inherited) had their marriage arranged, at the age of six or seven, they would reside with their future in-laws (p. 161).

The changes within the family norms were not taking place in isolation from changes in the society. Most of the historians of European societies, including those who with the help of demographers are now reexamining the preindustrial household and its composition, have concluded that the pattern of life was changed by two movements: early capitalism and the combination of industrialization and urbanization, which came later. Max Weber (1930), in a massive comparison of social systems and religions, points to the connection between *The Protestant Ethic and the Spirit of Capitalism*. Calvinism saw economic success as proof of divine blessing and its achievement came to dominate the lives of Europeans and, even more so, Americans, once the "boom" began. In a system that was to become known as cottage industries, early capitalists purchased raw material and "put it out" to women working at home (Shorter, 1975; Oakley, 1975; Laslett, 1973). In fact, Shorter reports a quiet revolution among young women who refused to marry the village boys selected for them because of their new economic independence. When, impelled by their desire to standardize production, entrepreneurs set up factories and expanded them with the introduction of steam, the whole family left the home and became involved with organized work for pay. It was not until the mid-19th century that protests against allowing children to work long hours under deplorable conditions resulted in child-labor laws that brought them out of the factories (Oakley, 1975). (The works of contemporary writers, such as Charles Dickens and George Sand, contributed to this reform movement.) Another reason for the expulsion of children from factories was the growing interest of men in these jobs.

The Protestant Reformation, the increasing industrialization and urbanization occurred within the centuries experiencing other complex revolutions, which wrought unprecedented changes in the structure of society and the life of its members. The power of the manor lords was broken and wars of centralization developed large and politically complex nation states. Such political states as Germany, France and Italy emerged with strong centralized governments that organized many smaller units through increasingly bureaucratized procedures. The need for an educated citizenship, supported by various political theories, particularly the idea of democracy, as well as by nationalism stressing the importance of a shared literate national culture, led to the institution and expansion of mass education for both boys and girls of all social classes (Znaniecki, 1952). The navigational and commercial revolutions, the technological and industrial revolutions and all the accompanying changes expanded the world of knowledge and social control. Work became organized into defined-time periods in large organizations that divided and integrated each person's contribution and rewarded it with a specified sum of money, to be used for the purchase of other goods essential to self-maintenance.

The victory of the reform movement meant that young children were now at home, and, with the home deprived of the many household members who in the past had helped keep watch over them, married women were being forced out of the world of work outside of the home. Concepts of childhood and motherhood began to develop and the idealization and glamorization of the marital state meant that henceforth women were expected at pregnancy to leave the public sphere of life—not returning unless forced by unanticipated tragedy (Shorter, 1975; Oakley, 1975). Oakley also reports that women were ousted from guilds, unions and jobs by highly competitive men freed from the pressure of the family line and dependence upon inheritance or membership in that work group. Men could now train for and sell their labor for wages, enabling them to maintain their own homes. In England, the drive to get women out of the public spheres of life was assisted by their weak legal and social position under common law and, as in other European societies, by similar restrictive rules. Thus, from being part of an economically productive unit, women and children became dependent on their fathers and husbands (Millett, 1970; Oakley, 1975; Stuard, 1976).

These trends affected widowhood in a wide variety of ways. In Western Europe wives generally remained in their homes after the death of the husband but their adult children were free to create their own lives, although at least one offspring generally stayed close to the parent unless she or he had previously emigrated to America, as many had done (Bott, 1957; Shanas et al., 1968; Young and Wilmott, 1957; Wilmott and Young, 1960). Many of the older widows had never worked for pay outside of the home; few were able to obtain occupational training if widowed prior to reaching retirement age. Most Western European societies introduced some form of social insurance, aware that widowhood has impoverished too many of their members. This insurance has enabled many widows to live independently, although within "soup-carrying distance," as Townsend (1957) calls it, ensuring what Rosenmayr and Kockeis (1963) refer to as "intimacy at a distance."

As a result of two major wars, most European societies have a high ratio of widows to women in other marital situations and to widowed men. Compared to the United States of the 1960s, when only 11 percent of the women were widowed, France had 16.5 percent, Austria 16 percent, and West Germany (excluding West Berlin) had 14 percent (Lobodzinska, 1970). The situation in Eastern Europe, which also suffered great losses, was somewhat different because of the policies of the communist states and because of delayed industrialization. Formally communist policy proclaims equality of the sexes, but at recent conferences several social scientists reported that women carry a heavy burden, working outside of the home for pay—getting little help from their husbands with the time-consuming tasks of shopping, housekeeping and child care. At a meeting in Moscow in 1972, the family research committee of the International Sociological Association devoted itself to the subject of women and work. Its meeting in Dubrovnik, Yugoslavia, in 1975, which focused upon sex roles, also heard numerous reports about the problem of combining work and home roles in the societies of Eastern Europe where most younger women must help augment the family income.

Generally speaking, the younger working women in urban areas rely on help from their mothers or other older women in the family. The traditional need for workers in rural areas has not diminished, and countries like Yugoslavia and Poland report a feminization of agriculture as a result of the increased work opportunities for men in nearby industry (Tutowski and Szwengrub, 1976). Because Yugoslav men are often absent for several years, working in other countries (mainly Germany), additional workers are welcome. Many Yugoslav states, such as Croatia, suffer from a shortage of schools. This has led to an exchange system whereby an urban widow shares her quarters with a young relative from a rural area in return for services and food from the farm. Yugoslavia also has whole villages that are populated by widows. Clad in traditional black, they are the survivors of wars and internal conflict that took the lives of their men.

Barbara Lobodzinska (1970, 1974) reports that in Poland grandmothers are frequently called on to care for young children, because almost all younger urban women must work outside of the home for pay. There are almost six times as many widows as widowers, and although the traditional cultural disapproval of the remarriage of widows, based on the demands of their late husbands' families on them and their children, has diminished because of the increased divorce rate, the probability of remarriage is low (Thomas and Znaniecki, 1918–1920). The housing shortage remains a major factor and only one-fourth of all urban and one-tenth of all rural households contain only one person (Lobodzinska, 1974). Because of the housing shortage, many married couples live with their parents or widowed mothers. Widows who do not share their

26

homes with married children usually visit them daily to take care of grandchildren, if there are any, and the home. Three-generational sharing of housing is, according to Lobodzinska (1974, p. 68) a matter of necessity, not choice, the result of the urban housing shortage, the fact that mothers of even small children must work; the inadequacy of social services for older people; and the loneliness of widowed women.

All in all, there appears to be a greater need for the services of older women; thus, a greater integration of these women and their families in work-related support exchanges than is true of Western Europe or the United States.

Historical Perspectives: America

Indians are the only group in the United States who are not descendants of immigrants in recent centuries. Voluntary immigration to America was mainly by young men who later brought their wives and children and/or siblings over, but rarely the whole kinship unit (Lopata, 1976a, 1976b). The decision to come to this continent, even when seen as a temporary quest for money with which to provide a better life back home, meant a willingness to loosen kinship and community ties. Although the immigrants included some upper-class political and religious emigres, the vast majority of Americans are descendants of landed or even landless peasantry, as well as some craftsmen. The earlier arrivals were more likely to settle on the land—the United States being predominantly rural as late as 1900. But the booming cities drew most of the immigrants; America became urbanized and industrialized, while the children of earlier arrivals tended to move westward.

Because of the shortage of women, the lot of widows in early America was relatively good, their skills as well as their property helping to make them attractive marriage partners. "Widows were quite popular, even those with children. One

27

reason was their economic status. The European custom of leaving the major portion of an estate to the eldest son did not survive in the colonies" (Murstein, 1974, p. 300). Murstein quotes Benjamin Franklin as saying that "a rich widow is the only kind of second-hand goods that will always sell at prime cost."[3] The situation of women was uneven; on the one hand the need for them as workers and producers of children was great; on the other hand, Puritanism and the strict morality of the time deprived them of certain rights, in spite of concepts of democracy. Dulles (1965) in his *A History of Recreation* and Boorstein (1958, 1965, 1973) in his three-volume *The Americans* conclude that women in 19th century America lost the status enjoyed in colonial days. Dulles found that they "were more and more condemned to a life separate and apart. . . . In colonial days they had been able to enter far more fully into both the work and the recreation of men" (p. 95). He goes on to say that, "Whatever their position in society, women were expected to devote themselves wholly to the duties of domestic life. Visitors from abroad often singled this out as a bizarre and unexpected aspect of the American scene" (p. 96). Thus, in the first half of the 19th century, "Seriousness of purpose was heightened by strong religious feeling: the average man locked himself in his office and his wife in his home" (p. 98).[4]

By the early 20th century, the United States was still largely rural and agricultural, but the picture changed dramatically after that. Brunner (1928, p. 15), studying foreign-born farmers as late as in the 1920s, found most of them settled in the Middle West. In 1920, "one person in every eight in the United States is a villager. Almost one in four of the rural people are villagers."

Although the women's-rights movements had begun in America in the 1840s, the struggle has been a long one, reflected in the rights of widows. Following the American Revolution, "First reforms gave a woman the right to control the property she had brought to the marriage and to dispose of it by will" (Murstein, 1974, p. 314). Yet, "The level of American women's expectations . . . rose more rapidly than their perceived gains from 1850 to World War I" (p. 325). Simultaneously, ideological developments on this side of the ocean built up into a "feminine mystique," as Betty Friedan (1963) labeled it, that barred greater involvement of women in society until the 1970s. The early American world had been divided into a male domain comprising all public, economic, political and even "serious" voluntary organizational life, and the female domain, which was restricted to the privacy of the family home. The economic institution was the predominant factor, while the family, religion and recreation were pushed back in the order of importance so as not to interfere with the man's work role. Even education was valued mainly in terms of its income-producing potential, and, as recently as the 1950s, Mirra Komarovsky (1953) felt compelled to defend the education of women in areas other than those designed to increase domestic skills. The role of education in achieving economic success encouraged former peasant immigrants to forego the immediate income or work contributions of their children that allowed them to attend school for long periods. They did this even when it became apparent that the educated children would abandon many of their customs and even the parents themselves, leaving the old neighborhoods as their income opened up opportunities to move to "nicer" communities.

Thus, not only across-the-ocean but internal migration helped weaken the ties of the extended family and the control of the neighborhood over each nuclear family. Households became designed for only the husband, wife and their young children. Almost all production moved from the home into factories and offices. Ma-and-Pa stores were replaced by supermarket chains and white collar jobs, still highly respectable, became concentrated in large employing organizations (Mills, 1956). The man was (or remained) the only breadwinner until recently, and thus spent many hours away from the home with his job and travel to and from work; and the woman remained restricted to the home, in spite of official rights. At

29

the same time, the social role of housewife lost whatever status it had in the past, the home being seen as a refuge for those who did important, often punishing work—to the psyche if not to the body—in the world outside. The home, instead of being the manor house, the place through which the life of society flows, became the place where nothing upsetting was supposed to happen, and the housewife, the woman who took care of this vacuous domicile, was downgraded in status (Lopata, 1971a; Sennett, 1973a, 1973b).

This arrangement of family life, dependent on the economic institution, supported by the religious and educational ideologies and based on the participation of the husband-father in a tightly circumscribed career in the labor market, created three difficult situations for women. This happened in spite of their steadily increasing life span, the decrease in childbirth mortality and the improvement in their general health and well-being. The first traumatic period for a woman begins with her withdrawal from full-time participation in life outside of the home prior to, or at, the birth of her first child. Having spent most of her life from earliest childhood away from home in school (later at work) and having married a man she met in the outside world under relatively egalitarian conditions, the woman suddenly finds herself as the sole adult daytime occupant of the home—facing problems of child care and child rearing for which her past life has not prepared her, lacking adequate support systems. For the first time in human history, in all but unusual circumstances (such as those of pioneer life), child rearing has been assigned to a morally and socially isolated person who receives only occasional "help" from the other parent when he is home and not too tired "to pitch in." From being one of a large group of people sharing work in and around the house, and sharing responsibility for the children, she has, for the largest part of the day, become the only adult occupant of a home managed independently, but isolated from supports. She has become the main adult responsible for rearing children, often in a hostile, or at least, an indifferent community—one which does not share all of her values, blaming her if the child does anything to displeasure others. Several "parenthood as crisis" studies deal with the trauma of this reversal of past life (Dyer, 1963; Hobbs, 1965; LeMaster, 1957).

The second difficult period of a woman's life, which in the past was blamed on somewhat mysterious menopausal biological changes, occurs when she is about 45 years old and her last child has left home for good, although actually this offspring is likely not to have spent much time at home before that (Neugarten, 1968). Left alone without enough physical work in the home to justify her existence, feeling she has no function in a function-oriented society that values women mainly for their role as mothers even after that role can no longer be performed actively, made incompetent to function outside the home in a prestigious economic role in society, the middleaged women until very recently found life depressing (Bart, 1973). In the meantime, her husband must work until retirement, often in an uninteresting or, at least, unsatisfying job, because he has to support the wife and their home, and he is too busy to understand or sympathize with a person who does not have enough to do. The isolated nuclear family does not provide her with on-the-spot companions, just as it had not provided the help she needed during the "full-house-plateau" years (Lopata, 1966, 1971a). Voluntary associations offer outlets, often of great value to the community, but they are not considered a serious involvement for any but the upper classes. It is only after the husband retires that the couple, sometimes moving to a retirement community, can function in a leisurely style without a feeling of guilt or shame.

All the changes in the lives of women become dramatically evident at the third stage of their life course—widowhood, which can be problematical. The life of a woman in modern urbanized America is likely to be disorganized by the death of her husband for several reasons. In the first place, her identity as a wife is shattered and there is no comfortable role of widow available to her as it is to widows in other parts of the world (Lopata, 1972). In addition, she often needs to "make herself over," from a dependent person, living vicariously through the husband and children, into an independent person. Often the husband's death breaks old ties with many people, his family, his work associates and the voluntary associations she belonged to with him or through him, such as women's auxiliaries of fraternal groups. Friendships must be modified if they depended on couple-companionate interaction (Lopata, 1975a). Widows report feeling like a "fifth wheel" when going out with married friends.

Housing arrangements tend to be independent, but lonely, for those not living with unmarried children—evidence of how much the family system has changed. Social security and paid employment enables the widow to maintain herself economically. Keeping the home and learning to do what the division of labor had formerly been assigned to her husband, she is able to utilize the resources of the society to continue modified contact with others and she is allowed, even encouraged, by the society to be relatively independent of anyone, even male members of the family. No male agnate of her late husband takes over responsibility for her; no one tells her what she must do. She may move and may even disassociate herself entirely from her in-laws. They have no legal and no moral rights over her or her children [see also Marris (1958) on London widows' relations to in-laws]. Seldom before in history have women been allowed to develop such independence. The question remains, however, how well are widows managing their lives and what support systems do they develop from the resources available to them?

The resources developed by society and the community for their members are enormous; the woman herself is apt to have developed her own resources in her life before and during her marriage. The societal and community resources provide goods and services for the economic support of herself, as well as her offspring. There are practically unlimited opportunities for social contact and for positive relational interaction and self-feelings, for the self to enjoy being, and to be doing things. Formalized methods of providing economic support proliferate, obviating the need for self-sufficiency in the production of needed goods to maintain any style of life, since in most urbanized homes, this is impossible—at least, a wasteful duplication of effort. Complex social structures provide opportunities for learning to understand societal complexity and for training in specific social roles. If specialized groups do not provide such services, these roles are woven into complicated and usually large organizational systems with their own recruitment and instant socialization. Participation in these roles and groups involves a behavioral interweave among people who have sufficiently similar backgrounds to be able to carry out duties and exercise rights that have a function in the system by helping it accomplish its goals, or else it must add intermediaries to serve as bridges between dissimilar peoples. Similarity is based on shared knowledge and, in most economic roles, no one cares whether the job occupant is a widow or not. If she can do the work, she can be hired if there is an opening and the occupation is not labeled as masculine. Training centers for adults exist, as do numerous employment agencies.

American society, aware that its members face a variety of problems, either chronic or acute, has evolved many "helping" procedures, professions and groups to assist people. Lawyers help solve legal problems, sometimes even without charging a fee. The government provides economic supports to widows and surviving children of workers covered by social security, or welfare assistance to those not covered but unable to earn enough to maintain themselves above the poverty line. Banks lend money and offer economic advice. Wills (Sussman, Cates and Smith, 1970), insurance and private pension plans make it possible for a man to set up economic safeguards for his family. Social workers, psychologists, and psychiatrists are trained to help solve a wide variety of situational and emotional problems. Priests, rabbis and ministers are called on to assist members of their congregations in need of help and church groups are supposed to offer help in times of crisis and continued contact throughout life. Voluntary associations providing regular contact and a variety of shared activities abound. Public transportation can substitute for the private automobile which the widow often gives up after the death of the man who, in the modern division of labor, has probably taken care of it. Illness, death and care for survivors is the business of the health professions, especially the personal physician. School personnel are available to help children suffering from the traumatic impact of the death of the father. Neighborhoods have people of similar socio-economic backgrounds who form a resource for services. American society idealizes friendship, particularly for people who no longer have a full-time commitment to the "important" social roles such as wifehood and motherhood for women; books, as well as various community organizations, offer instruction on how to form such relations. In fact, training courses abound on *How to Win Friends and Influence People* (Carnegie, 1936); grooming; how to apply for a job; how to carry on an intelligent conversation; how to train children without a second parent; and so forth. The "modified" extended family is still seen as a viable resource in spite of the dissolution of the nuclear family household (Litwak, 1965; Shanas and Streib, 1965; Sussman, 1965). Most American children are expected to feel some sort of obligation to provide supports to their mothers. There are some unmarried men, although their number dwindles as the widow's age increases, and others who, though married, are willing to provide companionship and a sexual relationship.

Demographic Perspectives: America

As of 1975, there were 75,345,000 women aged 18 and over in the United States, of which 10,104,000 were widows (U.S. Bureau of the Census *Statistical Abstracts* 1976, Table 44). By contrast, only 1,817,000 men out of a total of 67,869,000 were widowers, providing one obvious answer to the question why most widows do not remarry. There are few available single men in the age group in which women are likely to become widows. The most apt to remarry are the younger women. Although the number of widows has been increasing steadily since 1920, their proportion in the total female population of this country reached its peak in 1970 and has decreased since, hovering around 14 percent. The prior increases in the proportion of widows were due in part to the wars, in part to the increase in marriages since the turn of the century and in part to the increasing longevity of women. For example, only 13 out of 30 years between 1940 and 1969, inclusively, had a drop in the rate of marriages of all unmarried women aged 15 and over (U.S. Bureau of the Census, *Marital Status*, 1972).

The median age of widows is 68; for widowers, it is 71. This distribution reflects shorter life-span for men than for women. As stated before, the number of widowers is dramatically smaller. Women, particularly, have benefited from improvements in public-health services as well as in preventative and restorative medicine. At the turn of the 20th century, most women died before their last child left home—the life expectancy going from the decade of the 40s to over 75 years today. This change is due to the fact that many more women live many more years, to the reduction of infant mortality, death in childbirth, and death from communicable diseases. American men die at an earlier age than women, not only in wars, but also from vascular disorder, cancer and other chronic diseases. Recent research holds the life-style of modern males, psychological pressures at work, unhealthy diets, cigarette smoking and a lack of exercise as the most frequently mentioned causes. Although it is possible that changes in the lifestyles of modern, urban women to ones resembling those of men will narrow the gap between female and male life expectancy, it will take a long time for the effects to be felt. In the meantime, the older the husband (and the older he is than his wife, as now is typical of married couples), the greater the possibility of her becoming widowed. The percentage of women aged 14 and over who are widowed goes up from 25 percent in the 60–64 age bracket to over 75 percent for those 85 and over (U.S. Bureau of the Census, *Marital Status*, 1972). Although only one in ten women aged 50–54 is widowed, one in every 7 or 8 of all American women is widowed; the disparity is explained by the large number of older women in the society.

Because of the age of most American widows and the recency of this society's urbanization and industrialization, as well as the recency of the arrival of most of its population, the vast majority of these women were born either in rural areas here or in Europe, or, at least, reared by immigrants or in-migrants. Many of the cities were populated by rural or by nonurbanized peoples, who became a source of unskilled labor for their factories. Some of these people turned into true urbanites, but most remained "urban villagers," steeped in their traditional culture, a small frame of reference and a limited set of social relations (Gans, 1962). American population has multiplied almost threefold since the turn of the century—from 76 million in 1900 to 203 million in 1970. It has changed in its basic distribution, now mainly metropolitan, with 65 percent of its members living in and around cities (U.S. Bureau of the Census, *Current Population Reports*, 1971, p. 1). In 1900 the country was predominantly rural—just over 30 million of its residents lived in urban areas, while 46 million were scattered throughout its enormous rural spaces, with some clustering in towns (U.S. Bureau of the Census, 1960, p. 34–50). Furthermore, the numerical expansion, particularly that of its cities, was heavily dependent on the immigration of people from other parts of the world, people with a different cultural tradition than the country's, and different from each other's. Like the Polish peasants studied by Thomas and Znaniecki (1918–1920), many or most of these immigrants came from barely literate rural backgrounds (Lopata, 1976a). Instead of settling in similar environments, they poured into the cities.

They came with agricultural skills but went into industries. The cities survived having such a vast population with such backgrounds, but many of their life-styles and problems and the lives of their elderly are the outgrowth of this. As late as 1970, only 33 percent of American white women were native-born daughters of native-born parents, although only 6 percent were foreign-born (Kennedy, 1976). Still, since half of the widows in this country were 68 years of age or over in 1970, they were born in 1902 or before, and the probability of them having been of foreign stock is high.

What is surprising in view of the women's backgrounds is that so many are able to live alone, independent of their families, once they become widows. Chevan and Korson (1972, 1975) estimate that as early as 1960, over half of the widowed women in America lived alone and that there has been an enormous increase of such independence since 1940. They did, however, find great differences among ethnic and racial groups in the proportion of widows who live either alone, with their children, or with other persons. Widowed minority women are least able to live alone or to head their own households. According to the U.S. Census, a total of almost seven million, or 82 percent of the households not headed by a husband–wife team, have a female head (U.S. Bureau of the Census, *Statistical Abstracts*, 1976, Table 59). In spite of the publicity given to divorce-caused female-headed households there were over three times as many female-headed households managed by widows as by divorcees as late as 1960. The reasons for the publicity are threefold: the lingering disapproval of divorce, the greater probability that homes disrupted by divorce rather than by death contain young children and the dramatic increase in such households in recent years, especially since 1960. The increase in divorce is evidenced by the fact that 1975 figures showed 2,560,000 widow- and 2,108,000 divorcee-headed households. Over one-and-a-half million households are headed by widows below the age of 65, and almost a million by widows below the age of 55. That same year, widow-headed households surpassed divorcee-headed ones starting in the 45–54 age bracket.

Statistics documenting the various characteristics of women who are or have been widowed point to the fallacy of a common assumption, i.e., the men who die at an earlier age are generally the middle- and upper-class "business executives."[5] In fact, however, not that many men fall into the stereotypical upwardly mobile, executive-ladder-climbing, career category. Moreover, a careful study of census data reveals a disproportionate number of widows to be of disadvantaged background, of immigrant parents or themselves migrants from poorer countries or poorer sections of America to its cities and towns, or nonwhite, with all the concomitant problems. The widows are disproportionately found among the less-educated women, former wives of less-educated men, who had earned less money doing physically harder work than men in other marital categories. The minority or otherwise disadvantaged widows are younger—and their mates were younger at death—than the widows of white-collar workers. The figures show that we, as a society, have not as yet been able to counteract the ill effects that voluntary and enforced migration and lower-class constraints and habits have imposed on a relatively large segment of our population.

For example, the median years of schooling completed by widows is lower than true of all American women aged 14 and over in all age categories (see U.S. Bureau of the Census, *Marital Status*, 1972). Although younger women are now obtaining more education than their older counterparts, and although widows tend to be older women, only the married but separated women have a lower median year of schooling than do the widows. The nonwhites in all marital categories are much worse off in terms of schooling than are the whites, with as much as two years less of education, but there are some interesting variations within the groups. The younger black women, past the age of 19, in all marital categories, show a

38

greater gain in schooling over their older counterparts than the younger white women.

The lack of formal schooling above the ninth grade on the part of so many widows is reflected in the kinds of jobs they are able to hold. Their occupational distribution also reflects the probability that many dropped out of the labor force on marriage, or, at least, at the birth of their first child, so that whatever skills they possessed became outdated or rusty. About 25 percent of all widowed women are in the labor force; they account for eight percent of all women currently in the labor force, a low proportion considering that over 13 percent of all women are widows. The very young and the very old are not as apt to be working for pay, for different reasons, so that the peak of the working widows is reached among those between age 45 and 54. Their total of 67 percent in 1970 surpasses that of married women, husband present, which peaks at 58 percent in the 35–44 age range. The reason for the older age of the widowed workers is that these women must work, since they are too young for retirement, social security and generally do not have children young enough to qualify them for benefits as mothers of dependent orphans of the deceased worker. Most of these women are either private household workers or farm managers and farmers. They are also disproportionately concentrated in craft occupations or as managers or officials (two categories with relatively few women) and in service and sales jobs. They are underrepresented among professional and clerical workers, a reflection of their education and age, and among workers on farms owned by others.

The summary evidence about the characteristics of American widows is contained in census figures on the median and mean incomes of women aged 14 and over by marital status, age and race (U.S. Bureau of the Census, *Marital Status*, 1972). The U.S. Bureau of the Census lists the income of women in a very traditional fashion: married women with husbands present who are not themselves in the paid labor force are listed as having no income and they are included in the average for married women and for "all women,"—thus lowering the mean and median considerably.[6] It is not surprising therefore, to find the median and mean income for all American women aged 14 and over to be very low. By contrast, the women who are widowed and who receive social security or a pay check make a relatively good showing. However, their households are likely to be dependent on this as the sole income, with the husband dead and the children either too young to work, or out of the house and not contributing to it. Although there are fewer people spending money, expenses of a one-member household are not half of those of a two-person home. Another aspect of national income distribution of women needs explanation. Census tables with income means, which are averages, show them almost inevitably to be higher than the medians, i.e., the sum at which the population breaks in half. This is due to the fact that the incomes of women above the mean are more spread out than those below it. The presence of some very wealthy women brings up the average. The exception is for the black remarried and then divorced former widows aged 63 and over, who are generally so poor that those with incomes above the median are too close to it to outweigh the low-income half below it.

There is a great deal of internal heterogeneity in income by age and race, although the range is not great, with most widows being listed as relatively poor, both because of limited sources and because working women in America still earn much less than do working men. Black widows are the most disadvantaged of either race in all but one age group—that between 14 and 24. The differences in both mean and median incomes of blacks and whites are striking, in that white widows average and distribute above their counterparts in other marital categories, while blacks widows average and distribute below all black women. One reason is that more black married women than white are working and contributing income to their household, which narrows the gap between them and white married women due to discrimination, while fewer black than white widows are working. As now computed, with married women not in the labor force reported as having no income, white widows are better off financially than are other women in the population, while black widows are not only poorer than white widows, but they are poorer than black women in other marital categories in all age groups above the age of 34.

The highest personal mean income of all listed marital, age and racial categories is reported for white widows aged 25–34. The lowest mean is for black widows 65 years of age and over. Although the mean income of widowed women above 14 peaks at the 25–34 age group, the peaking for all women does not come until the ages of 45–54. This may be explained in two ways, each undoubtedly contributing its share. Widows with dependent children receiving social security are usually better off in terms of money (as surveyed by the Census Bureau) than other young women. Those young widows who do not enjoy such benefits are working and they have higher average salaries than married women, whose average income is lowered by the nonworkers [see also Mallen (1975)].

The overall educational, occupational and income picture of women in America supports the evidence from a variety of sources that they do not prepare adequately for employment, a specific occupation or a career, and do not take seriously the probability that they will have to earn their livelihood sometime after marriage. Their inflexible commitment to homemaking and child-rearing reflects the necessities of life at the turn of the century, when women lived within family units until their death, but it does not reflect the current needs of women who will live to about 75 years of age, with about 30 of those years without a child in the home and 15 vigorous years with no one else in the household. The habit of not taking seriously the involvement of American women in the world of work does not take account of either divorce or widowhood, or other emergencies and disasters, let alone the need for more than one income in a family headed by two persons. In 1970 terms, the fact that few women without a husband or with a limited income held well-paying jobs means that many of them fall below the poverty line (see Chapter 9, Supports from the Economic Institution).

American society is, of course, conscious of the problems of women unable to earn enough to support themselves and their dependents comfortably and it has developed various resources to help them. Widows with dependent children or those past retirement age eligible for social security as widowed mothers or as older widows receive monthly benefits which, although often insufficient, help stave off abject poverty and provide, at least some economic base. Instituted in 1939, these programs for widows of insured workers operate on the assumption that only a portion of the income needs to be replaced after the death of the husband. Recently research indicates that many women have no other important source of income so that their whole life is dependent on the social security payments, which are generally not enough to support the young widowed mother or the recipient of old-age benefits (Lopata, 1977; Kim, 1973; Lopata and Steinhart, 1971; Steinhart, 1975, 1977). Lucy Mallan (1975, p. 18) documents the eligibility and the consequences of such eligibility on the income of young widows (under age 60), with or without children, in great detail and concludes:

> No doubt, social security benefit increases since 1967 have lessened the likelihood that young widows with one to three children would be poor. Other widows, those with many children and those nearing age 60, have not done so well. . . . First, multi-child families are at a disadvantage, in that their total incomes are held down by a combination of the family maximum on social security benefits and the mother's difficulty in working when there are several children.

Others whom she finds to be at a disadvantage are the widowed mothers of one child who had worked before the death

42

of the husband and widows approaching the age of 60 who do not work.

The changes in the life-styles of widows in America and of women throughout their lives, such as better education and greater independence not only from in-laws but also from adult married children, can be expected to increase in the future, even if commitment to working and to earning income is lagging. Chevan and Korson (1975, p. 52) come to this conclusion from their analysis of widows and widowers in the public use sample of the U.S. Census with regard to independent housing:

> Future generations of widows and widowers are not only likely to have higher incomes, but are also likely to have more education, greater participation in the labor force, past and present, more marriages, fewer residing in rural areas and more residing in the West, fewer children and there will be fewer foreign-born among them. . . the implications for an increase in the proportion of the widowed living alone is clear.

The same conclusions can be reached about future use of other resources in support systems involving widows in America.

Summary

The theoretical, comparative, historical and demographical overviews lead us to expect a great variety of life-styles of urban American widows. Because of the changes just described, we are not likely to find many women under the strong control of and actively supported by the family of the deceased husband. The widows are likely to have led typical lives, having withdrawn from active participation in the labor force and dependent on the husband as the only, or at least, the primary breadwinner. Depending on their age and the age of the other survivors, they either return to the labor force or rely on social security for household maintenance. They most likely head their own households, living alone or with un-married children.

In spite of certain similarities among the women, the recency and the rapidity of change in modern urban America can lead us to anticipate great heterogeneity in the support systems of various types of widows, depending on their ability to engage voluntaristically in new social roles and relations and to modify the old ones after the death of the husband, as well as on the availability of traditional supports that surround traditional women. We can expect some widows, possibly first- or even second-generation immigrants, to continue to cling to and have available family members as the sole providers and re-ceivers of supports and to be unable to develop other kinds of relations. There will be socially isolated individuals, or widows with restricted social life spaces of roles and relations. We may also expect a wide range of women with expansive life spaces, dependent upon a great variety of factors, active in friendship, neighboring, work roles away from the home, voluntary associations and in contact with various relatives. To understand their support systems, we must first find out something about the women who are widows in the United States as a whole and in the metropolitan Chicago area in particular, where we will be studying their lives in greater detail.

NOTES

1. For the purpose of this section and the chapter in the Cowgill and Holmes book (1972) I used *The Human Relations Area Files*. These contain references from a variety of sources to the norms governing the behavior of widows or women wanting to divorce their husbands in regard to their children. Most societies specify that women must leave their children with the father's family, sending back the child they are still nursing, if they leave before she or he is weaned. In cases where there are no children, widows can occasionally return to their own families, depending on the economic arrangements made at the time of marriage. Their families may not want

them back if the return necessitates the return of the bride price. The husbands' families may not want them to leave if they have the right to take their dowry with them.

2. The code of Manu specified the following regulations for widows:

They be deprived. . . of every gold and silver ornament, of the bright-colored garments, and of all the things they love to have about or on their persons. . . . Among the Brahmans of Deccan, the heads of all widows must be shaved regularly every fortnight. . . . The widow must wear a single coarse garment, white, red or brown. She must eat only one meal during the twenty-four hours a day. She must never take part in family feasts and jubilees with others. She must not show herself to people on auspicious occasions. A man or woman thinks it unlucky to behold a widow's face before seeing any other object in the morning. A man will postpone his journey if his path happens to be crossed by a widow at the time of his departure. A widow is called "an inauspicious thing" [as quoted by Sarasvati (1888)].

3. Recent research into European and American history may change this image. Sicherman (1975), in reviewing such research, points to one study relating directly to widowhood.

By closely analyzing marriages and widowhood in one community, Alexander Keyssar has challenged a favorite piece of historical wisdom: that widows occupied a favored place in colonial society by virtue of their wealth, their capacity to take over family businesses, and their freedom from male control . . . (p. 465–466). He found that widowhood was an important problem (since the marriages were more often terminated by the death of the husband than of the wife), that it often proved permanent or, for those who eventually remarried, lasted an average of seven to ten years, and that the widow's economic situation was precarious. . . . Although Massachusetts law entitled her to one-third of her husband's real property for life use—and the courts sometimes allowed more for those with slender means—the widow's estate was smaller than the town average, certainly no inducement for prospective fortune hunters. Moreover, because of the labor shortage in the colony, she could not hire the necessary hands to help her run the farm and thus rarely continued in a productive economic role. Instead although she might be subsidized by the town, she was most often dependent on her adult children, living perhaps in the "westerly end" of the family farmhouse as stipulated by her husband's will (p. 465–466).

4. The position of women in the history of American society has undergone some very interesting shifts and is reflected in the situation of widows, but it has not been very positive until recently. There is much evidence of an antifeminine tenor in the culture, reflected in psychology by Helene Deutsch's *The Psychology of Women* (1944) and Lundberg and Farnham's *Modern Women: The Lost Sex* (1947) and in popular literature by Philip Wylie's *Generation of Vipers* (1955). Sicherman's review of women in American history quotes a number of studies describing the image of "true womanhood" which separated the world and human personality into two sex-segregated spheres. It is interesting to note that many European observers found that the men and women of this society actually lived in these separate worlds. Masson (1976, p. 304) begins her paper on the conceptions held by Puritans of women with the statement that, "As de Tocqueville observed, nineteenth-century America differentiated very sharply between roles appropriate for men and women." Of course,

the travelers coming here were generally of the upper class, and it is quite possible that democratizing Americans simply adopted a lower-class image of the home and the homemaker, which they then extended to all women. It is this very restricted view of the adult American woman that initially started me on my study of wives—later of widows [see *Occupation: Housewife* (Lopata, 1971a) and *Widowhood in an American City* (Lopata, 1973a)].

5. The most useful sources of data on the American population are the U.S. Bureau of the Census reports. In addition to the *Detailed Characteristics, United States Summary* (Final Report PC(i)-Dl) and the state summaries for each decade, there are special reports such as the one on *Marital Status* (PC(2)-4C) and *Current Population Reports* (Series P-20). Data on past decades are contained in the *Historical Statistics of United States, Colonial Times to 1957* updated to 1962 and revisions; and data on each year are found in the *Statistical Abstracts of the U.S.* The U.S. Department of Health, Education and Welfare Public Health Service often issues pamphlets of the National Center of Health Statistics on subjects such as *Marriages, Trends and Characteristics* (HSM 72-1007) or *Remarriages, United States* (HRA 74-1903). There is a public-use sample available for purchase on one of a 100 or one of a 1,000 cases. It is this sample that Robert Kennedy and the team of Al Chevan and Henry Korson use for their national analyses.

6. It is possible that the feminist movement may change this, since various schemes are being proposed to redefine the occupational participation of the wife who stays at home to care for the house and children, as simply being the internal component of a two-person career. In that case, half (or some such proportion) of the income he earns is seen as contributed by her efforts. Pay for housewifery is also being considered [see Nona Glazer-Malbin's *Old Family, New Family* (1975)].

TWO

Resources and Support Systems of Widows

Before examining the personal resources and support systems of the widows who form the subject of this book, we must look at the larger community in which they are located, i.e., metropolitan Chicago, whose people, organizations, culture and resources provide the facilitators or constrains for the social engagement of these women at every stage of their lives, but especially in widowhood.

Metropolitan Chicago: The City and Its People

Hog Butcher for the World,
Tool Maker, Stacker of Wheat,
Player with Railroads and the Nation's
    Freight Handler;
Stormy, husky brawling,
City of the Big Shoulders.

CARL SANDBURG
Chicago, 1916

Carl Sandburg's paean to Chicago focuses on its economic base, whereas the very title of Farr's book, *Chicago: A Personal History of America's Most American City* (1973) emphasizes its people. The city's "Americanness" is inherent in its location near the center of the country, its function as a hub of transportation and communication, the diversity of its economic base and of its population, its socio-economic, ethnic, racial, and religious heterogeneity and its long-standing image as the "melting pot" *par excellence*. Chicago's anthem proclaims, "There she stands, beside the inland sea, with outstretched arms to welcome you and me," a reference not only to its location, but to the fact that it has recruited and accepted a comparatively large number of immigrants and domestic migrants. Its industries at the turn of the 20th century (for Chicago is a relatively young city) needed many workers, and neither skill nor familiarity with American urban life were prerequisites. Until recent decades, the city expanded rapidly in proportion to its environs, in spite of the devastating fire in 1871 that wiped out most of the wooden structures, housing a large part of the new arrivals. As of 1970, less than half of the population of the northeastern Illinois counties of the Chicago Standard Metropolitan Statistical Area lived in the city proper; the rest were dispersed to a number of communities outside the official city limits in "six counties, 249 incorporated suburban municipalities" (Opperman, no date). There are also some 3,000 square miles of unincorporated areas. Two of the counties are in the neighboring state of Indiana.

The rapid expansion of the city has been achieved mainly through the absorption of rural or small-town people from the surrounding areas and from the American South, particularly along the territory reached by the Illinois Central Railroad, and of foreigners. As late as 1930 25 percent of its population were foreign-born and 40 percent native-born of mixed or foreign-born parentage, leaving only 28 percent as native-born of native-born parents. At that time, the predominant foreign-stock nationalities in Chicago were Poles, Germans, Russians (mostly Jews), Italians and Swedes. There were few blacks or members of other nonwhite races in Chicago in 1930; the heavy influx began about the time of World War II. Of recent years, the number of Spanish-speaking peoples, primarily from

Puerto Rico and Mexico, has increased sufficiently to warrant special attention in the census reports.

The age distribution of the city's 1930 population indicates the newness of its population, as the median age was only 29 years; the elderly accounted for only four percent of the total. The figures keep changing over the years as the population continues to age; the proportion of in-migrants to the total already residing here is decreasing and younger families move to the ever expanding suburbs. The median number of school years completed by Chicagoans has increased from 8.5 for both sexes in 1940 to 11.25 for males, and 11.9 for females in 1970. The 1970 median is below the national 12.2 figure. Chicago has been a city with a relatively large proportion of single-family detached dwellings, together with the "two flats" and the "three flats" which the residents see as typical.

The population of the city and its surrounding suburbs is not homogeneous, nor are the housing, work and shopping areas scattered throughout. To understand the city in which the widows we will discuss reside, we need two constructs: the "natural local communities" into which the University of Chicago sociologists found it to be divided in the 1930s and Burgess's theory of concentric zones.

Louis Wirth and Eleanor Bernert explained the local communities in their introduction to the second *Local Community Fact Book*, published in 1949:

> The modern metropolis is a city of cities, a mosaic of little worlds and aggregate of local communities, each one differentiated from the others by its characteristic function in the total economy and cultural complex of city life. . . . In the course of research extending over a generation at the University of Chicago, it has been found useful to view the city as made up of seventy-five component local communities, each of which has a history of its own, and is marked off from the others by distinctive physical and social characteristics and by natural boundaries. The names of these seventy-five communities have acquired considerable currency and renown and evoke among the inhabitants a sense of identification if not of loyalty (p. vii).

The 75 local communities they identified and the suburbs can be grouped into five concentric zones, which Burgess found typical of modern cities—for which Chicago served as a model. The zones are distinguished from each other by distance from the center, by concentration of activity and density of people, by industry and by other resources. The first zone is the "central business district" (Gist and Fava, 1964).

This is where skyscrapers, department stores, cheap variety emporia, hotels, restaurants, theaters, and motion-picture houses are concentrated to meet the needs of downtown shoppers or transients. The inner zone is essentially an area of retail trade, light manufacturing and commercialized recreation. In Chicago it is called the "Loop" (p. 108).

The term, "Loop," comes from the circle formed by the elevated tracks around the zone, but the community extends beyond this business district to include some residents. In 1970, the Loop contained a disproportionate number of older people, with 30 percent of its population being 60 years of age or older, while the city itself had 15 percent. It thus has the highest concentration of elderly in Chicago, but the number itself is not large, as only 1,462 people were living in this area in 1970.

The second zone of modern cities, modeled after and definitely appropriate to Chicago, is the "zone of transition." This encompasses a heavy concentration of lower-income people, inhabited in pre-World War II years "by Old World immigrants and rural migrants, by unconventional folk, and by social outcasts such as criminals and prostitutes. Typically, the zone of transition also contains some high-cost living, the "Gold Coast" (Gist and Fava, 1964, p. 108). The contrasts of the zone of transition attracted sociologist, Harvey W. Zorbaugh, who described them in *The Gold Coast and the Slum* (1929). In fact, many books—sociological, historical and fictional—have been written about the diverse groups who have inhabited this zone over the years.

The other zones of Burgess's theory of the structure of modern cities have been generally neglected in sociological research. The third zone is that of "workingmen's homes." Because it borders on the zone of transition, its residents are most apt to be the upwardly mobile workers who have acquired private homes as part of a movement to the upper segment of the lower class. Many are first-generation migrants from rural areas or other countries or their second-generation adult children.

The fourth zone is that of "middle-class dwellers." It is "populated mainly by professional people, owners of small businesses, the managerial group, clerical forces and the like. There are hotels and apartment houses here, and detached residences with spacious yards and gardens" (Gist and Fava, 1964, p. 109). Richard Sennett (1970) reported on life within the fourth zone in the early history of the city in *Families Against the City, Middle-Class Homes of Industrial Chicago, 1872–1890* (see also his "Genteel Backlash: Chicago 1886," 1973). His focus is upon the fear and rejection of new immigrants and other lower-class residents of Chicago by those who had already achieved sufficient social status to move out of the first zones into the fourth, which they then tried to protect against incursion by less fortunate urbanites with callous disregard for the problems of the city.

The fifth, or "commuters' zone," forms the "outer periphery of the city." It includes the suburblike city neighborhoods and community areas, as well as the suburbs and exurbs. Although the exurb is a concept that was developed for another city, it applies to Chicago. It was coined by Spectorsky (1955) to describe the upper-class communities around New York City, with low population density, expensive homes on farm land or wooded acreage (see his *The Exurbanites*).

The various descriptions, sociological or fictional, of Chicago's population document their lives as they moved into the inner zones, met with disorganizing influences but somehow survived, and, usually in later generations, moved out to the

51

suburbs to build more middle-class lives or to escape the city's problems and new groups. Many people, particularly the elderly, never left the areas of original settlement, either compelled to stay in homes of such low market value as to rule out a move, or moving only a few blocks as conditions changed.

Life in Chicago for the new urbanites at the turn of the century, and in recent years for the black, white and mixed migrants from Appalachia and the South, from Puerto Rico and Mexico, has been compressed in the inner belts, full of ethnic flavor, tainted by crime, violence, political corruption and other problems. This compression provides many opportunities for human contact in congested housing units, along crowded streets and stores, in large work organizations, in churches or national organizations and in parks and beaches. In the early years of a group's settlement, neighbors tended to be from the same country, often from the same village or locality. This does not mean that all neighborhoods were necessarily homogeneous, only that there were enough of one's "own" people around to support ethnic communities with a whole complex of institutions (Breton, 1964; Lopata, 1976a). Neighbors of other racial or ethnic identity were either ignored or labeled as strangers—treated either with cautious or open hostility. The ethnic neighborhoods of older immigrants groups are, for the most part, in the process of vanishing, with their former residents dispersed into clusters of secondary settlement or along spokes of class-varied, individuated communities. Despite an increasing segregation of blacks and whites, many older white widows still are nestled in changing or predominately nonwhite areas of the city.

RESOURCES OF THE METROPOLIS

Chicago has become the second-largest city in the United States and its structure has been modified from that observed by Burgess in ways other than the dispersal of some of the older ethnic groups. It is no longer the "hog butcher of the world"; its stockyards closed down sometime ago. Although steel mills still operate on the far south side of the city and in the industrial northwest of Indiana, much of industry and business has become decentralized and the city's population around the Loop is changing as slums are razed and replaced by high-rise buildings, inevitably shifting the composition, as old-time residents cannot afford the new housing. Economic life is moving out, generally skipping the intermediary zones and settling in the formerly stereotypical "bedroom" suburbs. The industrial plants are decentralizing and moving in smaller units beyond city limits on the heels of their white workers, creating transportation problems for their black and other minority employees who are basically confined to the inner city. Traffic, outbound from Chicago in the morning and inbound after work hours, is now almost as dense as the reverse. There are more than 100 business and shopping districts in and around Chicago. The post-World War II suburban housing boom was accompanied by a proliferation of shopping malls. These are now being followed by apartment complexes, almost self-sufficient in the services they provide, insuring work-free and safe environments and "escape from loneliness" in suburbs, designed for the young with small children and the retired or almost retired who no longer want detached homes.

The city's skyline has undergone a dramatic change, with high-rise buildings positioned on a strip along Lake Michigan—both north and south of the Loop. Some of the lake has been filled in to create better land space for this northward expansion. Many of these buildings house the wealthy in apartments which are rapidly being converted from rentals to condominiums. Others contain small units designed to attract young singles [see *Singles in the City* (Starr and Carnes, 1973)], retired couples, and the widowed or divorced. Further west, at some points within two blocks of this strip, are found the slums or the near-slums. These now extend northward to Uptown, beyond the original zone of transition, which is now

53

occupied by such a great a variety of problem-ridden people that it has been selected as a Model City area for the focusing of problem-solving community resources. Uptown, like the Loop, contains a disproportionate number of elderly, the not-so-impoverished residents living nearest the park bordering on the lake and the very poor and often isolated in the blocks stretching west. A number of the elderly, including widows, now live in public housing in the area, in middle-income apartment buildings and in a variety of apartment hotels. The same is true of several areas near the lake on the south side of the city. Chicago's housing authority has also built complexes for the elderly, apart from other age groups or in low-rental housing for different age groups, within the black belt or belts, extending south and west from the Loop.

The suburban widows are concentrated in older communities, such as Oak Park, where women aged 65 and over form 11 percent of the population, in centers of more heterogeneous, larger suburbs such as Evanston to the north, where they constitute only nine percent of the population. They can also be found in the younger communities with specially designed apartment or other housing combinations made attractive to people of their needs or tastes. A major problem of widows living in the suburbs is transportation; these communities rely on automobiles, and public transportation other than commuter trains is sadly deficient. People without cars must live within walking distance of existing services or these commuting spokes.

Within Chicago itself, however, the public transportation is extensive, reputedly among the best in the country. Chicago also offers its residents a fine park system with numerous recreational programs, many of them specially geared toward the elderly. City resources also contain many medical and health-service facilities, including numerous hospitals, although many of them are concentrated in the older areas of the city. Some have almost become geriatric centers simply because of the nature of their clientele. However, many of these areas have high crime rates, so that an undetermined but possibly high proportion of the population dare not use them as health resources. These complexes, often connected with medical schools, have numerous clinics.

Churches abound in Chicago and its environs, replete with clubs and voluntary activities. An extensive network of organizations provides a wide range of contact and opportunities for shared activities. There is a Catholic group called NAIM for the widowed, clubs like Parents without Partners, Spares, Widow-to-Widow and others for the formerly married. Employment agencies, both private and state-run, are available for people seeking or wanting to change jobs. Legal aid, travelers' aid and emotional help resources are extensive, with social workers ready to help those who are unable to reach out to the resources.

On the negative side of the ledger, as far as the quality of life is concerned, several factors directly affect many widows. One of these is Chicago's weather, often uncomfortable enough to prevent leisurely outdoor activity and casual social contact. Bad weather works a particular hardship on lower-class widows, whose social life is built on informal contacts with neighbors rather than on more formal invitational visiting. A second negative factor is the high rate of mobility and the disintegration of the local community areas [see *The Eclipse of Community* (Stein, 1960)]. The minority groups now coming to the city differ physically from the older population and this visible difference has met with a great deal of prejudice and fear [see *The Rise of the Unmeltable Ethnics* (Novak, 1972)]. Many of the foreign-stock groups, as well as the native-born children of native parents still in the city, are openly resentful of and resistant to the efforts of the city, state and federal governments to provide resources to the racial minorities, which they feel go far beyond those offered them when they were at the bottom of the socio-economic ladder. They have "made it" partly up this ladder; they want to rest on their achievement without competition from below. In recent years, elderly women of Chicago have often banded together to protest the busing of minority children to their neighborhood school and feelings run high on this issue. As in the families described by Sennett (1970), many white families in Chicago hold stereotypical views on crime in the streets; they see a clear connection between race and crime, forgetting how they themselves were stereotyped in the past. Crime is of concern to the elderly, both white and black, and the widows of both races tend to restrict their lives to a limited social life space, going out in the daytime only if absolutely necessary—never alone at night.

Widows in Metropolitan Chicago

The Chicago Standard Metropolitan Statistical Area contained in 1970 a total of 2,670,045 women aged 14 and over, 324,925 of whom are widowed, with an additional 54,465 women known to have been widowed in the past (U.S. Bureau of the Census: *Detailed Characteristics: Illinois*, 1971, Table 152). The demographic characteristics of the widows in this area reflect the national urban situation. Only nine percent of all the "unrelated" widows, or those not living in families or subfamilies, forming five percent of all those listed by family type, are inmates of institutions, compared to the national 10 percent. Two-thirds of those living as heads of families do not have children under the age of 18 living in the household and most of the remaining ones have only one or two offspring of that age. Over half of the widows live as "unrelated individuals," in fact, as primary individuals, which means that they live alone. Except for the effects of climatic differences and some regional cultural variations, we do not expect to find great differences between the Chicago area women who are widowed and their counterparts in other cities of America, although there are probably differences in supportive networks and support systems between them and the widows living in more stable smaller towns in states like Missouri,

Washington, or South Carolina (B. Adams, 1968; D. Adams, 1969; Berardo, 1968, 1970; Philblad and Rosencranz, 1968). Some of evidence indicates a greater potential for social isolation of older and less educated widows in metropolitan Chicago than in more stable small communities, because of the mobility and heterogeneity of the population. This difference may be historical, due to the presence of so many "urban villagers" not surrounded by villages in modern cities.

The widows in metropolitan Chicago whose support systems are discussed here are not fully representative of all women residing in the area who are or have been widowed because of the method by which they were selected for interviewing. They are representative only of women who are current or former beneficiaries of social security as widows of entitled men and/or as mothers of that man's children.

We have five categories of widows: beneficiaries with dependent children or mothers of offspring between the ages of 18 and 22 who attend school (*widowed mothers*); older widows who receive retirement benefits (*retirement widows*); *mothers of adult children* who are no longer eligible for benefits; and *remarried widows*, who lost benefits because of remarriage. Finally, we have a sample of women, *"lump sum" beneficiaries*, who received a single payment to help defray funeral costs. Not included in the sample are the women whose husbands had not earned sufficient quarters of credit in the system to qualify for social security insurance benefits, those who were dropped from the rolls prior to the time the sample cut-off was set, those whom we could not reach in spite of valiant efforts to locate and those who refused to be interviewed.[1] The material used in the study of the support systems and networks of metropolitan widows is based on two-hour interviews with a random sample of these former or current social security beneficiaries, conducted by trained, middle-aged women interviewers, who spoke to a total of 1,169 women. The form of the interview itself is contained in Appendix B.[2]

One way of checking the sample and also of providing the reader with basic information on our Chicago area widows is to compare their distributions on a few critical characteristics with figures on the total number of widows in the metropolis obtained from the U.S. Bureau of the Census as presented in a public use sample for 1970 (see Table 1). The differences that exist reflect the method by which we obtained the sample. The list from which the respondents were sought was drawn up by Social Security Administration statisticians, with guarantees of confidentiality from contracting agencies, that is, the Center for the Comparative Study of Social Roles of Loyola University of Chicago and the Survey Research Laboratory of the University of Illinois, which conducted the interviews. Some addresses of former beneficiaries were very old, and the remarried widows were especially hard to trace. Older widows had the highest rate of refusal. As a result of the complications of tracing and obtaining permission for the interviews, and the limitations of the list itself, our sample contains more affluent widows than are present in the Chicago population at large. Younger widows are overrepresented, due to our oversampling of remarried women and mothers of dependent children. The latter category was especially easy to trace and cooperative. The racial distribution reflects the general population, but proportionately fewer younger women in our sample are in the labor force, mainly because, as recipients of social security benefits, they are able to stay home with their dependent children. The fact that fewer women of our sample, aged 55–64, are working may be due to the presence of dependents. All in all, however, the sample represents 82,085 women who are widowed and, although missing the highly disadvantaged, it contains a sufficient number of the very poor to rule out an extreme bias.[3]

Six out of 10 of the widows whom we interviewed, whom I call "Chicago area widows" throughout, are now 65 years of age. However, only one-fourth of them, including those who were widowed more than once, had been that age at the

TABLE 1

*The Number of Chicago SMSA Widows by Age, Race, Education,
Income and Labor Force Participation*

	CHICAGO SMSA (1974) LOPATA WIDOWHOOD SURVEY SAMPLE OF SSA BENEFIT RESPONDENTS		CHICAGO SMSA (1970) SAMPLE OF U.S. CENSUS BUREAU	
	%	N	%	N
Age:				
44 or under	8		6	
45–54	14		11	
55–64	19		21	
65–74	32		32	
75 and over	28		30	
Total	100	81,502	100	327,600
Race:				
White	86		84	
Nonwhite	14		16	
Total	100	82,078	100	327,600
Education:				
8th grade or less	38		55	
Some high school	20		16	
High school graduate	28		19	
Some college	8		7	
College grad or more	5		3	
Total	100	78,822	100	327,600
Income:				
Less than $3,000	33		59	
$3,000 to $5,999	30		23	
$6,000 to $8,999	15		11	
$9,000 to $14,999	13		5	
$15,000 and over	9		2	
Total	100	70,897	100	299,400
Labor force Participation:				
44 or under	47	2,939	61	12,609
45–54	65	7,174	69	25,201
55–64	47	7,234	56	40,966
65 and over	11	5,456	11	20,781
Total	28	22,803	31	99,556

time of death of their husband. They have been widows for an average of 10 years, with 15 percent having been in that status less than four years. Only about six percent, mainly younger women with children, have remarried. Most had been married a relatively long time, half of them 30 years or over, with only a quarter having been married less than 20 years. Some aspects of their relations with their late husbands, as reconstructed in memory, and the circumstances of their husbands' death, are discussed later.

All but 15 percent of the widows are white, and although neither young nor recently widowed, most of them are not at the final stage of their lives, which helps explain their apparent independence. These women reflect their historical generation in that only about four out of 10 never went beyond grade school, and only 13 percent obtained at least some college education. We will examine their income in detail later but we must keep in mind during the forthcoming discussion that one-third are living on less than $3,000 annually. Just over one-fourth are in the labor force.

Personal Resources

There are three types of resources from which social relations and support systems can be drawn. The first set of resources available to a person contains all the attributes, abilities and skills of that particular individual. Two of the major hypotheses guiding our analysis of widowhood are that length of urbanization and amount of education have important bearing on the development of support systems of widows and that their support systems differ significantly because of great variations in these factors. Race and ethnic background are also important influences on the lives of women, and therefore of widows. The ability to utilize community resources is based on habitual skills in behavior toward these different external resources developed during socialization and education at home and in school. A second set of resources is the current assets that facilitate social engagement, such as income and housing. The third set of resources includes all the people and groups with whom the person has an established relationship, such as parents, siblings, in-laws, children and other relatives, friends, boyfriends, neighbors, comembers of voluntary associations, co-workers, and members of helping professions such as ministers, rabbis, priests, doctors, lawyers, social workers and so forth. The interview was so designed as first to obtain information about all the resources available to the widow and then to find out who is actually involved in support exchanges with her.

THE SELF AS RESOURCE

Many widows are not using the available resources of Chicago as a metropolitan center to build complex support systems and networks because they lack a background in urbanized living. Very few of their fathers and only 10 percent of their mothers were Chicago-born. In fact, only one-third of the fathers or mothers came from any city with a population of 50,000 or more. More than four in 10 fathers and mothers had been born in villages, farm towns or on a farm. Over half of the parents were foreign-born. However, only one-fifth of the women and their late husbands came from rural farm or non-farm areas. Only a third of the husbands, but almost half of the wives, had been born in the Chicago area. Thus, in many cases the husband's mobility was greater than the wife's. Seven of every 10 women born outside of Chicago were adults, that is, 18 years of age or over, when they came there.

There are strong age differences in the urban backgrounds of the women. For example, one or both parents of almost half of the retirement widows were born in a village or on a farm; and one-fourth were married to men of similar background. An overwhelming proportion of parents of these older women were born in another country or another state. All in all, the widows being studied here tend to be first- but mainly second-generation migrants to metropolitan Chicago. Familiarity with settlement patterns of migrants to Chicago indicates a high probability that even the second-generation in-migrants resided in the less affluent, educationally poorer, multiproblem areas of the city. In fact, many of the widows have a strong ethnic identity, typical of Chicago. There are very few Mexican or Puerto Rican, Japanese, Chinese, Indian and similar groups in the sample because of the recency of their migration. The main groups represented are Germans, Scandinavians, Scotch-English among the older women, and Irish, Polish, Italians and Jewish among the younger.

Some of these women grew up in households in which only a foreign language was spoken. In over 14,000 homes, English was not spoken at all, and in more than 16,000, two languages were spoken. An additional 20 percent of the women were raised in homes in which English was not the primary language. Studies of ethnic groups such as the Poles (Obidinski, 1968; Mostwin, 1972; Lopata, 1976a, 1976b) indicate that if more than one language is spoken in the home, the parents use the foreign tongue, and the children use English. In such homes, the likelihood that the parents will be able to hand down knowledge and skills of American urban logic and behavior to their children is minimal. In addition, many of these children went to ethnic schools taught by foreign teachers, or teachers otherwise not deeply steeped in American culture (Greeley, 1971; Rossi and Greeley, 1968; Lopata, 1976a). In many ethnic communities, girls were not encouraged to pursue the sort of education concerned with the acquisition of abstract knowledge and ideas needed for complex and flexible life patterns.

Most of the parents born outside of metropolitan Chicago, and even many born there, had inferior educations. This emerged from answers to the question about the years of schooling completed by the parents, quite apart from the quality of their education. Only 48 percent of the widows were able to answer the questions as to the fathers' years of school-ing, and eight percent simply stated that they did not know. Sixty-six percent of the women who answered the question credited their fathers with eight years or less of schooling. Interestingly enough, more (59 percent) of the widows knew their mothers' school history. Most of the mothers—66 per-cent—who told their daughters about their schooling had eight years or less.

The reason for including all these figures is to show that we are dealing with older women and that the historical gener-ations they represent tended to have a rural American or for-eign background, whose education was not designed to de-velop personal resources for voluntaristic engagement in a complex social life space. The same, of course, is true of the widows from the black community, since when most were growing up, the parents came from or even remained in the rural poor south, and few black children obtained an education from parents, the community or the school—designed to meet the demands of cosmopolitan life [see Jencks (1972)].

POSSESSIONS AS RESOURCES: MONEY AND HOUSING[4]

The death of the head of a household almost inevitably changes the amount and sources of income available to the survivors for their own maintenance and for other support exchanges. No urbanite can exist without some source of money or gifts of food and clothing. Most people must meet payments for rent or mortgage, property taxes, utilities, med-ical and other expenses. Few widows live with their married children or in circumstances requiring no expenditure on their part, and, as we will see, few are engaged in economic or service support systems that could substitute for a steady in-come. Yet the amount of income of the Chicago area widows and the sources from which it is drawn vary considerably.

The interview contains two measures of income—one in a precoded question on the total income the year prior to the husband's fatal illness or accident, and in 1973, the year prior to the study. The second measure is a detailed set of questions on the amount of income received in 1973 from specified sources (see Chapter 9, "Supports from the Economic Institution").

The heavy dependence of wives on the earnings or social security of their husbands is evident in Table 24, which documents the drop in income after they became widows. The 1973 aggregate income figures show that half of the widows lived on a total family income of less than $3,500, and about 40 percent of the women are living close to poverty by either the Social Security Administration or the U.S. 1970 Census Cutoff, as we shall see in Chapter 9. The more income sources and, especially, the more earners in the family, the higher the family income. The married women are especially well off, compared to the widows, as are other women with a male head of the family. Social security benefits, usually in the form of survivor benefits, are the most frequently mentioned source of income, with three-quarters of the widows being recipients. Earnings and interest are next in frequency; the income from rentals, employee pensions and veterans' widows pensions are not readily available. Public assistance, private insurance and other sources appear least often. Social security benefits, however, do not bring as much money to the household of a widow as do earnings—or only about half of what she can earn, for a median of only $2,292 in 1973.

The home is an important resource in a woman's life (Lopata, 1971a). It is a symbol of ownership and, in widowhood, of independence. The Chicago area women with no dependent children or other dependents tend to live alone—generally by choice—and they are possessive about their home. The dwelling and its location can give a sense of security or bring fear and anxiety. If located in an area with compatible, sociable neighbors, it can provide many supports. Its location can also serve as either a constricting boundary or facilitating tie to other resources.

Over half of the women in our sample are living in the same housing unit now as they did the year before the husband's fatal illness or accident.[5] The most recently widowed are the least likely to have moved, but still many of the older retirement widows have stayed in the same dwelling. An additional 12 percent had previously lived in the same neighborhood—and all but nine percent in the Chicago area. This contradicts the frequent assumption that women pick up and move far away after the death of the husband. Of course, even those who moved nearer to their children did not have to go too far, as almost all of them have at least one child in the Chicago area. Almost two-thirds of the women are now living in a private house, only seven percent fewer than when the husband was alive. This is typical of Chicago, and it does indicate independence, at least as far as residence goes. The remarried women are the most apt to live in a house—85 percent of them. Not surprisingly, the women now receiving retirement social security are the least able to afford a house, nine percent fewer than when the husband was alive (56 percent and 65 percent, respectively). Very few of these couples had lived in retirement hotels, nursing homes or any other institution, whereas more widows do now, but the proportion is low—lower in fact than for the city or country as a whole (two percent). Again, this reflects the fact that the current and former social security beneficiaries are better off on the average than the total of women in this marital category.

Not only are the majority of widows living in houses rather than in multiple-dwelling units, but over half of them own their place of residence (53 percent), a drop of only six percent from the time prior to the husband's last illness or accident. Furthermore, ownership is much higher than the group's average for all categories except the retirement beneficiaries. A third of the widows are renting, while only 13 percent (or one percent more than before widowhood) have made other living arrangements, which means in households owned or rented by other people. These numbers are indicative of a much greater degree of independent living than anticipated, and they reinforce the Chevan–Korsen (1975) thesis that dependent residential arrangements for widows are decreasing, as all but the elderly are highly independent. Twenty years ago, Peter Marris (1958) found that many younger London widows (at least those whose husbands were below 50 years at death), were also independent in their housing and other aspects of their lives; this is the same for the Chicago area widows.

There are three changes in the housing conditions of the women who are now widows: these concern the headship of the household, the number of people and the number of rooms. Eight of 10 widows are heads of their households, and the proportion ranges from 91 percent for the women not eligible for any social security benefits except for the lump-sum payment, to only 22 percent for those who are remarried and who thus tend to list the new husband as head. A total of only five percent have a husband who now heads the household; only 12 percent defer to an offspring as the head. This distribution reinforces all the prior findings about American widows. Even among the retirement widows, that is women who were 65 years of age in 1974 or drawing reduced benefits at 62, the rate of those heading their home is 78 percent.(The age for reduced eligibility dropped recently.) Not surprisingly, 90 percent of the women represented by our sample designated the husband as the head of the household the year prior to his fatal illness or accident; eight percent claimed the role for themselves; and only two percent lived in residences headed by other people. The number of people contained in the household now has changed in two ways. In the first place, there is a shift from two people to one person since the women with healthy husbands were not living in one-person households; now 43 percent of them do. Twenty-four percent are now living in two-person homes, while 21 percent had lived in three-person residences. The second change is due to the fact that many years have elapsed since the husband was well and the children had moved out of the mother's house. That is, 13 percent of the widows now live in three-person dwellings and 19 percent in homes with four and more persons, while in the past, 38 percent were in four-plus households.

Also, the number of rooms within the widow's household has tended to shrink since before the illness of her husband, since those who moved generally went into smaller quarters. This does not apply to the remarried, who have expanded their living space, with 55 percent now living in seven or more rooms, as compared to only 26 percent previously. Generally speaking, one-third of the widows are now living in units of one to four rooms (a drop of 10 percent). Forty-nine percent have five to six rooms (a drop of seven percent) and 18 percent are in larger units, a change of only three percent.

In order to determine the kind of surroundings in which the widow now finds herself, the interview included a scale calling for interviewer estimation of certain characteristics of the unit and of the block in which it is contained. This scheme was possible because the interviews took place in the household of the respondent, and the judgments are of interest not only to those of us concerned with the living arrangements of widows but also to urban sociologists. Although many of the respondents did know of the interviewer's visit in advance, some did not, and yet most were found to maintain neat and clean residences. At least two-thirds are evaluated at the positive extreme slot between the "neat and clean" category and "messy and dirty." The same cannot be said about the judgments on appearance of the residence in terms of wealth and poverty. The interviewers tended to refrain from either extreme (four percent each), and slots near the poverty end were slightly underused. Even then, over 15 percent of the respondents were found to live in surroundings that the interviewer judged as close to poverty. There appears to have been an atmosphere of moderate tension in many of the homes, although, here again, the interviewers did not venture far into the negative extreme.

Almost two-thirds of the widows live in residential areas

with no commercial or industrial ventures on their block and with clean streets. However, less than half live in extremely well-kept blocks with mainly single-dwelling units, and only a third in areas with much open territory. The picture that emerges is one of neither slum nor gold-coast extremes. On the other hand, the pattern of Chicago is reflected in the fact that these women live either in areas of single-dwelling units or in sections dominated by apartments. Relatively few live in mixed blocks.

PEOPLE AS RESOURCES

Although some women are socially isolated, or at least lack close associates, most have people or groups who can serve as resources for support systems. In view of their composition, however, few still have parents living or available for contact. Only 14 percent have living mothers and eight percent living fathers. Not surprisingly, the older the woman, the less likely she is to have parents available as contributors to her support systems. Only 13 percent of the almost 12,000 mothers, and eight percent of the more than 6,000 fathers, are living in the same dwelling as the widowed daughter, although many more shared residences at some time after her marriage. Less than 20 percent of the widows have a mother and/or father in the neighborhood, while over one-third of the mothers and almost half of the fathers reside outside of metropolitan Chicago. Thus, many living parents are not near. The contact rate is low; only three percent of all the widows are able to see their mother daily, and even fewer, their fathers. Their parents-in-law for the most part are dead and those still living are seen infrequently. Few widows are remarried and few have living parents-in-law from this marriage.

Only 19 percent of the widows are without a sibling. However, many of these relatives are not able to contribute to the support systems, for one-third of them do not live in the area or in Illinois; some live abroad. Thus, in spite of recent liter-

FIGURE 1

Frequency of contact with children and siblings living away from home and with old and new friends by Chicago area widows

Widow group	Several Times a Year (3)	About Once a Month (4)	Several Times a Month (5)	About Once a Week (6)
Widowed mother	3.66 (S)	4.17 (OF)	5.14 (Ch)	6.03 (NF)
Retired widows	3.22 (S)	3.86 (OF)	4.69 (Ch)	5.81 (NF)
Lump sum beneficiaries	3.62 (S)	4.50 (OF)	5.23 (Ch)	6.21 (NF)
Remarried widows	3.41 (OF) 3.53 (S)	—	4.78 (Ch)	5.42 (NF)
Mothers with adult children	3.52 (S) 3.74 (OF)	—	4.81 (Ch) 5.13 (Ch)	5.70 (NF)
Total	3.37 (S)	3.93 (OF)	4.81 (Ch)	5.84 (NF)

Legend: OF = old friends, before husband's illness (23,116 or 28.1% have none). NF = new friends, since husband's death (44,225 or 54% have none). Ch = adult children living outside of mother's home (20,590 or 25% have none). S = siblings living outside of widow's home (16,097 or 20% have none). Not presented in figure are the extreme positions: never = 0; less than once a year = 1; several times a week = 7; daily = 8.

69

ature that claims close contact among adult siblings, particularly in old age, most of the brothers and sisters of the widows are scattered and involved in their own lives, having spent years building their homes and families.

Children are more numerous and are seen more frequently, although they, too, tend to be dispersed and involved in their own lives. All but nine percent of the widows have at least one living child, but contact with those who are not in the home tends to be asymetrical, the mother seeing one child more often than the others, so that the average frequency is not high, being a few times a month but less than weekly. Not surprisingly, the younger the woman, or, in the case of a somewhat older one, the more children she has, the higher the probability that at least one offspring is still living with her. Thus, women aged 44 or less have an average of more than three children still living at home; those between 45 and 54 an average of fewer than two; and older women at most one, if any—the average being less than one.

Other resources are friends, both the "old friends" predating the husband's fatal illness or accident and "new friends" made since widowhood. All but 25 percent were able to list at least one close personal friends before widowhood, for an average of almost four for all widows who claimed such relationships. Although they still consider them close friends, they do not see them frequently, for a variety of reasons, which I will discuss in the chapter on friendship. Forty three percent of the widows represented by our sample have formed new friendships since the death of their husbands. Of course, the time period involved is a relatively short one for some women and some of it was devoted to grieving and rebuilding their lives. However, since the average length of widowhood has been 10 years, it indicates a slowing up of efforts or less success in making friends. However, new friends are seen often.

Chicago area widows have been faithful to the religion in which they were socialized in childhood. The only shift is a decrease in the number of women who identify with an unusual parental religion and an increase of those who do not identify with any faith. The number involved in such shifts is small and very few belong to any religion other than one of the major faiths. Almost half of the women in our sample are Protestants; almost the same proportion is Catholic; and a minority four percent is Jewish. Although fewer than two percent have no religious preference, only 83 percent of the total claim to be practicing their faith, and only 78 percent belong to a church. Almost half of the women regularly attend religious services once a week, one in eight never does and an additional four percent less than once a year. Altogether, almost a third attend services occasionally. This discrepancy between identification with a religion and active involvement in its ritual is typical of urban America, although of males more than females, and we had expected a higher rate of attendance on the part of widows.

Over half of the Chicago area widows do not belong to any voluntary association, club or group other than a church. Some of the active women (23 percent) belong to only one such group and 12 percent belong to two. This lack of involvement is a reflection of their ages and class background. The organization most frequently mentioned is a church club—followed by ethnic societies, auxiliaries of men's groups, sports and social clubs. Only a few list professional or other occupational affiliations. Those who specify membership in a particular group are apt to attend meetings several times a year.

In sum, the metropolitan Chicago area has many resources for developing individual abilities, opportunities for increasing personal resources, and support systems and chances for maintaining and expanding social relations and roles. Although the urban American world that emerged out of rural and immigrants backgrounds is increasingly based upon voluntaristic action of each individual member, vestiges of former life-styles persist. Some women, lacking the abilities and skills to engage in the society, continue to rely on the automatically engaging neighborhood or family. Ethnic or recent migrant backgrounds can provide supports which do not require voluntaristic engagement in widowhood. Some of the recent Mexican, Puerto Rican, black and white Appalachian migrants to Chicago retain close kinship ties and settle near people they knew in their old homes. Traditional families tend to make stronger attempts to keep the unit together than do some of the more individuated families. Traditional widows may be more willing to undertake grandparental and housekeeping duties to help adult daughters to keep a job. Polish Americans, though more apt to have geographically and socially scattered families, enjoy a history of active involvement in voluntary associations, even within classes generally inactive in such groups (Lopata, 1976a, 1976b). Strong religious identification can result in an active church life even in the absence of other contacts or can provide strong emotional supports. The black family reputedly maintains close ties with the mother and the grandmother, living together and supporting each other. At least, much of sociological literature suggests that old forms of social integration sustain the individual until she or he is ready to enter new support systems. However, it is quite possible that many people are ready and able to create new ones for themselves. How do the societal, community and personal resources of Chicago area widows translate themselves into support systems?

Support Systems Involving Widows

The support systems involving Chicago area widows discussed here include five economic supports she receives from others (inflow); five gives others (outflow); the in- and outflow of 10 service supports; the sharing of nine social supports; and of 13 emotional supports she received the year before her husband's fatal illness or accident plus the 13 she is receiving now. Each respondent could list up to three persons; that is, she had three "chances" to list a person, a group or something as esoteric as "my faith" as contributors or recipients of each support in each of the four systems. The interviewers and coders were instructed whenever possible to separate the references in cases of multiple listings, as when a widow names "Tom and Janet" as a couple with whom she is friendly. This means that each respondent could list up to 30 persons in the economic, 60 in the service, 27 in the social, and 78 in the emotional support systems, for a maximum total of 195 persons.[6]

All four of the support systems initially included the "before" and the "now" time segments, but we finally eliminated the "before" segment of all but the emotional system. Two reasons guided this decision, the main one being the lack of significant variation in the responses. From the vantage point of widowhood, the late husband simply appeared too frequently during pretests in the three systems—economic, service and social—especially in the sex-segregated areas of life, to make the retention of that part of the interview worthwhile. In addition, the interview was much too long and we did not want to lose details of the current supports. On the other hand, very interesting variations appeared in the emotional "before" system, which, in cases of remarriage, made possible comparisons with a living new husband. A private reason was my desire to relate the emotional contributions of the late husband, as remembered by his widow, to a newly created "sanctification scale."

Most of the widows do not take full advantage of all the chances in all the supports, often explaining that they do not engage in the activity or listing only one person as provider or recipient of such a support (see Table 2). The mean, or average, of the total number of listings per respondent is 25 percent of the 195 chances. In addition, a number of women list either themselves or "no one" as supppliers of some of the supports, so that only little over one-fifth of the opportunities to list significant others and groups are used. In other words, widows tend to limit the number and variety of people

TABLE 2

Frequencies with Which Categories of People Collapsed,
by Their Relation to Chicago Area Widows,
Appear in Their Support Systems

Persons	Mean	Median	Chances for that Category to Appear	% Never Appear
Self	4.1	3.9	65[a]	15
No one	3.2	2.6	65[a]	12
Late husband	8.0	8.8	13[b]	4
Present husband	0.9	0.0	52[c]	84
Boyfriends	0.5	0.0	156[d]	92
Children	8.4	17.4	195[e]	8
Parents	1.0	0.1	195	83
Siblings	2.9	0.4	195	54
Other Relatives	3.5	2.2	195	28
Friends	6.1	3.9	195	24
Other persons, groups	3.2	1.8	195	28
Sum	48.6	46.7	195	—
Others (no self)	44.5	42.6	195	—
Others (no self or no one)	41.3	—	195	—

[a]The "self" and "no one" can appear only once in each component of each of the four support systems for a total of 65, "before" and "now."
[b]The late husband can appear only once in each of the "before" components of the emotional support systems (although a few widows listed him also "now").
[c]The present husband can appear only in the various components of "now" support systems (although a few widows listed him also "before").
[d]Boyfriends can appear in all three chances of all "now" components of the support systems (although a few widows listed them also "before").
[e]Children, relatives, siblings, parents, parents-in-law, friends and neighbors and all other persons and groups can appear in all three chances of all "now" components of all four support systems as well as in the "before" emotional system.

with whom they exchange supports.[7] Caution should be used in drawing inferences from the "never appear" column of Table 2, because it obviously combines women who do not have such resources with those who do yet do not involve them in their support systems. For example, 54 percent of the widows never mention a brother or sister in responses to any of the questions, although only 19 percent do not have living siblings. The significance of the memory-constructed husband is evident from the fact that only four percent of the women do not mention him as part of the emotional system the year before his fatal illness or accident. There is a very close correlation between the percentage of women who have no living children (8.6 percent) and the proportion who do not list a child as part of the systems (8.4 percent); some childless widows list stepchildren. Parents are dead and hence not mentioned in the support system; the failure of one-quarter of the respondents to name other persons such as relatives outside of the family of orientation or procreation and friends or neighbors reflects the support system, not the resources set.

The contributions to the support systems of many of the Chicago area widows are highly concentrated. Although the format provided for only 13 listings of the late husband, since only the emotional supports are obtained for the "before" period, he appears most often of all people at that time, sometimes as providing supports even after death. Children appear quite frequently, but the mean and medians for them are kept down by the widows' interesting conceptions of economic and service exchanges. Homemaking activities or exchanges of goods that are part of the "normal" flow of daily life in a household are often not defined as "help." More details of this tendency will be given in the section on specific supports.

Friends appear relatively often in the supports, usually in the social system, and more often among the middle-class than the working-class women. Next in importance as contributor to the widow's supports is she herself. That is, many of the women are aware of themselves as a resource supplying supports. A careful reading of the interview indicates, however, that this designation can express both positive and negative affects, usually, but not necessarily by different women. On the positive side, the woman sees herself as the major provider of a self-feeling such as independence or self-sufficiency; being obviously pleased that she is able to obtain this support from herself. The negative feelings come out when widows expect or want other people to provide a support, but lack the resources or fail to recruit potential contributors. For example, several women complain that they did not like to travel or go to the movies alone, but that they have no alternative if that was what they want to do. Even more likely to be negative is the woman who answers "no one" to most items of the emotional system. A widow who replies, "No one," when asked whom she most enjoys being with is not expressing a positive attitude toward her social world.

The least likely to appear in the supports of the Chicago area widows are a new husband, boyfriends, parents or parents-in-law, simply because they are not available as resources. Siblings, other people or groups not connected through family lines, such as coworkers, comembers of voluntary associations or professional helpers such as ministers or doctors are only occasional contributors to the support systems of widows, as are relatives outside the immediate nuclear line of the family of procreation, although they exist as untapped resources.

ECONOMIC SUPPORT SYSTEM

The vast majority of the Chicago area widows have no economic supports other than the direct income from current or past work by themselves or by their late husbands (see Table 3).[8] In addition, few give such supports to other people outside of their own household. When asked, "In addition to your regular income, are you presently receiving (or giving, in a parallel set of questions) any of the following kinds of financial help," very few claim to give or receive gifts of money, payment or help in payment of rent or mortgage, food or payment for food, clothing or payment for clothing, payment or help with the payment of other bills (medical, etc.) or expenses (vacation, etc.). Moreover, the women do not list financial exchanges not covered by our questions even when offered

TABLE 3

Percentages of Total Listings of Significant Others Contributing to the Inflow and Outflow of the Economic Support Systems of Chicago Area Widows

				CONTRIBUTORS—ALL WIDOWS						
Economic supports	Number of First Listings[a]	Number of Total Listings	Boyfriends[b]	Children	Parents	Siblings	Other Relatives	Friends	Other People, Groups
Inflow									
Gifts, money	7,210	11,477	2	83	2	5	4	2	0
Rent	7,201	8,915	4	70	2	5	0	13	6
Food	9,193	10,427	4	77	1	7	2	0	8
Clothing	4,685	6,099	1	92	0	5	1	0	1
Bills	6,168	7,655	6	58	2	4	0	0	38
Outflow									
Gifts, money	10,844	17,160	0	43	2	4	29	1	20
Rent	4,380	5,193	0	81	5	10	3	1	0
Food	4,523	6,029	4	67	5	14	5	1	4
Clothing	2,811	3,638	0	60	1	9	17	2	11
Bills	3,554	4,151	0	68	3	8	10	8	4

[a]Most widows do not exchange selected economic supports.
[b]Present husband is eliminated from this table for obvious reasons.

the opportunity to do so. Table 4 details the contributions to this system of various significant others, organized by the relationship to the widow (the late husband, children, etc.), which will be discussed later. This chapter covers only the overview, but obviously the economic supports of whatever nature are highly concentrated on the children. Also, unlike the service support system, the widow here feels that she is the giver of economic help more often than the receiver. The "other relatives" category generally refers to grandchildren, although occasionally nieces and nephews are mentioned. The "other" category refers mainly to charitable organizations in the case of the outflow, and governmental agencies in the inflow, particularly in the help with the payment of bills, although some widows are given assistance by private agencies. There tends to be a significant association between poverty and financial assistance, but being poor does not guarantee economic supports, as evidenced by the fact that so many of the women living below the established poverty cut-off report no such aid.

SERVICE SUPPORT SYSTEM

Most of the metropolitan Chicago widows also are not involved in extensive service supports, either as receivers or as givers, although more participate in these exchanges than in the economic system (see Table 4). The question eliciting this information stated: "Now I will read you a list of things people often do for each other in daily life or in solving special problems. Does anyone do any of these things for you? Does anyone. . . ." The various services found to be common during exploratory and pretest research were then read, followed by a parallel question and a listing of services in which the widow can appear as giver rather than as receiver. These included the provision of transportation, household repairs, help with housekeeping, help with shopping, yard work, child care, car care, sick care, help in decision-making and provision of legal aid, in that order.

There are several probable reasons why relatively few widows are reported as involved in most of these supports. An obvious one is that many women have no need for the specified type of help, nor do their associates need it. The guidelines used in our discussion of economic supports is the established level of family income considered the minimum necessary for comfortable living, in fact, a level below the poverty cut-off. In terms of services, however, we cannot establish any criteria for need, but can only record whether or not a widow receives or gives one of the mentioned supports and with whom she is involved in such exchanges. A woman who does not have a yard obviously does not need help in its maintenance. The same holds true for child care, and most of the widows no longer have offspring requiring supervision. It is somewhat more surprising to find so few of the widows helping with child care, but it is impossible within the framework of this study to determine whether this is due to the absence of small children in the network, to their unwillingness to care for them or to alternate arrangements made by the parents of such children. All we know is that only 20 percent of the Chicago area widows help take care of children. Most of this help involves the care of their own grandchildren.

The second reason for the lack of involvement in service supports is the traditional sex-segregated nature of everyday American life. Almost no women help anyone in the care of an automobile. Nor do they assist in legal problems or with household repairs. These are tasks that fall into the man's domain in the usual family division of responsibility. If widows do perform such services, the recipients are most likely to be their parents or friends, people with even less experience in these areas. The widows also are not providers of transportation, since being unfamiliar with cars, they usually get rid of theirs after the death of the husband. Hence, they also do

TABLE 4

Percentages of Total Listings of Significant Others Contributing to the Inflow and Outflow of the Service Support Systems of Chicago Area Widows

Service Supports	Number of First Listings[a]	Number of Total Listings	CONTRIBUTORS—ALL WIDOWS							
			Present Husband[b]	Present Husband, Boyfriend	Children	Parents	Siblings	Other Relatives	Friends	Other People, Groups
Inflow										
Transportation	44,771	54,355	56	5	57	0	8	6	18	7
House repairs	34,863	38,676	77	11	55	1	9	11	4	10
Housekeeping	18,702	20,548	42	4	69	3	2	7	5	11
Shopping	32,060	34,119	57	5	67	1	5	4	12	6
Yard work	25,836	28,537	63	11	55	2	4	13	2	14
Child care	2,806	3,682	61	17	28	21	4	9	12	10
Car care	10,787	11,876	70	17	50	2	4	6	5	17
Sick care	45,732	51,924	50	4	65	4	9	4	8	6
Decisions	33,663	39,440	89	9	70	2	10	5	2	2
Legal aid	15,670	16,002	20	2	19	0	8	10	5	55

TABLE 4 (*cont.*)

Outflow

Transportation	14,768	18,794	2	0	19	8	7	10	39	16
House repairs	1,320	2,041	8	4	34	25	3	9	20	3
Housekeeping	9,842	10,512	0	0	56	8	10	8	12	6
Shopping	10,727	11,395	0	0	13	20	9	8	34	16
Yard work	2,948	3,223	9	2	23	17	20	6	13	17
Child care	16,689	19,943	0	0	52	0	3	30	8	6
Car care	108	189	0	0	0	68	6	18	8	0
Sick care	29,302	36,320	15	2	44	10	10	10	14	16
Decisions	14,694	17,298	26	4	44	6	11	7	24	4
Legal aid	504	644	0	0	35	22	2	9	24	8

[a]Many widows do not exchange selected service supports.
[b]Remarried widows only.

not need help in the care of a car—another consequence of a sex-segregated society.

A third reason is the infrequency of services rendered across household thresholds in modern urban America, except along the direct lines of ascent or descent, and even then, mostly in unusual circumstances. Some of the sociologists of family relations have developed a thesis of a "modified extended" family, as opposed to Parsons' theory of isolated nuclear family, as typical of American society (Litwak, 1965; Shanas and Streib, 1965; Shanas et al., 1968; Sussman, 1962, 1965).[9] The thesis claims frequent exchanges of services among members of the extended family operating from geographically dispersed households. A careful reading of the research upon which it is based shows it to have been limited to inquiries about help given married children in the early years of their household formation or to parents in their health-restricted old age. Help given other older relatives was not examined. In some of the studies, people were asked if they "ever" had given help to selected relatives, or if they helped them during the past year. There is a great difference between the responses of people when asked if they had ever, or within the last year, given or received help from their children and when the query focuses on consistently given support. The study of Chicago area widows indicates that widows are seldom receivers, or givers, of services in major areas of life involving people in physically separated households. This conclusion reinforces findings from previous studies that show Chicago area housewives or older widows rarely involved in borrowing or lending even among their neighbors (Lopata, 1971a, 1973a).

The final reason for the infrequency of listing of service exchanges on the part of Chicago area widows lies in their tendency to think of "help" in these areas only in situations of extraordinary or specifically arranged assistance outside the normal field of work. This becomes apparent when we find women with children or even a new husband in the home who claim they do not receive or give help with housework, shopping, decision making and so forth. A woman cleaning her own home apparently does not consider this as help to the children living in it. She will think of herself as providing such services only if she does so in someone else's home or, if living in a home managed by another housewife, helps her with the work. In the same vein, many widows list help given to them in the management of their home by children or a spouse only when it is consciously arranged, and in such a case she clearly indicates that she is the person responsible for the work getting done and that the others merely help her (Lopata, 1966, 1971a). This is the traditional image of the role of housewife against which some modern feminists are rebelling. It may be the new trend for all persons living in a household to share in its maintenance, but many Chicago area widows have not organized their homes that way and do not feel this way, either doing all the work themselves or getting "help" with certain chores from people living with them by prearrangement. The combination of attitudes distinguishes between the ordinary routine of managing one's own domain and "helping with" an activity managed by another person.[10]

A careful look at Table 4 highlights the infrequency of service exchanges, the asymmetry of different support involvements, and the great variations in the interaction with people in different relationships to the widow. Help given to her most frequently involves care in case of illness or transportation. Sick care is also her most frequent contribution to the supports of others.

SOCIAL SUPPORT SYSTEM

Many of the current and former beneficiaries of social security do not engage in the social activities that the teams preparing the interview and the pretest respondents found to be the most frequently shared leisure-hour activities of urban American women (see Table 5). We asked the respondents if they participate in selected "social activities that people can

83

TABLE 5
Percentages of First and Total Listings of Present Husband, Children and Self and Total Listings of Other People Contributing to the Social Support Systems of Chicago Area Widows

Social Supports	Number of First Listings[a]	Number of Total Listings[a]	Present Husband[b] 1st	Present Husband[b] T	Present Husband, Boyfriend 1st	Present Husband, Boyfriend T	Children 1st	Children T	Self 1st	Self T	Parents	Siblings	Other Relatives	Friends	Other People, Groups
Public places	40,243	59,944	89	63	16	12	27	28	4	3	1	6	6	38	6
Visiting	64,869	110,063	30	19	3	2	30	29	2	2	2	11	10	40	5
Entertaining	48,964	88,970	14	8	3	2	24	23	0	0	1	6	19	43	5
Lunch	51,399	79,607	27	19	5	4	18	18	3	2	1	7	5	51	12
Church	62,078	79,318	65	46	4	3	29	35	41	33	1	6	5	15	3
Sports, cards and games	34,337	56,709	36	25	6	4	10	12	4	2	0	5	10	58	8
Travel out of town	48,460	68,046	84	62	8	6	32	35	27	21	1	11	9	15	2
Celebrate holidays	73,853	142,108	38	23	4	2	58	52	0	0	2	10	25	7	2
Other activity	3,291	4,064	23	6	4	3	15	17	57	47	1	0	2	24	6

CONTRIBUTORS—ALL WIDOWS

[a]Many widows do not engage in selected social supports.
[b]Remarried widows only.

84

do with others?" and, if they do, with whom they do these things, and how often. If the woman states that she does not engage in the activities, we asked her why not. The specific activities are: going to public places such as movie houses, visiting, entertaining, going out to lunch or eating lunch with someone, going to church, engaging in sports, cards, and games, traveling out of town, celebrating holidays and doing anything else that the respondent wishes to mention.

There is, however, considerable variation in the proportion of nonparticipants in the total number of widows represented by our sample, depending on the activity. The variation reflects not only constraints such as income, the presence of small children or other dependents, health, and so forth, but also facilitating resources such as socio-economic or class habits of leisure activity; self-confidence necessary for the development of "polite companionship" interaction during marriage and in widowhood; and the availability of others willing to do the same (Znaniecki, 1965; Lopata, 1971a, 1973a, 1975a). Over half the widows claim never to go to public places such as movie theaters or to engage in sports, play cards or other games. Four in 10 never "entertain" or travel out of town and a similar proportion always have lunch alone. The most frequently engaged in activity is the celebration of holidays, followed by visiting and attending church. Even here, however, more than one-fourth claim never to go to church. Many of the widows perhaps define "entertaining with" differently from "visiting with," because there is a gap of 20 percent between the proportion who claim not to entertain while at the same time admit to "visiting." (The word "with" may be the main factor in the difference.) Of course, it is possible that these women lead asymmetric social lives, by visiting but not entertaining.

EMOTIONAL SUPPORT SYSTEM

The emotional support system that was finally incorporated into the interview has two main segments, called "relational sentiments" and "feeling states." The first set of questions refers to the sentiments that arise in people as a result of aspects of their relations with others. Thus, we asked women what persons are closest to them, whom they most enjoy being with; to whom they tell their problems; who comforts them when they are depressed; who makes them angry most often; to whom do they turn in times of crisis; and what person makes them feel as an especially important person. The last question is actually a transition to the second segment of the emotional support system introduced with the following questions, "Now I am going to read some 'feeling states' that many people think are important for a full life. What persons or groups make you feel that way? (then we read each word separately). Respected, useful, independent, accepted, self-sufficient and secure." Feeling states are more solid aspects of a person's identity than are the relational sentiments, although it is obvious that the sentiments can be brought forth through memory reconstructions of the situations in which they initially arose or are usually experienced. Both sets of emotional supports are related and emerge in interaction as well as from the way people are treated throughout life (Mead, 1934; James, 1900; Cooley, 1922; Berger and Kellner, 1970; Berger and Luckman, 1966). The questions are split into several locations throughout the interview to decrease response set. They were asked both for the year before the husband's fatal illness or accident and for now.

The internal differentiations among the emotional supports both the year before the husband's fatal illness or accident— as remembered by the Chicago area widows—and now are interesting. So are the contrasts between the "before" and the "now" periods (see Tables 6 and 7). Although the late husband dominates the "before" emotional supports, he appears with varying frequency in the different supports. Almost all of the women list someone in each of the supports, although this varies by the sentiment or feeling state, some women specifying that no one made them feel that way. These tables

TABLE 6

Percentages of First and Total Listings of Late Husband, Children and Self and Total Listings of Other People Contributing to the Emotional Support Systems of Chicago Area Widows the Year Before the Husband's Fatal Illness or Accident ("Before")

Emotional Supports "Before"	Number of First Listings	Number of Total Listings	Late Husband		Children		Self		Parents	Siblings	Other Relatives	Friends	Other People, Groups	No One
			1st	T	1st	T	1st	T						
Sentiments														
Closest	82,037	158,709	67	39	16	33	0	0	5	8	6	9	1	0
Enjoy	81,462	135,052	78	50	10	28	0	0	1	4	5	10	2	1
Problems	81,715	101,052	58	50	7	13	4	3	3	5	4	8	3	13
Comfort	81,119	105,712	58	46	7	15	2	3	2	7	5	8	4	14
Important	80,054	118,889	75	53	9	27	2	3	2	7	3	5	2	7
Angry	79,027	88,778	23	21	13	19	0	1	1	2	4	2	5	52
Crisis	80,182	102,842	62	50	3	10	1	1	4	10	7	5	3	9
Feeling States														
Respected	80,316	141,239	65	40	1	2	3	2	2	2	5	7	11	3
Useful	80,937	132,882	69	46	11	31	7	5	3	1	3	2	7	2
Independent	80,053	93,895	40	36	2	8	39	36	1	2	2	1	3	15
Accepted	78,200	124,650	58	38	7	21	6	4	2	2	7	12	11	5
Self-sufficient	79,437	96,010	40	35	4	9	42	37	1	1	2	3	5	8
Secure	80,289	101,754	75	61	4	14	11	10	2	1	1	3	3	5

CONTRIBUTORS—ALL WIDOWS

TABLE 7

Percentages of First and Total Listings of Present Husband, Children and Self and Total Listings of Other People Contributing to the Emotional Support Systems of Chicago Area Widows at the Present Time ("Now")

Emotional Supports "Now"	Number of First Listings	Number of Total Listings	Present Husband	Present Husband, Boyfriend 1st	T	Children 1st	T	Self 1st	T	Parents	Siblings	Other Relatives	Friends	Other People, Groups	No One
CONTRIBUTORS—ALL WIDOWS[a]															
Sentiments															
Closest	82,044	144,277	31	4	3	65	60	2	1	3	10	9	10	2	2
Enjoy	80,706	145,463	43	7	4	53	52	0	0	2	8	13	16	3	5
Problems	81,664	112,996	54	5	4	37	42	7	6	2	9	4	12	5	21
Comfort	81,304	117,671	58	6	5	41	45	6	4	2	9	4	11	5	21
Important	79,630	128,246	53	8	5	52	57	6	4	2	4	7	9	4	12
Angry	80,320	89,275	15	2	2	18	22	1	1	0	3	4	2	9	63
Crisis	80,170	114,490	67	6	5	52	54	4	3	3	10	5	7	4	12
Feeling States															
Respected	81,035	144,162	40	5	4	54	52	7	4	2	4	7	12	13	4
Useful	80,459	126,334	40	5	4	46	50	16	11	2	4	2	7	9	13
Independent	79,819	97,652	31	2	2	13	20	61	50	0	4	2	3	7	7
Accepted	77,698	128,472	37	5	4	37	40	11	5	1	4	6	19	14	10
Self-sufficient	78,953	100,142	35	3	3	14	21	61	49	1	4	3	6	5	10
Secure	79,883	111,801	59	6	5	28	36	40	30	1	4	7	4	9	10

[a]Remarried widows only.

demonstrate the significance of listing both the first mention and the total, because they show the concentration of attention on certain significant others. That is, certain people, such as the late husband in the "before" period, come immediately to the widow's mind, while others, such as friends, rank second or third in importance. Few women admit feeling angry at anyone in the past—even fewer in the present. The widows draw qualitative distinctions among the different sentiments and feeling states, so that people appearing in one are not necessarily contributors to another. For example, the enjoyment of being with someone definitely expresses a different relational sentiment than feeling close to, and it does not necessarily lead to transforming that person into a confidant or comforter.

The present emotional support system is more dispersed, although children pretty much take over for the late husband. In the few cases of remarriage the current husband often plays a different role in the system than does the remembered late husband.

LACK OR FAILURE OF RESOURCES

The discussion of the service support system spoke of some of the reasons why the Chicago area widows fail to mention involvement in such exchanges—or to see a certain activity as a service to someone else. What remains is a glance at the failure in the support system due to lack of resources or lack of action on the part of identified resources. A woman can feel that someone, somewhere, should be helping her, or else she may expect some form of assistance from specific persons. Of course, the support she expects may not be the support these persons or the societal resource offer her. Consequently, a woman may experience or define herself as experiencing failures of supports. Several sets of information in the interview give us clues on such feelings. In the first place, the women were asked to rank the degree of helpfulness of selected persons and societal resources in establishing a new life in widowhood. Next, they were asked if there was any kind of help or advice they wished people had offered them but had not received at that time. Third, many of the explanations for lack of engagement in the social activities supports may be taken as indications of failure of resources. Finally, the response, "no one," in the emotional systems seems to be a clear indication of a lack of supports in vital aspects of life.

The lack of personal individual and economic resources restrict many widows in their social activities. Health problems bother one-fifth to one-third of the women, depending upon the activity, out-of-town travel being the most affected. Lack of money is given as the main reason for not engaging in "polite companionship" activities with others by about one-fifth of the women, again depending on the activity. Lack of time and energy are also listed by that same proportion of women. Generally, the main reason given by the women for not entering the social support systems is lack of interest or desire. Since this is definitely a self-imposed limitation, it shows that the self can be both a resource for social engagement and a constraining force.

As mentioned earlier the "no one" answer in the emotional support systems both while the husband was alive and well and at the present time is indicative of the type of emotional isolation discused by Weiss (1973) and Townsend (1968; see also Lopata, 1973b). The one place it might not be indicative of Townsend's "desolation" is in the response to, "Who makes you angry most often?" Still, close relations with significant others are bound to produce some sort of emotion. As sociologists who depend on survey research, we cannot be sure whether these women really do not feel angry at anyone; do not admit to such feelings even to themselves; or will not publicly admit to them in a society that supports "coolness" of temper as the ideal.

Leaving the feeling of anger aside, we still find a relatively large proportion of women (from one-fifth to one-tenth) who list "no one" as their current confidant, comforter, person to whom they would turn in crisis, or who makes them feel important, useful, accepted, self-sufficient and secure. Thus, the resources have failed to match some of the needs for the relational sentiment and feeling state supports available when the husband was alive and well, usually supplied by him. The children have grown and lead their own independent lives; the person who made her feel important died. On the other hand, we must again note the increased contribution of the self to many of the feeling states. Two different types of women generally report the "self" and "no one" as contributors to the emotional support system, although there may be an overlap of angry or frustrated widows who wish someone would provide some of these supports and who are not happy to be their own main suppliers.

Summary

All in all, although a variety of people are involved in the support systems of the Chicago area current or former beneficiaries of social security, the main contributors are a husband, children and the self. Friends enter the social system, but often on a superficial level; they do not become confidants to whom problems are told; serve as comforters; or provide important self-feelings. Table 8 documents the number of significant others, organized by their relation to the widow, who appear in each support of the three current systems. The self as a source of supports can appear only when the question is not prefaced by a screener eliminating all women who do not get a service. Women tend to report going to church and traveling alone, although they usually meet other people in these activities. Not surprisingly, the self is most frequently reported as the provider of feelings of independence and self-sufficiency. What is equally interesting is that some of the women feel they can receive these two self-feelings from other

TABLE 8

Numbers of Significant Others, Self Designations or "No One" Responses of Chicago Area Widows in Their Service,
Social and Emotional Support Systems

Support System	Children	Siblings	Other Relatives	Friends	Other People, Groups	Self	No One	Total[a]
Service—In								
Transportation	30,749	4,169	3,292	9,730	3,592			54,355
House repair	21,373	3,329	4,147	1,485	3,655			38,676
Housekeeping	14,199	389	1,351	979	2,200			20,548
Shopping	22,958	1,679	1,417	3,989	2,205			34,119
Yard work	15,596	1,251	3,758	486	4,098			28,537
Child care	1,025	142	315	453	359			3,682
Car care	5,885	447	667	560	2,009			11,876
Sick care	33,734	4,822	2,158	4,196	3,005			51,924
Decisions	27,683	3,804	2,075	951	697			39,440
Legal aid	3,056	1,348	1,649	814	8,741			16,002
Social								
Public places	16,925	3,808	3,619	22,991	2,875	1,937		59,994
Visiting	32,323	12,254	10,933	43,821	5,199	1,782		110,063

TABLE 8 (cont.)

							Total
Entertaining	20,346	5,622	16,968	38,319	4,368	165		88,970
Lunch	14,631	5,424	3,897	40,689	9,421	1,407		79,607
Church	27,601	4,461	3,659	11,711	2,461	25,989		79,318
Sports, cards, games	6,897	2,847	5,597	32,987	4,407	1,357		56,709
Travel out of town	23,831	7,743	6,207	10,000	1,050	14,312		68,046
Celebrate holidays	74,185	3,597	35,406	9,804	2,448	223		142,108
Emotional								
Closest	87,123	15,093	12,387	14,983	2,289	1,520	1,650	144,277
Enjoy	74,858	12,189	17,748	23,811	4,076	15	3,730	145,463
Problems	47,752	10,185	5,117	13,726	5,763	6,570	17,219	112,996
Comfort	52,840	10,566	4,810	12,841	5,855	5,275	17,330	117,671
Important	72,400	5,130	9,990	12,059	5,408	5,118	9,549	128,246
Angry	19,532	2,615	3,758	1,763	7,750	883	50,401	89,275
Crisis	62,315	10,993	6,392	8,345	5,138	3,745	9,470	114,490
Respected	74,772	6,008	9,855	17,352	18,857	6,500	3,172	144,162
Useful	63,758	3,586	2,658	8,456	11,606	13,429	10,698	126,334
Independent	19,235	5,561	1,876	3,055	6,813	49,254	5,181	97,652
Accepted	51,030	3,724	9,036	24,615	17,522	9,397	7,705	128,472
Self-sufficient	21,050	4,817	2,948	5,649	5,053	49,334	8,458	100,142
Secure	40,776	4,142	8,518	4,458	10,182	34,007	8,156	111,801

[a]All the categories of people are not included in the summary table, therefore the total is larger than the sum of each row.

people. The question about whom they most enjoy being with draws the largest number of listings. Almost equally many responses concern the sentiment of closeness and the self-feeling of being respected. The most frequent social activity is the celebration of holidays, not only because so many women do make them into special events, but because so many other people are involved. The complexity of the support network varies considerably, some widows being relatively without contributors, others relying on a very few people for most of their supports; and others weaving a complex network with different people who contribute to different supports. As we will see, the widow's age, the ages and location of her children, her education and race are important factors influencing the personal or societal resources drawn into the support systems of different networks. The myriad of community resources, especially in the form of helping professions and groups, are relatively unimportant in the support systems of most widows living in metropolitan Chicago. There are women, in fact, who fail in their efforts to convert resources into supports at various stages of widowhood.

NOTES

1. Gloria Heinemann (1977, Appendix A3, p. 16), the project director for the interviewing agency, who is at the Survey Research Laboratory of the University of Illinois, Circle Campus, computed the proportion of completed interviews to the total eligible sample as 52 percent. Two factors accounted for this low response rate: (1) The method of drawing the sample by SSA, which resulted in addresses as old as 12 years, with the consequence that a large number of widows had moved and could not be located. The contact rate was, nevertheless, 75 percent, due to the persistence of interviewers. (2) The large number of widows who refused to be interviewed.
2. This method of obtaining data on individuals enables us to determine not only the major characteristics of a population, but also how these combine into networks and systems and the factors which influence their distribution. In this case, we want to know which widows use

94

which of the numerous supports typically involving urban American women and the composition of their supportive networks. The product of survey research is heavily dependent on the quality of the interview, in terms of its internal theoretical consistency and the extent to which it reflects the life of the people and picks up the importance of differences among them. Thus, it results in a different kind of picture of widowhood (in this case) than does a case study or a biographical account such as Lynn Caine's *Widow* (1974). Survey research does show the prevalence of different action and feeling patterns. We need many sources of information to understand subjects as complex as human beings living in different situations and locations.

3. The use of a multiframed sample with different ratios was dictated by the fact that a regular probability sample would yield too few young and remarried widows. There is no overlap among the frames. The individual samples selected are differentially weighted to reflect the different selection ratios. Thus, the 1,169 widows in the sample, when appropriately weighted, represent a universe of 82,085 Chicago area former or current beneficiaries of social security. The weighting procedure is the same one as used by the U.S. Census.

4. The data on income was analyzed by Gertrud Kim and details are available in Chapter 4 of the final report to the Social Security Administration on the "Support Systems Involving Widows in a Metropolitan Area of the United States." The chapter was written by Gertrud Kim, Henry Brehm and myself.

5. Those of us involved in the study of the support systems of widows of all ages spent some time establishing the appropriate way of asking about the period that before the husband's death remains as "normal" in the woman's memory. We finally asked her to give us the year before the illness or accident which finally caused his death; few respondents had difficulties specifying such a year. We then kept referring to that calendar year whenever eliciting data about that period.

6. We really had 201 chances, but so few women listed "other" economic supports in answer to an open-ended question that we dropped these six chances. The different supports contained in the interview are a product of extensive exploratory and pre-test interviews and discussions with Chicago area widows. Using a social-role framework, we asked initially what were the rights and duties they exchanged regularly with significant other people. We then tested these.

7. Obviously, the self, the late husband, the present husband and "no one" could be mentioned once by each woman in each set of chances, while different children, relatives, even parents and parents-in-law and other people or groups could appear more often.

8. The next six tables will be used throughout the book as we examine in detail the contributions of various significant others in the support networks.

9. Sussman (1965, p. 63) summarized the research of several sociologists, including his own.

> The theoretical position assumed in this paper is that there exists in modern urban industrial societies, particularly in American society, an extended kin family system; highly integrated within a network of social relationships and mutual assistance, that operates along bilateral kin lines and vertically over several generations.

The studies whose findings he presents point to the existence of a very active and viable extended kin network in that "extended family get-togethers and joint recreational activities with kin dominante the leisure time pursuits of urban working-class members," and that, "Kinship visiting is a primary activity of urban dwelling and outranks visitation patterns found for friends, neighbors, or co-workers" (p. 69). In addition, the kinship group performs services, " regularly throughout the year or on special occasions" and these include shopping, care of children, advice-giving, etc. (p. 70).

This chapter and the others referred to throughout this report provided a guiding hypothesis for the study of the support systems involving widows; the results are startling. Why this study so strongly contradicts the hypothesis of the viability of the extended kin family system is hard to determine, but future research must continue testing the alternate views and in-between formulations of networks. Of course, many of the researchers include adult children in the extended kinship group and do not separate their contributions, although talking of the larger unit. Chicago may be very different from Cleveland, for example. Our widows represent all social classes, not just the working class. They are also of all ages, although the majority are older. Widows may have a much more restricted social sphere than married men and women. A lot of possibilities occur as hypotheses. Ideally, longitudinal studies of actual kinship patterns and changes in specifically delineated support systems could contribute to our better understanding of contributions of specific relatives to the supports of a variety of Americans.

10. A very interesting tendency of many housewives is to define the father's playing with his children, particularly before mealtime or while the mother takes care of another child, as "help with the children," as though this was not a normal part of a father's role (Lopata, 1971a).

THREE

Widowhood and Husbands in Memory

The women here are or have been widows; at least one of their marriages ended with the death of the husband, and it is this marriage and its consequent widowhood on which we will focus. Widows subsequently remarried, were included in the sample because we wished to find out how the late husband's contributions to the emotional support systems, as remembered by the widow, compare to those of the present husband. We will later compare the support systems of the women who remarried to those who did not.

For the most part, the marriage that ended in widowhood was the only marriage of the Chicago area, current or former beneficiaries of social security represented by our sample. Only two in 10 women have married more than once, and only two percent entered such a relation more than twice. Most of the first marriages ended in widowhood rather than divorce, a distribution representative of the ages and historical generations of the majority of the women. A small proportion (2 out of 100) of the widowed women were separated or divorced from the husband at the time of his death. The majority of those who remarried, including those previously divorced, again were widowed, although 25 percent are still married. The most unhappy are former widows who entered a marriage that ended in separation or divorce.

The mean age for the women entering all marriages is 26 years; the magnitude of the mean is accounted for by the older ages of second and third marriages. Despite the general belief that widowhood is a phenomenon of advanced age, the mean age of the wife at the time of her husband's death was 56, with half of the total 58 years or younger. (Most were in their 50s or 60s.) One-quarter were less than 50, and three-quarters were under 65 years of age when becoming widowed. In view of the American cultural norm of men marrying women younger than themselves, the husbands generally were somewhat older at death, with a mean age of 60. Still, half of the husbands were below age 61 when they died. Looking at the life-styles and support systems of widows everywhere, it becomes apparent that many continue to be strongly influenced by their late husband—and their life together. Marriage in general, and marriage to that particular man, provided facilitating and constraining resources for building support systems and relational networks. The circumstances of life prior to his fatal illness or accident; the circumstances of his death; the ensuing problems and the solutions arrived at by the widow bear on the degree of disorganization produced by this series of events and the resources with which the widow can form new supports or modify old ones; or breaking ties with the past and building a new life. Finally, the memory of the past, reconstructed by selective recollection, provides a cushion for the new life or a set of self-images and behavioral constraints that immobilize the widow and even prevent effective help from her network, regardless of its scope. Thus, the widow's use of currently available resources in her support systems and networks has been influenced by her late husband's contribution to her past supports and his provision of background resources.

Causes and Circumstances of
the Husband's Death

We will see in Chapter 9 that the total median family income
the year prior to the husband's fatal illness or accident was
$7,360 in terms of constant 1973 dollars. This income came
mainly from the man's wages; over one-third of the families
was totally dependent on this source; an additional fifth received the largest part from the wages or salaries of the husbands, with some funds from other sources. Thus, a total of
58 percent of the families drew all or much of their annual
income, and a total of 69 percent at least some, from the
earnings of the male head of the family. The fact that wages
constituted so high a proportion of the total family income
indicates that most men were holding full-time jobs at the
onset of their fatal illness or accident. The majority of men
(other than those who died suddenly) were unable to perform
the same work that they did before illness, and only one-
fourth returned to their regular jobs. Over one-half were unable to work at all. A fourth of the families received Social
Security from the husband's record and, although one-third
of the women earned some money, half of the wives with
income contributed much less than a half of the total family
income. The occupational distribution of the late husbands
reflects their historical generations, with one interesting variation. Eleven percent were professionals, and 14 percent
managers, officials or proprietors, which reflects the national
distribution for males aged 55–64 (see U.S. Bureau of Census,
Marital Status, Table 5, for basic figures for this group). The
highest occupational concentration, over one-third, was in
crafts—high, relative to the American males in that age group
for 1970. The national percentage of men in crafts is 22 but
the economy of metropolitan Chicago apparently has a greater
demand for craft skills than that of other areas. Seventeen

percent of the late husbands were working as operatives with percentages dropping to six or less in the other occupational categories.

The most prevalent cause of the husband's death, reflecting national trends, relates to vascular problems, heart attacks, strokes and related disorders. Over half (51 percent) of the men died from these complications, cancer being the second most frequent cause of death (18 percent). One-tenth of the men died as a result of accidents—the majority involved automobiles, although job-related accidents are included. The large number (even though only two percent) of men who died violently at the hands of others or through suicide, reflects life in metropolitan Chicago. Only one-third of the violent deaths occurred in war times. Combined illnesses contributed to nine percent of the deaths. The "other" causes of death vary widely, the most frequent being cyrrhosis of the liver, followed by pneumonia, tuberculosis and such rare diseases as yellow fever (10 percent).

Only three in ten men died suddenly, usually the younger husbands of younger wives. Half of the men had illnesses lasting six months or more. There is much debate in the literature on grief as to which form of death, sudden or lingering, is more painful for close survivors. Parkes (1964a, 1975) and the team of Glick, Weiss and Parkes (1974) have consistently maintained that "untimely and unexpected bereavements constitute a special risk to psychological and social adjustment" (Parkes, 1975, p. 119). Bernice Neugarten (1968) concludes from her studies of the middle-aged and aging that "rehearsal" for widowhood, lessening the impact of the death of the husband, is not possible if the event takes place "off time." However, the researchers who worked with Paula Clayton claim that the difference in the effect of sudden versus anticipated bereavement vanishes after a time—generally within 13 months after death [see especially Bornstein et al. (1973), also Clayton (1973, 1973b, 1975)]. The Chicago area widows described here were interviewed after at least a year had passed so it was impossible to measure the psychological and physical effects of grief. In addition, my prime interest, as a sociologist, is in the support systems and networks that are developed in widowhood. At the same time, the death of the husband and the circumstances surrounding it can have important long-range effects on the survivors. For a variety of reasons we asked the widows to describe the circumstances of the husband's death: we wanted to give the respondents an opportunity to review this event as a catharsis. The women, having received letters and telephone calls making the appointment, knew that the interviews focused on widowhood and we discovered during the pretest that they grew impatient with background questions, wanting to talk about the death of the husband. We were also interested in finding out how the death is preserved in the memory of the widow. The question is completely open-ended—one of the few times we indulged in that luxury— "What were the circumstances surrounding your husband's death?"[1]

Most of the respondents are no longer in the acute stages of grief, having worked through the shock and initial pain as reflected in physical symptoms, such as weight loss, sleeplessness, illness, etc. (Weiner *et al.*, 1975; Glick, Weiss and Parkes, 1974, Clayton, 1973a, 1973b, 1975). They have been successful to varying degrees in cutting ties with the deceased and developing identities as partnerless persons (Lindemann, 1944; Maddison and Walker, 1967). As part of the process of grief they went through what psychiatrists call an "obsessional review," in which the survivors of a traumatic event, such as the death of someone important to them, continue to discuss the circumstances surrounding the death, offering explanations and justifications—selectively reliving what happened. Provisionally, we coded the answers to the open-ended question about the death into four sets of data: where the onset of illness or the accident took place, where the death occurred, what the wife was able or needed to do during this time, and her reaction to the situation as part of the scene or as the recipient of the news.

In one-third of the cases the place in which the onset of illness occurred is not a significant aspect of the death, at least in the memory of the widow, and is therefore not mentioned in the description of the circumstances. In another third, it took place in the home, specifically so located. About a fifth of the men were already in a health-care facility at the onset of the final attack. The widows list a great variety of public places as the locales of attack or accident, including work or recreational centers, highways, a store, etc. Only a few men became ill in locales defined by the activity rather than the specific place. Typical for this is the response, "He died in the war." Road accidents usually involved cars, suicides committed in the home or the car, stabbings in taverns or on the street, and so forth. Two men were shot during a robbery, although the wives do not specify whether they were the robbers or the victims.

The American way of death is evidenced by the comparison of the site of the onset of the fatal illness and of the death itself. More people die in hospitals or nursing homes than suffer fatal illness or accident in such places (41 to 18 percent). They tend to be stricken at home or in public places, being taken to a hospital—the established modern site of death. Only nine percent of the men died in a public place. However, a quarter of the men died at home, the place where people died in the past. A quarter of the women leave the location of the husband's death unspecified; these often involved cases of sudden death, in which only the site of the attack is mentioned. In the case of sudden death, whether in a public place or the home, the man may simply not have reached the hospital in time. Judging from comments by the widows who now reconstruct the circumstances of the death, few men make a conscious decision to die in the home. However, knowing that death is imminent, some leave health-care facilities, preferring to be at home.

There is a tendency for the widow not to report involvement in the circumstances of her husband's death, less than half making some reference to their own actions. One-tenth of the women simply state that they were not present; 13 percent report having found the body. One of the women had shot her husband. All in all, there are few women who feel that they might have been able to do something constructive to prevent the death or assist the dying. Ineffective help is reported by one respondent: "He got up to go to church, went to the washroom and dropped. We tried to revive him, but couldn't. We also called in the fire department pulmolator squad, his doctor and a priest."

Sixty-three percent of the women do not report their reaction to the death as part of the circumstances surrounding it. This exclusion supports the general psychiatric theory that the first reaction to the death of a significant other is shock and numbness (Clayton, 1973a, 1973b; Glick, Weiss and Parkes, 1974; Lindemann, 1944; Maddison and Walker, 1967; Parkes, 1964, Silverman, 1972); it may also be a form of denial. The death happened to the husband—not to her. Later grief comes to her.

Having read Peter Marris' (1958) study of widows in London and their reported anger at the doctor, the hospital and others, we expected more frequent expressions of anger. However, our society does not encourage expression or even admission of anger. As we saw in Chapter 2, many of the widows, unlike Lynne Caine (1974), do not admit to a feeling of anger with anyone. The following two quotations are really not expressions of anger over the death itself as an event happening to the man or to survivors. One woman is irritated over a lack of financial compensation:

Nobody knows how it happened. He was a crane operator and an #18,000 steel roll rolled and killed him. I can't believe this is the way it happened. I don't think they told me the truth about his death and the way it happened. I haven't received any special compensation because of his accidental death.

The other woman expresses irritation at the late husband: the way he died was simply symbolic of their life together. She combines all elements in the description of the circumstances:

I was out baby-sitting. My husband always spent a lot of his money with his friends going out drinking. While I was baby-sitting he went out and got drunk. It was very cold. He fell down outside the home and froze to death. The neighbors called the police and the police came and told me that he was dead, that he had frozen to death. He had heart trouble; they think he probably had a heart attack, too. May be that is why he fell down first or maybe he was drunk and then his heart stopped.

The Chicago area women who describe the events surrounding the death of the husband and the aftermath indicate that suddenness is not the only factor weighing on the survivors. Each type of death has its own set of tragedies, experienced differently by different women.

Some typical patterns emerge from the interviews. A long-term illness may be a preparation for grief, but it may also involve prolonged, taxing care at home by the wife:

He died from emphysema, had an enlarged heart. He was sick for over six years and I had to take care of him, even feed him. He couldn't do anything for himself towards the end.

Death from cancer is frequently a painful process, not only for the patient, but also for those close to him:

He worked up to about five months before he died. He did not feel well and went into the Illinois Research Hospital and they discovered he had cancer of the tissues that hold up the organs. They operated. He was in the hospital four weeks, came home and died in four months. Just a skeleton.

The trauma of cancer is felt in the account involving a 46-year-old husband and his 53-year-old wife:

He was operated on and three weeks later he was passed as OK, under medical care. The doctor was pretty sure he got the cancer all out, but he didn't. He was draining and the doctor had to clean it all the time. He had a hole in his back and it was bleeding. I called the fire department and went to the hospital. A day later they called me to get there. Doc said he'd have to open him up again, but didn't think he'd live, but wanted to give him a chance. The operation wasn't performed again cause he was too full of cancer. He died the next day. I was there.

Death from heart attacks tends to be sudden, even when there is a history of previous attacks. The reaction is shock. One man simply collapsed by the side of a pool while he and his wife were visiting friends. Fatal heart attacks happened in a greater variety of places than other forms of death because its victims were generally living active lives—likely to be stricken away from home.

The hardest-hit women seemed to be those whose husbands died violently, especially in cases where they were callously informed of the death. For example: one woman, who ended up needing psychiatric help for three years, received a telephone call from a friend who told her that her husband was with four other men in a speeding car and that he and two of the others were killed instantly. Very frequently, the violent deaths that involved knife or gun fights were associated with taverns and drinking, some of the wives expressing relief. The type of man who becomes the victim of a murder is likely to have been violent at home, too:

He was at a nightclub and was shot outside the nightclub in Waukegan. I could go out with men again (in new life). I wasn't even talking to them before that. My husband made me hate men.

The widows of suicides are the most likely to report traumatic aftereffects. One woman was informed by the police that her husband had died from carbon-monoxide poisoning in a garage. She was incredulous, especially as he had not left a note. Another woman's reaction to the suicide of her husband was embarrassment, to the point that she moved out of the neighborhood to a community that was not familiar with her marital history. Another respondent, now happily remarried, spoke in negative terms about her late husband; his death was a relief, even though he died "messily." (By the way, she does not say how he was found or by whom.)

> He was home alone—shot himself in the head. He had been very moody for the past month. He gambled a lot, drank a lot, worked when he wanted to, was physically cruel to me most of my married life. I guess it all caught up with him.

A pathetic combination of life-and-death circumstances was experienced by a 22-year-old widow. She married a young man whom she had known to be a drug addict, who she assumed was trying to kick the habit.

> He had a terrible auto accident and a lot of surgery and became a drug addict when he was in his early teens. He'd been on drugs for nearly 10 years when we met. Then he went to the Illinois Drug Abuse Clinic and started on their methadone program and that got him off heroin, but he kept popping pills. He had gone to get methadone as he did daily, but he evidently took other drugs, too, that day, and died that evening. The inquest showed the presence of several drugs.

Although married only one year, this girl had had a miscarriage and a stillbirth, going through everything with little help from her in-laws or others. The people close to her want her now to pretend that she had never been married.

One of the complicating factors that surround the husband's death is that it does not occur outside the normal flow of life. That is, problems do not disappear and daily activities must go on, regardless of the upsets and needs occasioned by the illness and death. One woman, for example, experienced the loss of her mother, father, brother and sister all within a short period of time. While this was happening, her husband lost a leg, dying shortly afterward. Other woman were pregnant and either lost their babies or delivered them after the death of the father. One woman who had had a hard childhood, living with foster parents until her mother remarried (strongly affected by the death of a teenage friend), was four months pregnant with twins when her husband died. Her marriage had been a happy one and she felt at sea after her husband's death.

Early Problems and Changes in Widowhood

One-sixth of the respondents state that they had experienced no problems when asked by the interviewer either, "Right after your late husband's death, what were the three main problems you faced where you needed help?"—if the death had been sudden; or, "During your late husband's illness and right after his death, what were the three main problems you faced for which you needed help?"—if the illness had been prolonged.

These responses are difficult to understand unless the death had been anticipatorily experienced and all arrangements had been, or could be, made with no difficulty. The problems that get the most frequent first mention are funeral arrangements and financial matters. Emotional problems, particularly loneliness, are mentioned first by one-fourth of the women— the proportion increasing somewhat as second- and strongly as third-listed difficulties. They appear also later in the interview, when the time period involved was more removed from the actual death. That is, the process of the husband's dying and death created immediate practical problems, in the form of needs for funds and services [see Peterson and Briley (1977) for a list of both problems and solutions]. The respondents

107

who report more than one problem interweave practical and emotional difficulties. The processes of dying and death often necessitate help in the solution of everyday, acute problems, such as care of, and response to, emotionally upset children, the need for a job, movement from or to another place, personal health problems and the like.

The widows specify 122 different sources of help in meeting the first-listed problem, with high concentrations on the self (13 percent), on different children and their spouses (34 percent) and on siblings (11 percent) as providers of solutions. A surprising fact, in view of the prevalence of resources in the Chicago area, is the absence of professionals allegedly trained to provide first-line supports during traumatic crises. Only eight percent of the women list such people as providers of solutions to problems during the husband's illness and immediately after his death. Another eight percent mention governmental and private groups and agencies. In fact, seven percent of the widows, in addition to the women who turned to themselves for the solution, state flatly that no one helped them solve the problem or that the solutions come naturally from the problems.

The widows used 97 different resources to help them solve second-mentioned problems, although 40 percent of the women do not list more than one problem; 17 percent list none; and 23 percent give only one. Again, these problems tend to be practical ones of finances and services. One hundred different suppliers of solutions to the third problem are mentioned, and these tend to be emotional much more often than is true of the first two categories (39 percent, opposed to 25). All in all, despite the presence of numerous ministers, priests and rabbis and church groups in America whose function it is to help their parishioners in time of crisis, their aid is not evident in the discussion of the problems during and following the death of the husband. As we shall see, such people are not active in the current support systems and they certainly were greatly underrepresented during the process of becoming widowed, despite acute need.

A "NEW LIFE?"

Generally speaking, unless a husband was living away from home, not part of everyday life and the social and emotional life of the wife, we can expect her to experience great changes after his death. Not only must the widow undertake the complex process of "grief work" by which she breaks ties with the deceased and establishes herself as an independent (or at least partnerless person) but she must also reorganize her life on many levels. Current resources and needs must be reexamined; new resources must be located, training or informal learning or new skills must be obtained, old roles must be modified and new ones must be entered and adjustments made within the whole role cluster. Whatever obligations the widow, children and others still have to the deceased, these actions do not add up to total social roles. However, many women are not that conscious of changes, nor do they plan their future in a long-range rational manner. When we asked the older women in our first study how they and their social life have changed since they became widowed, we found that 46 percent reported no change in the self and 42 percent no change in their social life (Lopata, 1973a, 1973c). I concluded, in "Self-Identity in Marriage and Widowhood" (1973c, p. 414), that, "The respondents who report no change in themselves as a result of widowhood are less educated, more socially isolated and less dependent in their social life on the presence of their husband than are the women who have consciously experienced identity reformulation" [see also Maddison and Raphael (1973)]. Education and social isolation are also significantly associated with the reported absence of change in the social life of a woman that follows the death of her husband. These are women like the present and former beneficiaries of social security discussed in Chapter 2, whose lack of education prevents voluntaristic behavior vis-à-vis roles outside the home.

Because of the previous responses to the questions on change and the possibility that the concept of change is itself threatening, we substituted the concept of "new life" in a series of three questions: "In reviewing your life since you became a widow, how helpful have each of the following persons or groups been in your building a new life?"; "How long did it take you to establish a new life?"; and "In what ways do you feel this was a new life?" As mentioned earlier in the section on failures of resources, most women feel that several of their resources were "generally very helpful" or at least "helpful in special situations"; adult children were judged as very helpful by 86 percent of the 77 percent of the widows who have such children; and parents and siblings by 53 percent of the 55 percent who have such relatives, although only 33 percent of the in-laws are so evaluated by the 56 percent of the total number of widows with in-laws. Friends are seen as more often helpful than other relatives, neighbors, work associates and other people or groups. That is, 53 percent of the 92 percent of the widows who see friends as a resource, found them generally very helpful when they were building a new life and 43 percent of the 91 percent who see neighbors as a resource so define them. Seventy-five percent of the widows evaluate "other relatives" but only 33 percent of these women found them helpful. Only 36 percent of the widows had their own work associates and 35 percent of them list them as helpful at that time. Finally, only 36 percent of the women look to co-members of voluntary associations or clubs as potentially helpful and only 38 percent of these respondents judge such resources as generally quite helpful.

The questions concerning the length of time required for building and defining a new life draw interesting responses. Only eight percent of the women say they do not have a new life. The woman whose husband froze to death explains that her husband had not been at home much; she continued to work and live as before. It appears, however, that most widows equate the building of a new life with overcoming the heaviest part of grief as an emotion rather than with grief work as a process and to ignore the building process. As many as 14 percent state that it took no time—less than two months. Of course, some may not be leading a new life, either having introduced all essential changes prior to the husband's death if he had been ill long, or not having as yet completed the transition, unaware of the changes they will have to make. This latter assumption is underscored by the tendency of the "lump-sum" beneficiaries, most recently widowed, to report not having built a new life or a short grief period. Thus, one woman, aged 53, states that it took her one week to establish a new life, explaining:

> I felt like a young mother. I lived every day as it came and kept busy (Probe). My neighbor lost her husband shortly before I did and she set an example for me. (How?) She worked around the house and yard and when I looked at her I said: "If she can do it, I can." I had a happy marriage and I'm thankful for the years we had together.

Most of the women, however, report a longer time to get over their grief, as they seem to have carefully considered the question that dealt with the development of a new life. Twenty-five percent feel that it took between two and 11 months, 20 percent say a year; 23 percent fall anywhere between one and two years, with a strong concentration on the two-year mark. Only 16 percent believed that it took them more than two years, some insisting they never will be able to establish a new life:

> It's so different. You're never the same. I don't go out with couples. I can't stand to look at them and be by myself. I see people we knew but it's not the same anymore. Getting a job and working around the house keeps me real busy. That's the only way I can explain it to you.

This woman defines any style of living that is not a duplication of the past as none at all. A few others concur: "I just work."

The conclusion that the widows have equated getting over much of their grief with the building of a new life is supported by the definitions many give of what that new life would be. Getting over grief, accepting the situation and making the best of it are seen as symbols of a new life by 12 percent of the respondents, while 15 percent list learning to be alone and doing things alone. A more positively phrased change is given in the definitions of the new life by the 19 percent who believe that they learned to be independent—able to handle responsibility in the various aspects of life. These more holistic answers are offset by specific symbols of change on the part of the other women. Over ten thousand women represented by our sample went back to work, and they look on this change as the watershed. Eleven percent cite other specific actions, such as going back to school, taking a trip. buying or selling property and so forth.

A few women speak of changing relations with other people, such as dropping or being dropped by old friends, developing new relations, returning to social activities with friends and so forth. Some felt that their new life began when they started getting out of the house, "becoming involved," while others specify symbolic activities such as dating or dancing as indications of change. Remarriage as the establishment of a new life is reported by only a fourth of the women who actually entered such a new relation, leaving almost three-fourths who do not report their remarriage as a sign of a new life, obviously considering other processes prior to taking that step as more symbolic. Twenty-three percent list specific actions such as returning to work as another proof of having built a new life, although getting over grief is mentioned. In general, however, the widows are able to speak of themselves as having developed a new life, reporting this situation in much more positive terms than appeared in answers to the change questions in the previous study of older widows.

The process of creating a new life should not be seen as simple; many women in making purposeful changes went through complicated situations and demands by the self and by others. The following interview illustrates a negative and problematic set of circumstances, but elements of it reflect the problem of many other women mastering grief or at least other complications created by the death of the husband. The respondent, born in 1920, had been divorced from her first husband and widowed twice since. She spent a long time with the interviewer, who summarized her situation:

This lady's husband shot himself in the bedroom. They had been married only two and a half years and she had been helping him build a new seven-room ranch house. He was working as an electrician. She became ill with a vascular problem—terrific headaches and her doctor put her in the _____ hospital. Her husband came only once to see her. When she got home, he told her he didn't want to be saddled with a sick wife. He needed her to help build the house. Also, now that she was ill, she cramped his life-style. She also found out he was going with another woman all the time he was married to her. The house was in his name, the insurance policies, $10,000 and $3,000 and another one at work, were all in his daughters' names. Mrs. _____ had to resort to a lawyer, and in the meantime she had no income and was too ill to go to work.

The respondent herself explains her problems, expected and wished-for changes and her new life:

(Problems after husband's death:) "Finances. The insurance was in his daughters' names. He had no will. The house he had in his name and his daughter refused to use the insurance money to pay for the funeral, so I had to sell his truck to bury him. My mother gave me a little money. I didn't even have food to eat. It was two years before I got social security."

She wanted to go back to the beauty shop to work, having worked there one to two days a week before she became sick, but her health would not allow that. In the meantime:

My husband's daughter wanted me to stay in the house in _____ and keep up the payments on the house and keep the yard work done. Just so she could get more money. (Why didn't the respondent do that?) I was physically unable to stay out in the country alone on four acres and do all the heavy yard work. Financially, I couldn't do this either.

In commenting on the interview, the respondent further explains her problems:

I'd like to know what it means "disabled woman's payment" and why I got my social security so late. _____ died in February, 1971, and I received my first social security check in September, 1973, and my disability started in November, 1973. I nearly starved to death. I was ill and unable to work and too ashamed to tell anyone about it or go to ask for welfare.

Many women did not introduce purposeful changes in their lives—in spite of inadequate income and frequently restricted resources for the support systems. In fact, many women simply do not visualize life as changeable through their own actions, according to numerous locus of control studies (Phares, 1976). Only 24 percent of the widows give affirmative answers to the question, "During the time you were trying to establish a new life, were there any major things about your life that you wanted to change?" Those with the least desire to do so were the older retirement widows. The younger women are much more ready to term unsatisfactory some aspects of their situation after becoming widowed. These women cite 61 specific changes they wished they could make related largely to housing. The financial arrangements of selling or buying homes, businesses and other objects draw about an equal number of comments. Some women want to undertake very specific acts, such as going back to school or work, getting out of the house, starting new activities, etc. Getting over grief and accompanying emotional problems draw fewer comments but are mentioned. They make surprisingly few references here to children and relations with other people. Only about a half of the women wishing to introduce changes in their lives at that time were able to do so with at least moderate success. In 38 percent of the cases they succeeded completely, at least, by their own definition, a disproportionate number of them being the remarried widows. It is possible that younger women who end up in another marriage are more involved in their environment, in general. They may have a different approach to life than women who do not enter into another marriage, remaining as widows. Lump-sum beneficiaries are the least likely to report that their wishes for change had been fulfilled, but then they are most apt still to be hurting and unadjusted. Most of the widows who were unable to make the hopeful change claim an absence of opportunity. Typical of this is the woman above whose health prevents her from returning to even part-time work. Others are too busy, too tied down with dependents or the victims of inhibiting advice or action by others.

PRESSURES FOR CHANGE

Many of the autobiographical or applied psychology literature dealing with widowhood cautions against taking advice from people who "do not understand" (Peterson and Briley, 1977; Caine, 1974; Green and Irish, 1971; Silverman, 1972; Kreis and Pattie, 1969; Glick, Weiss and Parkes, 1974; Lopata, 1973a). In fact, the original Widow-to-Widow program and current efforts to organize similar groups are based on the premise that people in the support network of a wife offer mainly bad advice to her when she becomes widowed. Not having experienced the processes of widowhood and grief work themselves, they are apt to define the situation of the widow from their own vantage point failing to understand her feelings and vantage point. Many of our respondents feel that they were asked to make changes they neither wanted nor were able to make. Some of them, for example, have a strongly

115

internalized image of themselves as lacking the skills necessary to function in the world outside the home without a husband; no amount of persuasion to get them to join organizations or to train for a well-paying job will have much effect. Others feel that the advice they received would benefit the adviser more than them, as in the case of the woman who feels only the stepdaughter herself would benefit from the course of action she advised.

However, specific pressures from others to change are reported by only 23 percent of the women. Most of the widows who feel that they were pressured at that time are well-integrated in a network that had definite, although often contradictory, ideas about what they should do. The retirement widows are the least likely to have felt pressure for change with their environment; the younger women are the ones who were subjected to outside pressures. Change was expected of them after the death of the husband in 52 areas of life—mainly in the same areas in which they themselves had desired changes, in housing arrangements, buying or selling of objects, etc., but there are several new subjects which were never or seldom mentioned as changes they themselves desired. The two main areas focused upon by others were relations with men and their children. We had expected the sources of pressure for change to be quite concentrated, but it happens that 74 persons or types of people were involved, ranging from parents, siblings, children and various in-laws, aunts, uncles, cousins, to friends, neighbors and co-workers. The variety of suggestions for change and of persons making suggestions implies a situation with a great deal of strain in the form of role overload (too many demands), intersender inconsistencies (conflicting demands from several persons) and person-role strain in which what is expected conflicts with personal feelings and desires. Some of these strains are evident in the reasons given by the widows for failing to make the expected changes. A total of 86 percent of those women who report change expectations from their network did not make changes.

The reasons are primarily unwillingness or inability. With few exceptions, what is stated or implied in the open-ended answers to this question is that significant others expecting a specific change simply did not understand the widow or her life definitions. Fortunately, only 10 percent of the respondents made decisions that they later regretted, while in the process of establishing a new life. Decisions most frequently regretted were often in areas highest in advice from others or in steps taken too soon after the husband's death. Selling the home and/or moving away from a familiar neighborhood or other residential changes are mentioned frequently—also financial or child-related matters.

All in all, however, most of the widows are not unhappy now, even those who had been happily married and whose bereavement was followed by grief and problems of readjustment. In fact, when asked for the degree of agreement with the statement, "I am very satisfied with the way my life is going now," 40 percent say that they *agreed* strongly and an additional 39 percent "agree," without the added emphasis. This leaves 16 percent who disagree and six percent who strongly disagree. This response does not mean that they are not sometimes lonely or that they do not idealize their late husband and their marriage—sometimes even to the point of sanctification.

LONELINESS

The prior study of the older urban widows demonstrated that the feeling of loneliness is experienced differently by different women (Lopata, 1973a, 1973b). Robert Weiss (1973) organizes the forms of loneliness around two themes: social and emotional desolation. Interviews focusing on the role changes of the older widows indicate that a woman may consider her late husband a unique person—a love object—a person to whom she was a love object or at least an important and unique individual, a partner in companionate activities, an escort, a member of a couple team in couple companionate interaction, etc. Working-class women tend to explain that they miss being able to organize their work and time around their husband; cooking is what you do for others, not for the self. Much like retired men accustomed to getting up in the morning and going to work, they feel lost when dependent on themselves to structure the day. Many women have never before been alone in a home, having gone from the home of their parents directly into one they established with marriage. In addition, the whole round of activities and the social life space into which a widow ventures can be modified by the death of her husband. Lynn Caine (1974), although only representative of the small fraction of wives who are both occupationally independent and at the same time strongly influenced by the occupation and work demands of the husband, dramatizes, in the book, *Widow*, her prior dependence upon him and the changes introduced into her social life by his death. The Chicago area widows vary considerably in the extent to which they engage in activities of polite companionship or in more direct interaction with the work associates of their husbands [see also *Occupation: Housewife* (Lopata, 1971a)]. Going to conventions with the spouse and entertaining his co-workers or customers can be an important part of a woman's social life. Others are dependent on the husband's income for their social integration; once this income is no longer available, even sex-segregated association with former associates becomes impossible. As we will see, when discussing friendship, married women are often reported as neglecting the widowed friend, unwilling to have an extra woman for dinner or risk having their husband subjected to the temptation of a lonely woman, and afraid of emotional scenes by the bereaved. Many of the Chicago area widows sell "the husband's" car, identified as such and are afraid to go out alone, even to organization meetings. Thus, the emotional desolation and the social isolation become intertwined, one feeding the other and making the woman feel like a deviant—

at least, like an undesirable human being (Townsend, 1968). After all, if she were really a lovable person, her husband would not have deserted her by dying. There are many other psychological problems accompanying grief and bereavement that make positive self-images difficult.

Many of the mothers of dependent children who participated in this study report other problems. Some had been in the process of working out (negotiating or renegotiating) their marriages when the husband died. According to Berger and Luckman (1966), marriage requires a reconstruction of reality, including the self and the marital partner. One of our respondents reported that she still argues with the deceased, finding him a much more interesting discussant in death than the live men she goes out with, in whose presence she acts passively. In fact, younger women reportedly have more problems dealing with loneliness and grief than the older ones (Glick, Weiss and Parkes, 1974). Neugarten (1968) states that older women have had an opportunity to "rehearse" for widowhood and have built into their lives safeguards against loneliness. Younger wives can be so involved in their new roles of housewife and mother as to neglect external systems. Finally, the whole situation of being restricted to one's own home with small children incapable of providing adult companionship, trying not to show excessive grief with them, tired from the routine of work with no one to share it and trying to be both mother and father to the children, is very difficult. Some attempt to solve the problems by returning to the home of their parents; others do try to retain independence—often at great cost. A number of the younger women with small children explain in detail this "pull" between loneliness and the burden of single parenthood with inadequate supports and the wish to independently run their own home and rear their own children.

The lonely widows say "no one" in answer to many of the emotional support questions. Other women find new social relations to compensate for the loss of the husband and for other consequences of widowhood. Most, in addition, assume that loneliness is a common experience. At least, when presented in the self-administered segment of the interview with a direct question, "How would you describe your present feelings about yourself?" followed by six precoded alternative answers, few define themselves as comparatively lonely. Only three percent of the respondents agree with the statement: "I am the most lonely person I know," and only six percent with, "I am more lonely than most people," in spite of the fact that so many of the older widows in the prior study had suggested that loneliness was a major problem of widowhood. A total of 29 percent of the former or current beneficiaries of social security agree that, "I am less lonely than most people"; 24 percent that "I rarely feel lonely", and 15 percent that, "I never feel lonely." The middle-range answers reflect a realistic view of the lives of other people and the general distribution is similar to that of people living in Nebraska in a variety of circumstances studied by Woodward and Woodward (1972). Several explanations may account for the fact that so many widows claim that they are never lonely. Some of the women may have become used to their greater isolation, finding life to be calm and relatively undemanding—compensations for the absence of their companion (Lopata, 1973a). Others may have sufficient and satisfactory social relationships to stave off social and emotional desolation. Another explanation for the frequency of this extreme answer may be denial, as indicated by the high association between the specified level of loneliness and the answer to the question, "What persons made (make) you angry most often in 19____ (now)?" Women who claim not to be lonely also claim never to have been angry at anyone, neither the year before the husband's fatal illness or accident nor now. At the other end of the continuum, women who claim to be more lonely than other people (or the most lonely person they know) tend to list some person, often more than one, as a frequent object of anger in the emotional support system—past and present. It is impossible to determine whether the women claiming both anger and loneliness are simply less prone to denial or if the anger produces, or is in turn produced by, loneliness. Of course, women relatively lonely now also may have been lonely in marriage.

Husbands as Supporters

CONTRIBUTIONS OF THE LATE HUSBAND
TO THE WIDOW'S SUPPORTS

The most unfortunate woman would seem to be one who does not have positive memories of her late husband and her life with him, unless, of course, she is currently involved in a positive support system, relieved by the termination of a bad marriage, and satisfied with life as it is now going. She may or may not be remarried. Later we will examine the relation between attitudes of those widows who remarried toward the new husband and their memories of the late spouse. Most widows, as we noted earlier, claim a strong contribution of the late husband to their emotional support system the year before the illness or accident that caused his death. Table 6 details the percentage of first total references to the late husband. The total numbers of persons whom the widows represented in our sample list in first place and altogether are included to show the base for the percentages. This table reveals not only that the husband appears often in most of the "relational sentiments" and the "self-feelings" segments of the emotional system, but also that he comes first to mind when widows are asked to name the closest, most enjoyable and so forth, person in their lives at that time. He is much less often relegated to second or third place after mention of someone else. This is significant, since being only one individual, he may be mentioned only once by the woman in each support category, while children and friends may be listed separately, a different one appearing in each order of mention.

In spite of this, we find the late husband dominating the emotional supports. No other person or category of people contributed to the supports to the extent that he did, at least in the reconstructed past (Berger and Kellner, 1970; Berger and Luckman, 1966; Lopata, 1973b, 1977a). It is impossible to determine the actual contributions he was making while alive but he lives in her memory as having been highly supportive. The possibility of memory transformation is indicated, however, by the widow's unwillingness to list her late husband as the person who made her angry most often. Only one-fifth of the total number of references to sources of anger are to the husband, although half of the references to the person closest to the widow are to him. But then, as mentioned before, very few women admit to any feelings of anger, this sentiment drawing the lowest listing of people.

There is an interesting variation in the contributions made by the late husband to the wife's emotional supports, as remembered by her from perspective of widowhood. In order of frequency, the late husband appears first as the person the wife most enjoyed being with—the one who made her feel important and secure. In addition, two-thirds of the widows list him as the person closest to them the year before the illness or accident that finally caused his death. However, 16 percent of the women do not think of the marital partner first when asked for people closest to them (usually listing children) and 17 percent of the total number of references do not mention the husband at all as being one of the people closest to them. The husband appears proportionately infrequently in the total references to close associates because the women list so many other people in addition to him. This sentiment draws a larger listing of supporters than does any other one. An even larger proportion do not mention the husband first or ever as the person to whom they told their problems, to whom they turned in times of crisis or who comforted them when they felt depressed. These findings support some of the conclusions of family sociologists and social gerontologists that women

use other women as confidants and comforters, usually daughters or friends, more often than men, including husbands
(Blau, 1961, 1973; Lowenthal and Haven, 1968). This observation must be kept in mind during the analyses of the sanctification scale, which points to a greater tendency to sanctify
the late husband as a person than as a marriage partner. In
spite of the difference in the percentages of women who enjoyed the husband as a companion and those who considered
him a confidant in the first order of listing, he tends to appear
much more frequently in second place, and fewer other people
are listed second or third, so that the proportion of total references to the husband as confidant is the same as for companion, and both are higher than for the contribution to the
feeling of closeness.

Two-thirds of the women feel that their late husband provided them with self-feelings of being respected and useful,
but fewer of being accepted. This is an unexpected distinction,
and the probability of the man appearing second or third in
order of mention is quite low for all three feelings. Four in 10
of the husbands furnished the self-feelings of independence
and self-sufficiency. From the point of view of symbolic interaction, the process operating here is similar to that described
by Cooley (1922, p. 183–184) [see also William James (1900);
George Herbert Mead (1934)] as the "looking-glass self." The
wife seems to feel independent and self-sufficient if she thinks
that her husband sees her as that kind of person. As we saw
in Table 6, there are about as many women who draw such
feelings from their perception of their husband's judgment as
from their appraisal. In the latter case, the "I" part of the self
observes the "me" and evaluates the behavior as that of an
independent and self-sufficient woman. Again, this is in recollection. All in all, the late husband is remembered as the
most important provider of most of the emotional supports
the year prior to his fatal illness or accident, although he may
not have been so much the major comforter, confidant, the
person to whom the wife turned to in times of crises or who

imbued her with self-feeling of being accepted, independent, and self-sufficient as he was an enjoyable companion who made her feel important and secure. He is apt to come to mind first, as the main provider of emotional supports or not at all.

HUSBAND SANCTIFICATION

The dictionary defines "to sanctify" as "to purify or free from sin" and "to set apart as sacred." Several observers of the American scene have commented on the tendency of many widows to idealize their late husband—so extensively as to make him appear like a saint in retrospect. Jessie Bernard (1956, p. 6) states in *Remarriage* that the relation to a second spouse is influenced by how the prior marriage came to an end:

> To criticize a deceased person constitutes a breach of taste. The first spouse may be so idealized and memories of him may become so selective that he becomes virtually sanctified. In retrospect, the past often seems better than it really was.

Rees (1975, p. 146) feels that this is a temporary phenomenon: "Early in bereavement these memories were marked by obvious idealization of the husband and the marriage." However, our exploratory research with the Chicago area widows indicated that even women widowed for years may continue to idealize the late husband to the point of sanctification. The widows' stress on the major contribution of the late husband to their emotional supports the year before the fatal illness led me to hypothesize that much of this reconstruction of the past could be tested through a "sanctification scale," so as to determine the degree to which widows idealize their late spouse and the factors affecting this tendency, or conversely, the factors that deter women from sanctification if that should prove to be the case.

Sanctification is partly built into American culture, as well as into the cultures of the societies of immigrant forebearers.

Rituals like wakes, funerals and *shiva* are devoted to purifying the deceased. His life is reviewed through the selective recollection of positive incidents; his "good" features are stressed. The tendency to idealize the past is further buttressed by the relative deprivation experienced by the widow after the husband's death. Many men die while still "in the prime of life" or at least before totally incapacitated by age and while the wife is still in the "young-old" rather than "old-old" age category (Neugarten, 1968). Life prior to the fatal illness or accident is likely to have been relatively satisfactory for most couples who remained married for a long time—or at least the wife was adjusted to whatever unhappiness or stress existed in the relationship. The children were apt to have established their own lives and to have "turned out all right" (Lopata, 1971a). Any possible conflict over them is likely to have abated, and the financial strains of early marriage and parenthood to have diminished. In addition, conditions following the death of the husband can easily lead to feelings of relative deprivation. Income often declines, adjustments in housing and personal relationships must be made (Lopata 1969, 1977). The woman is deprived not only of her daily companion, but also of an escort in her contacts with others. All the features of deprivation experienced as loneliness are present. Memory tends to reconstruct the reality of the past from the perspective of the present, and it is not surprising to find that widows see their life with the late husband as superior to the present. This definition would tend to reinforce the idealization process by which he is seen as the provider of all (or most) of prior satisfactions and supports.

Husband sanctification performs many important functions, other than giving the widow an ideal past. It increases her status, at least in her eyes, at a time when her morale needs a boost. After all, if such an ideal man had married and lived with her, then she must not be as unworthy a person as her depressed moods make her seem to be. A major function of the process is help with "grief work," at least with its tie-breaking aspects. Basing their analysis on Freud's "Mourning and Melancholia," Eric Lindemann (1944) and other psychiatrists (Maddison and Walker, 1967) have defined this grief work as follows:

> A widow is faced with two concurrent tasks; she is required, through the processes of mourning, to detach herself sufficiently from the lost object to permit the continuation of other relationships and the development of new ones; at the same time, she has to establish for herself a new role conception as an adult woman without a partner.

The process of grief work is a difficult one, particularly for women who were deeply immersed in the role of wife. In addition, there is a double-bind element to it because of the high importance American society assigns to the marital relationship and its personal nature. That is, men and women select their marriage partners and continue in the relationship without divorcing or separating allegedly because of choice. One of the few obligations carried into widowhood, and widowerhood for that matter, is the obligation to remember the late spouse and to mourn for him or her. This is one of the ways people achieve immortality, or social existence beyond physical life, and each of us wishes to exist in the memory of those who play a significant part in our lives. In spite of the secular nature of our urban world, the deceased are frequently perceived as "hovering" over the survivors. Widows often report a "feeling of presence" of the late husband, sometimes defined as hallucinatory experiences (Marris, 1958; Rees, 1975).[2] On the other hand, grief work requires tie-breaking and both psychiatrists and close associates expect widows to cease mourning after an "appropriate time." There are other social roles and relations that demand attention once the period of profound grief is thought to have passed. It is my hypothesis that the sanctification process is an effective means by which the widow can continue her obligation to the husband to remember him, yet break her ties and re-create herself into a person without a partner. Over time, with the help of mourning rituals and associates, she purifies the husband of mortal jealousies and demands for continued attention. He becomes saintly, safely out of the way in daily life and noninterfering as she goes about rebuilding her support network. Sanctification moves the late husband into an other-worldly position as an understanding, but safe and distant, observer.

The sanctification scale is so constructed as to make it easy for the woman to define the husband as close to ideal in order to find out which women resist the temptation of doing so. It is self-administered and contains two parts, the first being a series of semantic differential statements by which the widow may define the late husband, including: good–bad, useful–useless, honest–dishonest, superior–inferior, kind–cruel, friendly–unfriendly and warm–cold. The second segment of the scale, labeled "life together" consists of seven statements for which strong or moderate agreement or disagreement was sought. These start with, "My husband was an unusually good man," and go through, "My marriage was above average," "My husband was a very good father to our children," "Our home was an unusually happy one," "My husband and I were always together except for working hours," "My husband and I felt the same way about almost everything," to the extreme of, "My husband had no irritating habits."

The sanctification scale proved interesting in many ways, in the frequency with which women idealize their late husband to the extreme, in the variations among the items, and in the characteristics of those who do so and of those who moderate their judgment or go in the opposite direction. The two segments of the scale drew different patterns of responses and have to be kept separate. That is, the widows tend to be more extreme in their idealization of the husband as a person than of his relation to them as wives (see Tables 9 and 10). This difference is partly a consequence of the format of the questions—the widows are obviously more drawn to circling the extreme level of the semantic differentiation than of the

TABLE 9

Semantic Differential Evaluations of Late Husband by Chicago Area Widows: Part I of Sanctification Scale

Characteristic: Positive Extreme	LOCATION OF LATE HUSBAND[a]							Characteristic: Negative Extreme
	1 %	2 %	3 %	4 %	5 %	6 %	7 %	
Good	76	8	6	5	2	1	2	Bad
Useful	73	8	9	5	2	3	3	Useless
Honest	82	6	4	4	2	1	1	Dishonest
Superior	55	14	13	13	2	2	2	Inferior
Kind	79	7	5	4	2	2	2	Cruel
Friendly	79	7	5	5	1	2	2	Unfriendly
Warm	77	7	6	7	1	1	2	Cold
Total: Section	74	8	7	6	2	2	2	**Total:** Section

[a]Percentage bases vary from 78,375 to 80,301.

TABLE 10

Evaluation by Chicago Area Widows of Life Together with Late Husband:
Part II of Sanctification Scale

	LEVEL OF AGREEMENT				
	Strongly Agree %	Agree %	Disagree %	Strongly Disagree %	%[a]
Husband an unusually good man	64	25	9	2	100
Marriage above average	45	37	15	3	100
Very good father[b]	69	26	3	2	100
Ours was unusually happy home	54	30	11	5	100
Husband and I always together	50	27	18	5	100
Husband and I felt same way about almost everything	35	36	24	5	100
Husband had no irritating habits	28	28	36	8	100

[a]Percentage bases vary from 73,704 to 80,384.
[b]Ten percent of the widows found this question inappropriate.

agree–disagree combination. However, that explanation is not sufficient and this intriguing variation remains. Another interesting aspect of the semantic-differential segment is the unwillingness of almost half of the women to be extreme in the superior–inferior differential. In fact, the judgments of the husband form several almost mutually exclusive packages. The highest associations, as measured by gammas, are between the evaluation of the husband as good and kind, warm and kind, and warm and friendly (all the gammas are .90 out of a perfect association of 1.00). Women who place their late husband high on the superior end of the continuum are not as apt to define him in these softer terms. Honesty, goodness and kindness are also apt to be closely related to each other in the way the widow remembers her late husband.

The most extreme statement in the "life together" segment of the sanctification scale, "My husband had no irritating habits," drew disagreement from 44 percent of the women, with eight percent disagreeing strongly. This means that over half of the widows agree with this statement, including the more than a quarter who are extremely on the agreement side. It would be interesting to see how many wives of a living husband would go that far in idealizing him. All but 11 percent of the respondents judge their late husband as having been an unusually good man, supporting their prior evaluation on the semantic differential continuum between good and bad. A very low proportion of women claim their husbands to have been a poor father, at least only five percent disagree with the statement that he was a very good father. Other statements in this segment of the scale draw less frequent extremes. Close to a fifth of the women agree strongly that the husband had been an unusually good man yet refuse to evaluate their marriage as above average. Complete sharing of nonjob-related activities during marriage is claimed by half of the women, with an even smaller proportion claiming identical feelings about "almost everything." All in all, when we look at Table 10, it seems apparent that the formal aspects of roles and the man himself are seen ideally more often than are his relations with the wife. The highest "strongly agree" percentages are in the judgment of the late husband as an unusually good man and good father. Mild agreement is most apt to be expressed with definitions of the marriage as above average, involving the sharing of feelings. Most apt to bring disagreements is the statement that absolves the husband of any irritating habits and one demanding similarity of feelings. The latter statement may not be a negative evaluation, but it does point to the possibility of conflict or strain in the relation or compartmentalized interaction. More than one in six widows do not judge their home as having been unusually happy when the husband was well, although only one in 20 is willing to go to the extreme of a strong denial that there was happiness in the home.

When trying to see which of these statements are most closely tied together, we find that women who define their late husband as an unusually good man are the most apt to describe their marriage as above average (gamma=.91) and their home as unusually happy (gamma=.87), with the association between the positive judgments of the marriage and the home having the third-highest association (gamma=.86). A happy home is also highly associated with the widows feeling that the husband had been a good father (gamma=.84). There is a strong association between the feelings that the home had been happy and that the husband and wife felt similarly about things (gamma=.82). By contrast, the association between the husband having been a good father and having shared activities between the husband and wife is low (gamma=.65, or the lowest within the scale). In general, there emerges an interesting combination of judgments in the minds of widows who reflect on their married life. Women who feel that the man was a good father seem to have lived in a more sex-segregated world, with set expectations of men's habits and activities, as well as feelings that were not shared by the couple. Once they guarantee sanctification of the husband as a man in general and as a father, these widows are able to differentiate qualitatively between aspects of his relation to them and of their life together.

What remains now is to examine the association between items in the two segments of the sanctification scale. The indications are that, regardless of how strong the tendency toward sanctification, widows who persuade themselves into defining the late husband as "superior" are apt not to have felt close to him or to have shared activities and feelings with him. At least there is a much weaker association between his definition as a superior human being and his wife's recollection of shared feelings (gamma=.54) or activities (gamma=.77). On

the other hand, the man defined as an unusually good husband is also apt to be judged as a good (gamma=.89), honest
(gamma=.85) and kind (gamma=.82) man in general. A good
man is often a contributor to a good marriage (gamma=.80).
A good father is most apt to draw praise as an honest man
(gamma=.80) and honest men contribute to happy homes
(gamma=.80) much more consistently than do superior men
(gamma=.66). The greatest variation in associations exists
between the combination of honesty and good fatherhood on
the one side (gamma=.80) and good fatherhood and superiority (gamma=.59). Superior men seem to lack empathetic
relational qualities in the eyes of their widows.

Although several characteristics of the widows, such as age,
age at widowhood and income, influence their tendency to
sanctify the late husband or their unwillingness to do so, the
two most important turned out to be education and race.

The most significant difference between categories of widows in their scores on the sanctification scale is between the
white and the nonwhite (mainly black) social races. The differences are particularly strong in the semantic-differential
segment of the scale, both groups being more realistic in the
relational or life-together segment. The largest gaps between
the mean scores of the whites and nonwhites are in the definitions of the late husband as superior, honest and good in
general. Blacks are much less willing than are whites to assign
first rank on these items. For example 58 percent of the whites
and only 32 percent of the blacks place the husband at the
positive extreme of the superior-inferior continuum (gam-
ma=.53). Between 80 and 83 percent of the whites and between
41 and 54 percent of the nonwhites evaluate the late husband
as perfectly good, kind, friendly or warm. The gammas run
from .42 for the useful–useless continuum to .67 for the
honest–dishonest. These are statistically quite significant differences. The highest gamma is .54 in the association between
social race and the life together segment of the scale, occurring

in the statement "my husband was an unusually good man," supporting prior conclusions. The lowest gamma, of .28, is between social race and the claim that "my husband had no irritating habits," because the whites also refused to agree strongly with that statement. The greatest variation in mean scores between the two social races occurs in connection with the statement that the husband and wife did everything together during nonwork hours. Another somewhat similar distribution among agreements of the women in both races occurs in relation to the statement that the late husband had been a good father (gamma = .32). On the other hand, only 44 percent of the nonwhites and 73 percent of the whites agree strongly that theirs had been a happy home in marriage, 25 percent of blacks and 48 percent of the whites that the marriage had been above average, 33 percent of the blacks and 58 percent of the whites that the couple had felt the same way about everything.

Many factors contribute to these differences in judgments of the late husband by widows of the two social races, in addition to the possible cultural differences in the obligation to sanctify the deceased husband. Interesting patterns to these differences are found when we run some of the other variables such as age and education controlling for race. The nonwhite widows are less likely to have achieved higher levels of schooling. However, schooling has much stronger effects on the black than on the white widows. That is, the higher the schooling of the black widow, the more likely she is to sanctify the late husband (gamma = .26), while the differences for the whites are not strong (gamma = .09). The main differences among the whites are between the women with less than an eighth-grade education and the others, as evident in the total sample discussed before; after that the relation is not linear. Not only are the years of schooling more consistently important for the blacks than for the whites in the scores on the husband sanctification scale, but so also the possession of a diploma or degree (gamma=.38) for blacks, gamma=.11 for whites). For example, black widows without a grade-school diploma are less apt to sanctify the deceased husband than are their white counterparts.

However, age is more important for the whites than for the nonwhites, particularly in influencing the semantic differential segment of the scale (gamma=.25 to .10), while it has the opposite effect on the life-together segment (gamma=.14 for whites, .23 for nonwhites). The older white women tend to sanctify the late husband but not the relation, in spite of differences in education. The more educated nonwhites, on the other hand, tend to sanctify the late husband, regardless of age. Age has less effect on the whites than on the nonwhites in the extent to which life prior to the husband's fatal illness or accident is positively defined. There is another variable which indicates a difference between the whites and the nonwhites, i.e., place of birth (gamma=.38 for nonwhites, 0.6 for whites). Eighty-eight percent of the nonwhite widows were born outside of Illinois and these women tend not to be the sanctifying respondents unless they are relatively educated. The differences in the influence of education, age and place of birth of the white and the nonwhite widows do not, however, account for all the differences in the extent to which the two races sanctify the late husband and relations with him. There remains the possibility that subcultural variations, in addition to the hardships of life play a role in contributing to the differences.

There tends to be an association between age and education, with the elderly generally being less educated than are the middle ages and all but the very young. We expected the elderly white women to be more traditionally sanctifying the deceased husband than would the younger women. However, the least sanctifying are not necessarily the younger but definitely the least educated, or those with less than an eighth-grade education. The gammas indicating association between education and the sanctification items are not as high as in the case of race because of internal variations by level of schooling but there are interesting patterns. The least educated and the most educated (16 years of schooling or over) women are not only different from each other, as expected, but also from the remaining women. They most resemble each other in their refusal to claim that the husband had no irritating habits, only 20 percent of the least, and 18 percent of the most schooled strongly agreeing with that statement. On the other hand, both sets of women are willing to give the late husband good scores for having been a good father (54 and 60 percent, respectively). Ninety-two percent of the most educated and 71 percent of the least educated rank the late husband in the extremely positive position when it comes to honesty, 68 percent of the former and only 39 percent of the latter claim they had been married to superior men. Actually, although there is a trend for positiveness of judgment to increase as education of the widow increases, the most educated are not the most positive. It is mainly the high-school graduate or the woman with some college who is the most sanctifying on several items, the grade school finisher being also positive and very different from the grade school dropout or person who was unable to finish for whatever reason. Evaluations of the quality of the marriage tend to increase with increased schooling, from a low of 31 percent among the least educated to 54 percent of the most educated, with a dip to 47 percent among the college dropouts. The evaluation of the home as having been happy does not follow a similar trend. Thirty-six percent of the grade school nonfinishers, 60 percent of the finishers, 64 percent of the high school dropouts, 59 percent of the finishers, 49 percent of the college dropouts and 45 percent of the college finishers agree strongly with that statement. All in all, the least educated are not apt to define their husband as having been superior, useful, or extremely good. They resemble the highly educated in their refusal to agree that the late husband had no irritating habits. They are also the least apt to remember sharing activities with him or having an above average marriage. The main positive judgment the women with less than an eighth-grade education make about their late husband is that he was a good father, but even here only about half were extreme in their praise.

The eighth-grade "finishers" respond quite differently to all items than those with less schooling, converging only in the infrequency of agreement that the marriage had been above average. They generally do not go beyond the second of the seven slots in the semantic-differential segment of the scale, and their scoring means are at times higher and others lower than those of the high-school dropouts. These two groups are similar in many distributions but those that did not finish high-school are much less likely to agree that they and their husband felt the same way about things. The high-school finishers and college dropouts are also similar, both in the precentages of extreme judgments and in the means, except that the latter do not as often claim to have shared all activities with or felt the same way as their late husband than do the former. There is also a difference in their definition of the home as having a happy one and of the husband as having been a good father— the college dropouts being less willing to voice strong agreement with these statements. Widows who had completed 16 years of schooling or more are least likely to judge the husband as having no irritating habits; they are below the average in agreeing strongly that their home had been an unusually happy one, that the husband had been a good father, or that the marriage had been above average, but they are at least as extreme as the group as a whole, and often much more frequently extreme, on the semantic-differential scale.

It appears, thus, that women whose lives were restricted by childhood home circumstances, be they located in an ethnic or racial ghetto or other places with inferior education, married similar men and existed in marriage in situations making sanctification of the late husband and the home created with him difficult. While the most educated women refuse to go to extremes, they are much more positive than are the least educated about their marriage and husbands, while the elites of the blue collar world, the grade school and high-school finishers may be encouraged by subcultures and relatively good lives in marriage to push evaluations to the extreme. We shall examine the effect of schooling on other aspects of life in greater detail in Chapter 8.

The Chicago area widows are consistent in their view of their late husband as a past contributor to their emotional support system and their evaluation of him as a person or of their relation as measured by the sanctification scale.[3] We have four sets of items we can compare here to validate the system and the scale. The emotional system, it must be remembered, contains the "relational sentiments" and the "feeling states" parts. The associations between the frequency of appearance of the late husband in the emotional system and his evaluation on all items are above .24 when we use the gamma measure. There is a .27 gamma association between the semantic-differential segment of the sanctification scale and one of .24 between the "life-together" segment and the sentiment part of the emotional support system. This means that the women who rank their husband less than perfect in the sanctification scale tend also not to mention him in that part of their emotional supports that focuses upon his relations to them as a person who was close, enjoyable, a comfort and so forth. The more positively he is defined on the sanctification scale, the more frequently he appears in this part of the emotional system, although the interview includes these two measures in different places, presenting them in different forms.

The association between items on the sanctification scale and the appearance of the husband in the sentiments segment of the emotional system is much greater than the association of scale items and the appearance of all other people, with a few exceptions. In all cases, the judgments involving him show at least a gamma of .24. The strongest associations occur between the frequency with which the late husband appears in the relational segment of the emotional system and his judgment as friendly, (gamma=.36) an unusually good man, (gamma=.35 kind, gamma=.34) and good in general (gamma=.34). Although most of the associations between frequency of contribution to this part of the emotional system are higher in the semantic-differential segment of the sanctification scale than in the relational segment, women who claim that their marriage had been above average (gamma=.35) and that their home had been a very happy one (gamma=.31) also tend to list the late husband frequently. Definite patterns exist here. The husband is either judged as the highest level of warmth or he does not appear at all in the emotional system. Men whose wives evaluate them as closer to the dishonest than the honest end of the continuum also do not appear often as emotional supporters.

Other contributors appear to be associated with the sanctification scale occasionally. For example, the self tends to appear more frequently if the husband is not evaluated as extremely useful or warm and if the wife disagrees with the statement, "My husband had no irritating habits." The wife also tends to turn to people or groups outside her immediate family and friendship network if the husband is not defined as extremely warm. Although only 20 percent of the women mention a brother or sister in this segment of the emotional supports, there is a tendency to combine the evaluation of the husband as a good father with the inclusion of siblings in the emotional supports. The appearance of people outside the closest network is also associated, although to a lesser extent, with the good-father judgment. The use of friends in the emotional support system is associated, though rather weakly, with the judgments of the marital life only if the widow agrees that she and her husband felt the same way about almost everything.

Rank of Role of Wife

There are a number of hypotheses as to the location that widows would assign the role of wife, when asked to rank this social role in order of importance in comparison to other roles women perform. Such a question was included in the self-administered segment of the widowhood interview, duplicating the question asked of the suburban and urban housewives and some working women in a series of studies conducted in the late 1950s, until 1065. The question read: "In your opinion, which of these roles is the most important for a woman to perform? Which is the second most important and the next?" The list of roles they were asked to rank included: daughter, worker or career woman, wife, housewife, mother, member of society, member of religious group, friend and grandmother (see Table 11). Several of the hypotheses as to how often women who are no longer performing the role of wife would still rank it as the most important a woman can perform can be tested because of the comparative data with the housewife study. The expectation that the role would not be as important in the eyes of widows as for wives is only partly born out in the right side of the table. Fewer widows than wives place it in the top four positions. However, turning now to the separate ranks given by widows, we see that the role of wife is given first place more often than any other role, including that of mother, and that the role of mother is more frequently emphasized than among housewives. Interestingly enough, however, the housewives ranked the role of wife among the top four only when directly faced with the list such as presented to the widows. Earlier interviews used an open-ended question as to which are the most important social roles of women, and many of the housewives being interviewed at home during the day, forgot to mention the role of wife or to refer to duties or rights involving the husband. It seems somewhat sad that so many widows consider the role of wife

TABLE 11

*Rank Order of Social Roles Most Important for a Woman to Perform,
Given by Chicago Area Widows and by OCCUPATION: HOUSEWIFE Respondents*

Social Role	RANK ORDER, WIDOWS									WIDOWS		HOUSEWIVES[a]	
	1	2	3	4	5	6	7	8	9	Top 4	Bottom 4	Top 4	Bottom 4
Daughter	5	5	21	25	17	10	7	5	6	56	28	47	5
Worker, career woman	3	2	5	7	10	11	12	16	34	17	73	7	39
Wife	50	23	10	5	4	2	2	3	1	88	8	96	2
Housewife	5	12	25	12	10	12	10	8	5	54	35	27	20
Mother	32	46	13	4	3	1	1	1	0	95	3	85	3
Member of society	4	2	4	6	8	11	18	30	18	16	77	8	32
Member of religious group	2	2	6	8	8	14	21	20	18	18	73	10	30
Friend	1	3	7	17	22	25	16	6	3	28	50	10	16
Grandmother	3	6	13	18	19	13	9	8	11	40	41	13	20

[a]SOURCE: Helena Znaniecki Lopata *Occupation: Housewife*, New York: Oxford University Press, 1971, pp. 51 and 57.

so very important for a woman to perform when they themselves are no longer able to be involved in it, except in memory.

Summary

The women whose support systems in widowhood we are studying tend to draw upon their past in several ways. The past provides them with current resources, in the form of a home, finances, and a support network of children, other relatives and friends. The traditional patriarchal obligation for a widow to continue filiating her children to the male line of her late husband has decreased with mutual marital choice and the establishment of an independent household. There remains, however, a personal obligation to the husband to remember him—to keep him alive in memory. This obligation combines with the personal needs of the widow and cultural norms to produce a memory support system. That is, many women who have gone through the agonies that accompany the death of the husband and the related problems of widowhood, including loneliness, seem to have been successful in idealizing the past and the former mate, some even to the point of sanctification. Reliving the circumstances of the death and reviewing their life in marriage, widows tend to select certain items of the past and weave a new fabric to present a positive image of their past and of the man who made it possible. The late husband is seen as the main contributor to their emotional support system the year before his fatal accident or illness and as an ideal type of a man. Such sanctification performs many functions which provide comfort, a sense of having been important to an important man and a feeling of having had a good life in a happy home. Simultaneously, sanctification evolves the widow out of the double bind of having to mourn the late husband while simultaneously reestablishing herself as a partnerless person and rebuilding her support systems without him. Purified of mortal jealousies and other feelings, he is seen as a benevolent saint, blessing her efforts at a full life without him. Of course, not all women are able to convert formerly mortal men into saints, the effort being too unrealistic for women whose married lives had not been good. Many other factors contribute to lure some widows away from the rather pervasive tendency toward sanctification into a more realistic definition of the pluses and minuses, or at least imperfections, of the late husband.

The reworking of the past has an internal consistency, in that women who now define their husband as having been an effective supplier of emotional supports when he was alive will also tend to be more positive in their definition of him as a person and of their life together than are women for whom he was not a major emotional supporter. Warmth, kindness, friendliness and "goodness" in general appear to be more important to the widow as she looks back on her late husband than are superiority or usefulness. Although many women claim that their spouse had no irritating habits, the more educated and the nonwhite younger women do not take such as extreme stand.

NOTES

1. Exploratory interviews during the first year of a research project are always open-ended, in that the interviewer asks very broad questions, such as, "What are the major problems of widowhood?" and tries not to interrupt the respondent or interject his or her own ideas. Such interviews are usually taped and many such tapes are then analyzed for major trends. Gradually, a pattern emerges and questions might become more specific, pointing, for example, to a time period, or an area of life such as relations with children. There is a constant interplay between the theoretical framework guiding the research and the results of interviews that show how people experience what we are examining. In order for the research to turn into a survey of the population testing the actual distribution of the experiences of the different people, we need to standardize the questions, train interviewers to ask them exactly the same

way, drawing a random sample through a variety of methods and interviews. When dealing with a large number of the interviews the need for standardization is not only scientifically motivated, but also a practical necessity. It would be impossible for us to get coders who would code the answers in exactly the same way without the cost being prohibitive. The chance of error in coding is enormous. The interview at the end of the book will show the reader the usual format of survey interviews.

2. It has been pointed out to me that the concept of hallucinations is used in psychiatry in conjunction with mental illness and that the widow's momentary feelings that the husband is present are really a normal reaction—more of a memory lapse than a symptom of serious problems. Paula Clayton (1973b, 1975) is also critical of the tendency of people dealing with or researching the bereaved to treat them as if they were, at least temporarily, ill and she recommends looking at grief work as a normal process.

3. Future research will have to determine to what extent married women also present their husband publicly, or at least in response to such questionnaires, as practically saintly (see Table 11 and next chapter).

II

MAIN CONTRIBUTORS

F O U R

Boyfriends and New Husbands

American society as a whole has not developed institutionalized norms either enforcing or forbidding the remarriage of
widows (Bernard, 1956). There is no system of suttee, levirate
or widow inheritance that maps out a woman's future once
her husband dies. Her relations with men outside her family
and her nonsexual friendship network grow out of a combination of a variety of personal factors and structural constraints, as are relationships entered into voluntaristically. Jessie Bernard (1956, p. 116), in her study of American remarriages
in the 1950s, found five basic sets of forces "that help select
those who remarry." These same forces bear on whether or
not a woman enters the "courtship" stages preceding or aimed
toward marriage, or even a close relation with a man without
such a specific goal. They are: (1) the desire to enter into such
a relationship, (2) an absence of inhibiting influences, (3) the
opportunity for meeting prospective intimates, (4) community
and family pressures inhibiting or pushing a no longer married
woman in that direction, and (5) "all the personal qualities
and nonpersonal factors that make one attractive to prospective mates."

Of course, these forces are interdependent. The desire to
enter into a close relationship with a man can be strongly influenced by the awareness of the statistical probability of doing
so. People are also aware of the image they project compared

147

to the standards of the ideal mate in the society, or they may be so depressed as to assume that they can no longer be attractive to members of the "opposite" sex. Community and even family pressures for or against boyfriends or marriage depend largely on the stereotypical notions about the right age for romance and marriage, about who is an attractive prospective mate, about "proper" ways of meeting people with whom rapport can be developed, and so forth. Many people in America have restrictive attitudes that influence the way a widow sees herself and the manner in which she consciously or subconsciously develops new social networks and support systems allowing or excluding the possibility of intimacy with a man and of remarriage. Bernard J. Cosnect (1970) found that only a quarter of the women studied in his "Family patterns of older Jewish people" would even consider remarriage. The vast majority of older Chicago widows previously studied did not expect to remarry. Most of them stated that they did not wish to enter such a new relation (Lopata, 1973a, p. 319). Among the reasons given for rejecting remarriage was the refusal to give up the advantages of their current status, such as independence, or their doubts about finding a man "as good as" the late husband. Many women refuse to develop a close relationship with a man because of fears of being taken advantage of. Some do not wish again to take on the burden of work and care of a husband, particularly since he also may become ill and confront them with the same problems of care as the late husband, including the emotional repercussions. As one woman stated, "They ask me why I don't want to remarry. I had a sick husband all my life. I don't want to bother. I worked like the devil all my life." By the way, she classifies her husband in the sanctification scale as having been completely useless: "He couldn't do nothing, just cough, cough all the time."

As the author of *To Love Again* (Kreis, 1975) explains, many widows fear new close relationships because of the high probability of being hurt again, of losing a new love object, someone to whom they become important, of having to go through the pain of grief again (Bernard, 1956; Caine, 1974; Peterson and Briley, 1977). Such feelings are particularly strong among women who sanctified the late husband, or whose memory construction or reconstruction has gone in the opposite direction. Of course, it is impossible for sociologists involved in survey research to know if the officially listed reasons for not wanting to remarry are "real" or whether they are justifications for not being able to remarry. As sociologists know, however, such justifications are the essence of life if they are believed by the woman herself. In fact, many of the American subcultures contain warnings against remarriage, especially in the case of women with inherited wealth. The family and the community may add to these admonitions if they stand to gain from the women remaining widows (Bernard, 1956). The woman herself may feel it wrong to make available to another man the monies earned by the late husband. This attitude helps explain the legal contracts and the many precautions encouraged in the subcultures followed by some widows, and widowers for that matter, to ensure against economic exploitation by a new partner.

There is also some evidence that many women in America benefit psychologically from not being married and that they are aware of these advantages. At least, Jessie Bernard (1973) argues strongly in *The Future of Marriage* to support her conclusion from a variety of research sources that many women benefit psychologically from being unmarried, while many men benefit from being married. Indices of personal disorganization, such as depression and other physical and mental health problems, suicide, alcoholism and so forth, are used by Bernard in conjunction with evidence that husbands and wives actually experience two kinds of marriages, living in separate social life spaces.

The obvious inhibiting force that prevents many widows from developing a close relationship with a man or from remarriage is the lack of opportunity caused by the demographic distributions of the American population. We do not have sufficiently exact and comparable figures over the decades as to the statistical probability of remarriage for widows of different age groups to permit a dependable presentation of trends. The various researchers using the U.S. Bureau of Census data tend to combine age categories inconsistently. Nye and Berardo (1973, p. 606) were dependent upon Jacobson's data published in 1959, collected much earlier than that. The best prior statistical overview of remarriage rates is contained in Bernard's (1956) book, but it is impossible to compare these rates to recent figures. However, the general situation seems to be clear. Rates for all other marital categories of women and for men are higher than those for widowed women, but there is great variation in the rates for widows by age. Widower rates are higher than widow rates for remarriage, especially at late ages. "Three factors, the shorter life expectancy of males, the higher remarriage rates for men than for women, and the tradition of men marrying women younger than themselves contribute to the imbalance of women over men in this category." (United States Department of HEW, *Remarriages*, 1973). There are, as mentioned in Chapter 1, more than five widows for each widower in American society. In addition, men here marry women younger than themselves not only the first time, but in subsequent marriages as well. In fact, the age gap between the husband and the wife increases in later marriages. This trend reflects the bargaining power of men, although the logical step would be for women to marry men younger than themselves, thereby decreasing the likelihood of repeated widowhood (see Nye and Berardo, 1973). Since widows tend to be older than divorced or never married men, a sizable proportion of eligible males is not available. In addition, as Morton Hunt (1966), Jessie Bernard (1956), and Nye and Berardo (1973) point out, never-married men, particularly divorced men, tend to avoid dating widows, mainly because they cannot compete with the idealized deceased husband, but also because they are going through a different emotional shift than the widows. The set of all these factors means that younger widows have a better statistical probability of meeting eligible men and, since they are less apt to sanctify their late husband, a better change of relating positively with men.

Unfortunately, we do not know too much about the process of building close heterosexual relations on the part of widows. There is some recent literature on marriage among people who have been married before, but it is sparse. McKaine (1969) focused on *Retirement Marriage* and Bernard (1956) frequently refers to the differences in the courtship of the divorced and of the widowed, but much of the other literature on second marriages is concerned with the divorced. Dating, romantic love, courtship and similar subjects are usually covered in discussions about youth. In fact, as McKaine (1969) and Nye and Berardo (1973) point out, many a community acts as if it were somehow improper for older people to be interested in sexual relations or romantic attachment. Actually, in spite of the lack of societal approval or even tolerance of such emotions by any but the very young, there is evidence as early as the 1950s that sexual activity is prevalent among the nonmarried middle-aged and elderly Americans. "It is probable, however, that sexual exchange occurs more frequently during courtship among the remarriageable population than among the young unmarried persons," notes Bernard (1956, p. 158), referring also to Kinsey's conclusion, "Sexual involvement leads to serious emotional involvement to a greater degree in the middle than in the lower classes" [see also Scanzoni and Scanzoni (1976)]. Morton Hunt (1966), in *The World of the Formerly Married*, claims that this group has reversed the courtship sequence in that sexual intercourse often precedes psychological intimacy, if the latter develops at all. Of course, the young have also changed their patterns of intimacy-building preceding, or as an alternative to, marriage in recent years.

The negative attitude toward the sexual feelings and behavior of the elderly, which is expressed even by some of the widows, reflects the rampant agism in America. Many of the interviews show ambivalent feelings toward men, especially toward sexual intimacy, although there were no direct questions dealing with such relations. The main reason for the lack of direct information as to sexual activity of the Chicago area widows was the hesitancy of many people connected with formulating the interview and the approval stages of this study to deal with this subject. When the widows themselves mentioned sexual intimacy as part of their relations with boyfriends, the answer could not even be precoded in fear of what the "watchdogs" of American privacy would say if they found reference to sexual behavior in an interview of widows. Sexual concerns are considered "improper" for the middle-aged or elderly generally, but especially for widows, regardless of age!

Boyfriends

Information about relations with men since widowhood appears indirectly in answer to other questions. Few women were as open in explaining such relations as was a young widow with an illegitimate child. Her late husband was killed instantly in a car accident while serving in the Marine Corps. One of his friends told her of the circumstances and helped her while the government investigated her status because the late husband's family claimed that they had been divorced. The contention proved to be wrong but, in the meantime, she had developed a strong attachment to this friend, Charles. The following is her explanation of what happened:

> Charles was divorced when he lived with me. When I told him about my pregnancy, he was leery about it. It was a situation in which my doctor told me I couldn't get pregnant when I was first married to John. Here, five years later I was pregnant. Charles and I discussed marriage and we were going to get married, but he was in the Army, was stationed in Chicago and was ordered to go to Vietnam. So we decided to wait and get married when he came back. I'm glad I waited. We went for counseling to a

priest before he went back to Vietnam, before the baby was born. The priest looked at my side, why I wanted to wait. At that time, Charles was having difficulty with his Army pay. I figured that if he had any more complications we couldn't meet the bills. So I continued to work and receive my government check from John's death. The priest said it was to be my decision. When Charles came back from Vietnam, he saw the baby. You know he was already married and divorced three times when I knew him. So I noticed both our personalities had changed. I had found myself more independent. I lost respect for Charles. He gave no support for the baby during my pregnancy or after little Charles was born, even though he had promised that he would. So that's why there's no more Charles.

Aside from such insights in some of the interviews, we are dependent for our knowledge of the widows' relations with men upon a limited set of questions beginning with, "Since your late husband's death, have you had any close male friendships or relationships?" It appears from the answers to following questions, particularly in the descriptions of shared activities, that the respondents interpreted the question exactly in the way it had been intended. We wanted to know about boyfriends, not cross-sex friendships that resemble same-sex relations devoid of any sexual connotations. As we shall see in Chapter 6, American society discourages cross-sex friendships, having adopted what is really a working-class European assumption that men and women can relate to each other only through family roles or with sexual goals in mind [see Scanzoni and Scanzoni (1976), and Gans (1962)]. Women listing friends of the year prior to the late husband's fatal illness or accident predominantly offer the names of women and, if a man appears, it is as a partner in couple polite-companionship interaction (Znaniecki, 1965). Only 22 percent of the widows claim to have had a close male relationship since the death of the husband. One woman felt obliged to explain that the man she often had dinner with is "just a friend, a shoulder to lean on." Widows who eat lunch with male coworkers, usually professionals, often felt obliged to explain to the interviewer that there was nothing "personal" in it. In other words, most women take "a close male friendship or relationship" to mean dating.

Two-thirds of the women who had a close relationship with a man since widowhood have limited themselves to only one such associate, a quarter having had two, and only about one in ten list several boyfriends. These men were met in a variety of situations, mostly in public places such as bars, dance halls and other recreational areas, work, church or other group locales (25 percent). I had expected more of the men to have been known to the widows in the past. After all, one would think that an already established relation can be shifted into dating interaction more easily than can a stranger be turned into a boyfriend. This did not prove to be the case; only nine percent of the boyfriends were known in the past and six percent had been friends of the late husband. It would appear that such a shift in relations is difficult, the man, and possibly the woman herself, seeing her always as "Tom's widow" rather than as a partnerless person. Surprisingly enough, only eight percent of the boyfriends were met through relatives; neither are children good sources of contact with future boyfriends, no boyfriends were met through them. Friends are much more useful as connecting links, in spite of the constant complaint by widows over matchmaking efforts, of being "paired" at dinners and other social functions (Caine, 1974; Bernard, 1956; McKaine, 1969). One-quarter of the widows credit friends with introducing them to the boyfriend. Of course, not all contacts through friends are of the matchmaking nature; more casual introductions are possible. Since half of the women moved after being widowed, neighbors who become boyfriends may have been met when the woman was already without a partner. It is less likely that boyfriends are former neighbors, unless the man also becomes widowed. This is an unexpectedly frequent occurrence in the case of remarriage. That is, women are not apt to date a neighbor unless that relation results in remarriage.

Initial contact with first-named boyfriends tends to have taken place many years ago—29 percent of them before 1960. This helps explain the fact that 44 percent of the first-named relations and 50 percent of the second ones have already been terminated. This leaves only one in six widows with current boyfriends. Many women married their first boyfriend dated in widowhood. Relations with close male friends were terminated most frequently through death or because of incompatibility. Some of the men were married and returned to their wives. Anger is often expressed by women who either did not know of the marriage or were led to believe that a divorce was imminent. The role modification study of older widows focused on the feelings of women who were sexually propositioned by husbands of their women friends (Lopata, 1973a). In fact, questions about such action as well as about jealousy of married women friends formed a major component of a Relations Restrictive Attitude Scale. The problems created by sexual propositioning by such men are complex. Many of the widows are lonely and want intimacy with men, but they do not wish to ruin their relations with the female friend. In addition, as much as a woman may want sexual relations, she is usually more desirous of total romantic, multilevel interaction with a man. Finally, even if she wants intimacy, she often feels adultery to be wrong, especially if it involves the husband of a friend. Of course, these comments apply only to women openly interested in the sexual aspect of relationships with men. Those not interested would prefer psychological rewards which they usually cannot obtain from already married men, especially from husbands of friends or other acquaintances. Some women terminated friendships with men with the explanation that they did not want to remarry, implying that the relation could only go in that direction if it continued.

Relations with boyfriends tend to be rather intensive, in that three-quarters of the first-named men are or had been seen at least weekly. Women who list more than one male associate tend to see them less frequently—four in ten less than once a week. Shared activities depend, of course, on the degree of intimacy between the partners. Sexual intercourse is seldom openly mentioned, but shared meals at home, talking and watching television are listed. Not surprisingly, couples who see each other often tend to share several different activities. The widows usually mention public, traditional and recreational activities they do with boyfriends first; over a third tell of going out to dinner, 12 percent going to movies and other public places, and 17 percent engaging in sports or attending sports events. The less formal activities, which are also more intimate, such as going to each other's homes, are mentioned next. One respondent carried on a long-distance romance, flying to Philadelphia for weekends. Another explains that her boyfriend spends a great deal of time in her home, but that much of it is taken up with playing with the children, bathing and putting them to bed, helping with the dishes and so forth.

Although there are over 10,000 current boyfriends of the widows represented by our sample, in addition to the forty-six hundred new husbands, these men friends tend not to appear in the main support system of the women unless they are living in their home. Those who make contributions, moreover, do so selectively (see Tables 4, 5 and 7). Less than one-fifth of the boyfriends provide the widows with transportation, and that all other forms of service supports show even less evidence of boyfriends. That is, although 9,570 boyfriends are listed by the widows, most of them do not help in the major areas of life. Husbands are much more helpful, but their contributions vary considerably by the traditional division of labor. A surprising 43 percent of the husbands do not help take care of their wives in illness. All in all, although husbands help in household and personal care much more than do boyfriends, at least in the judgment of the women, neither are deeply involved in any but a few supports. Married women who do go to public places most decidedly go with their husband, and boy-friends are more active here than in other supports. One-fourth of the widows eat lunch with a boyfriend. Interestingly enough, very few women are accompanied by boyfriends when they go to church. Visiting others in the company of boyfriends is also rare; more women entertain with them in their home. By contrast, husbands are much more apt to go to church with their wives and wives are accompanied in their travel out of town by husbands much more often than widows by boyfriends. The latter reflects the reality of leisure-time life for all but the very recent "modern" women.

The fact that boyfriends are not as integrated into the lives of women as are present husbands is indicated by contrasts in the emotional support system. If boyfriends appear here, it is mainly as people who make the widow feel important and with whom she most enjoys being. Only one-quarter of the women obtain comfort from boyfriends when they are de-pressed, but even this is a high proportion compared to their contribution to other supports. A small number of women list boyfriends as the person closest to them; only six percent mention him first. By the same token, boyfriends do not often anger the women; more husbands are the source of such sen-timents than are men with whom irritating relations can be broken comparatively easily. There is another interesting ten-dency of the widows who receive emotional comfort from their boyfriends to list them in second or third order of mention rather than in the first. This reinforces a prior assumption that the boyfriends really exist at the outside perimeters of the widow's life space, the central core being filled by everyday affairs, particularly, as we shall see, by her children, job or friends. Husbands, on the other hand, move into the lives of the women, sharing the home and, if not its work, at least its social and emotional supports with her.

Remarriage of Chicago Area Widows

Although only six percent of the widows represented by our sample have remarried, 13 percent report having had at least one opportunity to do so which they did not take. Some of these women later remarried but most remained widowed. Interestingly enough, men whom they considered marrying were generally met in different ways than men whom they only dated. The potential marital partners were much more apt to have been known in the past than were the date-only men (17 to nine percent) or to have been met through clubs, organizations or churches (13 to six percent). On the other hand, friends are a much less likely source of potential marital mates than of dates (eight to 24 percent). Otherwise, the distributions are similar, a quarter of the men the widows had the first opportunity to marry having been met in public places. The two most important reasons given for not marrying a particular man were the lack of desire to remarry and the undesirable characteristics of the man. Half of the women mention unwillingness to remarry; these are the least likely to choose a husband later. This means, however, that the women were willing to enter a relatively close relationship leading to the possibility for remarriage even though they then decided not to take that step. Eleven percent of the retirement widows say that they would not marry because if they did they would lose their social security, while six percent list health reasons.

This discussion about unwillingness to remarry makes it interesting to take a closer look at those women represented by our sample who did enter a new marriage after the death of their late husband. A few remarriages ended in divorce but not enough to permit an adequate analysis, so only women currently remarried are considered here. What are the differences in background between the women who remarried and those who did not? To what extent does the new husband serve as a resource contributing to the support systems of the wife? Does the remarried woman remember her late husband differently than does her still-widowed counterpart? What are the judgments of life and remarriage by the women who chose this marital status?

There are several basic differences between the women who remarried and those who did not that date back to early life. They form a set of characteristics that seem tied together. The remarried women are very likely to come from urbanized homes, in that both parents were born either in metropolitan Chicago or in another large urban center. If born outside of Chicago, the remarried woman herself is likely to have migrated here at a younger age than her still widowed sister. There is also a strong association between remarriage and schooling; the women who entered new marriages usually have finished high school at least, or completed any schooling system they started without dropping out. The same holds true of the educational achievement of both the late and the present husband. Consequently the men they married have or had relatively good incomes. Furthermore, the income of the remarried women when their late husband was well was higher because almost eight of ten of the men were working at their regular jobs when they were stricken, compared with six of ten of the husbands of the women who did not remarry. Neither category of wives was apt to have worked themselves for different reasons; taking care of children was the predominant reason given by the women who are now remarried which indicates the presence of young offspring.

In fact, the remarried women tend to be younger, although many of the younger women are not remarried. They were younger at the time they entered the marriage that left them widowed and at widowhood than were the women who have not remarried. Very few of the women whose husbands died when they were 60 years of age or older have been able to remarry or were interested in doing so. The remarried women were mostly in their forties when they entered the new relation. However, they married men older than themselves, either having not learned a lesson about widowhood from their previous marriage or being unable to attract younger husbands. Fifty-eight percent of the new husbands were 50 years of age or older at the time of the marriage, compared to only 32 percent of the wives. In spite of their comparative youth, two-thirds of the remarried women had been widowed over six years, contrary to the common assumption that remarriage occurs very rapidly. The current marriage tends to be a very recent one, two-thirds being of five years or shorter duration.

Not surprisingly, in view of the age of these women at the time of the death of their husbands, most had young children still at home. Four factors may bear on the relation between children and remarriage. Given their age, the women able and willing to remarry could have no, or fewer, children at the death of their husband than the still widowed. A large number of small children may "frighten away" prospective husbands. On the other hand, the mother of several dependent offspring may be more anxious to find a father and breadwinner for the family. Finally, remarried women may decide to have children for the sake of the new relationship. Women who have remarried are more apt than the other widows to have been mothers. Less than one percent of these women had no children when their husband died, while the whole sample shows 8.6 percent of all the women to be childless. The women who remarried had an average of 3.6 children when their husband died, while the average now for the whole sample is 2.7 and

3.0 for all mothers. Not surprisingly, the more children a woman had at remarriage, the younger the last tended to be. The mean age of the eldest child when the widows remarried was 22 years, and the most frequent age, or the mode, was 35 years. The age drops steadily till the seventh child, whose average age was seven years at the time when the mother remarried. The remarried women, by the way, have a total of more than seven thousand offspring in their new marriages. Some of these children came with the husband but most were born in the present marriage.

All in all, these women were younger, better educated, married before to better trained men earning better incomes than were the women who remained widows. It also appears that having children, especially dependent ones, serves as a spur, rather than a deterrent, to marriage.

The presence and ages of the children help explain another difference between the two categories of women, i.e., those who are now remarried and those who are not; that is their work history since widowhood. Although not apt to have been working when the husband was well, more than seven out of 10 of the remarried women entered the labor market after his death, compared to less than half of the widows. In fact, 43 percent of the women with a new husband are still working, not necessarily because of money. Their current income is quite high and the main reasons they give for continuing in a job are personal, one of the few situations where such justifications appear even in first place out of three reasons. As we shall see in Chapter 9, the presence of several earners almost automatically increases family income, particularly if one of those earning money is the man. In addition, the women who remarry are much more apt than the still widowed to be living in a house, generally a large one. Interviewers found that their homes seemed more affluent and relaxed. Their neighborhoods also drew more frequent positive judgments than those of the still widowed, who mostly live in single-dwelling, open-spaced and residential blocks.

THE LATE HUSBAND AND THE NEW HUSBAND

How does a widow who has remarried handle her previous marriage and late husband in memory? Several sets of information provide such insights. We can compare the frequency with which the late husband appears in the emotional support system of the remarried women and of those who have not. In the case of the remarried widows we can also compare the contributions of the late husband to the former emotional support systems to those of the present husband to the current system. Finally, we can compare the tendency to sanctify the late husband, that is, to idealize him to the point of sainthood, by women who do and those who do not have a new husband.

There are, obviously, two overall possibilities. One is that the remarried woman is less likely to remember the late husband as a major contributor to her emotional support system or to sanctify him and their relation than is her still widowed counterpart. The second possibility is the reverse. There are many reasons to believe the validity of either alternative. The remarried women are younger, and, as we saw in Chapter 3, increasing age is associated with an increasing tendency to sanctify. Younger women may also have been too busy with children and the complications of widowhood to go through the process of sanctification. Besides, their marriage may have been under greater stress than that of older women who can then remember theirs as peaceful and good. The current life of the remarried widows may guard against extremes of idealization of their past life and allow for a greater degree of realism. Women with a living husband may find that excessive sanctification of the late spouse, even privately, may disturb their own peace of mind and, moreover, create tension in the new marriage. The former widows with whom I talked at length during the exploratory phases of this research project were very conscious of the danger of even implicitly comparing husbands or making the dead appear superior to the living. The appearance of the remarrieds as less given to sanctification could also be a function of the tendency of the still widowed to be extreme. Excessive idealization might stop women from realistically viewing men with whom they come in contact as potential replacements for the late husband, thereby diminishing the willingness to remarry. Also, it tends to antagonize men.

However, two sets of mutually exclusive factors can contribute to a new wife's extremely positive attitude about her late husband and marriage. Remarried widows may simply be positive in their judgment of people; their feeling that life had been good may account for their willingness to remarry. American culture works on the assumption that happily married persons who become widowed are willing to marry again. Those who fail to remarry may have a less positive memory of their past marriage; they may feel so relieved at being widowed that a new marriage holds no appeal. A different situation faces the currently unhappily remarried woman. The new husband may not be providing the supports she expects either because they had been provided by the late husband or because she now believes that he had been very important in her life.

Of course, the comparative evaluations of the contributions of the late and present husband to the life of a woman may depend on the stage in her life course and the complexity of its support network.

SUPPORT SYSTEMS

The only system within which we can compare the remarrieds and the still widowed and the contributions of a new husband in the case of remarriage to that of the late husband is the emotional one. There are not many emotional supports in which the remarried women differ significantly from their still widowed counterparts in the frequency with which they list the late husband as a contributor to their supports (Table 12). However, they are less apt to mention him first as the person to whom they had felt closest the year before his fatal illness or accident, as the person to whom they told their problems, who comforted them and who made them feel important and respected. They are the still widowed; obviously, we do not know if the relation had been different or if the remarrieds down play the contributions of the late husband to these emotional supports. Sixty-eight percent of the still widowed but 52 percent of the remarried list the late husband

TABLE 12

The Frequency with Which the Late Husband Appears in the Emotional Support Systems of Chicago Area Widows for the "Before"[a] Time Period and the Present Husband in the "Now" Period

Support System and Time	FREQUENCY							Mean[b] Frequency
	0	1	2	3	4	5	7+	
Sentiments *before* late husband								
Never remarried	4	7	8	11	12	19	39	4.42
Currently remarried	7	13	7	11	12	20	30	3.93
Feeling states *before* late husband								
Never remarried	11	7	11	15	17	16	24	3.63
Currently remarried	10	11	12	18	17	12	20	3.37
Sentiments *now* present husband	2	2	9	6	10	27	44	4.83
Feeling states *now* present husband	8	8	9	14	21	21	20	3.75

[a]The year before the husband's fatal illness or accident.
[b]There are seven relational sentiments and six feeling states both "before" and "now."

as the person to whom they felt closest the year before his fatal illness. Forty-nine percent of the remarrieds, compared to 60 percent of the still widowed remember the late husband as the main person to whom they told their problems, while 52 percent of the women with a new marriage, compared to 66 percent who do not have such a relation define the late husband as the main contributor to their feelings of being respected. Of course, there may be several reasons for the differences, one of them being the variations in ages. The remarried women are apt to be younger and to have been widowed at a younger age. Women at younger ages are apt to be mothers of young children who have not worked out their marital relations, or changes in them, sufficiently to consider the husband as a major confidant. During that stage of the life course, the focus and interest of husbands and wives are least alike and changes from prior relations are most dramatic. In fact, several studies by sociologists have been devoted to "parenthood as crisis" (LeMasters, 1957; Dyer, 1963; Hobbs, 1965).

There are also interesting variations in the contributions remarried women feel their new husband is making to their emotional support systems, in comparison to what they now remember their late husband provided. The strongest difference in the frequency with which the late and the present husband are listed first are to him as the person to whom the widow told or tells her problems, who comforted or comforts her, to whom she turned or turns to in crises and who made or makes her feel important and respected. In all these cases the new husband is much more apt to be listed than is the late husband. There is little difference in how often the husband appears as the person closest to the wife, whose company she most enjoys and who provides feelings of independence and self-sufficiency. The two places in which the late husband is more apt to appear than the new husband are as the person

165

who made or makes her feel self-sufficient and who angers her most. It is very interesting to note that one-quarter of the remarrieds are willing to list the late husband as a major source of anger.

These differences may be due to the qualitative variations in the marriages or to personality changes of the woman as a result of experiences of maturing and aging. On the other hand, it is quite possible that becoming and being a widow makes a woman appreciate marriage more than does the process of experiencing marriage the first time, especially during the rather trying family expanding years (Lopata, 1971). Widowhood-induced needs for being comforted and for a confidant, plus the process of entering into a new marriage, may change the nature of the woman–man relation so that the couple becomes more supportive than is true of a first marriage.

Table 4 and 5 show details of how the present husband contributes to the service and social supports of the Chicago area former widows. The first set of percentages are computed from the interviews of the remarried women only, and would have been even higher had more women engaged in these activities. Actually, 82 percent of the women who list help with household repairs give the present husband as the main helper but only 57 percent of all husbands render such assistance. Few women need help with child care, so only 29 percent of all husbands provide it, but their contribution constitutes 65 percent of all such care received. These figures apply to all the supports, but we will stick to the analyses as presented in the other chapters. Thus, only 29 percent of the present husbands of former Chicago area widows provide child care, mainly because it is not needed in the home or because other people provide it. The second set of figures shows contribution of the husband and the boyfriends as a percentage of total listings by all widows.

Table 12 answers some of our questions as to the differences women see in how extensively the late husband contributed to their emotional support systems and how the present husband now contributes by remarriage status. It becomes apparent that there are some women who are not husband oriented, in that they do not draw their emotional supports, or draw very few, from a husband. Those are the women who mention either the late or the present husband very infrequently, or even never in answer to the support questions. At the other extreme are the women who refer to a husband with great frequency. Thus, we see that the difference is not between husbands, past versus present, but among women in the extent to which they are husband-oriented. This is a very interesting finding, not anticipated initially because of a cultural bias leading us to expect the women to have to differentiate marriages by differentiating the contributions of each husband to their emotional supports. Table 11 also documents the variations between the women who have remarried and those who have not in their evaluations of the contributions of the late husband. The still-widowed women mention him more often than do the remarrieds.

HUSBAND SANCTIFICATION

The tendency of the remarried women to be less extreme than those still widowed in judging the deceased husband as the most important contributor to their emotional supports leads us to predict that, for whatever combination of reasons, they would also be less extreme in their sanctification scores. Table 13 supports this prediction. Although most of the women present both the late and the current husband very positively, the remarried are consistently less sanctifying than the still widowed. The greatest gap between the two categories of women is in their response to the statements that the husband had no irritating habits; that the couple spent all its

nonwork hours together; and in two judgments on the semantic-differential scale. The remarried women are much less
apt to give extreme credit to the late husband as honest or
friendly. The two groups are most alike in their feeling that
the husband was kind and warm, an "unusually good man"
and a good father. Although we have not mentioned previously the women who remarried but then divorced or sepa-

TABLE 13

*Mean Scores on Sanctification Scale Items, by Remarriage Status
of Chicago Area Widows*

Husband	Gamma[a]	Never Remarried (1)	Currently Remarried (2)	Difference Between (1)+(2)
Semantic Differential				
Good–Bad	.14	1.59	1.78	.19
Useful–Useless	.17	1.66	1.85	.19
Honest–Dishonest	.22	1.44	1.72	.28
Superior–Inferior	.10	2.04	2.15	.11
Friendly–Unfriendly	.22	1.50	1.75	.25
Kind–Cruel	.32	1.54	1.61	.07
Warm–Cold	.19	1.58	1.66	.08
Total	.24			
RANGE 1–7				
Life Together				
"Unusually" good man	.15	1.48	1.54	.06
Marriage	.15	1.74	1.90	.16
Always together	.22	1.78	2.08	.30
Felt same	.14	1.98	2.13	.15
Good father	.09	1.37	1.45	.08
Home happy	.16	1.65	1.81	.16
Not irritating	.28	2.22	2.60	.38
Total	.11			
RANGE 1–4				
N =		74,403	4,521	

[a]Gamma association between marital status as ordered in columns 1 and 2 and scale items. The
higher the score, the less positive the judgement.

168

rated as they are relatively few in number, we find an interesting variation in some of their responses. They are much less likely than are the other two categories to define their late husband as friendly or warm, and much more apt to place him at the positive extreme of good and useful. They are almost on the "disagree" level of judging the late husband as a good father. It would appear that these women are less happy with their past than are the women in either of the other marital situations.

Satisfaction with Life and Roles

All the evidence presented thus far seems to indicate definite advantages of remarriage for those women who do not then dissolve this relation through divorce or separation. There are financial, service, social and emotional benefits for many women, at least as far as the former widows in our sample are concerned. In addition, there appears to be a definite advantage as far as feelings of loneliness are concerned. The remarried are much more apt to feel lonely never or rarely than are the still widowed and especially than are the women who are no longer in the marriage that follows widowhood. Of course, it is possible that the currently remarried women would not consider themselves lonely even without a husband, because of their overall personality and social integration, but the presence of a husband undoubtedly contributes to assuaging feelings of loneliness. On the other hand, some of the remarried women judge themselves as more lonely than most people.

We asked other questions in an attempt to ascertain the relations between satisfaction with life and remarriage, including a direct one. The currently remarried women are the most apt to strongly agree with the statement, "I am very satisfied with the way my life is going now." The women who are most apt to disagree with that statement are the divorced or separated former widows; almost a third of them are not satisfied with their lives. On the other hand, 18 percent of the remarried women circle "disagree" or "strongly disagree" in response to this self-administered question. Remarriage does not guarantee satisfaction with life. About a third of the married women, however, agree that "many widows who remarry are very unhappy in this marriage," which means that 16 percent of the women must feel unusually lucky because they are satisfied, although they believe many others who remarry are unhappy.

What are the advantages as well as the disadvantages of remarriage from the vantage point of the women involved? The former widows were quite consistent in their answers. The advantages a remarried widow has over one who does not remarry include:

> The company of a man, someone to enjoy your cooking, someone to cook for, companionship. There is love, someone to care for and who cares for you.

> My opinion is that it's so much nicer to share a life with someone rather than to be by yourself; and better for children to have a father.

> Companionship and a little more security; there is less loneliness; you need someone to care for who cares for you.

Financial advantages are mentioned by only 16 percent of the remarried women, while 66 percent mention social supports in the form of companionship and 18 percent emotional supports in the form of love and caring. The advantages a widow enjoys over one who has remarried are also fairly consistent:

> Being able to travel; doing what they want to without getting permission. They don't have to feel guilty if they want a vacation for six months.

> She can develop a strong relationship with her children when they are young. And when they are older she can do what she

170

wants. She can be her own person, choose a career if the wants that.

If she has a career that is very important to her, this could probably fill the empty space in her life.

Financial advantages of not remarrying are mentioned by 20 percent of the respondents, but 73 percent mention independence in one form or another.

We also asked whether the women feel that their current marriage is different from the one that ended in widowhood and what advice they would give to a widow about remarriage. Although it seems incredible, 15 percent of the respondents claim that the two marriages are not different. Half of the elderly remarried women feel this way, which indicates the possibility that these relations are quite instrumental and role-constrained, rather than affective. Those women who found differences between marriages when asked, "Some women who have remarried feel their present marriage is different from their past marriage; others feel there is not much difference between these marriages. Would you say your present marriage is different or not different from your past marriage?'" offer several explanations for these differences. Some of these are positive; others are neutral.

We're closer. He is an understanding man. He's good and kind and there's not the turmoil there was with the drinking in my first marriage.

My present husband is an entirely different personality and it's more companionship now than physical attraction; it's not the same thing as growing up and raising a family together.

It's simply that any second marriage has to be different. One factor is children and a stepfamily. Then you are younger with the first and you kind of grow together. With the second husband you are set in your pattern and don't change much.

There is less social activity; less community involvement. We were very, very active in community affairs, had to attend them. I was

171

drawn into it because of him. . . . There is truth that there is an easier feeling in the second marriage. Less tension, you aren't afraid to say, "No, I don't want to do that."

Not all widows remarried well. One, whose late husband was killed in an accident, married nine months later, only to find out from the Social Security Administration that her new husband was still married to another woman. Another's new husband is ill, so that they do not go out together often even though her children are no longer small. A third explains a difference in this marriage in terms of the husband's inability to relate to her emotionally.

My marriage is different because my second husband does not play—there's not much sharing. He is emotionally deficient. He is most uncommunicative, no verbal communication.

The answers focus on the differences in the husbands or in the relation itself because of changed circumstances. The presence of children often enters into descriptions of marital differences. The last woman quoted above is very unhappy with this marriage. She had gone through a lot in the past, losing a husband whom she loved very much, having to fight herself out of alcoholism with the help of Alcoholics Anonymous, and marrying precipitously to get herself and her children out of the home of her parents. Generally speaking, however, the descriptions of differences between the marriages tend to present the current marriage as quite satisfactory, a finding supported by other research (McKaine, 1969; Bernard, 1956).

Advice that remarried women "would give to a widow about remarriage" definitely focuses on the choice of the mate and steps needed to ensure a good marriage:

Be careful, there's a lot of jerks in the world; don't jump from the frying pan into the fire. There may be problems with families, if he was married before.

Make sure he's the right man. You've got to love him, it's as easy as that. Wait for the right one, be careful.

Ask his children and his close friends how he reacts in anger, disappointment, and if he is honest about his feelings.

Wait long enough for the shock to wear off. Consider only yourself . . .do not marry for children or family. Place high value on yourself. I don't think widows should try to be nuns because of widowhood as far as physical needs. . . . Accept and satisfy these needs and don't think of neighbors. Certainly a woman who has been married needs this physical means; be yourself.

I think the second time around there would be advantages of living with a man, not for the first marriage, but it would possibly be a good idea to live with a second husband first for awhile to find out how well you get along. There has to be some part of love, there can't be marriage just for security. It's probably a different kind of love but there has to be a definite feeling for the man other than need.

Watch out who you marry. Take your time.

If you remarry, try to make a go of it. I'm grateful to Bob. He's great. He's a good stepfather.

Make sure their husband to be has a will made out; it would save a lot of problems if he has children. And, make sure he is in good health.

The advisers are obviously speaking from their own experience. The last-quoted wife is very bitter. Her new husband died five weeks after their marriage and there has been friction between her and his children because they think that he left her much money. Another respondent found on the death of her last husband that he had changed his will, which *had* named her the beneficiary, and named his children so that she received nothing until she brought the case to court—a long, costly process. Her anger is intensified by the fact that she had nursed this husband for several years, while the children, his main beneficiaries, did nothing to help her, although they lived in the same city.

173

The final means by which we tried to ascertain differences among remarrieds and the women who remained widowed is by asking for a ranking of nine roles relative to each other. There is some difference in the assignment of the role of wife, the remarrieds being more apt to give it top priority in the top three ranks and much less likely to put it at the bottom. The age differences are also apparent in the frequency with which the remarrieds place the role of member of a religious group and grandmother in the bottom ranks. Interestingly some widows refused to rank some roles, such as member of society or worker, while the remarried are more consistent.

Summary

Most women represented by our sample have been married only once and most of these marriages were terminated by the death of the man. Over half of the women had been widowed before the age of 60 and about the same proportion had been married 30 years or more. Less than a quarter have developed close personal relations with another man since widowhood— only six percent have remarried. These figures reflect the lack of opportunity to meet and develop intimate relations with eligible men, as well as the unwillingness of these women to re-enter a marital relation. Boyfriends are met in a variety of ways; the initial contact most likely being made in a public place or through mutual friends. The boyfriends are, or had been, seen quite frequently, in various settings, outside or in the home. Many such relations ended with the death of the man or because of incompatibile attitudes. There are indications that some women have strong negative feelings about remarriage, although it is hard to determine if these are due to unwillingness to resume the role of wife or to a realistic assessment of the low probability of remarriage and the high probability that the men available to them at this stage of their lives are likely to be undesirable.

The remarried women tend to be younger, with younger children, and also to have been more advantaged in their past. That is, they come from more urbanized families, are better educated, and had been more affluent in the previous marriage than their still-widowed counterparts. This holds true even for women who married later in life, and age itself is not a sufficient factor to explain remarriage—except for very young women.

Generally speaking, remarriage seems to have positive effects on the support systems and life evaluations of former widows. Of course, positively oriented women are more apt to enter a new intimate relation and to be positive in their evaluation of it. The newly created families are living on incomes primarily from the husband's wage or salary, with some contribution from the wife. The new husband appears often in the emotional support system of the remarried women, even more often than does their late husband or than does the late husband of the still widowed women. Although the new husband does not appear often as the recipient of the wife's services, he contributes more to her service supports than does a boyfriend not living in her home. His help is, however, mainly through the traditional division of labor. He appears unevenly in the social supports as the first-mentioned contributor, mainly being the companion in social contacts outside of the home, but even here he appears much more often than does a boyfriend.

Either the remarried widows never sanctified the late husband as much as did the widows who remain single, or the contributions of the present husband to her support system have diminished the tendency in that direction. There is a definite difference between the remarried and the still-widowed women in the extent to which they define the late husband as a major contributor to their emotional supports when he was well and in their idealization of him. The remarried women also seem for the most part satisfied with their life and marriage, though some are still lonely and unhappy. The least

175

satisfied are the women who remarried and then dissolved that union through divorce or separation. The frequency of termination of boyfriend relations and the caution about the importance of the choice of a new husband indicate that the remarried women have for the most part entered a relation with someone who meets their expectations for companionship, security and successful father substitution for their children.

F I V E

Children as Resources

However effective remarriage is in providing resources for all support systems and a companion, lessening the probability of loneliness and adding to life satisfaction, a vast majority of women do not either have or desire that option. As we saw in Chapter 4, the lives of those who did and who did not remarry differ substantially in many ways. However, one thing both have in common is the presence of children and their active contribution to the mother's support systems. Only 8.6 percent of the current or former beneficiaries of social security represented by our sample have no living offspring; the remainder has a total of approximately 221,600 children, or an average of three per mother. Most of the mothers actually have three or less, only 31 percent having larger families. In fact, 69 percent of the respondents have two children and 45 percent have three. More than 24,000 children of the widows have died, reflecting the higher child mortality rate of earlier years. Some of the women adopted children or took care of stepchildren from an early enough age to consider themselves as having "mothered" them.

Although most of the mothers were less than 65 years old when the husband became ill, the ages of the children ranged widely. Not surprisingly, the more children a woman has, the lower their mean and median ages. Half of the eldest children of these women were already over the age of 30 when their father became incapacitated, while half of the fifth or sixth children were only 13 years old or less. (The addition of offspring following remarriage has been mentioned in Chapter 4.)

Since the late husband had been the father of most of the widow's children, we asked the mother if "this child was (any of these children were) strongly affected by the death of their father?," later determining, "Were any of your children not strongly affected by the death of their father?" We added the second question because it would have been incorrect to assume that the children not mentioned in the answer to the first question were defined by the mother as not having been affected at all, rather than not being the most affected child. This turned out to be a wise decision since some mothers focused on the problems of one child only. The answers to both questions varied considerably by beneficiary status, with interesting implications. The women most apt to feel that at least one of their children was strongly affected by the death of the father are the mothers of still dependent or no longer dependent offspring (69 and 67 percent, respectively). The remarried widows, who also are likely to have had young children in their care when the husband died are somewhat less apt to feel that these were strongly affected by that event (59 percent) and the "lump sum" beneficiaries are similar in their judgments (56 percent). Finally, the retirement widows are unlikely to feel that any of their children were affected (34 percent). Only 46 percent of the widows think that any of their children were strongly affected by the death of the father, and 43 percent that at least one child was not strongly affected—a rather surprising finding.

At the other end of the spectrum, as far as the effect of the father's death on the children, are the women who state that at least one of their children was definitely *not* strongly affected. The most apt to make such a judgement are the retirement widows (46 percent) and the remarried women (46 percent), while the mothers of adult children are the least apt to feel this way (31 percent). The widows themselves give interesting explanations as to why some child or children were more affected than others—or why all of their children fell into one or the other category by level of affect. For the main part, these explanations are made in terms of the age of the child. Both very young and adult children are often portrayed as not having been deeply affected by the father's death, as indicated not only by actual statements, but also by the distributions. The most apt to state that their children were not strongly affected are the retirement and the remarried widows. It is, of course, impossible to determine how the children felt about the death. Adult children with their own families of procreation may have been sufficiently removed from their emotional and other forms of dependency on the father as not to react strongly. Adult children have other people besides the mother to whom they can turn and express their feelings and they may wish to protect her from knowing how much they were upset. Some of the widows explain that their adult children had been prepared for the impending death of their father by his illness. Younger children often express their feelings more openly and since they generally live at home, the mother can witness their reaction.

As a result of any of these factors, over half of the widows believe that the death of the father had no strong affect on the children, a conclusion reinforcing American mourning rituals that focus on the widow as the main sufferer in the death of the head of the household, more or less neglecting his offspring and doing little to ease their burden. Interviews with Loyola University of Chicago students who volunteered to talk about how their mother handled her grief indicate that this cultural tradition is prevalent and may be detrimental to the welfare of the children. The death of the father appears particularly difficult to two types of situations: if the child had been in conflict with the father prior to his death or if his death deprives the child of a major ally in the family. The students complained that they lost not only the father but also the mother, if she turned to a favorite child for comfort. Most families contain one or more dyads of members who are closer to each other than to the rest of the unit, and the child who loses his or her partner is doubly bereft. We had hypothesized that the mother would point to a son as the most upset of her offspring by the father's death—but there was no significant sexual difference in her evaluations. It is impossible to say if this is the actual situation or if each mother is simply juggling her guilt and perceptions of the feelings of her children. One clue as to their reactions appears, however, when we ask if any of the children developed problems in their relation with others as a result of losing their fathers. Although only 11 percent of the women respond with a "yes," 60 percent of those widows list a son rather than a daughter as the first child to develop such problems, 55 percent as the second, and 82 percent as the third.

When asked how the child was affected by the death of the father, the widows find it difficult to explain. The answers refer mainly to deprivation, to the loss of a needed person or to the child's feelings of sadness and longing for the deceased. Not all of the mothers were able to help their children during this time; 30 percent explain that they were too depressed themselves or that they could not reach the child psychologically. Most of the mothers who believe that they were of help to the children used talking as their primary method. They talked with the child about the death, explaining that it was what was best, considering the father's illness—or else in religious terms. Few went out of their own surroundings to obtain professional help or turned to people such as school personnel, religious leaders or other members of the helping professions to help the affected child. As in their own support systems, there is a great shortage of societal members helping mothers and children to cope with grief and other emotional turmoil, even though several books point to the importance of professional help for children who must deal with these emotions and lack the maturity to do so (Vernon, 1970; Kubler-Ross, 1977).

Of course, the death of a father can have other consequences for the children besides emotional ones and we wanted to know how perceptive the widow might be about the many changes the loss of the father has wrought in the life of the offspring. The loss of a family's main breadwinner can affect schooling, work or money available for other activities either by diminishing total income or by bringing in more money, or a large lump sum, beyond anything the father if alive could have earned during the years of the children's growing up. The death often removes the main disciplinarian from the family, shifting the responsibility for the children to the mother. We asked the respondent if she thought the "child's (children's) future was affected by being without a father?" and then specified the areas in which we wanted her to estimate if the offspring received more, the same, or less of the item than they would have if the father had not died. The answers are rather surprising in view of the fact that so many women had children below the age of 20 when the husband became ill or suffered the accident. Only 16 percent of all the widows state that the children's future was affected by the loss of their father; the rest either had no children or say that their offspring already had established the future at that time or are unaware of any consequences on their lives. Although mothers of young children were the most apt to replace the father by remarriage, very few of them do. It thus appears that these widowed women do not seem to have much understanding of their children's life paths. As stated before, there is, of course, the possibility that the future of the children was actually unaffected by their father's death, but it is more probable that many widows simply do not think in long-range terms; that they deal with the world day by day and do not see the alternative paths their children could have taken under different conditions. Whatever the reason, not only did few of the mothers consider their children's future altered in general terms, but few found any consequences in the life chances that we specified.

The mothers of dependent children apparently are not planning extensive educations for their children or they must assume that their current income will cover it, because 58 percent see no difference in how much schooling they would have obtained had the father lived. The mothers of adult children were widowed while at least one offspring was under 28 or under 22 if attending school (or they would not be in our sample) but they are only somewhat more aware than are the mothers of younger offspring. Of course, the answers of the retirement widows are less surprising. Even the mothers who believed that the children gained less schooling as a result of being orphaned do not necessarily translate this loss into employment consequences, 72 percent perceiving no change. Interestingly, about a third of the mothers of dependent children, retirement and remarried widows, believe that their children gained rather than lost money by the death. Almost half of the mothers of adult children must be considering insurance or other such funds. One respondent explains that her husband never brought home a steady income because of his drinking, so that the social security she now receives is a definite asset. Not surprisingly, the lump-sum beneficiaries are most apt to see the situation in terms of a financial loss for the offspring, although they do not project this into changes in schooling or working. They did not have dependent children at widowhood. The main area in which the widow judges that her children obtained more, rather than less of a circumstance as a result of the death of the father, is in regard to responsibility for her. That is, 66 percent of the women feel that the death of the father has resulted in their children having to take more responsibility for the care of the mother than they had when he was living. This is not a feminist stance, but it does reflect the actual support systems, strongly dependent on the offspring. There is certainly much agreement among the widows that the death of the father did not lessen the children's responsibility for the mother (only five percent thought it did).

The probability that the father had been the patriarch of the family is implied by the fact that a third of the widows consider their children to have gained in freedom and independence when he died. Only 14 percent feel they lost it. This is particularly true of the retirement widows who are most apt to have lived in such a family system. Sixteen percent of the widows agree that the children gained peace and quiet by the death, although one-quarter of the remarried feel that they lost this quality of life.

Some of the mothers do make the connection between the change in one area of their children's lives and another. For example, 72 percent of the mothers who believed that their children got more schooling after the death of their father than they would have had otherwise also state that his death increased the amount of money available to the family. On the other hand, 58 percent of the women who say that the children got less schooling also find less money in the household. (However, we are speaking here of fewer than three thousand women represented by our sample.) Other relatively high associations are between the amount of schooling gained by the children and the amount of responsibility over their mother they acquired. Some mothers think that the increase in responsibility decreased the amount of time children could spend on their education. However, less than one percent of the women concluded that the children received less schooling and needed to work harder. All in all, the responses went strongly against expectations. Our main concern was with schooling and employment, and we anticipated that many children lost years or fields of specialization in schooling as a result of financial and possibly emotional factors after the death of the father especially if they were members of larger families and in their teens. But either no such changes occurred or, as stated before, the mothers failed to see them, understating the impact of the death of the father on the children. It is hard to estimate, however, whether the widow perceives the effect egoistically as on herself only or whether she cannot visualize alternatives to what the children actually experienced.

Characteristics of Children Now

All this happened, on the average, 10 years ago and the eldest child today is again, on the average, 39 years of age. Fifty-one percent of all the offspring are females. The composition of the families of mothers is as follows: 18 percent have only male children and 21 percent only females; the majority, 61 percent, have mixed families. In only eight percent of the families are all of the children under age 21; 76 percent contain children over age 21, leaving only 16 percent mixed. This means that almost one-quarter of the widows still have at least one child under age 21. Going further we find that the children of 43 percent of the women are all married, of 18 percent all single and of 40 percent a mixture. This means that 58 percent of the women have at least one child who is currently not married— most of them never having been married, rather than widowed, separated or divorced. In listing each child, we find that 32 percent have never married; 60 percent are married now; five percent are separated or divorced, and only two percent are widowed. As to education, only 11 percent of the families contain children of all ages who have less than a high-school education; 65 percent with all the offspring finished with high school or more schooling and slighly less than 25 percent being mixed. Many of these are young children who have not yet finished their education. In view of the ages and education of the children it is not surprising that in 40 percent of the families all the children are working away from the mother's home, as housewives or in paid employment; in only 18 percent none are working; the remaining 42 percent of the families are mixed.

Fifty-six percent of all the women do not have any child living at home either because they are childless or because their children have moved away. (We are counting children who are away at school without a separate "permanent" residence or their own household as still living at home.) Twenty-seven percent of the mothers have only one child at home, an additional nine percent have two, and the remainder care for still larger families. Twenty-four percent of them have no children living away from the household, 26 have one and 22 percent have two. The percentages taper off after that. The combination presents the following pattern: 16 percent of the mothers have all their children still at home, 51 percent have all of them living away and 32 percent are in mixed families. This means that in almost half of the households at least one child is at home. The more children a woman has, the greater the probability that the younger ones will still be living with her. In addition, starting with the eldest, 37 percent of whom are in the home (or at least in the neighborhood), there is a gradual increase of such convenient proximity as the birth order goes up, with the unexplainable exception of the sixth child, who is apt to be either at home or outside of the immediate area. Thus, women with a large number of children tend to have at least one nearby, even if not living with them. This finding supports those of other researchers (Shanas and Streib, 1965; Shanas et. al., 1968; B. Adams, 1968).

The residential arrangements of these widows reflect the national trend toward their independence discussed in Chapter 1. Those widows who share a household with someone else almost inevitably have minor, or at least unmarried, children living with them, although the very old, the first or second generation ethnics, the blacks, the very poor and the poorly educated, are more apt to be dependent for housing on their married children, usually daughters. They simply cannot maintain themselves independently. The changes in the living arrangements of widows and the characteristics of those who live alone indicate a strong probability that they do so by choice rather than because their adult children reject them. In fact, several researchers have reached this conclusion (B. Adams, 1968; Berardo, 1968, 1970; Chevan and Korson, 1972, 1975; Lopata, 1971a, 1973a). The widows themselves give three major reasons for their desire to live alone or, at least, not to move into the household of a married child: a wish for independence, to avoid strain or possibly conflict in their relations with offspring and their families and to avoid work and "being imposed upon" (Lopata, 1971b). The detailed reasons focus on the importance that many women attach to maintaining their own household within which they can organize their time, work and the placement and use of objects. The right to their own space, symbolically and practically, for example, in the bathroom, is important, especially to older women. They also fear that by moving into an existing household they would deprive others of rights over space and be resented by the occupants. They want to be able to decide when and what to eat, rather than having to adjust to decisions of another woman—even a daughter. They do not enjoy the idea of being peripheral to the life in another home which, after all, had operated without them for some time. Some are uncomfortable with their children's friends, neighbors and neighborhoods. Many older widows are accustomed to a lower socio-economic life-style than now led by their children, thanks to the help they had given them in earlier years. The women are accustomed not only to their own "territory" in the household but also their own type of neighborhood. Even if they moved after the death of the husband, their choice was generally based on their own, rather than on the children's idea of where they would be more comfortable.

The possibility of strain with the children and their families is given as an important reason why widows do not want to live with them if they can be economically independent and well enough to keep their own residence. Visits or occasional more extended stays with adult children make evident the possibility for such strain. Mothers are accustomed to observ-

186

ing and commenting on the behavior of their children and grandchildren, but their comments are not always welcome, especially when they are seen as criticism or attempts to control. The cultural changes since the mother's grandmother's youth, and the unwillingness of modern parents to use "old-fashioned" methods in bringing up their children or running a home often lead to strong differences of opinion. Besides, the son or daughter is embedded in a web of relations which the mother may find unsatisfactory or which can produce adverse reactions to her presence and behavior. The daughter may be willing to put up with the widow's "advice," but the older woman knows very well that the son-in-law has no tolerance. Widows are afraid that they will not be able to desist from actions that may make them look like interfering or as undesirable housemates, causing problems with in-laws and perhaps with grandchildren.

Finally, widowed women seem often happy with their lighter workload, fearing being imposed upon if they move into a busy household. They object to "baby-sitting" which they define as passive, as opposed to grandparenting, which involves socialization of the grandchildren or great-grandchildren. They do not want to do housework while the younger woman enjoys herself or works for pay away from the home. They are perfectly willing either to hold a job themselves or just sit in their own home. Those widows who live with married children are apt to be there as a service to themselves rather than to the middle-aged generation or because the children insist on it. The widows' description of an ideal residential arrangement is similar to the one Rosenmyer and Kockeis (1963) called, "intimacy at a distance," in reference to relations between Viennese older parents and their adult children or to what Peter Townsend (1957) calls living within "soup-carrying distance."

Only about 10 percent of the children living away from the mother's home are seen daily—the mean frequency of contact with all such children being only about several times a month but less than once a week. Daily contact is most apt to occur with the offspring who lives in the same building or block. Not all sons or daughters who live in the neighborhood are seen daily but on an average of several times a week or weekly. Thirty-one percent of the mothers see all their children at least once a week, 34 percent see them less often, and 35 percent see some children at least weekly—others less often. Approximately two percent of the children are "never" seen.

Contributions to Support Systems

As we saw in Chapter 2, adult children are perceived by 86 percent of the Chicago area widows as having been "generally very helpful" when they were trying to establish a new life for themselves after the death of their husbands. Children of all ages also appear very frequently as contributors to the mother's four current support systems, with some also appearing in the emotional system of the year prior to the husband's fatal illness or accident. Many women have more than one child, and the opportunity to list each was given often, so it is not surprising that the children appear even more often than does the late husband, who is only one person and could be mentioned only in the prior emotional support system. Approximately 8.4 percent of the women do not mention a child at all, and since 8.6 percent of the women did not have any children—i.e., did not actively perform the role of mother to any in their youth—some women are obviously referring to older stepchildren. Half of the widows mention children 17 times or more often in the various support systems, the mean or average number being brought down by those mothers who rarely list their offspring. The strong variation between median and mean indicates a rather low use of children by some of the mothers.

Let us now turn to the details of the contributions of the children. Tables 2 through 8 contain summaries of the numbers of references to children and the percentage these numbers form of the total of people the widow lists for that support. The spouses of the children are counted separately, so that, "my daughter Mary and her husband, John," were counted as two children, since they usually function in the mother's support systems together and cannot be located otherwise. Although the weighted figures are difficult to deal with because of their size, they are needed because of the importance of learning how many listings are actually involved in each system.

ECONOMIC SUPPORT SYSTEM

The contributions of the children to the economic support system of the Chicago area widows in ways other than paying for their own room or board or turning over their wages and salaries, in other words, "help" given by them and so-defined by the widow, are very rare. Table 3 documents this, emphasizing the point made before that widows are economically either poor or living on a steady income—not dependent on their children (see also Chapter 9). Whatever help she and her husband gave the children in the form of gifts of money, payment or help in payment of rent or mortgage, food, clothing, or other bills, as recorded by other sociologists, the widow now perceives herself as receiving more of such help than giving it; the figures are not large in any case (Litwak, 1960, 1965; Sussman, 1965; Shanas and Streib, 1965). The 82,085 women represented by our sample list only 11,477 people from whom they are receiving help in the form of gifts of money from and that less than 1,000 of the helpers are her children. It must be remembered that the table contains percentages of people in each relation to the widow who help her in the designated ways, not the number of widows receiving this help. A single woman might get financial aid from more than one of her children. In fact, if she needs help in the payment of any of her bills, and has more than one child, the burden is likely to be shared. The children often meet in a family conference and decide together how much each will regularly contribute to the maintenance of the mother. These family conferences are not necessarily pleasant events and the few widows who are the subjects of such meetings usually know this. Of course, gifts of money can be special occasion rather than regular payments. The percentages also show that if a woman receives any such help it is most likely to come from her children. Only the government competes with them, and that in the case of medicare and medicaid.

Some of the more affluent widows list themselves as givers of money to their children, but we do not know the amounts involved here any more than we did in the cases in which they are the receivers. Payment for food and clothing is rare. Of course the women are talking of children who live outside of the home, since in America moving out usually means that they become self-supporting.

SERVICE SUPPORT SYSTEMS

As noted before, the widow generally believes that she receives the various service supports more often than she gives them. The one exception was child care (see Table 4). Because of the presence of so many middle-aged and older women, many more baby-sit for their children than receive such help. Over half of the references to a widow, performing child care services, are for her own children—that is, she takes care of her grandchildren. About a quarter of the women who need such service get it from older children with their siblings. The most frequent aid from children is care during illness, and over twice as many children are listed as givers rather than receivers, though this is also the highest number of out-services performed by the widow. Children also help their mother with transportation and decision making, particularly with the latter. Other persons, generally neighbors, friends or co-workers, are also mentioned as pertains to transportation. Transportation is often associated with help in shopping, although some women explain that their children will "pick up a few things" for the mother when they are doing their own shopping. Many of the older widows like to live in neighborhoods where they can do their own shopping, walking the rounds almost daily not only to buy their food and other items, but as part of a social ritual.

Housekeeping "help" from children usually means a specially arranged division of labor, although some of the children, mainly daughters, come in from their own homes to help their mothers clean for special occasions or periodically. Few women have cars and about half of the transportation by car is provided by children. The traditional role of women is evidenced by the fact that none of them helps an offspring in the care of her or his car. One set of figures that surprises me was the infrequency with which children make household repairs; of course, these are not skills generally possessed by younger offspring, and the older ones tend to be busy repairing their own homes and helping their spouses, etc. (Shanas, 1962). By the same token, the mother does not repair the homes of her adult children and any repairs she performs in her home are considered as part of maintenance, rather than as "help" to the children residing in it. Since many children are living with her, she does not, as mentioned earlier, count her normal housekeeping and shopping services as help. Some mothers leave their home to help their children in the maintenance of their homes especially during emergencies such as illness or birth of a baby. These are specifically listed by the widow, but they are not frequent activities, but take place only several times a year.

One of the interesting questions in connection with the support systems of widows is which of her children, son or daughter, is of greater help. An examination of the detailed answers to who is in the primary service supports, that is, the first-listed person, indicates two things: one, the preponderance of daughters over sons—the other, the sex-segregated nature of the area of service supports. Daughters are more important than sons in the areas of sick care, housekeeping help, transportation shopping, as well as decision making. Thirty-two percent of those listed as providing transportation are daughters, compared with 19 percent who are sons. Such service is provided at least once a week in 69 percent of the cases. In other words, it is a regular and important service. Daughters are listed in 46 percent of the cases as helpers with shopping, compared with 18 percent of the sons; the activity is carried out at least once a week. Where there is help with housekeeping, it is provided at least once a week in 84 percent of the homes, and 51 percent of the helpers are daughters while only 10 percent are sons. In the case of illness, the widow gets help from her daughters with 47 percent of the cases—from sons with 12 percent. However, this care, important as it may be, is not needed as often. Only 12 percent of the widows need such help at least once a week, although 8 percent require it daily. Decision-making help is also needed rarely, and the daughters are listed 35 percent of the time while sons are listed in 27 percent of the cases. Sons appear more often than daughters in yardwork and car care. Sons are main helpers in the yard 36 percent of the time, daughters 15 percent, and such care is provided at least once a week in 43 percent of the homes. Car-care assistance is provided rarely; only 9 percent of the widows who receive it require it at least once a week. Only 15 percent of the helpers, on the other hand, are daughters. All in all, the widows are much more dependent on their daughters than on their sons in basic aspects of life.

SOCIAL SUPPORT SYSTEM

Children are proportionately less often mentioned as contributors to social supports than to service supports because many other people are involved in leisure-time activities (see Table 5). The activities we chose came from women's descriptions of what they do with others and not as part of the "normal" flow of daily family activities, such as watching television. Thus, the activities finally selected are apt to involve boyfriends, other friends, co-workers and relatives other than the children living at home. Children tend to appear in all of the three categories, with the exception of being listed second or third more often than first as companions in going to church, but that is mainly because so few people are mentioned beyond the first reference. As we noted before, women tend to go to church alone and the children living at home or nearby, not too large a number, attend with them. Children are mentioned first as the people with whom holidays are spent. They are least apt to appear in sports or other game-playing, mainly because few women engage in them; this accounts for the small number of people but also because such games are usually played with young people and most of the offspring are beyond that age. The widows are unlikely to be playing games with their mothers but they may do so with their children. Only a third of the women travel out of town with their children, although they may travel alone to visit them. Although the gap between entertaining and visiting is lower than in connection with the contributions of other resource persons, the numbers are small in both cases. The fact that so few widows claim to entertain together in their home with their children is not surprising, since many shy away from the idea of "entertaining." It is more surprising that so many widows claim not to go visiting with their children to other people's homes more often. Admittedly, not many have small children who must be taken along when visiting, but it would seem that the lack of a car, fear of traveling at night in the city, and so forth, would lead to reciprocal visits. In any case, relatively few children accompany their mothers while the latter either entertain or visit.

As with the service supports of the Chicago area widows, so with the social supports—the daughters are much more involved than are the sons. This tendency is consistent throughout the first two orders of listing, the numbers of sons who are mentioned third are not able to offset the discrepancy in the first two. Daughters are mentioned twice as often as sons as people with whom the widow most often goes to movies or other public events, if she goes at all. They visit with her more than twice as often although both sexes of offspring are listed under "entertaining" at home. If the mother goes out to lunch with someone outside of the normal routine of family meal-sharing, it is predominantly with daughters rather than sons (14 to two percent). It is the female offspring who is most apt to accompany the mother to church (17 to seven percent) and on out-of-town travel (20 to nine percent), and it is with her and her family that the widow spends her holidays (25 to 12 percent). The extreme difference between the contributions of the sons and of the daughters is startling in a society which claims bilateral family relations. The only social activity besides entertaining in which mothers engage with sons almost as frequently as with daughters is in sports or other games. But these are rare and tend to involve young children living at home. Once children reach maturity, the sons seem to withdraw from involvement in the social support system of their widowed mothers, the daughters or a daughter and their families maintaining the major share of contribution to it, other persons entering it selectively, depending upon education, income, age and other characteristics of the widows.

EMOTIONAL SUPPORT SYSTEM

Children appear in the emotional support system much more often than in the social, in reverse of friends, but they are the most frequent contributors now than they were when the husband was still alive. (see Tables 6 and 7). They do not, however, appear consistently, there being a great variation by sentiment or feeling states and in the order in which they come to the mother's consciousness. In the "before" time period we

seldom found them as the first-named person, obviously because the late husband was apt to have occupied that place.
Nevertheless, more than one-sixth of the women list a child
as the person closest to them even when the husband was
alive; one in eight remember a child as the one most apt to
make them angry; one in nine or ten as the one they most
enjoyed being with; one to whom one would turn in times of
crisis or who made them feel respected or useful. The contributions of children to these supports increase when second-
and even third-order reference is examined so that almost a
third of the total number of references are to closest persons—
those who made the woman feel useful, while over a fourth
of the women gained feelings of being respected and important
from the children. Not surprisingly, these are also listed as
people they most enjoyed being with.

The *"now"* period is definitely monopolized by the children,
although they are not apt to be the ones who make the mother
angry or provide feelings of self-sufficiency and independence
in first order of mention or in the total. They most frequently
contribute to her feelings of closeness and enjoyment; they
are the people to whom she would turn in crisis; and they
supply her with feelings of being an important and respected
person. The content of the emotional system provides a great
deal of insight into mother–child relations and shows that
children do not necessarily need to provide services for the
mother in order to be considered by her the most important
people in her life. Interestingly enough, children do not appear
often as persons the widow is most apt to tell her problems to,
only 37 percent listing them first. This supports Zena Blau's
(1961) argument that women need same age and same level
of negotiative power confidants, and thus they cannot use
their offspring as sharers of their problems—at least not in
first order of mention. This is also partly because many women
claim not to reveal their problems to anyone. Considering the
large number of children represented by our sample, it is
obvious that many children are not used as confidants. It

would be interesting to find out if children also feel that mothers refrain from sharing problems and worries with them.

Again, the question arises as to whether daughters are more contributive to the welfare of their widowed mothers than are sons. Interestingly enough, some women refused to declare openly preference for one child or another as contributors to their emotional support system, insisting on answering "my children" or "all my children" in answer to the various support questions, regardless of whatever probing by interviewers. The interviewers had been instructed to get each child separately, so that they tried to "break down" generalized answers—often to no avail. It is in answer to these questions for the time period prior to the husband's illness that we find some of the dead children. Unfortunately, we do not know the year of the death of the children, although, as mentioned before, there is a sizable number of them, so that we cannot determine what proportion of the deceased were available the year before the husband's illness. Although aware that some widows tend to sanctify the late husband, we did not fully realize that mothers may also sanctify deceased children; hence, the interview was not designed to establish the frequency of this trend. References to a deceased child as the one who was the closest to the mother, whom she most enjoyed being with, provide some clues. A number of Loyola University of Chicago students told us that life was difficult for them at home because of constant comparisons to a dead sibling who, in retrospect, is made to appear angelic.

As we saw above, children do not appear as often in the emotional supports of the mother the year prior to the husband's illness or accident as they do now—at least, in her reconstructed memory. However, a couple of examples suffice to show that even then, daughters tend to be remembered as more important to the mothers than sons, although the differences are relatively small in the first order of mention. When asked about people to whom the mothers felt closest in the "before" time period, only four percent name sons and eight percent daughters as in the first place. Second place references to sons increase to 17 percent of the total, but those references to daughters rise to 25 percent. Boys outnumber girls in third place mention only (18 to 16 percent) but there are few women who name three persons as closest to them in that period of time. In other words, daughters are named as among the persons closest to the mother even when the father was alive — much more often than sons. However, it is important to note that sons are not absent from this emotional support.

The pattern repeats itself when we ask the widow with whom she most enjoyed being at that time. We had a tentative assumption that the mother might list a son more often than a daughter, even if she felt closest to the latter, because of the favorable status enjoyed by males in our society and because many women claim to miss the company of males. This proves not to be the situation. Girls are mentioned first by six percent of the mothers, boys by up to two percent; girls increase to 24 percent as second supporters and boys to 17 percent. Finally, in much smaller numbers, but there, sons contribute to the mother's enjoyment of company up to 17 percent, daughters up to 13 percent of people listed third.

Returning to the current emotional support systems where we found the children quite active, we immediately find the domination of daughters (see Table 14). There are only two supports in which sons outnumber daughters. Sons, more than daughters, make the mother angry most often. However, security is derived more from sons than daughters, though the difference is not all that great. Daughters predominate as the person with whom the widows feel closest, who comfort them, and whose company they enjoy more. The size of the difference in the number of daughters over sons in each support depends of course, on two factors: the number of children which are specifically listed in the support and the relative number of daughters and sons who enter it. Thus, not only do many children serve as the closest people in the world to the widow, but female children are more often closer than

TABLE 14

Contributions of Daughters and Sons to the Current Emotional
Support System of the Chicago Area Widows

Support	Total Number of References					
Sentiments	**Daughters**		**Sons**		**Surplus**	
Closest	41,892	–	27,745	=	14,147	
Enjoy	34,291	–	23,484	=	10,807	
Problems	24,537	–	17,104	=	7,433	
Comfort	29,156	–	16,150	=	13,006	
Important	32,280	–	26,923	=	5,357	
Crisis	31,201	–	23,673	=	7,526	
Feeling States						
Respected	29,221	–	25,735	=	3,486	
Useful	25,538	–	21,148	=	4,390	
Independent	7,048	–	6,546	=	3,799	
Accepted	20,322	–	16,523	=	3,799	
Self sufficient	7,655	–	6,385	=	1,270	
Sentiments	**Sons**		**Daughters**		**Surplus**	
Angry	9,653	–	5,878	=	3,775	
Secure	15,087	–	14,930	=	157	
	Daughters		**Sons**		**Surplus**	
Grand Total	303,949	–	236,156	=	67,793	

male offspring, in spite of the previously noted fact that the daughters do not outnumber the sons dramatically as resources. The pattern lends support to the Parsons-Bales (1955) thesis that American women are assigned or undertake the expressive functions of the family. Although a previous study of housewives documented the importance assigned by wives to both their own and their husband's instrumental obligations (see Lopata, 1971a), this study indicates that the traditional division of the world (in America) is reflected in the differences in many mothers' feelings toward, and sentimental attachments to, their daughters and their sons. Recent literature on the male role in American society points out that boys are taught to be nonexpressive and nondemonstrative (Farrell, 1975; Komarovsky, 1976; Pleck and Sawyer, 1974; Scanzoni and Scanzoni, 1976). It indicates that the image of the male in this society derives largely from European lower-class culture which is modified and accentuated in various areas by the American experience (Gans, 1962; Komarovsky, 1967). Many of these widows are first- or second-generation, relatively uneducated immigrants or migrants from rural America. Many of the black mothers live in a lower-class black subculture that reputedly nurtures hostility of men and women toward each other and brings out a feeling by the women that men cannot be depended upon in times of crisis. As indicated in Chapter 1, different images of mother–son relations emanate from traditional India and China, but these too may have changed with the decline of the rights and duties of the male line.

Details of the distributions of contributions of children by their sexual identification to the emotional support systems of the widowed mothers indicates the possible hostility toward some sons' failure at contribution only in the frequency with which they are the main source of anger. We must remember that such a designation is quite extreme, since so few women allow themselves to express feelings of anger, possibly because of their dependent situation. They do not want to drive away their remaining sources of supports. Aside from that main expression of hostility we cannot assume that the frequency with which daughters rather than sons are listed first in the various supports means a rejection of the sons. If the mothers had grown up with, and in turn socialized their sons into, the traditional male role, the fact that they now feel their daughters to be closer than sons would be simply a natural consequence.

Daughters appear first in the minds of the mother most frequently in connection with the sentiment of closeness, as the person whose company she most enjoys, as the one she would most often turn to in crisis, as her main comforter when

199

she is depressed, and as the one who makes her feel important. Our assumption that the mother would much more often turn to her sons than her daughters in times of crisis proved wrong. In spite of the stereotypical image of male strength, the kind of help a widow feels she needs in emergency situations is more often apt to be given by a female member of the family. This is an interesting comment on the bond uniting many of these mothers to their daughters. However, fewer of the widows obtained their feelings of security mainly from daughters, possibly because daughters are themselves in family situations that preclude constant support. Had the interview not been so long to begin with, we would have inquired specifically what different women mean by security: it is possibly an economically tinged concept. Daughters and sons are most similar in the extent to which they are not the primary providers of the feelings of independence and self-sufficiency, acceptance or security. The gap between them remains large in the second order of listing in the sentiment of closeness, enjoyment of company, comforting in depression or help in crisis. It is relatively small when women list the person to whom they tell their problems—who make them feel important, respected, secure, accepted and independent—as well as self-sufficient. It is interesting to note that more sons than daughters are second-order providers of independence, while the reverse is true of self-sufficiency. It is difficult to estimate why daughters are listed first or second as providers of the self-feeling of being a useful human being while the sons appear third, except that some women ran out of daughters to which to credit this feeling. The numbers are small in third place listing, as stated before, and sons increase their standing over daughters as contributing to feelings of closeness, enjoyment of company, confidants, comforters, and those making her feel useful, angry, and secure. This is a strange combination; undoubtedly different women make these indications. All in all there are 303,949 references to daughters and 236,156 to sons in the emotional support systems.

The Role of Mother

I commented in Chapter 4 that the widows ranked the role of mother consistently among the top four levels in order of importance, when given nine roles for ranking; only three percent place it among the bottom four (see Table 11). There is very little difference by remarriage status. In this they out-ranked married housewives with at least one pre–high-school child. When I wrote *Occupation: Housewife* (1971, pp. 64–66), I divided the women into several categories—three of which are relevant here: (1) the husband-oriented women, (2) the child-oriented woman and (3) the life-cycle woman. I had expected many of the widows to fall in the third category, focusing on roles other than that of wife (or even mother) after the death of their husband and the children had grown up. Of course, almost half of the women represented by our sample are not yet in the shrunken-circle of the role of housewife and are still actively engaged in the role of mother. However, the traditional American culture is so pervasive that it is mainly the roles of wife and mother that really stand out even in the minds of the older widows, three-quarters listing one or the other first or second. Since nine percent of the widows are not mothers, it is interesting to note that 95 percent of all the widows still believe motherhood is among the top four roles for a woman to perform. Alternate relations or career simply do not exist in the traditionally conditioned minds of many women.

Summary

The children of the Chicago area widows tend to be distributed along a wide range of characteristics. In six out of 10 families there are both girls and boys, in two out of 10 there is at least one child under the age of 21, and in six out of 10 families there is at least one unmarried offspring. Unmarried children tend to live in the home of the mother, even after reaching adulthood. In 56 percent of the widows' homes there is no child and 37 percent of the homes still house only one. The remaining residences have a larger number of offspring. Although contact with at least one child living away from home tends to be relatively frequent (several times a week), the average frequency is just about several times a month but not as often as once a week.

Many of the widows appear to be somewhat insensitive to the psychological and life chance consequences of the father's death and subsequent absence on the children. Other mothers were aware of the impact on their children but were able to deal with it only verbally. Few turned to societal or other resources in their network for professional help for their children. Of course, few sought such help for themselves.

Today's and future American women of child-bearing age may decide not to have children. They are apt to be more educated and more competent in the building of social roles and social networks and thus have complex support systems without children, but the generations of widows represented by our Chicago area interviews benefited from being mothers. Furthermore, although Americans obviously congratulate the parents of a newborn boy more heartily than those of a girl, daughters are much more significant in the lives and support systems of these widows than are sons. Daughters exist as resources only slightly more often than do sons, but they or at least one of them in each family tend to be closer both geographically and emotionally to the mother. The daughters are involved with the mother in exchanges of economic goods more often than are sons but the total is not so great. Most of the widows are economically and residentially independent of their adult children, especially if these offspring are no longer living in the parental home. They are also relatively independent of service exchanges with those who are not part of the household.

Children contribute to the social supports of the widows, particularly through joint celebration of holidays, visiting and entertaining. The interaction tends to be asymmetrical in that not all children or even all daughters are equally involved. It is within the emotional support system that the children, especially daughters, are supportive, as they are unquestionably the people the widow feels closest to. She enjoys them and they make her feel important.

Among the Chicago area widows, motherhood definitely ranks either as the most important role a woman can perform or in second place in a ranking of nine roles.

SIX

Friends

Popular American literature on friendship leads to the expectation that friends would be most contributive to the support systems of urban widows. *The Oxford Universal Dictionary* (1955, p. 752) defines a friend as, "one joined to another in mutual benevolence and intimacy."[1] The concept of intimacy contains the basic components of what is assumed to be "true friendship": self-disclosure, trust, total personality involvement, empathetic sharing of feelings, comradeship, confidant exchanges, comforting and so forth. A friend is someone to whom you are important and who makes you feel important. Friends are people to whom you turn to in times of crisis for help and comfort and in normal times for services. True friends can be expected to give up their lives for each other, or at least to give "the shirt off their back" to the other.

In spite of the idealized image of friendship, or possibly because of it, most Americans do not expect to experience such mutual devotion in adulthood, recognizing constraints and impingements from other relations. In fact, they are really somewhat fearful of developing intense intimacy and are uncomfortable when they see it in others. Such a strong emotional tie is seen as potentially dangerous because it can lead to the neglect of other relations. Total commitment to friendship can effect performance of other roles deemed important to the society. It is seen as appropriate for the young because of its contribution to the growing-up process, as long as it does not lead to ganglike violence and vandalism. Too close friendship between adult members of the same sex is often viewed with suspicion because of possible homosexual overtones (Seiden and Bart, 1975; Pleck, 1975). Cross-sex friendship after childhood is definitely frowned upon unless it is part of a courtship pattern with the appropriate mate. Husbands and wives are supposed to be "best friends" in modern America and no other adult relations are supposed to interfere with the fullness and complexity of the ideal modern marriage (Glazer-Malbin, 1975).

Not only is "total personality" friendship constrained by the ineligibility of many partners and the competition of other roles, but restrictions are even placed on situational friendship (Maines, 1973). Most research shows that limited types of intimacy are developed in many living or work situations but these tend to be compartmentalized and not carried into other spheres of life. Even these relations are subject to controls. Bureaucracies fear that personal interaction may interfere with the smooth operation of the communication and authority lines (Ritzer, 1976). Industry has traditionally attempted to prevent the formation of cliques among its workers (Etzioni, 1964; Grusky and Miller, 1970). The military establishment frowns on friendships across rank boundaries and, although it encourages the "buddy system" during combat, it demands the partners return to "normal life" when back "at the base" so that their relationship does not interfere with other duties and roles (Little, forthcoming). Even prisons discourage friendships among women inmates (Nelson, forthcoming).

In other words, the basic constraints on friendship as idealized by American popular culture lie in the reality or life—seen as having no societally significant functions, they are defined as potentially interfering with "important" spheres of life. Sexual connotations are present because of the fears that psychological and social intimacy among people who should not engage in sexual intercourse with each other may move in that direction, but the basic concern is that friendship will not encroach on other social roles.

One of the problems in discussions of friendship is that it has a great variety of meanings; the content and the importance assigned to this concept by different Americans varies. Some speak wistfully of childhood friendships that resemble the ideal of total commitment and submersion, feeling that they do not have "true" friends any longer since the old ones have ceased to be available. Others read books like *How to Win Friends and Influence People* (Carnegie, 1936). Still another aggregate calls anyone they socialize with over the weekend, "friends" or even "everyone in this town," as one of the Missouri oldsters studies by Pihlblad in Rosencranz (1968) reported. *The Oxford Universal Dictionary* shows this variety of meanings in the definitions following the one given above:

> Applied loosely, to a mere acquaintance, or to a stranger; also used by members of the "Society of Friends" as an ordinary mode of address . . . .
> One who wishes (another, a cause, etc.) well; a sympathizer patron, or supporter . . . .
> One who is not an enemy.

A basic reason different Americans attach different meanings to the concept of friend is the variety of their origins. Descendants of kin-oriented immigrants model their expectations on the idealized duties and rights of fraternal relations—lifetime friendship being guaranteed to anyone who joins a fraternity or fraternal order (Znaniecki, 1965). Others base their expectations on the norms of behavior and organized activity of "polite companionship" developed in the courts of Europe and then diffused among upper and middle classes of both Europe and the United States (Aries, 1965). Znaniecki (1965) explains the origin of such interaction and the relations it involves:

> The progressive separation of the companionate and playful aspects of court life from its *important* [italics mine] practical aspects

was due to two influences: first, the participation of women in companionate intercourse; second, assimilation into courts of prominent men of letters, thinkers, artists and musicians [p. 175].

Those Americans who identify friendships in terms of participation in activities of "polite companionship" have evolved very complex rules of etiquette, games and pastimes.[2] Long training prepared the youth for such leisure-time intercourse and for the relations drawn from a pool of eligibles. They generally separate friendships from kin relations outside of the immediate family, although in the past extended kin were often included. Until recent years "leisure-class" women in American society developed sex-segregated friendship circles involved in formalized social events or informal interaction at specified times. In addition, both continents developed complex rules of polite companionship for couples, such as dinners and a variety of amusements. These kinds of interaction sequences, have been primarily "fun" oriented and do not necessarily involve intimate emotional supports. They have sometimes been extended to people with whom other relations are also carried out, sometimes simultaneously, as at business dinners or golf games.

A third historical foundation for interpersonal relations that some people identify as friendship lies in the easy familiarity among villagers or neighbors who know each other practically from birth, see each other frequently, and cannot "hide secrets" (Simmel, 1950). Such relations, as well as the other types, may include exchanges of services on a continuing basis or in an emergency, including those services that we have separated out as economic supports. Community friends have been known to offer food and other goods, (even their own labor) when, for example, a member of a household becomes seriously ill.

In *A History of Recreation*, Dulles (1965) concludes that much of the gaiety of polite companionship interaction among the upper classes of Europe did not thrive in colonial America—

due to several factors including Puritanism and the "serious-ness of purpose of pioneering life." Hard work was revered, and the main function of leisure time was to "re-create" energy for the next day's work [see also de Tocqueville (1835)]. Even now, people who are forced into leisure through retirement or diminished demand for their services often have problems in filling time, or in "wasting it"—by past standards. In ad-dition, most urban Americans are still first- , second- , or third-generation immigrants of lower socio-economic background that does not include intensive socialization into the subculture of polite companionship.[3] The majority of working-class Americans do not engage in formal, event-focused "friendly" interaction, such as dining by invitation at home (or at other locales), game-playing or just conversation (Rubin, 1976; Lo-pata, 1971a; Gans, 1962). The study of housewives in the sub-urbs and city that started this series of research projects found all forms of both friendship and neighbor contact to be class-based. Working-class women are much less apt to speak of friendships than are middle- or upper-class women and they are usually restricted to informal outdoor interaction, season-ally regulated in northern climates, with those who live nearby, and then only if the neightborhood is defined as friendly, which often it is not (Lopata, 1971a, 1973a).[4] Leisure-time socializing is limited to relatives or religious events. Rubin (1976, p. 194), points out that working-class couples do not often go out on social occasions. ("Less than one-fourth of the couples go out without the children as often as one Saturday night a month.") Also, although "entertaining adults who are not family members seems to be on the increase in working-class families," they do so far less frequently than middle-class families, so that only "more than one-third say they do so at least four to six times a year. But the dinner party—the back-bone of middle-class social life—is almost nonexistent (p. 195)."

The combination of generalized and situational constraints on friendship in terms of historical and social class back-grounds has produced some interesting complications. Lower-

class European and working-class American cultures encouraged friendships of the same sex (Lopata, 1971a, 1975; Gans,
1962; De Hoyos and De Hoyos, 1966; Nelson, 1966). Yet the
image of the ideally egalitarian marriage of partners, who are
also supposed to be best friends, has pushed such interaction
into the background, even discouraging it completely. Lillian
Rubin (1976, p. 192) finds that sex-segregated friendships
among working-class men are decreasing, "The days of regular
'nights-out-with-the-boys' seems to be past—gone with the
compliant 'little woman' who should sit patiently and wait for
his return." In addition, close same-sex relations are discouraged for both men and women during socialization for adulthood. Women in "rap" groups explain that they were socialized "not to like" other women after their "teen" years of
confidant interaction (Seiden and Bart, 1975). They were
taught that their whole life would be dependent on their ability
to maintain a relation with a man and that other women were
simply competition. Working in isolated households, married
women often feel unable to develop new or maintain prior
friendships of any but casual couple companionate depth.
Men, on the other hand, are taught to turn to women, not to
other men, to meet their intimacy and other emotional needs,
so that it becomes difficult for them to enter friendships of any
depth with each other (Pleck, 1975).

All this discussion would lead us to affirm the statement at
the outset of this chapter. After all, most widows are women
now deprived of the major relations that American society
sees as important enough to push potentially disrupted friendship into the background. Their parents are apt to be deceased;
their siblings dispersed and no longer demanding extensive
supports; the husband is dead; and the children are for the
most part involved in their own lives with their families of
procreation. Most are not in search of new husbands and so
should not feel competitive. This means that they now ought
to be free to concentrate on relations with friends. There are
other reasons leading us to expect such involvement. Zena

Blau (1961, 1970) found that the kind of interaction which leads to friendship, especially to confidant exchanges, requires equality of status and power, difficult to achieve in mother–child relations but possible among women in the same age cohort. People of the same sex, same age and same marital status are the best candidates for such friendships. Lowenthal and Haven (1968) reinforce this conclusion, and both Hochschild (1973) and Rosow (1967) find that older people of the same sex and marital status tend to live nearby and to develop relationships and service supports. Thus, the widow seems to be the ideal person for developing multifaceted friendships, involving such relations in a multiplicity of service, economic, social and emotional supports. At the same time our knowledge of the forms of interaction among non-kin associates of Americans leads us to anticipate great divergences among widows, based mainly on socio-economic variables (Harvey and Bahr, 1974). We must examine the social networks of the Chicago area widows to determine their friendship patterns and the contributions those friends who are in the networks make to the actual support systems of these women.

The interview contains a number of questions concerning the friends of the Chicago area widows, both for the year before the husband's fatal illness or accident and now. Interviewers were instructed to probe for as many as five friends in each time period, but we ended up with at least ten for some women, because they gave names of couples, especially for the "before" time period. Each person is coded separately, so that we have the sexual distribution of the friendships and can trace each person in the support systems.[5]

Sixteen percent of the widows claim to have had no friends in the year before the husband's fatal illness and to have none now. An additional 7 percent define their past as lacking friends, realizing that they have made new friends since widowhood. Thirty-eight percent list old friends but no new ones, leaving 39 percent with both old and new close associates. We must remember that these women have been widowed for an average of 10 years so that most of them have had time to develop new friends if they had the inclination and if circumstances had favored this.

The Friendless Widow

One in six widows believes that she was friendless before the husband took ill and that she has not made friends during widowhood. There are basically three types of these women (Lopata, 1977b). There is the woman who does not consider friendship to be part of her life. She is basically family oriented and does not attempt to make "strangers," or even acquaintances into intimates. In fact, many of her efforts are spent in preventing people from knowing much about her. She will never invite nonrelatives to her home or divulge any of her problems. She does not exchange services with neighbors or others. She is not likely to venture into voluntary associations.

The second type is aware of the possibility of friendships but does not have the self-confidence and social skills that are needed to develop such relations. She is apt to be surrounded by constraining forces. Having been born in a nonurban setting, often from another country, she is the typical "urban villager" so well described by Gans (1962), except that she does not have the kind of a neighborhood in which she has lived for a long time surrounded by people with whom she feels comfortable. She needs facilitating opportunities for continued contact of that type and does not have them.

The third type of the friendless widow may have internalized the idealized image of friendship, expecting from associates commitments they are unable to make for a variety of reasons. Being disappointed in her efforts at achieving the depth of intimacy and the complexity of support systems she desires, she may define herself as devoid of friends. Obviously, the definition of friendship itself influences whether a woman answers affirmatively when asked if she has or had close

211

friends. Most women have a sufficiently realistic idea or else are sufficiently worried about being classed as friendless to answer affirmatively to these questions and to cite friends. We will need to examine their support systems to determine the viability of such relations.

The characteristics of the friendless widows become apparent when we look at some of the figures. Although forming only 16 percent of the total number of widows, they form 22 percent of those who were 65 years or older when the husband became ill and 20 percent of those now in that age bracket. They are disproportionately likely to have had many children; very few of them have none or only one child. In spite of the "Porgy and Bess" imagery of warm friendliness in the black community, 21 percent of the black widows, as compared to 15 percent of the whites, list themselves as totally friendless during these two periods. However, the most important factors bearing on the question are education (gamma = .27), total family income when the husband was well (gamma = .24), and total family income now (gamma = .24). As pointed out earlier, it takes the social and planning skills developed in school to reinforce or offset those acquired in or absent from the home to build a foundation for social engagement. Women with more schooling marry men earning a better income in a higher-type occupation and together they develop a middle-class lifestyle that involves non-kin friendships: the differences are rather dramatic. Friendless women are most apt to have only an eighth grade education or less. Thus, 30 percent of grade school dropouts and 27 percent of the finishers claim to be friendless, compared to one percent of those with 16 years of schooling or less. The presence of both old and new friends increases as soon as we reach high school graduates. Very few of the women who hold professional or managerial positions and none in sales jobs, before widowhood, state that they neither had nor have friends. Housewives, women in household service and operatives, and especially laborers, are apt to declare an absence of friends. The first two categories of women are most apt to be socially isolated. Women currently in these occupations are also apt to be without friends. In fact, relatively few of them have made new friends. Again, it is the saleswomen who are most likely to have established new relations of such closeness. Surprisingly, it is the friendless women, besides those whose husbands worked as laborers or operatives, who are most likely to have been married to the working-class "aristocrats," the craftsmen.

Labeling oneself as being without friends near the end of the marriage and now has some very interesting (somewhat unexpected) attitudinal consequences. In the first place, there is a very strong association between such definitions and the evaluation of friends as helpful during the time when the widow was creating a new life. Thirty-nine percent of those who believe they are friendless state that friends were never helpful, and 24 percent that there were rarely people in the network who, at least at that time, had been defined as friends but who proved not to have met the expectations. These women are bound to fall into the third category of friendless widows—those holding expectations which former or potential friends fail to meet, a strong indictment of such associates. On the other hand, 22 percent of the "friendless" felt that there had been friends and that they were generally very helpful, while 15 percent found associates who were helpful "in special situations."

However angry or at least disappointed the widows were with people they now define as not having been friends, there is no significant association between the presence of friends in either period, before or now, and the wish for more friends. That is, over half of the friendless do not want "more" friends, with only 14 percent strongly agreeing that they prefer some. By contrast, the most likely to disagree strongly are women who claim both old and new friends. This does not mean that all the women with friends are satisfied; 33 percent with both types of friends wish for more. There is also no significant statistical association between a lack of friends and satisfaction

213

with life. As we saw before, most widows agree, whether strongly or not, that they are satisfied; the same proportion of women with, as without, friends are found on the positive side of that attitude, supporting the prior contention that some of these urbanites do not consider friendship as part of their life style. The distributions on the loneliness scale are not significantly related to friendship, except that the woman totally lacking in friends is most likely to consider herself the loneliest person she knows or more lonely than most people. On the other hand, 57 percent of the friendless consider themselves "less lonely than most people," "rarely lonely" or "never lonely."

Friendship helps alleviate loneliness for women who have both old and new friends. The middle categories of widows are not unusual, except for the women with only new friends, who are disproportionately likely to consider themselves either more lonely than other people or never lonely. There is no significant difference among the women with or without friends, before or now, and their tendency to idealize the late husband to the point of sanctification on either segment of the scale.

Characteristics of Friends

Almost three-fourths of the 220,930 old friends and 81 percent of the 102,304 new friends of the Chicago area widows are women. The men appear as husbands of the female associates or as partners of couple friendships, especially while the husband was alive. Current boyfriends are so identified and separated from the less sexual or nondating listings. Unfortunately, the English language does not distinguish adequately between these two forms of friendship, although the culture shows distinctly different forms of interaction within these relations. There is also a definite tendency of Americans to distinguish between friendships and kinship and not to list

214

a relative as a close friend. The few relatives included as friends, and they come to only one percent of the total, are usually siblings and their spouses, with an occasional niece or nephew or even in-law. Parents, children or grandchildren are almost never listed as friends, the women either feeling that these relations should not be confused with the role of friend, or simply because these are different kinds of emotional attachments. The norms set are similar, though obviously much less severe, to those of incest. It is possible that ancestral or collateral relatives are not included in the friendship circle of couples because of their asymmetrical attachment to one member of the dyad.

There are fewer friends by far in the "now" (1.25 per widow) than in the "before" (2.69 per widow) period. The relative scarcity of new friends may be due to any one, or a combination of, four reasons: the recency of widowhood (thus a shortness of time in which to make new friends); the tendency of women to develop friendships earlier in life; the dependence of married women on couple companionant interaction not available in widowhood; or the absence of social roles which ensure continued contact leading to increasing intimacy. As we saw earlier, housewives are apt not to list as many friends as do women in more socially involving occupations. The hypothesis that friendships are formed in earlier stages of life is partly supported by the fact that at least a quarter of the old friendships go back 31 or more years, a half at least 21 years. The fact that younger women are represented by our sample is evidenced by one-fifth of the friendships dating back 10 years or less. New friends were often met within the shortest time frame, that is, within 10 years, and many of the women widowed a long time ago tend not to be friendship oriented.

The resources through which the Chicago area women made initial contacts with people who became friends do not support the much-quoted Babchuk and Bates (1963) study of husband dominance. Relatively few Chicago area wives or former wives credit the husband with having initiated the contact with future friends (Lopata, 1971a, 1973a, 1975, 1977a). The widows credit only nine percent of the more than 216,000 friends who predate their husband's death to him. Only three percent of the new friends are former associates of the late husband or were brought in by the new husband of boyfriend. The women definitely credit themselves for the contact or refer to current or former neighbors. Several reasons exist for the differences between the Chicago and Nebraska figures, which credit the late husband with initiating contact with old friends. One factor may be different styles in friendship behavior, another the different time of the studies, and a third the methodology used. Babchuk and Bates asked their respondents for sources of couple friendships, whereas we asked the widows how and where did they first meet each friend. Yet our findings are more believable, not only because of their consistency over several studies, but also because all evidence pinpoints the wife as the developer and maintainer of social contacts and social relations (Berardo, 1968, 1970; Blau, 1973; Glick, Weiss and Parkes, 1974).

The neighborhood is the primary resource for both old and new friends (37 percent): next are clubs and organizations, particularly the church (16 percent), work (10 percent), other persons (15 percent) and the woman's childhood acquaintance (10 percent). As we noted before, the last of these resources is not surprising in the case of younger women. Interestingly, a lower proportion of new friends are brought in by "other people," meaning mainly relatives and other friends, than was true of boyfriends. This is largely due to age differences. Also, boyfriends tend to have been met in social or polite companionship situations, which usually involve existing friendships. Work and organizations take on increasing importance as resources for friendships after the woman becomes widowed, and remoteness from childhood is evidenced by the dramatic drop of this source of new friends.

Several characteristics of actual or potential friends can facilitate the formation and maintenance of such a relation. One is similarity of marital status. Eighty-three percent of the friends of the wife when the husband was alive were married; only 10 percent were widowed. Many of these have since become widowed, so that the percentage of those still married drops to 71 and the widowed friends increase to 21 percent. New friends are even more apt to be widowed, with 33 percent so identified, while only 55 percent are still married. Of course, the largest proportion of women in all but the very old age category is married, so that the widow is much more apt to come in contact with women whose husband is still alive than with those already widowed. Also, these women, as we saw above, tend to draw heavily on the neighborhood, voluntary associations and work resources for friends, and these sources tend to contain mainly married people. The fact that the old friendships were often couple-companionate is evidenced in that 92 percent of the prior-to-widowhood friends are identified by the women as having also been the friends of the late husband. That is high incidence, considering the sex-segregated nature of past working-class social life.

Times have changed for many of the Chicago women and their friends since the death of the husband. Old friends had been seen on an average of about once weekly in the year before his illness. Now they are seen less often, averaging close to once a month. (In fact, 45 percent of them are seen less frequently.) Contact diminishes for a variety of reasons, including change in the life-style of the widow or her friends, residential dispersion, lack of transportation and strains developing in the relations. If the widow has moved or sold her car, arrangements for transportation to the homes of friends for an evening visit may prove bothersome. Many of the widows of the first study agreed that married friends were jealous of a nonsingle woman in the presence of their own husband (Lopata, 1973a, 1975, 1977). Strain also develops in cases in which a friend felt a greater attachment to the husband than to the wife. One respondent related an incident and then commented on the whole situation of widows:

We had some friends before my husband died. They were my husband's friends. Then they moved out of town. After he died I went to visit them one day. The wife had to go somewhere and said if I didn't mind waiting, she'd be back at 9:00 p.m. So I waited. During that time, the husband got obnoxious with me. I never told the wife about this, but I rarely go there anymore. I never considered them my friends. They're not people I would turn to. It becomes a more complicated life because the social position changes after a mate's death. Women are not as welcome into the home of a couple known before the death. Therefore, the social position changes.

Another widow commented similarly, as she and her husband had associated with couple companionate friends. She reports a failure of social supports after becoming widowed.

The circle of friends we had before the death of my husband were [sic] not as friendly, especially the wives of our neighbors. I wasn't invited to any social gatherings anymore.

She also reports sexual advances by men as a problem:

How to handle past friends' husbands who invariably try to get fresh without any encouragement. This is always a shock and hurts deeply.
  A widow should expect to be dropped from past social ties. This always happens, and the sooner she decides what she's going to do with her life, the better off she is.

Feelings of relational strain begin to develop during the grieving period; friends reportedly not wishing to witness grief are antagonized by the sanctification process and feel awkward over their obvious failure to help the widow emotionally (Caine, 1974; Glick, Weiss and Parkes, 1974). The relation, often based on couple companionate interaction is made difficult not only by the absence of the male partner but also by the manner of his "dropping out." Death is generally a topic avoided in American society (Gorer, 1967). The failure of friends in early widowhood led to the formation of the first widow-to-widow program, which followed research with young widows by Harvard Medical School. Silverman and her associates (1972) point to the need for emotional supports from people who "understand" because they have gone through the same experience. The book, *Bereavement: Its Psychological Aspects* (Schoenberg et al., 1975), makes repeated reference to problems between widows and their still-married friends.

The infrequency of contact with old friends of so many of the Chicago area widows indicates the probability that these strains are not always resolved and the relation disintegrates to the point that efforts to maintain it wither. On the other hand, many women modify their relations with married friends into sex-segregated ones, while others do not mind being the "fifth wheel" in the company of couples. Of course, some of the women never did engage in social activities that would be skewed by the absence of the late husband, while others find new partners and continue the couple-friendships, even in widowhood or after remarriage.

Interestingly enough, despite the decreased frequency of contact with old friends, the Chicago respondents insist that the persons involved are still their friends. Only four percent of the old friends are no longer considered friends by the widow. Twelve percent of old friends are dead.

New friends are still found primarily through the neighborhood (35 percent) and clubs or organizations; while the job increases its contribution (16 percent) over the before period. New friends are seen very frequently, on the average of once a week, even more often than all of the children. They also appear in the support systems of the widows, as are some of the old friends.

Contributions of Friends to Support Systems

An examination of Tables 2 to 8 will referesh our memory as to the contributions made by friends to the support systems of the Chicago area widows, as compared to those of other associates. We see that friends are almost never involved in economic exchanges nor are they generally providers of services. They are proportionally greater receivers of services from the few women who consider themselves as providers. They are the people with whom the widows often engage in social activities but this involvement does not necessarily translate itself into emotional supports.

Adding up the appearances of friends in each support system of the Chicago area widows, we find that only one percent of the women report an in-flow or out-flow of economic supports involving friends and only 16 percent exchange at least one service with a friend, 10 percent of them mentioning such an associate only once. These findings go against the American image of the importance of friendship as a resource for economic and service help.

Involvement in the social system is much more frequent. Even here we note the absence of many people who had been listed as friends. That is, only 16 percent of the women define themselves as friendless, but twice that percentage (33) do not engage in the defined social activities with a friend and do not list other activities. On the other hand, almost half of the women are involved with their friends in several different activities or else they list more than one person as companions in a single form of interaction. The numbers in the sentimental and feeling states segments of the emotional support systems uphold the previous statement that involvement in the social supports does not necessarily translate itself into feelings of closeness or other emotional supports, since between 67 and 69 percent fail to mention a friend in either segment. This means that half of the women who actually engage in social activities with people previously defined as friends do so on a superficial level of polite companionship while turning to other people, mainly children, and the husband if there is one, for basic emotional supports. This fact underlines some of the earlier comments that concerned the various meanings that Americans attach to the concept, "friend." About half of the widows list at least one friend when the husband was alive (not critically ill) or added to the social network in widowhood and then fail to think of that person, or those people, when given 39 opportunities to do so in the current emotional support system. At the other extreme are the women who feel that their friends make major contributions to their basic self-feelings and relational sentiments. (It is interesting to speculate about the women who mention a single friend only once.)

Total figures are also indicative of the varied ways friends contribute to the support systems of the widows in that the extremes are quite apparent. One-quarter of the women do not mention a friend at all, whereas almost four in ten are rather extensively involved in their relations with people they term as friends. Table 2 indicates that the contributions friends make to the social supports and to the emotional supports in which they do appear are sufficient to bring their mean of appearances up to 6.1 which is higher than that of anyone else with the exception of children and the late husband. Let us now examine the various support systems, except the economic one, concentrating on the current network only.

SERVICE SUPPORT SYSTEM

The widows who engage in service exchanges are most likely to receive help with transportation and shopping and these are also services they provide their friends (see Table 4). Going shopping together is a favorite pastime of women whose main occupation is housewifery; these activities are easily interwoven. Some widows have friends who help care for them in sickness and they provide such care even more often. Interestingly, they feel that they help their friends with decision making much more than they credit such associates with the same service. (It would be interesting to know if the friends

221

define the situation in the same way.) All in all, however, the exchanges are rare and friendship in American society does not seem to be dependent on any of these services. This conclusion corroborates the data in the housewife study, which showed that most housewives do not often engage in such traditional actions as borrowing and lending things with neighbors (Lopata, 1971a, 1973a). Each household has become relatively self-sufficient; the norms of reciprocity seem to be diminishing in urban America. Of course, most of these women are no longer tied to a home with small children, so that they may have fewer emergencies requiring a friend's or neighbor's help. The infrequency of help with shopping is, however, rather surprising.

SOCIAL SUPPORT SYSTEM

The women who engage with friends in the activities included in the social support system are generally better off financially and have a background of middle-class or higher life than their less socially active counterparts (see Table 5). However, the activities do not evenly involve friends. For example, holidays are traditionally celebrated with family members; comparatively few women share them with friends. Of course, there are those who do not have close kin and have friends who are part of family holiday festivities. Out-of-town travel is not undertaken as frequently with friends as are game playing or attending sport events. If the woman travels with a friend, she is apt to list that person first but, since so few women list second or third companions in such activity, the proportion of widows naming friends increases considerably in these slots. The same is true of second-place mentions of friends as companions in public places such as movie houses or theaters. That, plus having lunch with each other, are activities more commonly shared by middle-class women. Visiting friends and entertaining with friends are also common.

Friends increase their contribution to the woman's emotional support system rather dramatically once she is widowed, mainly because the late husband is no longer the principal contributor of such aid (see Tables 6 and 7). The increase is not only in the total mentions but also in the frequency with which friends appear first. However, there are strong variations by support. Looking at the present system only we find that friends are most apt to be listed as people who make the widow feel accepted and as those whom she most enjoys being with. These two supports reinforce the thesis that friendships are based on mutual acceptance of equal-rank persons (Blau, 1961, 1973). However, such enjoyment does not necessarily lead to deeper forms of supports. Widows are less likely to tell their problems to a friend than to engage in pleasurable social activity such as sharing a meal. This emphasizes the social, rather than the emotional, nature of the attachment. After all, when you know that these women list over 300,000 friends it is shocking to find that only about 13,000 such associates appear as people who comfort them, are their confidants or give them a feeling of importance. Feelings of closeness draw only 2,000 more names of friends, and the only other emotional support to bring more than 10,000 friends is the self-feeling of being a respected human being. Very few women would turn to their friends in time of crisis or obtain their feelings of usefulness, independence, self-sufficiency or security from allegedly intimate associates. The distributions raise serious questions about American women's definition of a friend and their notion of friendship as an intimate relation. Of course, the other possibility is that these widows feel they must enumerate their children and other family members as people to whom they feel closest, so that a friend, although providing emotional supports, may be excluded from answers to formal questions about contributors to basic emotional aspects of life. Friends are not even listed as people who make the widow angry the most often, but then acquaintances or friends who became sources of an emotion so strongly negated by these women would probably have been dropped in the past. What is startling is the absence of many friends from the other emotional supports.

Evaluation of Life

The question remains as to whether or not the level and form of interaction a widow has with her friends and their contribution to her support systems influence her evaluation of life. There are several indications of such judgements. In the first place, we asked the repondents for their degree of concurrence with the statement, "I wish I had more friends." As said earlier, over half (58 percent) of the women with no friends in either the before or the now time period disagree with this statement. In other words, they do not have friends and they claim to be quite satisfied with this situation. In this they resemble the other three categories of widows, those with only old friends, those with only new friends and those with both. Only 15 percent of the total group strongly agree that they wish for more friends, and these are most apt to be women with new but no old friends (21 percent) rather than those with both new and old (11 percent). These differences are significant although the association between these two aspects of life is generally not strong. Over one-quarter of the women simply agree with the statement leaving 46 percent disagreeing mildly and 10 percent disagreeing strongly. Those with such definite feelings are more likely to have both kinds of friends than not.

Next, we need to know how the desire for more friends relates to the actual involvement of such associates in the emotional support system both when the husband was living and now. There are some interesting patterns in the distributions. Women who strongly agree that they want more friends tend not to have relied on such relations in the past, depending heavily on the late husband, who appears in most of the emotional supports. It is possible that they have not been able to find substitutes for the kind of support the husband gave because they do not know how to develop intimacy with friends. Those who disagree with this statement actually fall into two groups: some consistently involved with friends, relying less on the late husband, and those more child oriented. Those who disagree "mildly" are more friend oriented, and those who disagree "strongly" tend to have had a limited support network. In addition to children they are much more apt to list "no one" as having provided emotional supports. In addition, those not desiring friendships are much less apt to sanctify the late husband, while those who agree strongly with this statement are extreme in their sanctification.

When we look at the association between the presence or absence of old or new friends and agreement with statement, "I am very satisfied with the way my life is going now," we find that having friends does not necessarily contribute to that feeling. The proportion agreeing is remarkably similar for women with no friends, with old but no new friends and with both kinds of friends. However, the women with no old and only new friends are disproportionately concentrated in the "strongly-disagree cell." The distributions indicate the possibility that these previously friendless women may be expecting too much from the people they now identify as friends, or at least that such relations cannot offset other negative aspects of their lives. This is not so surprising in view of the infrequency with which friends appear in the emotional support system. The pattern repeats itself when we look at both the semantic-differential and the "life-together" segments of the sanctification scale. Women who did not have friends the year before the husband's fatal illness or accident are very likely to have a "lower" score in both segments. The percentage of women with only new friends who score low on the semantic-differential segments is five times that of those with both old and new friends (two and 10 percent) and dramatically more on the life-together segment (20 and three percent).

The Role of Friend

The fact that all but a quarter of the women list at least one friend; that most of them do not have living husband or parents; and that their other relatives, except children, are not supportive (see Chapter 7), does not automatically mean a high regard for the role, friend. Going back to Table 11 of the rank order of role discussed in the chapter about the husband in memory, we find that the role of friend is ranked in the top four positions by almost three out of ten widows, while half of them list it in the bottom four positions. This is not a particularly good showing for the role of friend. On the other hand, this role did better among the widows than among the housewives and working women studied in the late 1950s and early 1960s in the *Occupation: Housewife* research (Lopata, 1971a). The Chicago area housewives, the majority of whom were married are mothers of pre-high-school children, were even less willing to grant the role of friend an important place among the major roles performed by women than are the widows. The role is important to 18 percent more widows than to wives in the "full-house plateau" stage of the life course, but this is not an outstanding shift. Historical, rather than biographical, changes may account for this difference, while the main point of the discussion is that so few women rate the role of friend as one of the important ones women can perform.

Summary

The analysis of friendship patterns among Chicago area widows points to the tremendous diversity of definitions and involvement in such relations among American women. The friends whom widows list for the time they were wives are primarily women or else couples involved in polite companionate interaction. Relatively few are remembered as contributing significantly to the respondent's emotional supports at that time, mainly supplied by the late husband and children. In fact, most of the old friendships and even many of the new ones developed in widowhood never actually penetrate into the emotional support systems sufficiently to warrant first listing. However, this does not apply to all women. In fact, we can develop a rather open-bounded typology of widows from the standpoint of their friendships:

1. *The friendless widow*, who claims no friends predating the husband's fatal illness, accident or since his death. Some of these women are simply not oriented toward this role, either because they are focused on the family and have never considered external friendship or because they do not have the self-confidence and social skills needed to enter such relations. Others feel discouraged from previous attempts at developing supportive interaction with people and now define former associates as never having been "true" friends (Weiss, 1973).
2. *The casually interactive widow*, who lists friends but who is not very active in the polite companionship interaction typical of middle- and upper-class Americans. She usually limits exchanges to informal occasions, depending often on contact in the neighborhood without planned or home socializing. She usually does not include these people in her emotional supports.

3. *The polite companionship widow*, who meets socially with her friends, carrying out traditional middle-class activities such as going to public places, having lunch together, playing sports or other games and so forth. However, she does not include such associates in her primary emotional support system ahead of her family or does so only as the persons whom she most enjoys being with or who make her feel accepted.

4. *The widow in multifaceted friendships* lists at least one friend, usually more, whom she meets frequently and who contributes to several of her emotional supports as a confidant and comforter, to whom she would turn in times of crisis, and who provides her with some of the positive self-feelings.

N O T E S

1. See also my discussion of friendship in Nona Glazer-Malbin's *Old Family/New Family* and in Lillian Troll, Joan Israel, and Kenneth Israel's *Looking Ahead*.
2. Aries (1966) discusses the evolution of etiquette books in Europe since the 17th century as larger numbers of people acquired the income enabling them to emulate the manners and pastimes of the older nobility. He bases much of his knowledge of medieval, 17th and 18th century European art. Veblen (1899) drew an ironic picture of what he called the "leisure class," in which he stressed that leisure did not mean a lack of activity but only of productive activity.
3. Millions of dollars are spent in America not only on etiquette books but also on lessons and other methods of acquiring the skills for engaging in polite companionship. These range from instruction on what spoon and fork to use at formal dinner, to bridge, golf or dancing lessons [see Lopata and Noel (1967), *The Dance Studio: Style without Sex*].
4. *Occupation: Housewife* and *Widowhood in an American City* contain chapters or sections on the role of a friend and on neighboring.
5. These friends are identified as "first female friend," or "spouse of first female friend" if the woman is listed first, and the other way around if she gives "Tom and Janet."

SEVEN

Others

Here we will examine the contributions to the support systems of the widows by people other than the members of her family of procreation, boyfriends (seen as potential husbands) and friends. For all the women represented by our sample, the family of procreation includes the late husband (in memory), the new husband (in the case of the remarried women) and her children. These intimates seem to be generally very supportive for most widows. Tables 2 to 8 reveal that the next most contributive persons to the support systems are friends; all other people or groups appear less contributive. The "others" referred to include two sets of social units: relatives other than the husband and children and those people or groups in the society who could be brought into the supports.

Contributions of the Extended Family

Sociological literature of the 1950s and 1960s marshaled considerable evidence against the thesis that urban American consists of isolated nuclear families (Litwak, 1959–1960, 1960a, 1960b, 1965; Sussman, 1962, 1965; Shanas and Streib, 1965). The existence of such units, independent of extended family networks, had been hypothesized by a variety of theorists, i.e., Goode (1963), Wirth (1938), but especially by Parsons

(1943), as the inevitable consequence of changes in the macrosystems of modern societies. Sussman and Burchinal (1966) summarized the evidence that documents extensive support systems across household thresholds within what Litwak (1960a, 1960b, 1965) termed the "modified extended family." Sussman reexamined the data and argumentation in a volume edited by Shanas and Streib (1965, p. v). Sussman's (1965, pp. 62–92) review of the modified extended family research is prefaced by the following statement:

> The theoretical position assumed in this paper is that there exists in modern urban industrial societies, particularly in American society, an extended kin family system, highly integrated within a network of social relationships and mutual assistance, that operates along bilateral kin lines and vertically over several generations.

His summary claims, the existence of active economic, service, social and emotional support exchanges among kin-related nuclear families: "Help patterns take many forms, including the exchange of services, gifts, advice and financial assistance" (p. 68). In addition, "extended family get-togethers and joint recreational activities with kin dominate the leisure time pursuits of urban working-class members" and "kinship visiting is a primary activity or urban dwelling and outranks visitation patterns found for friends, neighbors or co-workers" (p. 69). Finally, the service that the kinship group purportedly performs are carried out "regularly throughout the year or on special occasions," and these include shopping, escorting, performing household tasks, advice-giving, etc.

This generalized picture has dominated much of family sociology, although the research to which it refers is based on a much more limited set of relations than is implied by the concept of "kinship network" (Shanas and Streib, 1965, p. 5; Sussman, 1965). The limitations are in the composition of this network and in the situations under which supports flow among family members. Most of the research focused on supports flowing up or down the parent–adult child line only— not on external relatives. Much of the help that is reported occurred during the crises or life course transitional stages. For example, the help that Sussman and Hill studied was given by parents to young families who were just establishing themselves in their households (Sussman, 1953, 1962, 1965; Hill, 1965). It is not surprising that both generations reported a downward flow of a variety of supports at that time. Activities of other kin members were not studied by these researchers. In addition, the same, and other, studies used an extended time period, a year in Sussman's (1965) work, and "ever" or an indefinite period in Hill's research. Kerckhoff's *Mutual Support Index* (1965, p. 101) contains only such questions as, "Have any of your children helped out when either of you were sick?" From the not surprising response that children have contributed such help sometime in the past have come some of the assertions that the extended family provide regular help and that the children in particular are so involved on a regular basis.

The summary tables discussed first in Chapter 2 make it apparent that members of the kin network, such as parents, brothers, sisters, "other relatives" meaning grandparents, aunts and uncles, cousins and granchildren are generally unavailable and rarely appear in the support systems of the Chicago area widows represented by our sample (see Tables 2 to 8). Let us examine all facets of this situation.

CONTRIBUTIONS OF PARENTS TO SUPPORT SYSTEMS

Parents of the widows we interviewed are not found in the current support systems of most widows mainly because many of them are no longer alive and the few who are, are not available either because of distance or other impeding circumstances. (Only 14 percent of the widows' mothers and eight percent of their fathers are still alive.) Because the actual numbers of parents involved with their daughters offer a more graphic picture than do the percentages, we shall use them here. There are 11,771 living mothers of widows represented in our study, of whom only 1,496, or 13 percent, now reside with their widowed daughters. A total of 2,026 of the mothers live in the same building, the same block or in the neighborhood—mainly in the neighborhood. This accounts for 17 percent of the living mothers, so that a total of 30 percent are within easy contact distance. An additional 3,757 (32 percent) reside in the Chicago metropolitan area. Thus, only 7,279 of the 11,771 (61 percent) mothers live within reasonable distance to the widows. Of the 6,377 living fathers, even fewer are readily accessible; 486 (8 percent) live in the same building; 1,160 (18 percent) live in the area; 24 percent live in metropolitan Chicago and the rest (50 percent) live outside the area of metropolitan Chicago. In the comparison between mothers and fathers available as resources, two main reasons explain the scarcity of fathers in the support systems, besides the probability that they were never as close as the mothers: the greater likelihood of their earlier death and the greater likelihood that they live farther away. Apparently daughters and mothers more frequently live close to each other than daughters and fathers.

We realized that most of the widows did not have living parents, but we wanted to know what their relationship had been like and we inquired about the past shared living arrangements. The question, "Who has lived with you since your first marriage?" was asked of women who had shared their homes with others. Interviewers were requested to obtain the connection between any person listed and the respondent. Many assumptions about American culture and its subcultures are based on three generational households of its past, if not so much of its current, life-style. A number of social scientists have disputed this assumption and the widowhood study supports their findings (Shanas and Streib, 1965; Shanas et al., 1968).

Only eight percent of the widows in our study report a mother, five percent a father, three percent a mother-in-law and one percent a father-in-law as ever having lived with them since their marriage. We see that, as the number of living mothers dwindles, the proportion living in the home of a daughter increases, but also that few of the respondents' homes ever contained a parent, either in marriage or widowhood. Not surprisingly, in view of the historical shift of the home from one dominated by the male line into one dominated by the housewife, a far higher proportion of the woman's parents than the man's share the domicile. Incidentally, the statistical distributions of shared residences at any time resembled those of the elderly in extended health-care facilities, except that more of the elderly live with family rather than in institutions (Shanas, 1962; Shanas et al., 1968). That is, between only four and five percent of the elderly of America live in nursing homes and similar institutions at any one time, although a much higher proportion end their lives in such places. The tendency seems to be for parents, including widowed mothers, to live alone until the children decide that this situation is too precarious and they make other residential arrangements, either in the home of a child (usually a daughter) or an extended-care facility.

The residential distributions of parents lead us to predict two extremes in frequencies of contact. Almost half of the widows whose mother, and 40 percent of those whose father, are still living see her or him at least once a week. This tendency supports the contention of the contributors to the Shanas and Streib (1965) volume that the elderly in American society are not neglected by their children. If relations with the older generation follow the same pattern of those of the widow with her own children, we can assume that those widows who do not keep in close contact with a living parent have a brother or sister who lives closer and provides more frequent contact. On the other hand, not only have fewer in-laws lived with the daughter-in-law, but also fewer are seen with any frequency. This break of ties between the woman and the parents of her late husband reflects the breakup of the male family line as well as the independence of widows. Contact is maintained in cases of strong mutual benefit, supporting Winch's (1963) thesis of the connection between identification and rewards derived from continuity of affiliation with the family.

So, most widows do not have parents who are available for contact and for involvement in their support systems, mainly because of death and the in-laws are even less available.

Three-quarters of the women in our study were widowed before reaching the age of 65 and many more had living parents then than at present. We will first examine the emotional support systems of women the year before the fatal illness or accident of the husband to see if many more parents appear then than are in the current system. The answer is they do not; the difference is minimal. Only three percent of the persons listed by the respondents as the closest to the wife when the husband was still healthy, or before suffering the final illness or accident, is a parent, and only five percent of the total listings are such relatives. The mother, by the way, appears in the forefront of the emotional supports much more often than does the father—the women obviously having gotten over any alleged Electra complex by that time. Four percent of the supporters in times of crisis are seen as having been the parents and the other emotional supports contain even smaller percentages. Looking at this distribution numerically, we find that, although 11,771 women represented by our sample had living mothers, and 6,377 had living fathers at that time, making a total of 18,148 parents, only 7,385 parents are listed as being one of the three persons closest to the daughter, 4,185 mothers or fathers as the person she would turn to in times of crisis, 3,675 as contributors to her feelings of usefulness, 2,933 as those to whom she would confide her problems, 2,348 as those who made her feel respected, 2,318 as comforters when she was depressed, and 2,239 as contributors to her feeling of being an important person. All other self-feelings or relational sentiments involving a mother or father as one of the three main contributors were cited by less than 2,000 widows. Excepting the anger support, we have an average of 117,790 persons listed by the 82,085 widows per support, providing overwhelming evidence that most women do not consider either of their parents to have been strongly contributive to their emotional support system the year before the husband's illness. This finding suggests a very important convolution or asymmetry in the process of role reversal between parent and child during the life course (Shanas, 1962; Hill, 1965). The usual theoretical position of social scientists interested in the life course or span posits a heavy flow of supports from parents to children in the offspring's early years that is reversed in the older years of the parents' life. This study suggests that children draw away from their emotional dependence on their parents relatively early in adulthood (possibly when becoming mothers) so that there is always a greater flow downward from mothers to adult children than is true of the reverse. The widows of our study seemed to have drawn heavily on their children for their positive feeling states and relational sentiments, while they do not simultaneously report themselves as receivers of important emotional supports from their parents, even in middle age. There are several possible explanations for the scarcity of living parents in the emotional support systems of their married daughters before these women became widowed. American society defines maturity in terms of independence from parental influence. When a woman is married and is a mother, she is expected to devote all of her emotional attention to her family of procreation (Lopata, 1971a). Unlike traditional India, the wife-mother is not expected to return to her family of orientation for extended periods of time (Goldstein, 1977). Also, given the rapid rate of cultural change in this society, daughters often feel that their mothers lack the knowledge to serve as efficient problem solvers, and they turn to the peer group or to the mate more often than to a member of the older generation (Lopata, 1971a). The differences in life-style among generations typical of highly mobile Americans contribute to the decreasing importance of parental guidance for adult Americans (Cowgill and Holmes, 1972). Finally, there is the strong probability that the emergent, or emerged, middle-class love model has romanticized the parent–child relationship (Leslie, 1967; Scanzoni and Scanzoni, 1976). Without reference to Freud, we know that many women represented by our sample were raised in large families with stern punishment patterns and an absence of emotionally expressive parent–child relations. Such women are not apt to have developed close emotional ties even with the mother, much less, the father. We must also note that the absence of a parent, or anyone else, from listing as the primary contributor to the daughter's emotional support system before or after widowhood does not necessarily mean that she has not been close to them but only that other persons are seen as closer.

Younger widows, that is, women who were widowed at a relatively young age, tend to report more frequent closeness to their parents and greater contributions to their other supports than do the middle-aged ones. Over-all 53 percent of the widows define their family of orientation (parents and siblings) as generally very helpful during the time they were trying to build a new life. At the same time, one wonders about the close to three in 10 family members who are remembered as rarely or never helpful at that crucial time. Fathers help with funeral arrangements and financial problems; mothers provide emotional supports throughout as well as child care or other services during the husband's illness and after his death. Some women moved into their parents' home, overwhelmed not only by shock and grief but also by the enormity of the responsibility of living and taking care of small children without the help of the father. However, such situations are relatively rare, and tend to occur more often if the husband's death was sudden than if the wife had the time to develop new supports and strengths during the transitional period. Also, such cases were not necessarily successful solutions of stress, since it is very difficult for a woman who has already established her own residence and life-style to return to a home dominated by her mother. The parents are apt to have very definite ideas as to the behavior lines she should follow in the care of her children or in her relations with others, so that there is frequent tension. Several women feel that the decision to return to the family home was a mistake and that it pushed them into unhappy marriages in a effort to get away from the parents.

Coming to the current time, we found only an infinitesimal number of women who are willing or able to use their parents for their economic supports; two percent of the women represented by the sample claim to receive and to give money as gifts to parents, and generally even fewer exchange help in payment for basic-living needs (see Table 3). Five percent help parents with rent or morgage. Fewer parents are still alive since it is about 10 years since the husband's death and the contributions in other support systems are uneven. As we saw, 11,771 mothers and 6,371 fathers are still living, yet the most frequent help the widows get from a parent is in care during illness, but even then only 2,111 parents are so involved, while 1,649 women can turn to a parent for aid in legal problems (see parents in Table 4). All other supports list parents less frequently. Of course, the higher age of so many of the widows may explain the absence of parents from the inflow of supports, but we can expect a much greater outflow from the widow to them. And, in fact, more widows help parents than receive help from them, but the numbers are not as high as expected. The widow reports herself as most often helpful to her parents in taking care of their other children. This means that the widow is young and back in the home of her parents or at least able to help care for her siblings (6,042 parents listed). Care during illness (a support assumed to be needed by the older parent), was claimed to be provided by the widows to only 3500 parents, most women having listed the father and mother separately. In other areas of life, where the provision of help was expected, the numbers are still smaller, even when all three "chances" of listing are examined.

Parents are also seldom available for social activities, even for the celebration of holidays (see Table 5 for percentages of parents so listed in comparison to other people). This finding is surprising; only 2,963 parents are listed as sharers of this family activity, with only 1,750 women visiting with their parents, and 1,096 entertaining with them. As stated before, many women do not engage in the social activities about which we inquired. Still, parents are evidently not active contributors to the social supports of the Chicago area widows, mainly because they are not available at the present time. Finally, as we find, according to Table 7 few parents are still alive or able to provide emotional supports for their daughters. Whatever reasons may account for their absence when the husband was well and children were still in the home, widowhood has not impelled the daughter toward greater involvement with her parents because she cannot or she does not want to. Generally speaking, the proportion of parents in relation to other persons listed and the total numbers involved in either segment of the emotional support system of the current time period are lower than in the past. Thus of the 18,142 mothers or fathers, only 4,383 appear as the person the widow most enjoys being with, 2,416 as one to whom she would turn in times of crisis, 2,239 as the provider of feelings of being useful, and 2,239 as a comforter in depression. All other supports draw fewer than 2,000 references. Again, this points to a high rate of independence of the women even from living parents, in spite of the problems associated with widowhood. There are, on the other hand, some women for whom the relation with a parent, usually a mother, is of tremendous significance, and in such cases the parent appears in several locations in the support systems.

However minimal the contribution of the woman's own parents to her life at its current stage or before the husband's fatal illness, it is vastly greater than that of her parents-in-law.

As we saw before, fewer of such relations have been available at either period, mainly because the husband was older than the wife. He was also less likely to be residing near his family, being more mobile and less obligated to maintain contact. Since the initiative for social interaction in American society is usually taken by the woman of the family and since, despite the egalitarian, bilateral assumptions of the ideal middle-class family, family loyalties and jealousies tend to run along "blood lines," it is not surprising that there appears some strain in the relations between a wife and her husband's family of orientation (Leslie, 1967). The decrease in interaction after the death of the connecting link is evidenced not only by the infrequency of contact, but also by the absence of in-laws from the support systems of the widows (Lopata, 1973a). There are exceptions—the concluding chapter presents an in-law involved widow—but they are definitely exceptions in terms of the frequency with which parents and even siblings from the late husband's side of the family appear in the support systems of the widows.

CONTRIBUTIONS OF SIBLINGS TO SUPPORT SYSTEMS

Very few widows share their residence with a brother or sister, although such a solution to financial problems and loneliness would appear logical. Nor have many siblings ever lived with the widow since her marriage: only 3,845 brothers and 3,921 sisters having been listed as past coresidents. The few who moved in with the sister tend not to have been married at that time, since very few spouses of either the brother or the sister are listed as having shared a house. The time spent in the home of the sister was generally not extensive, with a few exceptions, such as in the case of the Greek family discussed in Chapter 10.

Interestingly enough, the brothers and sisters of these women and even their parents are not necessarily defined as very helpful to them during the time they were creating new lives as widows. Only half of the women place the family of orientation as having been generally helpful—one-fifth defining them as "helpful in special situations" and over a fourth as rarely or never helpful. That is a rather larger proportion and they obviously expected greater assistance than they were given. Still, the half who did receive the expected level of assistance is a much larger proportion than now report involvement of a brother or sister in the various support systems.

Siblings are quite inactive in the economic support system of the Chicago area widows, both as givers and as receivers (see Table 3). The highest number of references to siblings as givers in the service system occurs in care during illness, but even here fewer than 5,000 are involved (see Table 4). This small number is surprising in view of the fact that 66,138 widows represented by our sample have at least one sibling, and there is a total of 200,643 brothers and sisters, for an average of three per woman with such relations. The highest percentage of references to a sibling in the inflow of service supports occurs in decision making but that is because so few women use this support to begin with. The outflow of services to anyone is relatively low and the sibling is proportionately more apt to be a recipient than a giver. Still, at most, a sister or brother is listed as someone whom the widow helps about 3,500 times. Siblings do not often benefit from help with transportation, shopping, housekeeping, or the other routines of life.

The infrequency with which siblings appear in the economic and service supports of these women, even in the third line of mention, is repeated in the social support systems (see Table 5). Of course, as mentioned several times before, these women are relatively uninvolved in many types of social activities and some women both with and without siblings, fall into the category, "does not engage." Generally speaking, the siblings who appear there do so mainly in second or third order of mention. The highest proportion of references to siblings is found in connection with visiting and traveling out of town, but the numbers are quite different because different numbers of widows are involved in these activities (see Table 8). Thus, more than 12,000 brothers or sisters appear as people with whom the widow visits, while only 7,700 as someone with whom she travels out of town. On the other hand, the largest number of siblings are listed as cocelebrants of holidays. This activity is undertaken with many people, which accounts for the fact that siblings form only 10 perccent of the total listings. They appear very rarely as sharing other activities with their sister.

Finally, we see from Table 6 and 7 that siblings are also not part of the past or the current emotional support systems of the widows, in spite of frequent assumptions that childhood or "blood" bonds would retain their hold, even in the absence of economic and service supports or social contact, or that surviving members of the family of orientation would turn to each other for such supports once their marital and parental obligation have diminished. The failure of so many siblings to appear as major confidants and comforters of the widows was not anticipated in the planning stages of the study because of the statistical probability of age similarity. Zena Blau (1961, 1973) has maintained that a confidant is most apt to come from the same or a close age cohort, which would include many siblings, rather than across generational lines. However, the increasing division in American society between friendship and kin relations, noted in the previous chapter in reference to the naming of friends, and also by Marjorie Lowenthal (1968), appears to be operating here. Two factors decrease the probability that siblings will be major confidants: the expansion of couple companionate relations with mutually chosen friends during marriage, especially by the middle-classes, and the social and geographical mobility of widows and their siblings. Wives generally follow their husband, and he tends to follow work opportunities, so that a woman is apt to be geographically separated from siblings. Their life-styles can easily diverge so that they have less and less in common as they grow older. She may feel an obligation to keep geographically close to her mother, or the parents may move close to her, but there is no such obligation among most sibling networks. Of course, siblings may never have had a close relationship, due to sibling rivalry and age difference in a tightly age-graded social system.

Siblings hardly appear in the emotional support systems of the Chicago area widows the year prior to the husband's fatal illness or accident as far as feeling states are concerned; their main contribution is as persons to whom the sister would turn to in times of crisis, 10 percent of the references being to such a relative, usually in second or third place in order of listing. Although more siblings are listed in the current support system, there is no overwhelming movement toward them after the death of the husband.

These findings of the absence of siblings from the emotional support systems of widows do not support sociological theories that posit continued closeness after status dispersal, but we were dealing with widowed women while many of the other studies focused on men and their brothers (Litwak, 1960a, 1960b). It appears that biological closeness of the collateral family relation of these women is not necessarily translated into enjoyment of association, psychological closeness or into sources of feelings of being an important person, of comfort in depression or confidant interaction. Nor do siblings contribute substantially to the development or maintenance by widows of self-feelings of respect, usefulness, acceptance, security, independence or self-sufficiency. This conclusion is one of the most unexpected findings of this study.

CONTRIBUTIONS OF OTHER RELATIVES TO SUPPORT SYSTEMS

Because of the age of the majority of the widows and thus of their children and the infrequency of their living together with married offspring, it is not surprising that so few share a residence with grandchildren. As stated before, three-generational families are rare in American history (Shanas and Streib, 1965; Shanas et al., 1968; Chevan and Korson, 1975). Immigrants often arrive without their elderly parents and the availability of land in the New World made movement from the parental home much easier than it had been in Europe. But even there, people preferred to set up their own households rather than be dependent on the older generations, and any society that provides economic maintenance programs, such as social security, facilitates intergenerational independence (Shanas et al., 1968).

We find this tendency to live apart throughout the woman's marital history—only 1,568 grandsons and 2,274 granddaughters having resided with her since her first marriage. There is a greater tendency for black than for white families occasionally to share three-generational households or for the grandchild to live with the grandmother, but the total still falls far below the popular assumption of "grandmothering" by women of either race. In fact, Americans seem to have vastly exaggerated the relation of women to grandchildren, grandmothers, aunts and uncles, nieces and nephews. Most Chicago area widows according to our survey, either do not have such relatives or do not pull them into their support systems. Although 29 percent of the gifts of money going from the widow are directed toward "other relatives" (most often grandchildren), this represents only six percent of the total number of women (see Table 3). All other economic supports involve many fewer widows. The scarcity of service supports is also evident (see Table 4).

Although widows generally define themselves as "visiting with" more often then "entertaining with," mainly because so many live alone, other relatives are listed in reverse frequency (see Table 5). The main reason for this reversal is the tendency of the widow to feel that she is visiting mainly her son or daughter even when there are grandchildren in the home she visits. On the other hand, the widow makes a spe-

243

cific effort to entertain grandchildren, whether they come alone or with their parents. The only other activity shared with many other relatives is the celebration of holidays. Most of the 35,906 "other relatives" listed here are grandchildren, though some nieces and nephews appear in this social support.

There are enough relatives outside the immediate families of orientation and of procreation in the emotional support system to warrant separation. Table 15 gives the summary numbers on the presence of grandchildren, nieces and nephews, co-workers and other people who are the only other important contributors to the emotional supports of some of the widows. The figures indicate several things. In the first place, there is a dearth of either grandchildren or the children of siblings in these support systems, either because of their total absence as resources or the physical or social distance between them and the widow. Next, we note that these two categories of relatives are unequally involved in the supports. For example, many more grandchildren than nieces and nephews are listed as persons whom the woman most enjoys being with. On the other hand, nieces and nephews are more often comforters when the widow is depressed and especially persons to whom she would turn in times of crisis. Grandchildren are not only enjoyed, but they help make the grandmother feel like an important, respected and useful person. Thus, the relation seems to be quite different with these two sets of persons, the nieces and nephews taking more responsibility for her, probably because they are older than the grandchildren. The grandchildren generally appear as people who are enjoyed and cared for. The grandmothers refer to them differently than to the children of siblings. Still it is quite surprising to find only 8,205 grandchildren listed in the emotional support involving the highest number of them. If each widow lists only one grandchild rather than multiples, this would mean that only 10 percent of the widows have a grandchild they can list as one of the persons they most enjoy being with. These relatives are not very contributive to other support sys-

TABLE 15

Number of "Others" Contributing to Emotional Support Systems of Chicago Area Widows[a]

Emotional Support	Grandchildren	Nieces & Nephews	Co-workers	Church	Priest, Minister, Rabbi
Relational Sentiments:					
Closest	3469	3075	49	—	309
Enjoy being with	8206	1729	491	375	—
Tell problems	803	980	47	58	1357
Comforts when depressed	405	1729	34	—	597
Makes feel important	5072	1620	1858	381	1247
Most often angry at	958	69	1812	—	—
Turns to in crisis	528	2397	103	—	815
Feeling States:					
Respected	2236	1133	4368	3599	815
Useful	4742	928	4331	2264	128
Independent	80	561	2722	731	94
Accepted	447	909	4238	4002	259
Self sufficient	620	44	1522	1027	47
Secure	643	33	1686	318	94

[a]N = 82,085.

tems, in that so few are confidants, comforters, persons she can turn to in times of crisis or persons who make her feel accepted, secure, self-sufficient or independent. Again, it appears that American society has overestimated the importance of grandchildren or the children of siblings in the lives of widows. What is quite possible is that the relation provides intense enjoyment for only a brief time while the grandchildren are little, and that the generations drift apart when the grandchildren become strongly involved in their own lives. Since the widows are now at an average age of about 65, their grandchildren are likely to be in the midst of the "expanding circle" or "full-house plateau" stages of their family life cycle and thus unavailable to the widow for other emotional, social or service supports (Lopata, 1971a).

The Roles of Daughter and Grandmother

The Chicago area widows are not apt to rank the roles of daughter or grandmother in the first two ranks of importance to women, but there are interesting differences in the way these two roles fare after that (see Table 11). In spite of the age of most widows and the death of most of their parents, the role of daughter rates higher more frequently than does the role of grandmother. It is possible that the respondents are thinking of the obligations of their daughters to them, rather than of their own past relations with their mothers when assigning this role third or fourth ranks. The absence of grandchildren from their support systems is reflected in their ranking of the role of grandmother within the highest four ranks less often than mother, wife, daughter or housewife. However, they certainly are much more apt to list this role within the top four positions than were their married counterparts studied in the 1950s and 1960s. The latter were, it must be remembered, much younger since they were selected as mothers of at least one pre-high-school child.

Contributions of Other People and Groups

We have focused on the involvement in the support systems of the Chicago area widows of persons defined by American society as intimates, which generally is taken to mean a husband or "close male friend," usually called a "boyfriend," children, friends, parents and other relatives discussed earlier. A complex, urban, modern society, however, contains many other people whom a woman, widowed or not, can draw on to build her support systems. Neighbors are obviously present and we have seen that they are major contributors to friendships. Over a fourth of the women work, which means that they have co-workers, employers or supervisors and, though less frequently, employees and supervisees. American society is allegedly oriented toward religion, especially in its organized form, and we saw earlier that many of the women are members of parishes or congregations. Voluntary associations abound and there is a proliferation of "helping" professions, governmental and voluntary aid associations or agencies and formal or informal networks of resources. The question arises whether these resources are of real help to those who are going through crises or transitional stages or engaged in the rebuilding of support systems and networks. It is at this time that we must examine in detail the statements made earlier concerning the failure of societal resources to contribute to the support systems of many Chicago area widows represented by our sample, and in the next chapter we will carefully examine the personal characteristics that influence the extent to which a widow is able to function in the social structure in which she now finds herself. We have several sets of data for the analysis of contributions of "other people and groups." The first of these consists of the perceived levels of helpfulness of selected sets of associates of the widow when she was trying to build a new life. Also we have the summary Tables 2 to 9 which give the frequencies with which the woman lists contributors to the four support systems. Finally, we have detailed listings of those persons or groups who appear most often in these systems.

Neighbors are generally people whose style of life is similar to ones' own, with whom contact is almost guaranteed; and who are thus potentially close associates. The *Occupation: Housewife* (Lopata, 1971a) study devoted much attention to neighboring because of its focus on new suburbanites with prehigh-school children who were creating new styles of life in the post-World War II decades—partly because of the dearth of unbiased research [see the biases built into Spectorsky's *The Exurbanites* (1955), Reisman, Glaser and Denney's *The Lonely Crowd* (1950) or William H. Whyte Jr.'s *The Organization Man* (1965)]. This research analyzed forms of neighboring by the social class of residents and life cycle of the family as well as of the neighborhood. Metropolitan Chicago contains areas of anomie-based (having lost traditional mooring) noninteraction whose residents lack common norms as well as those of institutionalized noninteraction by common agreement. It also contains neighborhoods that involve various levels of contact between women only, between both men and women in sex-segregated exchanges or between couples. Such contact can be limited to casual encounters during the normal round of activities, casually planned exchanges or special joint activities in the homes or outside of the home (Lopata, 1971a, Chapter 5). The study of the older widows indicated a lack of involvement with neighbors, especially in connection with service exchanges [Lopata (1973a); see also Chapter 2 of this book]. On the other hand, neighborhoods outweigh all other locations for the formation of friendships, some even being retained after a geographical separation. In this particular study, we shall examine neighbors only when they are not defined as

248

friends, since the former relation is arbitrarily defined as more important to a widow.

The perceived levels of helpfulness of categories of people we identified for the respondents, shows that neighbors are often defined as having been very helpful to the widow when she was trying to create a new life after the death of the husband. More than four of 10 women (43 percent) made such a judgment. This leaves, however, a quarter of the widows who found their neighbors never helpful, 13 percent who found them rarely so, and 19 percent as helpful in special situations. This definition indicates a great discrepancy between expectations and actualities. It is possible that the unhelpful neighbors were either strangers or involved in their own lives, unwilling to permit the widow into their lives or to become involved. The constantly reported problems of bringing oneself out of grief and rebuilding life, even on the part of the women who did not have a particularly good marriage, may have been so great that expectations of help from those living nearby could not be fruitful. The judgment of level of helpfulness, as indicated before, does not refer to what the neighbors did but to the accord between what the widow expected or wished for and what was actually contributed to her support systems.

The neighbors do not generally appear in the support systems of the widow at the present time, unless they have been converted into friends. There is little service support exchange among people living near her, a finding supporting previous research (Lopata, 1971a, 1973a).

CO-MEMBERS OF VOLUNTARY ASSOCIATIONS

The widow's perception of the level of helpfulness of co-members of voluntary associations when she was trying to rebuild her life is about equivalent to that of work associates, other relatives, in-laws and "the government." Sixty-four percent of the women found the question not pertinent, either because they did not belong or because the form of involvement did not lead to expectations of help. Twenty-eight percent of the remaining women obviously held expectations that were not met by the people in clubs and other such groups, because they stated flatly that these people were "never" helpful, while nine percent define them as "rarely" so involved. This leaves 38 percent in the "very helpful" and 26 percent in the "helpful in special situation" judgments. Unfortunately, we do not know what type of help was sought, though previous statements indicate it was probably in the area of social contact. The infrequent mention of voluntary associations as helpful to the widow is surprising if we assume that providing supports to their members is a major function of such groups.

Few people identified as belonging to the same groups as the widow appear in her support systems. As with neighbors and co-workers those co-members of voluntary associations with whom close relations are developed tend to be identified in the resource network as friends. There are some women, as we shall show in the concluding chapter, whose whole life revolves around activities of a country, bridge, garden or church club. This kind of involvement is much more typical of the upper-middle-class woman than of her working-class or newly lower-middle-class counterpart. The exception to this is the ethnic, particularly Polish American, non-middle-class woman who tends to be active in ethnic community groups, and the black woman who is more active in church groups, if she belongs to anything at all, than is the white woman [see Lopata, *Polish Americans: Status Competition in an Ethnic Community* (1976a) and Chapter 9 of this book].

Interestingly enough, "the church" as a symbolic group or as an actual organization appears frequently, when compared to other nonintimates, in the emotional support system of the widows, or at least in the feeling-states segment (see Table 15). It is and is respected. This source appears less frequently in these supports than do the co-workers but more frequently than such personal relations as grandchildren, nephews and nieces. At the same time, one would expect that involvement in church activities would have contributed more to the feeling of usefulness and security.

THE HELPING PROFESSIONS

There is a surprising, dramatic failure of the helping professions in the support systems of the Chicago area widows represented by our study. Priests, ministers or rabbis were not frequent contributors either during the husband's illness, immediately after his death, in the life-rebuilding stage or at the present time. In fact, a minister or rabbi is hardly ever mentioned, the priest more often (see Table 15). Even so, the number is insignificant if compared to the total number of women who were involved. Only 1,357 women mention a religious professional as one to whom they tell their problems at the present time and these listings are fewer than those in all other supports. The absence of religious advisers from these supports is startling considering the supportive nature of religious promises. However, my frequent speeches on this topic to the widowed and to the significant associates of widowed persons indicate that this absence is typical because the priests, ministers and rabbis are simply not trained, and they are not able to provide emotional, social or service supports to widowed parishioners. Part of this failure is due to shunning of intimate contact with husbandless women, but many other aspects of parish or congregational life make additional barriers toward effective support. In fact, widows tend to be the invisible members of the community and its churches as they are oriented toward the young and toward "successful" couples. A few of the widows explain the failure in these terms when listing someone connected with a church or synagogue in the "other" category in the questions as to the perceived levels of help offered by people during the life-rebuilding period and then defining him, sometimes her, as having failed to do so.

251

Doctors are also expected to provide help to widows during the traumatic period of the husband's death, yet relatively few appear as positive suppliers of supports, despite the fact that relatively many women suffer from physical and psychological problems after the death of the husband, as reported by our respondents as well as in the literature dealing with grief (Glick, Weiss and Parkes, 1974; Clayton, 1973a; Parkes, 1964, 1965). Doctors are even not mentioned as persons to whom the widow would turn in times of crisis and very few of the respondents have consulted psychiatrists or other mental health specialists, although many report profound depression, ulcers and similar reactions to the death of the husband or to their attempts to restructure their life.

Finally, another source of comfort mentioned by widows, aside from immediate associates, is "God," "religion" or "faith." God is listed as the one to whom a woman tells problems by 1,830 of the 82,058 widows represented by our sample, while 2,560 derive comfort from this source when they are depressed, and 2,290 turn to God in time of crisis.

All in all, however, the women living in metropolitan Chicago who lost a husband, often under difficult circumstances, have not been able to turn for supports to societal resources, even ones developed to help people in a crisis.

The Role of Member of Religious Group or Society in General

One of the shocking findings to me (who came to America from a society in which members take very seriously their obligations for its survivals and development) of the housewife study was the infrequency with which Chicago area women took membership in the society as a major social role (see Table 11). Only eight percent of the married mothers of at least one pre-high-school child ranked it within the top social roles of a woman. Although twice that percentage of the widows rank it within the top four roles, it is obvious that it does not fare well in that it draws the highest bottom four ranks of any of the roles; 77 percent of the widows placing it there. The role of religious member rates about the same among all these women in spite of the fact that, as we shall see later, the black women are prone to consider it more important than many other roles available to women. There are enough white widows to offset such judgments and 73 percent of the women place church membership or religious affiliation within the bottom four ranks, 59 percent among the bottom three.

Summary

We have just examined the contributions of relatives outside the family of procreation and of people or groups outside the kinship network to the four support systems of the Chicago area widows. The main conclusion to be drawn is that assumptions of an extended family network, actively exchanging supports between separate households in American metropolitan centers, are not borne out for any relatives, other than children. Few members of the extended family lived with the widows or shared households in the past. Parents are simply not available to any but a few, usually very young widows. Kin members such as aunts or uncles and cousins, siblings, nieces or nephews, and even grandchildren are also not available, or at any rate do not contribute to the major support systems on a consistent basis. Even if they exist as potential resources or contributors, the life-style of American urban women makes continuous contact and exchanges of supports difficult during the busy marital and parental stages, and the diminishing of such involvement does not bring the extended family back together, probably because few members are going through parallel changes or are willing to give up their pattern of living. Even if the widow maintains some type of contact, such as the telephone or correspondence, about which we did not inquire, these are not sufficiently important to be converted into supports—even emotional supports. Being together on holidays or traditional family events, such as funerals or weddings, does not guarantee a wide range of day-by-day or other regular supports. These generalizations do not negate the fact that some widows are involved in interaction and support systems with a variety of relatives, or that some are intensively engaged in many exchanges with one or a limited number of relatives outside the mother-offspring line. The evidence is strong, however, that the extended family is not tremendously active, in fact, that it is really quite inactive as a major contributor to the four main support systems of most Chicago area widows. Parents, siblings and grandchildren, not expected to be of great assistance, are either dead or otherwise unavailable, or they have developed their own worlds that do not include the widow in major exchanges. In addition, kinship interaction and emotional involvement, when they exist, tend to be sex-segregated, as was true with relations with the offspring.

Other people and groups, neighbors, co-workers, co-members of voluntary associations, including churches or synagogues, are also relatively underrepresented in, while religious personnel and members of other helping professions are almost absent from, the support systems of the Chicago area widows. Frequently seen associates become friends but other depersonalized associates do not contribute to many supports, except occasionally to supply positive self-feelings. Few women turn to societal resources for help, except in the case of the Social Security Administration, generally evaluated as helpful. Neighborhood networks, recommended in the concluding chapter, may help offset the failure of social resources in reaching women who do not have the know how or are not accustomed to utilizing societal agencies, although the availability of traditional helpers and support suppliers has diminished considerably. ·

EIGHT

Personal Resources and Supports

There are many personal characteristics of a widow that can serve her as resources for building support systems and networks. Here we shall examine only her use of herself as a resource and the influence of age, race and education, although other aspects obviously influence her life. In the following chapter we will concentrate on employment and income as potential resources for social integration.

The Self as Resource

Although American society and its ethnic and racial subcommunities contribute toward making women feel dependent, incompetent and self-depreciatory, as feminist researchers and writers have repeatedly pointed out, many of the Chicago area widows present rather strong and independent images of themselves (Bernard, 1975; Chafe, 1972; Dulles, 1965; Glazer-Malbin and Waehrer, 1972; Lopata, 1971a; Reeves, 1971; Rubin, 1976). Several reasons may account for this feeling of independence and self-reliance, among them widowhood itself. Jessie Bernard (1973) concludes in *The Future of Marriage* that unmarried women in this society are better off in terms of mental and physical health than are married women. Basing this finding on extensive research, she states that the kind of socialization and adult dependency fostered on women in America takes a heavy toll in emotional health. Widows with grown children or no children can develop independence and lead their own lives. They may also find that the work involved in the upkeep of their home has decreased and that they now, probably for the first time in their lives, have more free time (Lopata, 1971a, 1966). Many respondents who speak of themselves as independent women, satisfied with themselves and their life at the present time, may have gained these feelings from awareness of being survivors of the often painful process of losing their husband and grief work. As pointed out elsewhere, some of the widows in the prior study of role modification reported a change in themselves since the death of the husband in the direction of increased competence, independence and self-sufficiency (Lopata, 1975b). They also feel the benefit of having completed that part of grief work that Lindemann (1944) and his followers identified as reconstruction of identity, that is, of the self, into a partnerless person. Finally, some of these women may not have encountered situations that would bring demeaning self-feelings, developing independence in their own environment and not involving themselves in any form of consciousness-raising. Of course, this is not true of all women, for some never felt dependent and lacking in self-sufficiency; others never went through the processes described above and never felt independent; and a third category lost the positive feelings about themselves with the loss of a protective husband or the security of being a wife. A look at some of the data dealing with the support systems of the Chicago area widows will offer some insights as to their emotional states.

The school of social psychology known as symbolic interactionism holds that a person can draw on her or himself for major self-feelings and evaluations. We are able, so to speak, to stand aside and watch ourselves in action, hear what we say, and note the reaction of others to us. The self can be an object of attention, sentiment, strong emotions such as anger and judgment or evaluation. Cooley (1922) [see also Smith (1953) and Mead (1934)] noted that human beings have a "looking-glass" self, in that we see ourselves in the eyes of others and respond with a variety of self-feelings to the evaluation we imagine the other is making of us and our behavior. In addition, we store those images of ourselves that we wish to keep, or that we cannot throw out, as well as the criteria we think were used in the evaluation by others with whom we have interacted in past or are now in our interaction network. Finally, we can use these criteria in our own experience of looking at ourselves. An excellent example of these three processes is found among widows who are aware of a timetable known to many Americans as to the supposed stages of widowhood, the symptoms of each stage, and the symptoms indicative of movement from one stage to another. Widows often report a concern that they are "off-time" in their grief work, especially if significant others tell them or imply that they should be moving on to the next stage. In fact, serious self-questioning by a widow is often experienced as to the depth of her grief as well as to its timing (Caine, 1974; Silverman, 1972; Glick, Weiss and Parkes, 1974).

It is this theoretical base that led to the creation of several items of the emotional support system, particularly to its "feeling states" segment. If we look at Tables 2, and 5 through 8, we find the theory to be relevant, with interesting variations. As mentioned before, these tables present the percentages of the reponses to the emotional support system questions. Since the respondents list themselves only once in each separate support, if they do so at all, the combination of such designations in any of the three chances gives the total number of women, rather than responses, who list the self for both the "before" time period and for the "now" (see Table 8). The table also contains the number of women who state that "no one" supplies such supports as a contrast to the self-designations. As stated in Chapter 2, women who answer "no one" in reply to whom they enjoy being with, as over a fifth of them do in the present time frame, are different than those who list another person, or even than those who state that they most enjoy being by themselves.

Starting with the "before" time period, we can see from Table 6 that the self appears relatively rarely in all supports except for the self-feelings of independence, self-sufficiency and security. The self contributed to the feeling of security of only one-eighth of the widows the year before the husband's fatal illness or accident, but four in 10 of the widows state that they were their own main source of feelings of independence and self-sufficiency even when the husband was well. The self is not a very frequent contributor to the feelings of being an important person, of being respected, useful or accepted. This means that these self-feelings must be based on inter-action and the looking-glass process, so that the widows can-not use internalized criteria to evaluate themselves, being de-pendent upon feedback from others. Of course, it is possible that doing useful things for another person rather than hearing or perceiving the other as making such an evaluation brings the feeling of being useful.

It is also interesting to note the distributions of "no one" responses. As stated before, half of the widows do not admit to feeling anger at any one person, either because they do not admit to anger at all or because the emotion is diffused, not being focused on one, two or three persons. The fact that one in almost seven widows claims "no one" comforts her when she is depressed has several alternate explanations. Some women may define themselves as never depressed, others as not letting anyone know about this emotional state. There is the possibility that some women simply did not have the type of relation with their husbands or other people for that matter, which allowed for comforting interaction. Many of the couples described by Komarovsky (1967) and Rubin (1976), who do not engage in extensive communication and have little mutual understanding, would be typical of relations in which the widow now reports that no one comforted her.

The same proportion of women do not receive feelings of independence from anyone and, since they do not list themselves, we can assume that their package of feelings about the self does not include that one. Many of the women who stated that no one served as their confidant to whom problems were told explained to the interviewer that they do not believe in talking about their problems.

When we move to the "now" time period, we see a definite expansion of contributions by the self as well as by "no one" (see Table 7). This dual flow indicates two different kinds of women. One type develops self-confidence, after going through the death of the husband and the grief processes, which increases positive feelings about the self, the other becomes desolated by these events (Townsend, 1968; Weiss, 1973). However, we cannot be absolutely sure that some of the desolate women are not in the "self" column. Telling problems only to oneself may be a sign of social isolation or independence. The same may be true of women who claim they turn only to themselves in time of crisis. The self appears much more often in the "now" time than prior to the husband's death in all the feeling states. The most dramatic jump, 28 percent, is in the feeling of being secure. Six out of 10 widows ascribe their feelings of independence and self-sufficiency to the self, and relatively few state that no one provides them with that feeling. In fact, many more women now feel independent than did before—at least in the memory-redefined past. The contributions of the self to other feelings did not increase very much in widowhood, again indicating that they are relationally or interactionally based. This hypothesis is further supported by the significant increase in the number of widows who no longer feel useful, or who at least indicate that no one provides them with that judgment. There is also a strong increase in the number of women who now lack a comforter during depression and a confidant to whom they can tell problems. Over a fifth lack such companions. The death of the husband and other events since then have resulted in an increase in the proportion of women who claim not to be angry with anyone. It is possible that some of these women are relatively isolated, while others fear feeling or expressing anger at anyone in their network. Admitted anger and admitted loneliness appear to go together. It is also possible that recent events have removed sources of anger in the lives of many women, with the husband and children residing at home being listed in the past.

When we look at other details of the appearance of the self in the support systems of Chicago area widows, we found some interesting tendencies (see Table 2). The women refer to themselves on an average of four times in the 65 separate supports, the infrequency being due mainly to the structuring of the questions. We asked the respondents first if they are involved in the in- and outflow of financial supports or services. This formulation was dictated by the logic of the support and ruled out the listing of the self. Thus, the woman could list herself only in social and emotional systems. She is likely to mention herself in two social supports, going to church and traveling alone; the social nature of those activities begins when she arrives at her destination. The main use of the self as a contributor to the supports thus occurs in the emotional system, particularly in the feeling-state segment, as discussed above. Fifty-six percent of the women did not mention themselves in the social supports, 79 percent made no such designation in the current time frame of the sentiment segment of the emotional system, but only 27 percent do not consider themselves as a main supplier of feeling states. In general, it is the older, or retirement-age widow who turns to herself in the emotional system more than the younger woman, either because of a lack of significant others or because of a positive view of independence. For example, the retirement widows form 66 percent of the weighted sample, but contribute 90 percent to the category of women who do not feel close to anyone besides themselves. Of course, this distribution is considerably skewed—only two percent of the elderly women felt this way. They are overrepresented among the women who listed themselves as the main comforter during depression, and the main contributor to the feelings of being important and useful the year before the husband's fatal illness or accident. At the other end of the age spectrum, when it is polarized into retirement widows and all the other beneficiaries obviously below 65 or at least 60 years of age, we found that none lists the self as the sole companion in social events, and 79 percent do not mention it in the emotional system. Age differentiates widows in more ways than those just mentioned and we need to examine these more carefully now.

Age as Resource

Age at widowhood can be expected to influence the manner and degree of disorganization of past support systems as well as the content of the new systems developed after adjustment to the new marital situation for several reasons. The very young with no children can slide into the single marital category with relative ease, although they may be plagued by feelings of unfairness and of being left with "unfinished business" in their relations with the late husband (Blauner, 1966). Young mothers and the younger middle-aged women, that is, those between the ages of 30 and 54, are likely to be hard hit by the death of the husband in that they usually have dependent children, experience widowhood "off-time" with most of their friends still married and need to make other important changes in their life-styles when the income earned by their late husband vanishes from the household. At the same time, such women may be able to remain in or re-enter the labor force, gaining all the supports such activity provides. The older women of this cohort have, as we shall see in Chapter 9, an average income that is higher than that of any other group, with the exception of the younger remarried one. Some of the women in this age group face the serious problem of having to deal with the grief of their children in addition to their own. The next age group, between 55 and 65 years, is apt to be without dependent children, and thus does not qualify for social security, although the age of reduced benefits has been lowered recently to age 60. If out of the labor force for any length of time, such women can become destitute (Mallen, 1975). With the drop in income they may have to reorganize their lives. Friendships with still-married women may be strained, and few male companions are available for the continuance of couple friendships to women accustomed to it in the past. The elderly widows can be expected to suffer less disorganization in terms of income and other social roles, but they may be left relatively isolated by the death of a husband who was a daily companion, especially if he served as a major link to other people. This situation is especially likely to develop if they had been socialized into passivity vis-à-vis social roles outside of the home.

Her age also exposes the woman to a variety of historical events at different stages of her life. Increased age in our sample usually means nonurban birth, often a second-generation immigrant background, less formal schooling, a limited employment history, the Depression, World War II experiences and traditional views on a woman's place. There is a definite association between age and education among the women represented in our study (gamma $= -.36$). Although widows aged 65 and over represent 59 percent of those for whom we have complete information on the two variables (age and education), they form 82 percent of those with less than eight grades of schooling and 80 percent of those with only a completed grade-school education. In all other categories they are underrepresented. There are few women in our sample who are aged 44 or less and they are not the most educated, simply because a disproportionate number of younger widows are minority group members with a limited educational background. The women who are disproportionately apt to be college graduates are those in the ages between

45 and 54, which helps to explain their high average income.

The younger women, that is, those in any but the "retirement age" beneficiary category, tend to have been widowed between six and seven years at the time of the interview, having entered the marriage that left them widowed in 1945 at the average age of 25. Forty-six percent still have at least one child under the age of 21, while 23 percent have at least one over that age. On the other hand, 19 percent are mothers of only children under age 21, while 44 have only older offspring, and 37 percent are in families containing children both under 21 and older. Thirty percent do not have any children living at home. The elderly are mainly living alone, with the exception of those with a foreign background or health problems.

The elderly widows are highly dependent on social security and have fewer sources of income than do the younger women (see details in Chapter 9). Although few respondents are involved in exchanges of economic supports with anyone, there is a very tenuous association between income below the poverty level, age and gifts of money or help in the payment for living expenses. In fact, the majority of the most destitute are also apt to be lacking economic supports other than income.

Interesting age variations appear when we look at the differences in contributions of significant others to the service supports. A present husband, boyfriends and parents are seen as contributors to the inflow of services mainly to women widowed while young and still relatively young. The same holds true for the outflow of services. Siblings also decrease in frequency of service exchanges both as givers and as receivers as age at widowhood increases, in spite of assumptions of increasing importance of siblings in old age.

We must keep in mind that the contributions of anyone but children, which increase with age at widowhood and current age, are relatively rare. There is little, or unsystematic, variation by age of the contributions of other relatives, friends and other people or groups. Younger widows and those who were widowed early in life are apt to have younger children in the home, so that they do not list as recipients of services considered to be part of the normal flow of work. The sociological thesis that the flow of services from parent to child reverses itself with increasing age of the parent is supported by the data on Chicago area widows (Shanas and Streib, 1965; Litwak, 1965; Sussman, 1965). The widows help their children across household thresholds mainly when these offspring are becoming established and in the early years of the grandchildren's lives, that is, when the widow is between the ages of 45 and 64. This assistance decreases when the widow reaches older age, while the offspring simultaneously increase their contributions to the service supports of the mother. The outflow of services does not vary much when we compare current age of the widow to her age at the time of the death of the husband. Friends are also less apt to receive services from the eldest widows or from the younger ones.

Some interesting variations but a lack of a single clear-cut pattern occur when we cross-tabulate the service support system by age and 1973 income, as given in the precoded question. Older women who were then economically destitute (living on less than $3,000 a year), were more likely to receive transportation, care in illness, shopping, yard work and decision-making help from others than were their younger counterparts. However, the wealthy widows of all ages, but especially the younger ones, report much more frequently that they receive help with household repairs and yard work than do their poorer counterparts. Rich widows of all ages report help with decision making and legal aid more often than do the poorer women, a nonsurprising finding in view of their economic situation. The highest association (gamma=.66) between age and a specific support occurs among women who fell into the $9,000 to $14,999 income category in 1973 in reference to transportation. Twenty-four percent of the respondents younger than 45 years of age, but 73 percent of those 60 years or older report transportation services from others. There are negative associations between age and child care, regardless of income, and between age and most service supports for the middle incomed women living on between $6,000 and $8,999. It is not apparent why the elderly among them are so apt to need, or at least to receive less aid, care in illness, help with yard work, shopping or household repairs than are the younger women managing on the same income.

A very definite pattern emerges when the social support system is considered, with a definite decrease in contributions of significant others with an increase in age both at widowhood and now. Present husbands, boyfriends, as well as parents and siblings are available as companions in social activities mainly to the very young. The most willing to engage alone in often shared social activities, such as going to church or traveling, are the women in the decade immediately under 64 years of age. Of course, they may face a combination of being more competent and independent than women of other age cohorts while having fewer associates easily available for such activities. Their friends and offspring may still be busy with their own families. They are also the most affluent. Women who were widowed earlier are apt to have children in the home and siblings in the home of the parents. They are also apt to have friends, but then, so do all the women except the elderly and those who were elderly at widowhood. For example, siblings are mentioned at least once in the social support system of 44 percent of women widowed at age 30 or below and by only 24 or 28 percent of women widowed at later ages. Friends are mentioned by 78 percent of the women widowed in the youngest age category and the drop does not occur until the eldest cohort of age 65 or over, when only 52 percent of the women mention a friend.

Interestingly, it is mainly age at widowhood rather than current age which influences the distributions of references to people other than the self. The age 65-plus cohort may have cut back on social activities or may have always been less involved. There is even a drop in the use of children in the social supports in the oldest group. The same holds true of contributions of other relatives. These women are also much more apt to state that they never engage in the activity in the first place than are their younger counterparts. The association between age and the absence of a new husband, boyfriends, parents and siblings from the social supports of widows remains true for the current age, but there is a peaking in the 55 to 64 age group in the frequency of reference to the self. Only 13 percent of the women currently in the under 45 age category mention undertaking some sort of activity by themselves, compared to 39 percent of those age 45 to 54, 59 percent of those age 55 to 64 and 44 percent of those age 65 and over. This probably means that some of the widows who were younger at the death of the husband and who were involved in socializing with friends have now reached the top age group, increasing its percentage.

Age at widowhood also influences the involvement of significant others in the emotional support system. This applies especially to the contributions of parents and siblings as well as of boyfriends and a new husband. Women widowed before age 30 are generally able to draw on their parents and, to a lesser extent, on their siblings. Siblings decrease in importance in both segments of the emotional system as age prior to widowhood increases. Women widowed at an early age are more apt to list a sibling than are older women, the reverse of the hypothesized tendency. In other words, whatever closeness existed among the siblings in youth gradually dissipates with increasing age, so that older women do not often use a sibling as the person they feel closest to, enjoy being with, tell their problems to, turn to in times of crises, etc. These figures definitely negate the assumptions of many social gerontologists of a regrouping of the kinship unit after the demands of the family of procreation decrease in importance. Age does not make any significant difference in the contributions of siblings to the feeling-states segment of the system, either "before" or "now," because they are absent at all ages. A similar pattern emerges when we look at the contributions of relatives other than parents, siblings and children. They decrease with an increase in age except for a lack of strong differentiation in the feeling-states segment of the "before" time.

There is an, albeit weak, association (gamma= −.20) between age at widowhood and the appearance of friends in the emotional supports but the pattern is the reverse of the predicted one. The older the woman, the less apt she is to list friends in any part of the support system while she was married. The trend may be partly accounted for by cohort differences, older women not having learned techniques for developing friends later in life, so that as early childhood associates become less available, they are not replaced with new ones. As we saw in Chapter 2, most of the friends of women who claim such associates are of long standing. Also, the younger women are more educated and there is a strong association between friendship and formal schooling.

The most apt to report their children as supportive when the husband was still living and at the present time are women who were widowed between the ages of 30 and 54. Those women who were even younger may have had children too small to contribute to the kinds of supports we are investigating. Beyond that exception, however, age at widowhood does not make a great deal of difference in the contributions of children—at least there appears to be only inconsistent variation. Age at widowhood also does not have an influence on the contributions the husband is said to have made before his death to the emotional supports of the wife, except that the very young women are less apt to have derived their feeling states from him than are the women widowed later.

As indicated earlier, the self appears mainly in the feeling-states segment of the emotional supports. It increases its contribution in both segments over age at widowhood. Younger women seem to have been dependent on other human beings to provide them with feelings, even of self-sufficiency, independence and security, while the more mature women derived such feelings from themselves.

There is an interesting pattern in the use of "no one" in the emotional support system of the remembered past, with a definite increase (from 50 to 71 percent) over age in the sentiment segment and a decrease (from 42 to 17 percent) in the feeling-states segment. The older the woman is at widowhood, the more apt she is to state that no one provided her with positive relational sentiments at the time when husband was still well, or does so now. Of course, there is the strong possibility that the frequency of the use of "no one" in this segment of the system is in response to the "who makes you angry most often" question. As we saw before, few women admit feeling angry with anyone. In addition, many older women say that they do not reveal their problems to anyone. However, many of the women responded with "no one" more than twice and the proportion increases with age. It must be remembered that these were not precoded responses but ones volunteered by the respondents themselves. However, the older the women at widowhood, the less likely they are to state that no one provided them with positive self feelings. Again, there is an indication here that young married women feel insecure and lacking in positive feelings about the self, while age increases self-confidence as a useful, respected and self-sufficient person even in marriage.

There is also little difference in the use of "no one" in current feeling states. The sentimental supports, however, show a positive association between age and the resort to the "no one" answer. That is, the older the woman when the husband died, the more often she states that she now has "no one" as confidant, comforter, resource in crisis and so forth. The percentages listing "no one" at least once rise dramatically from 53 percent among women who became widows below the age of 30 to 18 percent among those who were already aged 65 and over.

The combinations of uses of the self and of "no one" by women of different ages at the time of widowhood indicates that younger women are more able to develop social relations with which they are satisfied and which provide them with positive relational sentiments than are the older women. They use both self and "no one" answers less often than do their older counterparts in this segment of the emotional support system. It is possible that the married older woman depends so heavily upon her husband or herself that she does not replace close other associates as disorganizing events break the relation or make it difficult to retain at that level of intimacy. Women widowed younger have more personal resources with which to build a new emotionally satisfying network. There are strong indications that age brings greater reliance on the self for positive feelings of self-worth among women whose husbands remain alive, although such husbands are also re-membered as generally supportive.

Dividing the current age of the widows into four categories, but starting with age 44 and under, because the 29 and under category used for the age prior to widowhood yielded so few cases, we find a similar pattern to that just discussed. The use of the self as a supplier of emotional supports in the feeling-states segment increases somewhat by current age, but not as much as by widowhood age (from 67 to 76 percent). Fewer older women have parents, a new husband or boyfriends so it is not surprising that it is mainly the very young who refer to them. Children are again most likely to be listed by the young middle-aged woman (age 45–54: 95 percent) who is also more likely to mention siblings (39 percent) and other people or groups (32 percent) in the sentiments segment of the system. The "no one" response increases with an increase in age (from 54 to 83 percent), mainly among the answers to the first segment of the system. The combination of age and education influence social interaction (see also Tables 18 and 19).

Race as Resource

It is difficult to predict if, or in what ways, a particular racial identity and membership in a particular racial subcommunity is a resource or a hindrance in building support systems or networks. Recognizing that our nonwhite population contains a few nonblacks and that the variation among the nonwhite races is high, we nevertheless cannot separate these groups because of their low representation in the sample. There are certain facts about differences between the white and non-white widows that we already know. We already found that the proportion of American widows aged 14 or over who are identified by the U.S. Census as black or as of social races other than white tends to be higher than the proportion of widows among the whites. In addition, we have learned that widowhood comes to nonwhite women at an earlier age and that they die younger. These differences are reflected in our Chicago area sample: the mean age of the whites being 67 and that of the nonwhites 58. Three times as many nonwhite as white women were widowed below the age of 30 and the difference is even more startling in the 30 to 54 age category. By age 54, only 37 percent of the whites compared to 61 percent of the nonwhites had already become widowed. The same holds true for the age of the husband at death, with 29 percent of the whites, but 48 percent of the nonwhites dying before reaching the age of 55.[1] Although this is partly a consequence of the sample itself, the national figures support at least some of the age differences between these social groups. Dispro-portionately many of the nonwhites (most of whom are blacks) represented by our sample are current beneficiaries as mothers of dependent children.[2] Over a third of them, compared to half of this proportion among the whites, fall into that ben-eficiary category, a distribution reflecting their young age and thus their children's ages. Many are totally dependent on social

270

security, and a few even have to resort to welfare, as discussed in Chapter 9. The white women are much more apt to have reached retirement age as widows and thus to be receiving benefits based on that fact.

BACKGROUND CHARACTERISTICS AND RACE

As we saw before, place of birth and educational achievement determine the resources urban women have at their disposal on which to build support systems in marriage as well as in widowhood. By these criteria, black widows have fewer resources to draw on for support systems and networks than have their white counterparts. One advantage they have is their and their parents' American birth, although they are less urban and Chicago-based than are the whites. Over half of the white segment of the widows' population is apt to have a foreign background, with the mother or father, or both, having been born outside the United States. Only about a fifth of the white widows are second-generation Chicagoans, with a quarter having been born in another state. By contrast, and it is important, none of the parents of the black widows were born in the Chicago area, although almost all of them were born in America but outside of Illinois. The differences in the size of the community in which the parents were born are less dramatic than this difference in distance from Chicago. There is a .38 gamma association between social race and location of place of birth in relation to Chicago for the mother and .50 for the father, but only .10 for the mother and .08 for the father when size of the community is being considered. Thus, although most of the parents were born outside of metropolitan Chicago, in much smaller communities or even in rural or village areas, the parents of blacks are more apt to have been born in the United States, although not in Illinois, while the parents of whites are likely to have been born outside of the country. The history of the urbanization process in America is reflected in these figures and the history of the family in the life patterns of the widows.

271

When it comes to the widow herself, we find that the white women are much more likely to be Chicago-born and to have married Chicago-born husbands, both the man who left them widowed and the man who they married subsequently in cases of remarriage. Only one-fifth of the white women are themselves foreign born, although a larger proportion of the late husbands were born outside the United States. The women of the black community and their husband(s) are not apt to have been born in the Chicago area, most of them having come here from another state. Interestingly, the few black women who have remarried, frequently chose a man from another country, often from the Caribbean area. Thus, their personal background is very unlike that of the white women in terms of a history of familiarity with, and involvement in, the Chicago metropolitan area. Half of the white women, as compared to only 12 percent of the blacks, were born in large cities, but the blacks were disproportionally likely to marry men of urban birth, while the whites married men less likely than they to be born in smaller communities. One-fifth of the black widows were born on a farm and another 15 percent in village communities, for a total of one-third. An additional 28 percent were born in small towns. Thus, a total of 64 percent of the black women, and 55 percent of the late husbands came from communities no larger than a small town. Only 36 percent of the white women were born in small towns or rural areas, and 40 percent of their late husbands were born outside of cities.

The educational level of the parents of the Chicago area widows reflects their place of birth, and the percentages are not very different for the whites than for the blacks, mainly due to the time and place of their birth. There is one important difference between the educational background of the two social races. When we compare the total numbers from which the percentages are computed for the parents with the totals for the widows, we find that the black figures for the father come from only 37 percent of the daughter, while the white figures are based on 52 percent of the daughters. There is thus a large proportion of black women who do not know or refuse to give the number of years their fathers, and to a lesser extent their mothers, attended school. We must assume, as we did before, that the parents of women who do not know the schooling completed by them were relatively uneducated.

Although the education of the mother and the father, when known by the daughter, are quite similar, the two social races are very different in the level of schooling the widows and their husbands achieved. Only 17 percent of the black widows completed high school compared to 29 percent of the whites, and only eight percent of the blacks, compared to 15 percent of the whites, went beyond that. Forty-eight percent of the blacks, compared to 37 percent of the whites, never went beyond grade school. The tendency of the black community to send girls further in school than boys, because of the whole employment discrimination situation, while the white community favored the boys, is reflected in the differences in the educational achievement of the late husband. One-quarter of the white men had gone beyond high school, compared to six percent of the black men and these figures have different relations to those for the women when each race is compared. Fifty-two percent of the black men, compared to only 39 percent of the white men got no further than grade school. This reflects the national scene.

Thus, although the white and the nonwhite widows came from different backgrounds, with the nonwhites generally disadvantaged in terms of personal foundations for support networks, there are many hypotheses floating around in sociological circles that would lead to an expectation of greater social integration and fuller support systems among blacks. After all, families in the black community are portrayed as matrifocal and mutually supportive out of necessity and because of the presence of a supportive community (Moynihan, 1965; Billingsley, 1968; Bernard, 1973; Jackson, 1973). The extended family is reportedly more apt to share residences and less apt to isolate elderly women than is allegedly true of the white urban families (Staples, 1971; Jackson, 1973).

To test these ideas, let us look at the life-styles of the women in marriage and in widowhood and then at social integration by race.

LIFE-STYLES IN MARRIAGE, WIDOWHOOD AND RACE

Generally speaking, the life-styles of the black and white women are much more similar in widowhood than they had been in marriage, mainly because of changes in the economic situation of the white women. This situation exists despite the differences in the age distributions at marriage of the two races. More of the nonwhites than whites in our study married very young, and more of them married and divorced before entering the marriage that left them widows. They were much less apt to be living in a home rather than in a apartment the year before the late husband's fatal illness or accident, than were the whites (44 to 71 percent, respectively; gamma = .53), but the association between race and housing is less dramatic for the "now" time period (gamma = .26). There is no significant difference, however, in the size of the unit they were or are currently occupying (gamma = .11 and gamma = .13, respectively). Although twice as high a percentage of the blacks than whites define themselves as heads of the household before the husband's illness, the percentages are small (15 and seven percent, respectively; gamma = .20). The vast majority of respondents list the late husband as having been the head of the household, thereby negating much of the largely lower-class-focused literature on blacks. Most women of both races have now taken over as heads of their own household, and the differences between the races are almost nonexistent (80 and 79 percent, respectively). Again, this similarity goes against expectations. The age distributions within the two subsamples are apparent, however, when we examine the size of this household at both time periods. A much higher proportion of whites than blacks were living in two-person households before the husband's death (44 and 26 percent, respectively) and are now living alone (47 and 22 percent). By contrast, the blacks were and are much more likely to be in households containing five or more people (42 and 19 percent before, 21 and nine percent now), although the husband's death and other factors have caused a decrease of size in most homes. Since most of the people living with the widows are unmarried offspring, the numbers involved help explain the economic plight of many black women. At the same time, the residential composition provides more support resources to the blacks than to the whites.

Although we found race to be an important variable affecting income of the widows at the present time, the drop caused by the death of the husband was even more severe for the whites than for the blacks, many of whom were already living below or near poverty levels. Although only 27 percent of the whites, compared to 52 percent of the blacks, were living on less than $5,000 before the death, the percentages change to 52 for the whites and 60 for the blacks in 1973. In view of the inflationary trend and the mean length of widowhood of our sample of just over 10 years, the decrease is severe, placing many white women close to the disadvantaged black women. The additional people living in the households of black wives before the husband's death were far more likely to be con-sumers rather than earners of income. The black family was much more restricted than the white family in the sources from which it was drawing its income when the husband was well (see Chapter 9). At the same time, there is a similarity of several income sources and levels of contribution that ne-gates many current assumptions about differences between black and white families. For example, there is little difference between them in the proportion accounted for by children's wages. Also, only nine percent more of the white than of black wives contributed wages to the family incomes. The same difference exists in the proportion of white and black husbands who were able to earn at least some part of the family income. Pensions were an insignificant portion of the income of both types of families, and all but one percent of either could not depend on that source at all. The differences, mainly explainable in age and occupational distribution terms, lie in the proportions of families in the two communities who could gain from social security and who had to depend on welfare. A quarter of the white families were able to draw on the husband's social security the year prior to his fatal illness while only 16 percent of the black families were able to rely on that source. Only one percent of the white families, but 16 percent of the blacks, had to use welfare to maintain themselves at that time. In sum, the income came from the husband's earnings for a total of 70 percent of the white and 60 percent of the black families, with 30 percent of the white and 39 percent of the black women contributing their own wages. (Details of the current economic situation of the two social races are available in Chapter 9.)

The occupational differences between white and the nonwhite husbands were even greater than the educational ones, reflecting the social structure of American society. The pattern is similar to that of the women in that a much higher proportion of whites than blacks held professional, other white-collar, and crafts jobs, which helps to explain the difference in family income prior to the husband's death. Overall, the man's income helped make the white family's economic life better than the black's and its loss accounts for the drop in family income in widowhood.

There are no statistically significant differences in the cause of death of the late husband by social race, but there are interesting substantive differences. The black men were more apt to die violently from accidents or homicides (15 to five percent), while more whites suffered heart attacks (53 to 40 percent), a reflection not only of age but the reality of life in the two communities. Only 28 percent of the total accident cases were job-connected, but 39 percent of the blacks' accidental deaths happened on the job, compared to only 23 percent of the whites. These figures reflect the difference in the types of jobs held by black and white men. There is a relationship between the length of illness that caused the death of the husband and social race (gamma = .20), with more whites than blacks dying suddenly, due to the frequency of heart attacks. Those blacks who did not die a violent death tended to have protracted illnesses.

Although the white women suffered a greater loss of income with widowhood than did the blacks, they have been able to continue to live in, or move to, neighborhoods that the interviewers rated as superior to those of the blacks. The University of Illinois interviewers, generally of the same race as the respondents, varied considerably in their evaluation of dwellings and neighborhoods. Black homes were less apt than the white to be judged as neat rather than messy (gamma = .34), clean rather than dirty (gamma = .40), rich rather than poor (gamma = .54) and relaxed rather than tense (gamma = .23). There is also a strong association between social race and the evaluation of the block in which the dwelling is located as having poorly rather than well-kept buildings (gamma = .47), littered rather than clean streets (gamma = .62), poor rather than rich appearance (gamma = .58), apartments rather than single-family dwellings (gamma = .28), crowded rather than open space (gamma = .22), commercial or industrial rather than residential buildings (gamma = .16). Given the relative recent movement of nonwhites to Chicago, the overcrowding produced by this migration, lower income and discrimination in housing, these findings are not surprising.

SOCIAL INTEGRATION, SUPPORT SYSTEMS AND RACE

There is a significant difference between the two social races in the number of friends each listed as having been close the year prior to the late husband's fatal illness or accident, the whites being more apt to claim friendships than the nonwhites. The difference diminishes considerably with regard to new friends, that is, those made since widowhood, largely due to the fact that whites generally have not made new friends rather than to an increase in the number of friends among the blacks.

Another interesting difference that emerges in other statistical analyses is that education has a positive effect on the number of friends listed by whites for the time prior to widowhood, but a negative effect on the blacks. The higher the education of the white women, the more friends are listed, with the widow with less than an eighth-grade education likely to claim no close friendships whatsoever (gamma = .25). Among the blacks, however, the women who did not complete eight years of schooling list the largest number of friends, while those who graduated grade school or had some high-school education more frequently spoke of a lack of friends (gamma = −20).

One way we can contrast the social integration of widows of the two social races is by averaging the frequency of social contact and involvement of people in the support systems encompassing the contacts. Thus, when a woman lists a child, sibling, old friend, new friend or boyfriend, or indicates attendance at a club meeting or religious service, we asked how often she saw that person or engaged in that activity. These are averaged out in Table 16 and given with the percentages upon which the mean is based. Mean contact with children is computed only for offspring living away from home, and mean contact with other people only for women who have such associates. The mean frequencies are based on the code indicated at the bottom of the table. We also calculated the mean frequency with which the widows are involved in exchanges or supports each time they say that they are so engaged.

With the exception of siblings, boyfriends, and church attendance, black women generally have fewer resources on which to draw for social contact, as evidenced by the per-

278

centages upon which the means are based. It must be kept in mind, however, that these women are younger and that they have more children living at home. Although the non-white widows have fewer contributors to their supports, they are in more frequent contact with those they have than are the whites (Table 16). Two patterns seem to emerge. One is a possible polarization of widows in the black community between those who are relatively isolated and those who maintain relatively close contact with their associates. The second

TABLE 16

Mean Frequency of Contact with Significant Others, Mean Frequency of Attendance at Organizational Meetings and Church Services by Widows Who Have Such Resources, and Mean Frequency of Use of Supports, by All the Widows, Computed for Whites and Nonwhites

Sources of Contact	WHITE		NONWHITE	
	$\bar{x}$ Frequency[a]	% with	$\bar{x}$ Frequency[a]	% with
Sources of Contact:				
Children[b]	5.89	77	6.23	64
Siblings	4.41	80	4.46	86
Old friends—seen before	6.77	79	6.80	64
Old friends—seen now	4.86	74	5.47	61
New friends	6.75	47	7.48	43
Boyfriends	7.12	20	7.18	34
Organization meetings	4.86	49	5.81	44
Religious services	5.38	98	5.80	100
Support Systems:				
Economic—in	1.12		1.10	
Economic—out	1.11		1.03	
Service—in	2.35		1.98	
Service—out	1.56		1.35	
Social	3.52		2.93	

[a]Code: 1 = Never; 2 = less than once a year; 3 = once a year; 4 = several times a year; 5 = once a month; 6 = several times a month; 7 = once a week; 8 = several times a week.
[b]Only for people actually listed by each woman, thus, no mean for children living at home; widows with no living children or with all children in the home not included.

279

is the possibility that many of the blacks have a smaller circle of associates, a more intensive relation and a greater dependence on fewer people.

The relatively frequent contact with significant others among the blacks (although the numbers are not dramatic in either group) does not translate itself into greater involvement in financial, service or social support systems. The whites show a higher average frequency of exchanges of supports than the nonwhites simply because the later often do not engage in such interaction. This means that the tendency for fewer women having more intensive contacts with a few others does not average out as greater involvement for the group than in the case of more women being involved in more supports with a greater number of people. A detailed examination of the support systems will bear this out. Whites go to public places as frequently as nonwhites (49 and 47 percent, respectively) and celebrate holidays (91 and 85 percent). The blacks are more apt to go to church (86 and 74 percent, respectively), but the whites are more active in all the other social supports, such as visiting (82 and 66 percent), entertaining (61 and 46 percent) and out-of-town travel (61 and 46 percent). They do not often list other activities. There may be many reasons, financial or cultural, for the differences, but the fact remains that some of the social supports tying urban Americans into a network involve fewer blacks than whites.

A comparison of contributors to the support systems of black and white widows finds them different in only some supports. Black women tend to have a more restricted variety of people and groups than have their white counterparts (see Table 18). As noted before, financial supports do not involve many people, and the blacks, despite their greater financial needs, exchange them with fewer others than do the whites. Only 16 out of the remaining 53 supports show a significant difference between the races in the people whom they involve. A basic difference is immediately apparent; the relatively infrequent mention of the late husband in four emotional supports. This distribution supports the prior conclusion that there appears to be a difference in the way in which blacks and whites remember their marriage. Among the blacks, the late husband is less often recalled as providing the basic emotional supports, being less often listed first as the person the wife felt closest to and whom she most enjoyed being with. He is less apt to have provided her with feelings of importance and acceptance. Moreover, the white widows are now much more apt than are the blacks to derive their feelings of independence, self-sufficiency and security from themselves, although there were no significant differences between them before the husband's illness.

The only reason the present husband and/or boyfriends appear as providers of car care relatively frequently is because so few women list such care, but the blacks receive this service more often than do the whites. There are also some basic differences in the appearance of children in the support systems of these women, partially due to the ages of the offspring. Thus, white women are generally more apt to receive sick care than are the blacks, but the blacks are much more likely than are the whites to get it from their children. Blacks depend more on siblings, parents and friends for care during illness, which again reflects age differences and the limitations of the support network. Parents and friends are also useful to the blacks in providing legal aid, while the whites get it and help in decision making from their children. The latter support also is more often rendered by the white widows than the blacks to their children, while the blacks involve more friends.

There is little difference among the people whom the two groups list as contributors to most social activities. As stated earlier, the main difference in the emotional supports of the "before" period is in the greater variety of persons listed by blacks as contributive to feelings of closeness, enjoyment, being important and accepted, because the whites concentrated so heavily on the late husband as the main contributor. The "now" time period finds the whites much more dependent

TABLE 17

First Listing of the Contributions of Others to the Support Systems of Chicago Area Widows, by Social Race When Difference Is Significant[a]

Support Systems	Self[b] W	NW	Present Husband W	NW	Children W	NW	Siblings W	NW	Other Relatives W	NW	Friends W	NW	Others W	NW	No One[b] W	NW	Gamma
Service Supports:																	
Car care (in)			12	22	51	33	4	0	5	11	7	16	0	0			−.35
Sick care (in)			4	3	69	49	8	15	5	2	5	19	7	4			.31
Decisions (in)			8	6	69	59	9	21	6	2	2	8	2	8			.20
Legal aid (in)			2	0	19	6	9	0	11	3	3	23	55	65			.30
Sick care (out)			1	3	31	54	10	8	13	16	19	5	5	8			−.22
Decisions (out)			3	4	42	20	12	5	8	2	24	54	5	0			.20
Social Supports:																	
Lunch	1	10	2	2	19	18	6	9	5	1	50	42	14	11			−.23
Games	3	2	3	2	10	20	2	7	8	2	57	66	12	1			−.20

TABLE 17 (cont.)

Emotional Supports:

Before:																	
close	0	0	0	0	16	16	5	8	2	4	4	9	0	3	0	2	.33
enjoy	0	0	0	0	10	14	1	5	3	8	3	5	2	3	0	4	.42
important	2	3	0	0	8	14	1	1	1	3	3	5	1	1	7	11	.27
accepted	6	3	0	0	7	10	0	1	7	2	8	5	10	14	3	13	.24
Now:																	
close	1	2	3	2	68	45	10	14	5	6	6	14	1	4	2	4	.34
independent	63	45	2	2	11	22	2	3	2	0	1	3	4	7	13	15	.25
self-sufficient	65	44	2	2	12	24	3	2	2	5	2	5	4	3	9	13	.30
secure	43	27	5	3	27	28	2	3	1	3	2	7	8	11	10	13	.26

[a]W = white; NW = nonwhite.
[b]Because of the formulation of the question "the self" and "no one" could not appear in the service supports and "no one" could not appear in the social supports.

283

on their children than are the blacks for the feeling of closeness. The nonwhites, on the other hand, gain feelings of independence and self-sufficiency from their children twice as much as do the whites. All in all, the strongest difference between the two races is the feeling of enjoyment of company while the husband was living.

There also appears to be a difference in the significance of religion and church participation between the two groups. The blacks are more frequently members of a specific congregation (gamma = .25) and more active participants. In addition, black widows are much more willing to assign the role of member of a religious group a higher rank in the list of nine roles than are the whites (gamma = .47). That is, 15 percent of the whites and 43 percent of the blacks placed the role of "member of a religious group" within the top four locations in the rank order of importance.

SUMMARY OF RACE AS RESOURCE

There are both similarities and differences in the backgrounds and life-styles of black and white Chicago area widows. The black widows in our sample, who do not fully represent all such women in the Chicago metropolitan area because the basic list was drawn from old, as well as current records of social security, and because of problems in locating and interviewing them, are generally younger than their white counterparts. They have more children, and more of these offspring are living at home. They married younger or were in a second marriage at the time of widowhood. Their age at widowhood was younger. Although the educational background of their parents was not very different from that of the white widows, because both groups came from non-urban areas in the American South or from another country, the education of black women (especially of their husbands) and their occupations were inferior (see Chapter 9).

The black widows are involved in less supports, with fewer people, than are their white counterparts, but they have more intensive contacts with significant persons in their lives. Fewer people are involved in their economic and service support systems and they participate in fewer social activities. Most of their voluntary association membership is in religious groups and religion in general seems to be of a different level and perhaps quality of involvement. A major difference between the two groups appears to be in relations with men currently and in the memory-reconstructed past, since fewer blacks feel as compelled to sanctify their late husband to the extent that the whites do.

All in all, in spite of differences in background and in the community in which they live, the black and white widows are not as different as some of the literature would lead us to expect. A major reason for this is the drop in income and other resources of white women with the death of their husband and with increasing age. This pushes them closer to the disadvantaged blacks, although the latter are younger. However, the past and present disadvantages have taken their toll in life satisfaction. When asked for degree of agreement with the following statement, "I am very satisfied with the way my life is going now" in the self-administered part of the interview, fewer blacks than whites strongly agree (42 and 25 percent). However, things are not too bad in the opinion of others, since only 27 percent, as compared with 21 of the whites, disagree with this rather strong statement of life satisfaction.

Education as Resource

The main thesis of this book is that family background in urban living, generally leading to better formal schooling, is the necessary precondition to voluntaristic engagement in a modern urbanized society.

Not surprisingly, the main background characteristics of the widows that contribute to their educational achievement are the place of birth of the parents and their education, as well as their birth place. The association between the place of birth of the mother in relation to Chicago and the education of the daughter is relatively strong (gamma= $-.33$) and of the father is somewhat weaker (gamma= $-.29$). Thirty-four percent of the women with no schooling had mothers who were born outside of Illinois and 66 percent who were born in another country. Almost identical distributions are present for the widows with less than an eighth grade education who form 18 percent of the sample and the grade school finishers, who form 19 percent of the sample. The higher the education, the more apt is the mother to have been born in Chicago but a disproportionate percent of the educated who went beyond college came from homes in which the mother was born in another state. Half of the widows whose mothers were foreign-born did not get beyond eighth grade, compared to 12 percent of those born in metropolitan Chicago. Distance from Chicago is not the sole factor; the size of the community also plays a role. The larger the mother's community where she was born, the more likely that the daughter continued in school beyond the minimum of grade school (gamma=.24). The effect of the mother's place of birth on her daughter's education is actually indirect, because it affected the mother's education and this affects the daughter's place of birth and thus the daughter's educational achievement.

The association between the mother's years of schooling and that of her daughter is even stronger than was the place of the mother's birth (gamma=.54). The association, however, is based only on cases in which the years of schooling of the mothers are known to the daughters, which is true of only 53 percent of the total number of widows represented by our sample. It is logical to assume, as stated before, that the mothers whose amount of schooling is not known to the daughters are probably not highly educated. Generally speaking, the widows tend to be better educated than their mothers. For example, 83 percent of the daughters who did not finish grade school had mothers with so minimal an education and although few daughters went beyond high school, those that did, and know their mother's education, come from much more varied homes than do the least educated. Some of the daughters failed to get the same amount of schooling as the mother, but the trend is to finish at least one higher level of education.

There is a strong association between the graduation diploma or degree earned by the father, when known, and that of the daughter (gamma=.61). Two tendencies are evident in the distributions of degrees. One is a parallel in the educational levels of the father and daughter. The fathers of nine out of 10 daughters with no diploma or degree were similarly uneducated while the fathers of six out of ten high-school finishers also were high-school graduates. There is, secondly, a general tendency for the daughters of the less educated men to surpass the father, while the daughters of the more educated often fall below.

The supposition that women born in the Chicago area are apt to be better educated than women of other backgrounds is generally supported (gamma= −27). Those with less than eight grades of schooling are most apt to have been born outside of Illinois, and even outside of the United States. Few of the women born in another country ever went beyond high school. In addition, very few of the widows who were born on a farm or in other rural areas went beyond grade school, while the women born in a large city are overrepresented among those who achieved additional schooling (gamma=.25 between size of place of birth and education).

The final set of evidence on the effect of background on the lives of wives and later widows, relates to the husband's education and occupation. There is a definite although not a perfect match between the education achievement of the wife and of the late husband (gamma=.65). Men in American society can and do marry below in status, that is, they marry women of a lower educational or socio-economic background. This tendency is true of many marriages of the Chicago area widows. Six in 10 of the widows with a college education or better married men of similar standing, while only three in 10 men with college degrees married women of similar education, over a quarter marrying college dropouts and an even larger proportion women who had not gone beyond high school. The strength of the association between the educational achievements of wives and husbands is apparent at the extremes, with no college-educated woman marrying a man whose schooling she did not know, and no man who finished high school or went beyond that level marrying a woman without any schooling. The women's educational efforts translate themselves quite well into the prestige level of their husbands' occupations, naturally linked to their education. Few women who obtained more than a high-school education are apt to have married craftsmen or anyone in a lower occupation. Five percent of grade-school drop-outs but 35 percent with 13 years of schooling or more married professionals. There is a relatively strong association (gamma=.34) between the level of the wife's education and the probability that the husband was working full-time at his usual job when he died, mainly a function of age.

In examining the relationship between the woman's education and her occupation, we found that it did not translate itself into job prestige as effectively as the husband's, mainly because of her work history and the ineffectiveness of job-search procedures.

SOCIAL INTEGRATION, SUPPORT SYSTEMS AND EDUCATION

There are definite and positive associations between the number of years of a woman's schooling and her social integration in widowhood, as measured by membership in voluntary associations, participation in social activities and the number and involvement of friends in the support systems. The evidence is quite strong but there are some interesting internal variations. Thus, 64 percent of women with one through seven years of schooling, compared to 34 percent with at least some college education belong to no voluntary associations. Single memberships do not vary as highly by schooling but multiple memberships go from 14 percent for the grade-school dropouts steadily up to 52 percent for the college finishers, with high-school finishers represented by 32 percent. Table 18 summarizing social integration data also contains important information as to the combined influence of age and education on social supports. Thus, schooling affects

TABLE 18

Associations Between Educational Achievements of Chicago Area Widows as Well as Percentages of Women at the Two Extremes of Schooling and Involvement in the Social Systems, a Religious Congregation and Employment, by Beneficiary Status

Social Supports	RETIREMENT WIDOWS			OTHER WIDOWS		
	Gamma	Percent Less Than 8	Percent 13 or Over	Gamma	Percent Less Than 8	Percent 13 or Over
Public places	.51	15	65	.38	25	81
Visiting	.19	71	80	.22	66	86
Entertaining	.45	33	65	.35	37	79
Eating lunch with	.49	30	75	.27	27	73
Play games	.30	28	60	.26	25	58
Travel	.45	35	85	.39	34	78
Celebrate holidays	.68	79	95	.23	81	95
Member of congregation	.10	90	80	.21	74	78
Current employment	.15	8	15	.32	26	69

the elderly women in their social engagement even more than it does the younger widows, especially at the extreme ends of the educational ladder. The internal variations among the supports reflect age, historical generation and education. The influence of education on the social involvement of the older women is particularly evident in the activities of going to public places, entertaining, sharing lunch, traveling out of town and celebrating holidays. These activities involve different proportions of the women, while the gap between the two educational extremes is smaller in visiting, membership of a congregation and in employment. Visiting is relatively frequent among the less-schooled women, although the most educated outdo them here as in all other activities that are part of the social support system. More uneducated than highly educated women belong to religious congregations. The contrasts are less extreme among the other widows, as evidenced by the gammas, with the exception of the influence of education on current employment. More of the elderly than the younger, least-educated widows list visiting and sharing lunch, playing games and traveling, but the differences are not as great as among the educational extreme categories.

The same conclusions can be drawn from Table 19. The presence of friends as resources and as contributors to the support systems is influenced by education, and the association is stronger for the elderly than for the younger widows in all but the self-feelings in the "before" time period. Friends, as mentioned before, are most apt to appear in the social supports, but even here over half of the least educated elderly women do not list them. The more educated of the two groups are similar in the infrequency of involvement of friends in the emotional support systems, but they make more use of friendships here than do the uneducated of both age categories. The most apt to have positive self-feelings at the present time is the younger educated woman who also lists new friends and involves them in the social support system.

TABLE 19

Associations Between Educational Achievements of Chicago Area Widows as Well as Percentages of Women at the Two Extremes of Schooling, the Percentages Lacking Friends and Not Listing Friends in the Support Systems, by Age

Support Systems	RETIREMENT WIDOWS			OTHER WIDOWS		
	Gamma	Percent Less Than 8	Percent 13 or Over	Gamma	Percent Less Than 8	Percent 13 or Over
Old friends (before)	.26	35	15	.24	28	7
New friends (since)	.21	71	50	.12	51	37
Emotional supports (before)	.35	94	65	.17	87	64
Emotional supports (now)	.27	81	57	.22	79	53
Self-feeling supports (before)	.19	88	5	.19	89	68
Self-feeling supports (now)	.26	81	70	.24	87	56
Service supports (in)	.14	92	90	.07	84	81
Service supports (out)	.38	92	80	.17	85	74
Social supports	.35	58	35	.28	45	11

When we look at the influence of education on the contributors to the support systems, we find the high-school graduates are the most apt to list the present husband as a contributor to the service, emotional and social supports. Of course, they are the most likely to be remarried. They are also inclined to mention boyfriends as providers of service and social supports, although they are outnumbered by those in the lower educational category in involving such men in their feeling states as receivers. The least-educated women are much more dependent on their children in the service supports than are the more educated, who are more often the providers of all of the services. The trend is definite and significant, accentuating the importance of the combination of age and education. The widows without skills in personal voluntaristic engagement or financial resources must depend on children for their services, while the more educated make more frequent use of a variety of people including siblings and other persons or groups, including professionals, service personnel and co-workers. Women at the two extremes of educational achieve-ment are the most apt to carry on social activities by them-selves, though these are often different undertakings. The least educated most often go to church alone; the most edu-cated go to church and travel alone. Interestingly enough, the most educated socialize with children more often than any of the other categories. On the other hand, the most educated do not meet as often with other relatives such as grandchildren as do the middle-schooled women. The use of friends in the social support system by the different educational categories shows the most significant, almost monotonic variations. Ex-cepting the fact that the college dropouts mention friends less often than those who finished grade school, higher education is strongly reflected in more frequent contact with friends.

The emotional support systems become even more complex when examined by educational categories. The self appears most often in the current feeling states of the most highly educated women, indicating great independence, but the other groups also register high. The high-school graduates were most apt to list the late husband as a past support. It is the least educated who mention him least often. The higher the educational achievement, the greater the wife's former emotional dependence upon her husband, while the less ed-ucated depended on their children almost as much as on their husband. The more educated women diffused the sources of their emotional supports after the death of the husband, not depending as heavily on their children and increasing their

involvement with friends. other people outside the family circle and their family of orientation. Of course, more members
of this last unit are available to them than to the less educated
women. There is a strong difference among educational groups
in the use of "other people and groups" as providers of feelings
of self-importance in the current period. In sum, the general
pattern is that of a strong dependence of the more educated
women on the late husband for emotional support and an
increase in the contributions of the self, friends and other
people after his death.

Summary

A major problem of widowhood, particularly in America since
marriage is so heavily embedded in a woman's life space, is not
just the loss of the husband but also the effect this has on
other social roles and relations. There are strong age, role
complex, racial and educational differences in the degree to
which wives depend on their husband as a supplier of social
and emotional supports and in how they change the system
once he is removed as a result of divorce, separation or death.
Some women were very independent and self-sufficient in
marriage and continue so in widowhood. Others find replacements for the late husband, in the form of another man, children, friends and so forth. There are many Chicago area
women who never were involved in a variety of social activities
and emotionally significant interaction that sociological literature and pretests found typical of American women, so that
the death of the husband does not change their life to a no-
ticeable extent, while others were active, not involving the
man in the network. Some women increase their dependence
on themselves, going to church or traveling alone and being
their own providers of positive self-feelings. The most desolate
are the widows who feel they have "no one" to turn to for
pleasurable and meaningful relations. Finally, some women

report that they now are able to engage in social activities and emotional supports that were not possible prior to widowhood.

The psychiatrists dealing with the grief work of widows have emphasized the importance of identity reconstruction from being a married to being a partnerless person (Linde-mann, 1944; Maddison and Walker, 1967; Glick, Weiss and Parkes, 1974). Many of the Chicago area widows fail to achieve this goal; they remain "the widow of" or substitute other people for the late husband as sources of identity and other emotional supports. Some of the women whom we inter-viewed had turned to themselves as suppliers of emotional supports even while the husband was alive and well, or at least before his final illness, and some only in widowhood. The use of the self as the source of feelings of independence and self-sufficiency, even security, can have two bases, and it is sometimes difficult to determine in an interview which is the appropriate designation. Many of the widows define dependence on the self for those feelings in a positive way, presenting a satisfied self- and life image, while others appear somewhat bitter over having to draw upon themselves for these feelings of self-esteem; they would prefer to depend on others for them. There are also two categories of women who do not designate themselves in response to the emotional support questions. One of these depends on other people, with varying degrees of satisfaction. The other are women who respond to these questions with "no one". These, too, can be divided into those who feel no need for such a support and those who wish they were involved in a relation providing it.

The significance of the self as supplier of identities and self-feelings needs greater focusing than possible in this study; this significance appears clearly, if in blurred forms, in the re-sponses to a variety of questions by different widows.

In addition to self-perceptions, -feelings and -evaluations, each widow can draw upon such characteristics as age at wid-owhood, current age, race and education as resources for building unique support systems and networks. Women widowed early in life usually have parents and siblings to fall back upon, and, once the period of grief is over, they can often find boyfriends who provide social supports or even a new husband who functions as part of the household. Both widowhood and increased age can bring greater self-confidence or self-reliance to such women, in that they are better able to develop important self-feelings of independence, self-sufficiency and security—feelings for which they relied on others when they were young wives, at least in memory. The younger women, with the exception of the very young, tend to be more educated; age tends to be negatively related and education positively, to complexity of the support systems. That is, the old and uneducated women tend to operate in a flat social life space, belonging to no voluntary associations if they are not members of a congregation, having few friends and involving few people in their support systems. Younger women engage in more social activities with more people, particularly if they have more than a grade-school education. The most active are women in their forties and fifties, though increased age brings forth an increase of service supports among the poorer widows, that is, those living on less than $6,000 a year. The pattern varies considerably among the very wealthy in several of the service supports, with the middle category of women with between $6,000 and $10,000 reversing the trend of the poorer.

The elderly, but particularly the uneducated elderly, tend to have been born outside of metropolitan Chicago, the blacks in the southern United States, the whites outside of the country. The blacks are younger and were widowed younger, unless theirs was a second marriage. In widowhood the white women tended to suffer a drop of income and constriction of social life more than did the blacks, bringing them closer to the nonwhites than they have been when the husband was still living. The blacks, not surprisingly, were dependent upon a more restricted set of sources of income than were the whites the year prior to the husband's fatal illness or accident. The combination of life circumstances of the blacks makes them less apt to be satisfied with their lives than are the whites.

Predictably, education bears directly on the social engagement and support systems of the urban widows, affecting the elderly even more than the younger women. The amount of schooling of a woman is influenced not only by her place of birth, but also by that of her parents, in terms of distance from Chicago and size of community. It is also influenced by the schooling of the parents, as measured by the number of years and by the diploma or degree earned. The achievement of the widow is reflected in the schooling of the man she chooses to marry and thus in his occupation and their income. All these variables affect the social engagement of the woman in marriage and widowhood, as evidenced by the number of friends and voluntary organizations, her involvement in social activities and the complexity of her support system. Less educated women tend to be highly dependent upon their offspring and to have a restricted social life. Because of the association between age and education we can predict that future generations of widows whose late husbands were not the victims of unusual disasters, will be able to maintain a wider social life and more complex support systems than do many of the elderly widows currently living in the Chicago metropolitan area.

NOTES

1. Throughout the discussion, it is important for the reader to keep the limitations of our sample in mind. The widows under analysis are women who were located and interviewed because they are currently or were until recently beneficiaries of social security. This eliminates all women whose husband had not worked long enough in an occupation covered by the social security system to earn the necessary insurance credit. The second limitation on the sample is imposed by the use of names and addresses of former beneficiaries who were terminated as long ago as 1968. The sample list was about a year old by the time the interviews

were conducted. Both of these factors eliminate women who have moved out of the area and left no forwarding address, those who moved often or so many years ago they could not be traced. Finally, as in all such surveys, the subject had to consent to the interview. This eliminated women too suspicious of this type of interaction or those "protected" by relatives. Consequently, widows represented in this study do not reflect the universe of widows in the metropolitan Chicago area, and the black widows are undoubtedly less represented than the whites. There is little doubt that the most disadvantaged urban black widow, the one whose husband's work lay outside the mainstream of the labor force, who is the poorest and the least integrated in the social system, who moves often and is highly suspicious of her environment and of middle-class interviewers, even black ones, is absent from this as from other population surveys. The same comments apply, of course, to nonblack widows, particularly the foreign-born and those marginal to the society for other reasons, but there are proportionately fewer of them in the Chicago area at the present time than blacks, because of the recency of the black migration to the city. The Mexican and Puerto Rican widows are also apt to be greatly underrepresented. Absent also are the white and black widows of federal employees, for they are covered by a different insurance system. Because the government has stringent controls to prevent discriminatory practices, proportionately more black employees than whites are likely to be missing from this study. Thus the widows in our study are apt to underrepresent the widows of both the most disadvantaged and of the relatively stable and well-off federal employees of the black community.

2. Most of the comments and statistics dealing with nonwhite widows are limited to blacks, who total 10,877 in the weighted sample, with an additional 939 women of Spanish, 59 of Asian and 47 of American Indian backgrounds.

N I N E

Supports from the Economic Institution

The support systems and networks of widows are strongly influenced by the relation between the societal family and economic institutions. To understand the uniqueness of this relation in urban America, we need to view its development historically, although not in detail. As Aries (1965) concluded from his study of pre-18th-century Western Europe, and as other social scientists discovered from looking at other times and places, the modern focus upon the nuclear family as a relatively isolated, economically self-maintaining, inwardly and privacy-oriented social unit is a unique occurrence. The basic social unit has generally been the household, containing a variety of maritally or biologically related and even unrelated members, the compound of several units cooperatively bound together or other systems of people in mutually interdependent social roles (Laslett, 1973; Laslett and Wall, 1972). Members' lives were public, with extended boundaries to others in the village, manor home or city house.

Women and Work

HISTORICAL TRENDS

Looking at the transitional stages of social change from medieval Western Europe to the capitalistic and industrializing societies that emerged there and in America, we find all physically able members of the basic social unit engaged in mutually interdependent sets of economic activities. Industrialization gradually removed tools and methods of production from the home or the small compound of workers to an increasingly large central location. As the pace of industrialization and urbanization increased, more and more households left the farms, (relatively self-sufficient economic units) and moved into urban complexes where they could maintain themselves only through the wages of employed members. As societies developed in this direction, ownership, management, work and consumption became increasingly segregated from each other. Although household members were originally often employed by the same organization as in company towns, they tended to work in functionally differentiated areas. The mushrooming of more than one major employing organization in the same locale brought with it the separation of members of the basic social units from each other during work hours. Aries traces the emergence in Western Europe of the family as a self-conscious and "privatized" or privacy-desirous social unit, separated from nonmembers and the larger society by definition and physical boundaries, to this early period of capitalistic and industrial development. This self-identified family shrank in size as the husband-wife-children unit cut its ties of economic dependency on the male family line with the help of new opportunities for self-support (Goode, 1963). This economic independence was accompanied by a decrease in the availability of the extended family for other social supports.

Changes in the family structure and interdependence of members were accompanied by ideological shifts. According to Aries and Shorter, prior to the 18th century, parents shied away from deep emotional ties to infants because of the high infant mortality rate; the surviving young children were viewed as miniature adults. They were acknowledged as members of the family usually only after they became contributors to its economic welfare (Thomas and Znaniecki, 1918–1920;

Lopata, 1976b). Until the 18th century the British sent their children between the ages of seven and 14 years to other people's homes to work and to be properly socialized (Oakley, 1974). Therefore, it is not surprising that both cottage industries and centralized factory employers utilized children as well as their mothers and fathers as part of the labor force (Shorter, 1975; Laslett, 1973). Reform movements, spurred on by writers, such as Charles Dickens in England and George Sand in France, protested the working conditions of children, and Western Europeans began slowly to develop a definition of childhood as a separate stage of life. With this change of perception came a new sense of parenthood, especially motherhood. Legislation removed children below a certain age from paid employment. Engels (1958) reported bands of such children roaming England. Public schooling, for greater numbers of children became more widespread not only to keep the children off the street but also in response to growing trends of nationalism and democratization. Capitalists supported kings in wars of centralization that broke the power of manor lords and freed the serfs, who left the land in even larger numbers and moved to the cities not only of their own country but also those of other nations in search of employment.

The rights of women to economic independence from their family of orientation or from their husbands, as well as rights of co-management of their property in Western Europe and America developed unevenly. During wars and crusades wives and mothers had to manage the farms, the manor homes with lands, the bakeries or other businesses (Oakley, 1974). Merchants traveled a great deal and their wives were often their business managers (Heilbronner, 1968). The biography, *The Merchant of Prato* (Origo, 1957), makes reference to exchanges of complex business information between husband and wife when he was away from home. Shorter (1975) reports that village women in France were among the first family members to become economically independent because of their work in cottage industries, with the result that many refused to marry the local men selected by their parents and flocked to cities for paying jobs. Unfortunately, Shorter fails to tell how these women were subsequently forced to give up their independence, but instead resorts to an "emergence of romanticism" explanation, implying voluntary submission. Aries (1965) also refers to the loss of women's rights to property management. Oakley (1974) documents that women could be found in many sectors of the British economy before the 1850s. But within a very short period they lost many rights, including membership in the guilds, their place in bisexual jobs, and control over women's occupations such as ale making and midwifery, and their rights to inherit or at least manage property in the absence or death of the husband [see also Laslett (1973)]. Oakley attributes this loss of economic independence to increased competition among men who had the political power to push women out.

Whatever the dynamics, the world of Western Europe, and especially of the newly emerging America, became very strictly divided into men's and women's spheres, with the women being assigned control over the home and related areas, while the men took over management of all public domains. Payment and other financial status rewards became the main measures of personal work worth, and these could be obtained only from employment in production or service organizations outside of the home. Paid domestic service gradually diminished in status, as did other benefits, and servants departed, leaving the housewife to this social unit, defined as economically nonproductive. The pressure to limit the woman, especially after she became a wife and mother, to the home and its related functions increased in strength in post-Colonial, Puritan America (Dulles, 1965). Cottage industries sprang up throughout the Connecticut Valley, and unmarried young women from surrounding areas came to the textile factories to work, living in closely supervised barracks. Once married, however, "good women" stayed home and cared for their families, unless their husband could not earn enough to support the family or unless they were upper-class and socialized into the role of charitable volunteer.

The restriction of the American woman to the role of housewife throughout her married life and the narrow definition of that role are somewhat difficult to understand in view of the contributions of the pioneer women and of the democratic foundation of the system. Various explanations have been offered, including the frontier image of the "macho male," freed from subservience to older family members and respect for the women whose cooperation was needed for survival. The peasant immigrants' image of women as easily tempted and as needing the social control of the family or village lacking in the "Wicked" city probably contributed to the attempt of the men to control women with laws and formal restrictions (Thomas and Znaniecki, 1918–1920; Lopata, 1976b, 1977; Dulles, 1965). The image of "true womanhood" was added to the idea that men could not understand women anyway (Gans, 1962), and further supported by the Puritan ethic (Dulles, 1965) and the *Freudian Ethic* (LaPierre, 1959). In spite of the suffrage movement of the 1920s, the restricted view of the "woman's sphere" reasserted itself in full strength in the post-World War II years, when women were again effectively pushed out of the labor force with the return of the veterans. Betty Friedan (1963) called the influences restricting the lives of women the "feminine mystique," and the publication of her book by that title appears to have spearheaded the trend toward an examination of the basic assumptions concerning the relation between the family and the rest of society, especially as it concerned women.

In the meantime, however, the restriction in the definition of work to paid employment and of a job as an occupational role within an employing organization, as far as the concepts of "earnings" and dependency are concerned, had some interesting consequences. These two concepts are of special significance in America because of the value placed on individualism, independence and "pioneer spirit" and the supposedly unlimited opportunity of earning a living through hard work. The image is, of course, masculine; the wife is shown, if at all, as the dependent helper of the man in his efforts to wrestle a livelihood from the land or the factory. The man is portrayed as invariably able to support his family, his wife and his young children, until the day he dies, leaving the survivors sufficiently well taken care of to see them through till the boys grow up and take over his economic function.

There are two types of people whom Americans define as dependents, meaning people dependent on someone else for their livelihood or economic survival: wives and children and people who for some reason cannot "pull their weight," either permanently or temporarily, or following active employment in the economic sector. More or less supports flow to the dependent person or unit, in proportion to defined need, evaluated prior or projected future "credit," the social value, benefits to the giver from the giving of these supports, and so forth. The emphasis on the economic institution in America, particularly on independence in economic supports from any source except earnings from the marketing of personal services, has created awkward attempts to provide "humanistically" determined need fulfillment, as well as multiple sources of strain within the family unit. Women are especially likely to be defined as problems vis-à-vis the world of work and its related social system. The U.S. Census, the Social Security Administration, employers and the society at large really do not know how to relate to a variety of women: full-time housewives, women who have a job although their husband brings in "good" earnings, divorcees or widows who must support themselves, and so forth. Several major reasons account for the discomfort of so many American public and private organizations in dealing with the subject of economic dependency and women. One reason is the rapid change the attitude of women toward the world of work is undergoing; a second is the heterogeneity of the population; and finally, there is the gap between policies and current realities. Social security is an excellent example of this. Throughout the 1920s and early 1930s, private pressure and public conscience pushed for policies that would ensure workers who were forced into retirement at a specified age and unable to save enough during their working years to support themselves on a regular source of income. The social security system was created in 1935 to ensure the retired worker against poverty and dependency on welfare. It was clearly an insurance system, in that the worker "earned" the benefits by prior work, with the employer contributing a share over an extended period of time during which the worker was getting pay. It was not until 1939 that society realized that the sum the retired worker received from social security was insufficient to cover the costs of maintaining a family that had become economically dependent on him in the past and especially in the case of the wife, who was unable to free herself from this dependency when the worker retired. The 1939 amendments to the Social Security Act insured benefits for people who had not worked but had been dependent on the worker, the justification being in terms of saving the family as unit. Thus, the base for the benefits shifted from earned income of the worker as a single unit to that of the worker as a head of a household. The wife and dependent children and/or parents were thus covered, as was the widow of a deceased worker and his dependent children. Yet the concept of dependency has been questioned of recent years by a variety of groups.

WORK HISTORIES OF CHICAGO AREA WIDOWS

In spite of the changes in ideology and behavior, the Chicago area widows for the most part followed the traditional pattern of movement from the world outside the home into the home upon marriage or the birth of the first child. Only about eight percent worked throughout marriage, or at least until retirement (see left side columns of Table 20). This means that some of the childless wives must have withdrawn from the labor force for at least part of the time, because some mothers con-

304

TABLE 20

Employment History: Percentages of Chicago Area Widows Working the Year Before the Husband's Fatal Illness, Since Widowhood and Now, by Beneficiary Status

	EMPLOYMENT HISTORY									
	DURING MARRIAGE					Year Before Widowhood	Since Widowhood	Now	TOTAL	
Beneficiary Status	All Years of Married Life or Until Retirement	Most Years	Some Years	On and Off	Never				N	%
Mothers with dependent children	6	31	14	14	38	39	70	54	15,784	19
Retirement widows	8	9	30	11	42	28	36	12	53,815	66
Lump sum beneficiaries	18	16	28	13	14	59	69	58	3,010	4
Remarried widows	10	11	27	19	33	39	74	44	2,497	3
Mothers with adult children	4	14	27	20	34	47	86	73	6,635	8
Percent	8	10	30	12	40	33	48	28		
N =	6,202	8,518	24,552	10,246	32,421	27,342	40,023	22,837	82,004	

tinued working, and only 8.6 percent of the respondents do not have children. Most of the women who were employed during marriage worked only some of the years or on-and-off. The most likely to have been consistently employed are the lump-sum beneficiaries, who were also the women most likely to have been childless. The retirement widows did not frequently work for pay after marriage. Mothers of children who were dependent at the time the husband died were also not apt to have been in jobs during marriage, some being employed only sporadically, but over a third never having worked at that time. Only a third of the wives were employed for pay the year before the husband's fatal illness or accident.

The reasons now given by the widows for not having been in the labor force during the year before the husband's fatal illness or accident reflect the traditions just discussed. Two-thirds of the respondents who were not employed at that time give the unwillingness of the husband to have them work as one of the three reasons for not being so involved. This surprising response is similar to that given by housewives in the same metropolitan area in the late 1950s and early 1960s, and does not indicate recent changes in work-related behavior or feminist attitudes. Disapproval by the husband is the answer most frequently given. Forty-seven percent of the women mention taking care of children—an explanation that appears most frequently as the most important one. Twenty-two percent give health-connected explanations as one of the three main reasons, although few were retired when the husband was alive. The "no need" (53 percent) and "do not want to work" (26 percent) reasons are interesting, because of the obvious implication that women work outside of the home only for pay and, if given sufficient income from other sources, will not do so.

All in all, a sizable proportion of women justify their non-employment when the husband was well in terms of anticipated conflict between the role of worker and the role of wife, or between the role of worker and the obligations of motherhood. We must await other studies to see if the rationales for not being in paid employment, as well as the level of commitment to an occupation and a career, are undergoing change (Lopata and Norr, 1974). The widows in this study tend to offer traditional justifications for not being employed when the husband was living. After widowhood, the husband obviously no longer figures as a force restraining the wife from working outside the home. The children are apt to be older and also do not appear as often as the main reason that wife cannot have a job. Increasing age appears as a more frequent factor, with 50 percent of the women reporting health restrictions, 15 percent with problems finding a job, and 16 percent being already retired. Forty-two percent of the women who have not been employed during widowhood do not want to work, and 41 percent do not need to because of other sources of income, mainly social security benefits as survivors or mothers of survivors.

A higher proportion of women were working in a job outside of the home the year before the husband's fatal illness or accident than had a steady work history earlier in marriage. The fact that one-third of the wives were already employed reflects the older age of the children and, in all probability, failing health of the husband, since most American married women with a husband present were not working in the 1960s, when most of the respondents were widowed. It is only in very recent years that the proportion of married women in paid employment rose to 50 percent. Of course, the women who were working when the husband was alive may be the more recent widows, as indicated by the high proportion of lump-sum beneficiaries, for they are the most recent widows. The total proportion of former wives who were working the year before the husband's fatal illness or accident is definitely brought down by the retirement widows. Almost four of 10 mothers of dependent children and the remarried women, and almost half of the mothers of adult children, were employed before the death of the husband.

307

The characteristics of widows or former widows who are now employed will be examined in greater detail, but it is interesting to note the changes in working status by stage of widowhood and beneficiary type. The death of the husband definitely persuaded many women to take a job, the proportion in each beneficiary category increasing dramatically, although the retirement widows are left considerably behind the others. Both agism and sexism are powerful influences keeping older women out of jobs, although the receipt of social security by decreasing need, may also serve as a deterrent. The mothers of adult children are most likely to have entered employment since widowhood, a not surprising finding since there is usually a gap between the time they cease to receive social security benefits as mothers of surviving children and the time they can get benefits as older widows.

Not all of the women who entered the labor force at widowhood have maintained this status into the present time, leaving open the question of how they are supporting themselves. The next most apt to be persuaded to work after the death of the husband are the younger women who then remarried. This new marriage allowed most of them to leave the labor force subsequently. Ten percent of the recipients of the only lump-sum payments have been added to the worker category in widowhood, not a large increase, and the number has now fallen back to the prewidowhood level. There are two alternative, not mutually exclusive, explanations for the absence of four out of 10 widows in this beneficiary category from paid employment. One is that many may not have had the time to obtain a new job in spite of the loss of the husband's income; the other is that insurance benefits are sufficiently large to rule out the economic motivation for paid employment. Mothers of dependent children increased the frequency of participation in the labor force during widowhood, although 16 percent returned to the role of housewife. One can only speculate that the social security benefits were simply not enough at first and that having several children often forces the mother into a job. Retirement widows, a third of whom worked since the death of the husband, are not apt to be in jobs at the present time, nine out of 10 being full-time homemakers, or at least not holding down a paying position outside of the home.

The relatively low level of educational achievement of the Chicago area widows and the sporadic involvement in the labor force are reflected in the kind of jobs they held in three periods of their lives—the year before the husband's illness, in widowhood, but not at the present time and now (see Table 21). Only one widow in eight is currently in a professional job, usually as a teacher or a nurse. Few who are in the professions entered a job in widowhood and then dropped out. Although two-thirds of the widows are in white-collar jobs, most of them are in clerical positions that are not highly paid. The shift of the American female labor force from unskilled or semiskilled factory work to office work is evident in the strong shift of these women from operative to clerical jobs from the time before the death of the husband to the present, although many had to take operative jobs early in widowhood. They are the older, less-educated women. Relatively few are or were in managerial or sales positions. Women in sales or clerical jobs are not likely to have worked much during marriage. There is also a concentration of these women in service occupations, with a decrease in private household servants. By the way, these distributions closely approximate those of all Chicago area women.

Not only were many women who had been full-time housewives pushed into the labor market by widowhood, but the change in their marital situation also encouraged them to increase the number of hours they work. Half of the almost 25,000 wives who were employed before the husband's fatal illness or accident worked less than full-time, with a quarter spending 20 hours a week or less on the job. Today, 45 percent

TABLE 21
*Occupational Distribution of Job Held the Year Before the Husband's
Fatal Illness or Accident, Job Held Since Widowhood but No
Longer Held, and Present Job*

Occupation		Before	Past Widowhood	Present
Professional		10	3	13
Managerial		7	9	5
Sales		8	6	8
Clerical		31	29	40
Craftsman		1	1	2
Operative		14	22	9
Laborer		0	1	0
Farming		0	1	0
Service		18	16	16
Household		10	13	7
Total working	$N=$	26,673	36,163	22,769
Housewives	%	68	28	73
	$N=$	55,412	23,152[a]	59,316
Total	$N=$	82,085		82,085

[a]Have not held a job since widowhood obtained by adding Present and Past-Widowhood and subtracting from 82,085.

of the women work 40 hours and an additional 17 percent are on the job 41 or more hours a week. They undoubtedly cannot afford part-time employment at the present time. In addition, many now have older children who are no longer a deterrent to work. Although paid employment provides many resources for supports, the work histories and economic situation of the widows make it increasingly apparent that many work mainly because they need the money. This is particularly true of widows not receiving social security benefits.

The rhythm of work has steadied now that the husband and his paycheck are gone. There is a definite increase in employment in "regularly" scheduled jobs—from 78 to 84 percent of the workers, with a decrease in unusual combinations. However, the widows are more willing to accept rotating work schedules now that they are no longer tied to their husbands' schedule. That is, only eight percent of the wives but 12 percent of the widows have flexible work hours, while 82 percent had worked regular daytime hours in marriage and 80 percent in widowhood.

A dramatic indication of the economic needs of the widows is found in the reasons they give for having taken paid employment since widowhood, compared to the reasons listed for the year before the husband's illness. A high proportion, almost half of the total number, of the widows claim to have been working only to help meet the needs of the family when the husband was the main breadwinner; this drops to 30 percent now. Now over half that, first and foremost, need to support themselves. This is seldom given second or third order of importance as a reason for employment. Only 13 percent of the women claim to have been the sole breadwinner when the husband was alive; now 38 percent of the women relate that they are the sole breadwinners of their families as a reason for working. Twenty-six percent of the widows agreed that "I worked so that the children could have a better life" when the husband was alive and only half that at the present time. The final economic reason, working for investments such as a house, apartment or car draws only 15 percent of responses for the year before the husband's illness and that drops to six percent for now. Personal reasons for working outside of the home, such as feelings of achievement, self-development, independence, the opportunity for contact with other people or just liking the work appear rarely in the first order of importance in the present time or the past, but increase in frequency once the economic reasons are taken care of. Very few women are career-minded to the extent of checking the statements, "I had chosen an occupation and I want to work in it." Interestingly enough, the shift of economic reasons from a subsidiary to a main source of support does not detract from the personal reasons for working outside of the home. That is, 33 percent of the women give contact with people as one of the three main reasons for working the year before the husband's illness and since widowhood; 25 percent list independence at both times. Liking the job is mentioned by 33 percent of the workers when the husband was alive and 32 percent of the widowhood workers. One reason for holding a job that increases, from 15 to 21 percent, is in "my job gives me a feeling of achievement." These are rather strong indications of commitment to the job. However, many women who worked both during marriage and in widowhood appear to have done so solely for economic reasons. It is, of course, impossible to determine if they were satisfied with the job and gave economic reasons simply because they are the only culturally approved ones or if they really worked for money only, without deriving any personal satisfaction at all from the job. We have some answers to this question for the current time period in that we asked for levels of satisfaction with specific characteristics of the job. Before discussing that, however, let us look at work histories, entrance into and aspects of the last job held, which applied either to a former or present job held in widowhood.

WORKING IN WIDOWHOOD

Few of the women who are now widowed and often economically restricted, trained in their youth for a specific occupation or set of related occupations. Few have more than a high-school education and only 20 percent obtained early work training. The effect of schooling on occupation is strong, as evident in Table 22. Although education beyond high school does not provide a 100 percent guarantee of employment in the top two categories of professional or managerial position, it certainly increases chances significantly and it almost always leads to a white-collar job. The least educated are the most likely to end up in service jobs, either in households or in business. Both high-school dropouts and finishers are likely to find themselves in clerical positions. It is also apparent from this table that widows follow the overall pattern of American

TABLE 22

Occupational Distribution of Chicago Area Widows in Present or Last Job Since Widowhood, by Amount of Schooling

OCCUPATION

Education	Professional	Managerial	Sales	Clerical	Crafts	Operatives	Laborers	Farm	Service	Household Service	Not Employed	Total N
8th grade or less	1	2	4	12	0	19	0	0	17	19	26	27,355
Some high school	1	9	11	21	1	21	2	9	12	3	20	15,665
High school	3	6	3	40	1	8	0	0	12	3	25	20,442
More than high school	28	11	5	36	3	3	0	0	5	3	6	10,731
Total N =	3,760	4,418	3,662	18,461	691	10,269	319	311	9,502	6,446	15,853	73,693

women in that those with more education are more likely to be employed (Lopata and Norr, 1974). Of course, there is the simultaneous tendency for the younger women to be the more educated ones.

Even though over four out of 10 widows did not finish high school, and so few trained for a job early in life, few of the total number got additional training in widowhood. The presence of the retirement widows, only one percent of whom have been trained since the death of the husband, of course brings down the total to seven percent who obtained occupational training. The most widows apt to have job training are the mothers of adult children (24 percent), the remarried women (19 percent) and the mothers of dependent offspring. In view of the relative infrequency of both paid employment prior to the husband's illness and occupational training since his death, we can assume that there are women who reentered the labor force subsequently, having been out of it for an indeterminated number of years without upgrading prior skills or training for new ones. Undoubtedly the sample also contains women whose earnings contributed little to the family income when the husband's wage or salary provided the major part and whose jobs are no better now, since nothing in their training had prepared them for becoming the major or even the only breadwinner.

The underutilization of occupational-training resources does not necessarily make traditional women yearn for that experience or be resentful of being unable to gain it. Many of these women do not have an occupational career "map" in their minds, with a set of directions as to the best ways of preparing for a job, getting it, keeping it and moving up the economic ladder.[1] Only one-fifth of the women represented by our sample answered "yes" to the question, "Is there any kind of training or retraining that you *wish* you had received to enable you to earn enough money to support a family since becoming a widow?" Of course, the women who responded are only those who have or had had some hope of entering the labor market or changing a job with the help of some training. This eliminates the elderly, those with various major handicaps and those who have not been economically or personally motivated to enter or reenter the labor force.

Those who wish they had taken occupational training specify 38 different kinds of jobs for which they would have liked to be prepared. Secretarial or nursing jobs were the most popular and a relatively large number of women would have liked to have had more schooling. Almost invariably, the women who said they wished for training wanted occupations of higher socio-economic status than those held by women with actual training. Age is an important variable influencing aspirations even if they are not converted into actuality.

Reasons for not obtaining additional training by women who wished they had are stated in terms of lack of time, energy, money, knowledge or motivation. The main obstacles are the presence of small children or the need to continue at a current job or to take whatever job is available because of immediate problems. Many women in other parts of the interview reveal great ignorance of societal resources such as training programs, and many assume that all forms of schooling are always expensive and must be paid for by the trainee.

Not only do most widows lack occupational skills and knowledge of available schooling and training opportunities, but they also go about finding a job in very unsophisticated ways. American society has developed a wide range of resources to match the needs of employer and employee. Many of these, such as employment agencies, specialize in this task, but they require self-confidence in marketable skills and planning for voluntaristic use. Only four percent of the Chicago area widows used either private or state-run employment agencies. Other sources of information about jobs impose rather severe restrictions of one sort or another. Following up on newspaper or magazine advertisements requires greater sophistication in processing information on the part of the applicant than does the use of agencies whose function is to do just that. But even these resources in job hunting are underutilized by the widows, with only 14 percent listing advertisements, and four percent saying that they got their job by seeing a sign in front of the employing organization. The remaining women depended basically on friends (25 percent) or relatives (eight percent), with 23 percent listing a wide range of resources, such as politicians or former employers, all of which are rather restrictive. The limitations imposed by such personal lines of contact to the world of work are of past or equally sex-segregated and lower-job horizons. Thus, women who need to work for pay because no one else is supporting them do not approach the occupational market with much more sophistication than do women who are not the main breadwinners of the family, at least as far as the actions of the Chicago area widows indicate.

WIDOWHOOD WORKERS

Frank Steinhart (1975, 1977) analyzed the factors affecting current labor force participation of the Chicago area widows represented by our sample and concluded that eight variables enable us to "differentiate between women who are working and women who are not working" (1977; p. 54).[2] These include enabling factors such as age, income adequacy, the presence of children at home and marital status, as well as facilitating factors such as education, prior work experience, additional post-school training and race. The latter set of variables are important but "show a varied influence" (1977; pp. 21–22).

The most likely to be working now is the widow with three children still living at home and with a history of having worked most of the years during marriage (94 percent). Another combination of variables that draws a high proportion of women into the labor force is the ages between 45 and 54 and history of having worked throughout most of the years of marriage (91 out of 100). Although the more educated women are the more likely to work, Steinhart found the combination of education and age to be very important. The widows range from only 16 percent of the youngest women—that is those 44 years of age or younger who have eight grades of schooling or less and are employed—to 82 percent of those aged 45 to 54 who have more than a high-school education. The only age group within which the percentage of women who are in jobs does not increase with extended schooling is not surprisingly in the eldest age cohort, which is low at all levels. Older widows have social security and are unable to hold jobs. Women with more education at younger ages can find jobs and they can earn more income than can widows with less schooling, so it becomes more worthwhile for them to be employed. The youngest have children in their care, but the 45 to 54 age group tends to work at all educational levels.

One of the strongest combinations of factors influencing a widow's participation in the labor force is that of income adequacy and the number of children living in her home (see Table 23). Steinhart computed income adequacy for this analysis by subtracting the wages of the employed women from

TABLE 23

Percentages of Widows Employed in the Chicago SMSA, by Number of Children Living at Home, by Income Adequacy Scale: 1974[a]

| Income Adequacy | NUMBER OF CHILDREN LIVING AT HOME | | | | | |
	0	1	2	3	4+	Total
0–.5	53	63	52	81	30	45
.5–1.0	18	31	68	67	48	32
1.0–1.5	8	57	41	39	52	18
1.5–2.0	12	32	60	58	49	26
2.0+	14	22	37	50	25	19
Total Percent	19	34	52	62	42	29
N =	7,047	6,561	3,614	1,545	1,381	20,148

[a]Gamma = −.43

317

the total family income and dividing what remained by the "Labor Department's income adequacy index for that size family" (p. 41). This enables him to determine how well, in comparative terms, the family could live without the widow's wages. The highest proportion of women workers, when income adequacy without her wage or salary is taken into consideration, is the mother of three children whose income would have been between .5 and 1.0 of the index. One of the reasons for the increased probability that a woman is employed if she has three children is the presence of a social security family maximum limit, which provides benefits to a widow and only two of the orphaned children, but not to additional ones. This policy, instituted during the Depression, creates economic hardship for mothers of more than two children since they do not get additional benefits for them. Thus, they are either pushed into the labor force or into welfare. Women with four or more children who are the most destitute, in that their income without wages is only half of the adequacy level as determined by the Department of Labor, are most likely not able to work for pay.

When combining education and income adequacy, we find one of the reasons why mothers with several children in the home are unable to work. The most apt to be employed are women with more than a high-school education whose income without wages would be less than half of the adequacy index (72 percent), while equally poor women with eight or less years of schooling are less than half as able to be employed (33 percent). Only four percent of the widows with 1.0 to 1.5 of adequacy index income and with only a grade-school education are now employed (Steinhart, 1977, p. 43). Of course, these are most apt to be retirement widows. None of the least educated women are as frequently in the labor force as are the more educated even if they are poor. For both the least and most educated women, the proportion who are employed goes down with increased income from other sources, but the pattern is not uniform for the middle two categories of education,

318

so that the total gamma is only −.14. Table 23 shows the association between income adequacy without pay and the number of children still in the home to be much stronger (−.43).

Race is an important variable influencing women's work involvement, because black women tend to have more children living at home and to be less able to find well-paying jobs. The largest gap between the white and nonwhite groups in proportions working is in the 45 to 54 age group. Nonwhites are apt to be in the labor force if they have two (62 percent) or three (58 percent) children at home, while whites are most likely to be working if they have three children in the home (56 percent), and they are more likely to be so engaged at all six family categories except that of two children in the home than are their black counterparts.

Steinhart (1977) summarizes the interweave of factors influencing whether or not a woman will work as follows:

> The importance of the relationship between income adequacy and the number of children at home is striking. The compensation the widow receives from the social security program is apparently adequate to the point where employment is a marginal consideration. However, the removal of such subsidy drives the widow into the job market quite rapidly. Conversely, the presence of the family maximum policy has the same effect on widows with large families. In the absence of children, age becomes a crucial factor. The respondents who have passed the usual retirement age of 65 are generally not employed, and when they are working they usually do not do so for primarily economic reasons (p. 53).

Job as Provider of Supports

Generally speaking, women who are now working outside the home or were employed any time during widowhood are satisfied with their job and working conditions. Over nine out of 10 widows agree strongly, or at least agree, that their working conditions in general are good and pleasant, that they like

319

their work, that it is interesting, and "that the people I know find my job interesting and they respect my position in it." Ninety-four percent consider their supervisors to be all right, and few say, "I have conflicts and misunderstandings with co-workers" (nine percent) or, "the place where I work is poorly organized" (18 percent). Not many women claim that the work is very tiring (seven percent) or that commuting to work is very hard on them (eight percent), although these two statements draw more mild agreements than any of the other negative ones. One positively stated feature of their working situation with which there is less agreement than with the others is the wage they are getting, but even here only one-fifth of the women disagree with the statement, "My work brings a good and fair wage." These are surprisingly positive attitudes concerning work and conditions of employment, considering that so many of these women are working in low-status clerical, service or factory jobs. Their evaluations go against much of the literature on occupational engagement of workers, which has been strongly influenced by Marx, through Chinoy (1965) and Blauner (1966), concerning the inevitable alienation of workers in low-status, nonproduct jobs. This expressed satisfaction exists in spite of the small income these women get from the job and the fact that so many are living in poverty or near the poverty level. This may be a reflection of the traditional passive and undemanding stance of women vis-à-vis the world of work. Either their job has sufficient rewards to offset what sociologists could consider inferior characteristics or it is simply not as unpleasant as the women expected it to be.

The information above points to several sources of supports derived from working, even if the levels of agreement and disagreement are moderate rather than strong. Liking the work itself brings the highest frequency of agreement at a strong level (36 percent) and in combined positive levels (95 percent). Only five percent of the women do not like their work and only 10 percent find it uninteresting and monotonous. Only

320

a fifth of the women feel that their work does not provide opportunities for self-development. These are intrinsic aspects of the job. Several of the other statements provide hints as to social supports, most women having co-workers with whom they get along and supervisors who are judged as good in meeting their obligations. Most jobs are carried out in the company of a more or less complex and integrative social circle. Because of the sex-segregation of many occupations, same sex friendships can be expected to develop on the job, proximity and similarity being major facilitators of such relations (Rosow, 1967; Newcomb, 1961). Operating in a similar way as contact with neighbors, extended contact can be socially and emotionally significant to a person. On the other hand, work situations can contain several factors that deter friendship. Work is supposedly task-oriented, and many employers discourage friendships on the assumption that they will interfere with job performance (Homans, 1961). Dubin (1956) also found that workers tend not to center their life interests on the work place and superficial "friendly" interaction does not deter them from changing employers without concern for peer relations. In the case of women, it is also possible that the separation of the work place from the home and the American emphasis on the importance of the homebound roles for women might lead to compartmentalization of life, especially while the husband is living.

Looking over the sources of friendship prior to widowhood (in Chapter 6), we found that work situation did not provide the wives with as many friends as did the neighborhood or voluntary associations, although it is one of the three main sources. The neighborhood is predominant perhaps not only because of the frequency of contact, but also because of its family base and the similarity of life-style. However close the relation among co-workers on the job may be, if they do not live near each other they disperse at the end of the day and leisure-time contact becomes difficult. Less than half of the number of friends developed through the neighborhood are credited to the work situation of the wife. Of course, fewer women were in paid employment at that time, whereas all had neighbors.

Co-workers as well as neighbors can appear in the support systems of the Chicago area widows in two ways: in the role indicated by those concepts or as friends. That is, a woman who has converted a co-worker into a friend is apt to list that person as a friend in the supports. Only those co-workers not converted into friends are identified under that label. We must keep this distinction in mind when we find that co-workers are not frequently mentioned in the emotional support system of the Chicago area wives while the husband was still living, at least in retrospect. Only 3,257 references out of a total of 826,825 are to people with whom the widow worked, and these tended to be listed by middle-aged women with grown children who were more likely to be holding a job and focusing on the work environment than were the younger women. Co-workers are more apt to appear in the feeling-states segment of the past emotional supports, but even here they are overrepresented mainly in the lives of middle-aged women who had worked most of their adult lives.

The proportion of new friends which come from work associations is higher now than for the time before the death of the husband, mainly because more widows have worked since that time and there are fewer friends in this time period. More who now work have made new friends than have women who are not employed or even than women who had worked in marriage. Friends developed out of work associations also increase their contribution to the emotional support systems of the widows, compared to their past and to women who are not working now. There are few references to co-workers in the supports of women who had worked in widowhood but are no longer employed. Co-workers appear most often as contributors to feelings of being useful or respected, but they are not often listed as people to whom the widow feels closest.

This means either that they have been converted into friends or that other people offer this basic support.

There appears to be an association between work history and the tendency to belong to voluntary associations, at least as far as women below the age of 65 are concerned. The least likely to belong to such groups are women who never worked (.64 average number of memberships), the constant workers (.69 average number of memberships), and the women employed only in widowhood (.77 average number of memberships). These distributions point to two types of women as far as involvement in organizations is concerned: those who are peripherally engaged in society, not working and not belonging to groups, and those who are too busy at the present time to maintain memberships. On the other hand, multiple memberships are most frequent among women of preretirement age who have not worked since the death of the husband (1.28 average number of memberships). Class differences operate here in that there is a significant association between education, working in paid employment and multiple membership in voluntary associations.

Finally, work experience since widowhood has a definite relation to the presence of one or more boyfriends in the lives of these women. The worker in widowhood is apt to have had at least one or more than one boyfriend (2.04 average number). The lowest percentage of women reporting boyfriends, and the fewest number of boyfriends by those to have had them, are among the widows who are not working at the present. The widows below age 65 represented by our sample who worked in widowhood but are not now employed list an average of 1.43 boyfriends, and those who now have a job list an average of 1.51.

Thus, we find that most of the widows did not work full-time during marriage, and only about one-fourth are presently employed. Income adequacy without her earnings and the number of children living at home influence the widow's search for employment. Education and occupational training help a widow obtain a job and probably reflect both an interest in employment and the ability of voluntaristic engagement in new social roles once prior social engagement is modified by changes in the life course. Work outside the home serves as a resource not only for money, but also for other supports, providing a pool of associates from which friends and positive self-feelings are drawn. Most of the working women are relatively satisfied with their job, even though their occupations are not highly thought of by American society. Either their expectations are low or the evaluations miss some of the sources of satisfaction which widowed women can draw from a job.

Sources of Money and Money as Resource[2]

The introduction of a money economy even prior to industrialization in Western European and American societies, and the restructuring of work into jobs returning earnings made people dependent upon money. Money is the main subsistence resource of urban society and this money usually comes from outside the home, either in the form of past savings or in current periodic inflow. Most Americans depend on money earned in jobs; only few are able to draw on unearned income. The source of income may be a person's job or a job held by another individual on whom that person is financially dependent. The wife, younger children and occasionally a disabled or elderly relative are those generally economically dependent on the head of the household. The death of that breadwinner almost inevitably introduces changes in the amount and sources of essential income available to the survivors and participation in support systems and social roles. The awareness that more than one family member may be dependent on a worker led American society to introduce benefits for dependent survivors of covered workers.

Of course, some survivors of a deceased main breadwinner may be able to shift the responsibility for their support to other persons or groups: an adult child, social welfare programs, private charities and so forth. There are other sources of money available to Americans. Some families with invested monies may draw interest from these investments. Others inherit enough money to keep them independent for many years. Aware of the variety of sources of money and related economic support available in this society, we focused a whole section of the interview on these matters.

As we have seen, few widows are either totally dependent on their married children or living in circumstances requiring no financial expenditure on their part. Few are engaged in economic support exchanges, aside from a job, which would substitute for a steady income. Information on the widows' actual income is contained in two separate measures.[3] One is a precoded question on the total income the year prior to the husband's fatal illness or accident and in 1973. The second is a much more detailed question: "During the past year, 1973, did you or any members of your family living with you receive income from any of the following sources?" If the answer was "yes" to any one source, we asked who the recipient was, the amount received and the frequency. The nine sources specified were: (1) wages and salaries; (2) rent from property, sales or special money-making projects; (3) social security benefits such as (a) old age, (b) disability, (c) survivor or (d) supplementary security income; (4) interest on savings, dividends, stocks and bonds; (5) veterans widow's pension; (6) employee pension; (7) private insurance; (8) assistance or welfare, public or private; and (9) other sources, public or private. Depending on the source, between two and four members of the widow's family living with her, as well as she herself, could be listed by her in any of the nine sources, for a possible total of 31 separate sums of money all the resources could bring into the household. The aggregate income is used in the discussion unless the subject of the analysis makes the use of the precoded amounts analysis.

About 13 percent of the women did not provide answers to the detailed income questions; 10 percent refused to name the amount contributed by a particular resource, and the remainder either did not answer the question or did not know the amount of money involved. The last-named women, relatively few in number, live in households in which the main breadwinner is another person whose amount of income the widow does not know. The refusal to disclose income is not surprising, since the study was sponsored by the Social Security Administration and all guarantees of confidentiality by the interviewers could not dispel the fear that information on income could result in the loss of benefits. The probability that this was the case is supported by the ignorance of these women about social security policies. Only a small fraction of the 1973 beneficiaries or former beneficiaries know how much they are allowed to earn without losing their social security income. Even fewer know that only wages and salaries are applied in the earnings test. Only 15 percent of the respondents know that the top amount which they could have earned without losing benefits was $2,400 in 1973 and that there is no limit once the widow reaches a certain age (72) or her family has a certain number of dependent children (2+). Once the family maximum in benefits is reached, it can be distributed among these children, without the widow receiving any benefits, so that she does not have to forego earnings. Only seven percent of the women know that only their own earned income is taken into consideration in determining eligibility. It is not surprising that women ignorant of the workings of the social security system would prefer to refuse to answer outright or simply state that they or their families do not receive money from a certain source. Of course, some women may have refused to answer because their earnings exceed the limit, but this seems a less likely reason among all but the more highly educated than is a lack of knowledge.

Table 24 contains three sets of income categories. For the time being we will ignore the third column (the income the year before the husband's fatal illness or accident), and we will focus on columns one and two. We do this for two reasons: one, to show the distributions of women within specified income categories, and two, to clarify the differences and similarities of the two methods used to obtain information on income—the precoded card and the elicitation of specific sums of money the widow or other members of her household obtain from specified sources. This table, complex though it is, is very important for an understanding of the financial resources or restrictions impinging on the Chicago area widows. The first fact to emerge from columns one and two is that a large proportion of the widows in 1973 were living on incomes of less than $5,000. The second fact is that widows are more extreme in estimating the total income on which they, or they and their families, live, when given a card with precoded categories rather than being asked for specific sums from specified sources. There is a strong possibility that the widows simply guess at the total income, without actually doing the additions we did. There is an interesting resultant variation between the means and medians and between the figures in each form of computation when both methods of income classification are used. The overestimation of income in the precoded question results in a higher average or mean income than obtained by the addition of all income sources. At the same time the aggregation shows a skew in that the sum at which half of the widows fall below (and half above) is much higher for the aggregated than for the precoded income, and higher than either of the means.

Table 25 shows the percentages of women reporting income from the sources we listed in the interview, as well as the differences in resource utilization according to several basic variables. The top row gives the proportionate frequency of use of each resource, while the columns show internal differences. Column two comprises the women who did not

TABLE 24

Percentages of Chicago Area Widows in Each Income Category at the Present Time, Aggregated from Separate Sources (A) and as Indicated from a Response Card in Precoded Categories (B); as Well as Income Before the Husband's Fatal Illness or Accident, Precoded (C); and Female Headed Households, U.S. [a]

| | TIME AND QUESTION FORM (1973 CONSTANT DOLLAR VALUE) | | | |
| Income | 1973 | | Before Widowhood[d] (C) Precoded[c] | US Population (D) Female Head |
	(A) Aggregated[b]	(B) Precoded[c]		
Base N	71,589	60,407	60,345	6,804,000
Missing %	13	14	27	
Under $1,000	4	1	3	4
$1,000–1,999	9	10	1	3
$2,000–2,999	26	22	4	4
$3,000–3,999	10	13	7	5
$4,000–4,999	8	7	4	6
$5,000–5,999	6	10	7	5

TABLE 24 (*cont.*)

$6,000–6,999	7	5	6	10
$7,000–7,999	3	5	7	8
$8,000–8,999	4	6	8	8
$9,000–9,999	3	3	7	7
$10,000–14,999	10	9	18	14
$15,000–19,999	6	5	14	8[f]
$20,000 and over	5	4	14	1[g]
Total	100	100	100	100
Mean Income	4100	6371[e]	11862	5797
Median Income	6714	4553	9580	7228

[a] SOURCE: Gertrud Kim and Henry P. Brehm, "Income as a Resource in the Lives of Widows," *Support Systems Involving Widows in a Metropolitan Area of the United States* (in Helena Z. Lopata et al., eds.). Report to the Social Security Administration, 1977. Tables 4–17 and 4–20.

[b] Aggregates include only women who report an income.

[c] The interviewee was presented a card with the categories listed here at the left side. Transformation to the constant dollar value (1973) is made by taking the middle value within each range.

[d] The year before the husband's fatal illness or accident.

[e] Means and medians are obtained from the mid-value of each range.

[f] Income range: $15,000–24,999.

[g] Income range: $25,000 +.

TABLE 25

Utilization of Income Sources by Chicago Area Widows, by Race, Age, Education and Dependent Children

Characteristics	Base	No Income Listed	INCOME SOURCE[a] (PERCENT USE)									
			SW	TW	RS	SI	IS	VP	EP	PI	PA	O
Total	82,084	13	25	33	12	74	30	9	10	2	4	4
Race:												
White	70,163	14	25	33	11	74	34	9	11	2	2	4
Nonwhite	11,922	9	25	28	18	77	7	7	7	1	19	3
Age:												
Under 45	6,241	8	43	59	10	86	26	19	4	3	10	7
45–54	11,041	7	60	69	13	67	31	24	9	2	5	7
55–64	15,345	11	44	54	14	55	35	5	16	1	6	7
65 +	48,873	16	10	14	11	80	29	6	10	2	3	2

TABLE 25 (*cont.*)

Education:

0–7	14,717	14	13	18	20	81	12	3	14	0	7	1
8	15,653	7	15	20	9	82	35	7	11	0	5	7
9–11	15,914	12	27	33	8	76	31	9	10	1	6	6
12	21,660	14	34	46	12	68	30	12	10	3	2	4
13 +	10,874	21	38	45	9	64	44	13	10	6	6	3

Number of dependent children (under 18):

0	68,056	14	21	27	12	72	30	6	11	2	4	3
1	6,277	9	56	67	10	82	30	20	10	1	1	7
2	3,596	6	53	61	13	94	25	31	7	5	10	14
3	2,065	8	34	54	15	89	24	26	5	4	2	9
4 +	2,141	7	31	54	11	86	36	20	6	3	26	4

[a]SW: own wages; TW: total wages; RS: rent, sales; SI: social security insurance; IS: interest, savings; VP: veteran's widow pension; EP: employee pension; PI: private insurance; PA: public assistance; O: other.

331

answer income questions. According to the top row, almost three-fourths of the women receive regular income from social security, either directly or through benefits coming to their children or other dependents in the household. In order to better understand the contribution of various resources, we separated the widow's income from wages or salary from that earned by all other household members. The column headed TW thus lists her earnings as well as those of a new husband, adult child or anyone else in the home. Almost a third of the women are drawing on earnings of at least one member of the household, with a fourth bringing in income from their own job. The totals indicate that social security based on past earnings of a family member, almost exclusively the late husband, and employment by present members form the foundation of support of most households. Only three in 10 widows can draw upon "interest on savings, dividends, stocks and bonds" (IS), but the sums from this source are not large. "Veterans widows' pensions" (VP) and "employee pensions" (EP), respectively, help only 10 percent of the women, while a widely held assumption that many widows benefit from "private insurance" (PI) is dispelled by the fact that only two percent of the Chicago area respondents obtain monies from this source. "Assistance or welfare, public or private" (PA) helps only four percent of the families or widows living alone, while less than five percent list sources we had not considered when drawing up our list (O).

Thus, even when encouraged to list contributions of nine major income sources for a total of 31 one-source-recipient combinations, most widows cannot come up with anything but social security or their own or their family members' earnings, with interest on savings contributing some funds to a third of the women. Assumptions underlying the initial Social Security Act concerning multiple sources of income of widows and their dependent children are thus incorrect for two reasons. The first one is that most do not receive much income, and the second, that most of these widows are mainly, or even totally, dependent on social security.

Race makes little difference in the utilization of income sources, except for rent, savings and public assistance. In 1973, almost five times as many whites as nonwhites received income from savings of one form or another. On the other hand, about 18 percent of the nonwhites, and only 10 percent of the whites, gained income from rentals. Nineteen percent of nonwhites compared to two percent of whites depend on public assistance. The difference in the resort to welfare is mainly accounted for by the youth, and by the presence of several small children in the home, of nonwhite women. The social security these widows receive is simply inadequate and many are unable to obtain a good job or leave the children in the care of others.

Age influences income mainly because it affects the chances of employment. The youngest and the oldest women are often unable to earn an income, though for different reasons. The highest use of own earnings is made by women in their forties who are more educated and less likely to draw social security benefits. This age group is also apt to have an additional earner in the household. The younger women have not had much chance to accumulate savings and property and the early death of the husband diminishes the possibility of employee pensions. A few, widows of soldiers who died during the Korean or Vietnam wars, receive veterans widows' pensions.

The probability of income from earnings and veterans widows' pensions increases, while income from social insurance and employee pensions decreases with better education, mainly because of age differences. Fewer of the least-educated widows have an income from savings than any of the other groups. On the other hand, it is interesting to note that the more highly educated widows tend to refuse to answer questions about income.

The number of dependent children affects the ability of the

widow to derive income from her own wage or salary. The pattern is somewhat different than that found by Frank Steinhart in his analysis of working widows, because he considered all offspring living in the home, while Gertrud Kim considers only dependent children. Thus, Kim finds that among widows with dependent children, the proportion drawing an income from their own earnings decreases as the number of children increases. While more than half of the widows with one dependent child worked for pay, only about a third of those with three or more dependent offspring do so. According to Kim (1977), the fact that women with many children are able to stay out of the labor force may be due to the help they are getting from both social security and public welfare (Kim, 1977). Steinhart (1977) found the drop-off in the frequency of employment after the total of three children living at home is reached.

About one-fourth of the Chicago area widows depended on only one source of income in 1973, while about 60 percent had more than one source. Of course, we do not know the resources of widows who did not answer the precoded or the individual source question. The more sources a woman has, the higher her income is apt to be, especially if wages and salaries of more than one earner are considered.

One-fifth of the widows in the 65-plus-years of age group with less than nine years of schooling are totally dependent upon social security, with no other source of income. They ran their household on $2,423 a year in 1973. Even worse off are the women with only veterans widows' pensions. Although they average 9.7 years of schooling and 65 years of age, their annual income in 1973 came to no more than $1,004. Private insurance brought women limited to this single source a total of $3,800, which is considerably more than the sums brought in by rent and sales. At the high level of income, not including the combined earnings of a male head or other member of the family and the woman herself, are the few who average $29,426 from several sources, such as social security, private insurance, interest on savings and investments, and rents and sales.

Although three-fourths of the Chicago area widows obtain benefits from social security, mostly in the form of survivor insurance, these sums are not large. Median income from this source ($2,292) is most definitely below that derived from household wages or salaries ($6,999) and even to that from the earnings of the widow herself ($5,000). On the other hand, social insurance contributes more income than do other sources of income. Widows with earnings from their own employment contribute a mean of 63 percent to the total income, while remarried women derive an average of 69 percent of the total household income from earnings, usually of the husband, but often also their own. Social security makes up 58 percent of all the women's total income, with 20 percent depending on it as their sole support. Other sources are lesser contributors to the widows' income; only one-fifth of the financial intake of women who have savings comes from interest. This means that women getting the interest from stocks, bonds and other investments can draw on a wider range of resources or else that their savings are simply not adequate to meet their standard of living. The widows with no dependent children are more apt to be dependent on their own social security than are the widows with several children in the home, mainly because they are older. Widows drawing only on their own wages are apt to be childless.

Most dependent upon social security in terms of share of total incomes are the blacks, who are also younger with younger children, the least educated, and living in households with the fewest earners. Lump-sum beneficiaries and remarried widows, as well as women in their forties, obtain the largest part of their income from total household wages and salaries.

Gertrud Kim used three sets of comparisons in determining the relative financial situation of the widows: their annual income the year before the husband's fatal illness or accident, the income of the American population in general as well as its female segment and the amount needed for "survival," as determined by the Social Security Administration's poverty level computations (Kim, 1977, p. 31) or the Bureau of Census cutoffs.

Comparing gain and loss columns of Table 26, we see that many of the widows are worse off now than they were when the husband was well and, for the most part, earning money. Both the mean and median incomes in 1973 came to only about half of what they had been prior to widowhood. Kim then computed the percentages of women who gained and those who lost income following the death of the husband, by age, education, the number of dependent children and beneficiary status, as well as the mean and median amount of income gained or lost. Only 22 percent of the women gained income, measured in constant 1973 dollars. In addition, both the mean and the median income loss were considerably higher than the same measures for income gain. There is also a strong negative association between the age of the woman and the probability that she will gain money in widowhood. That is, the older the widow, the more apt she is to lose money, while the younger women are more likely to improve their total family income after the husband's death, usually because social security benefits exceed the young husband's income the year before he died. Not surprisingly, the more dependent children the widow has, the greater the likelihood of higher income, but, as in age differences, we must keep in mind that there are few women in any of the categories who actually benefit economically from their spouse's death.

The best off financially after the husband's death are the women who remarry, while the worst off, in comparison to their prewidowhood state, are the retirement widows and the lump-sum beneficiaries. Social security cannot replace a man's earnings; neither can the other sources of income available to women in their middle years without dependent children.

TABLE 26

Percentages of Women Experiencing a Gain or Loss of Income in Pre-and Postwidowhood Times, and the Mean and Median Gain or Loss, by Race, Age, Education, Number of Dependent Children and Beneficiary Status[a] (1973 Constant Dollars)

Characteristics	Base N	GAIN			LOSS		
		%	Mean	Median	%	Mean	Median
Total	60,344	22	4852	2267	78	7766	5675
Race:							
White	49,868	21	5261	2711	79	8360	6000
Nonwhite	10,477	27	3299	1870	73	4727	3747
Age:							
Under 45	5,516	43	7125	4969	57	6814	5863
45–54	9,754	34	5895	4227	66	8847	6516
55–64	12,535	16	4952	3775	84	6544	7478
65 and over	32,253	17	3370	1175	83	7310	5310
Education:							
0–7	11,591	22	2393	1468	78	5445	4243
8	11,558	21	3480	830	79	6295	5163
9–11	11,407	24	4789	2538	76	6859	5678
12	15,543	26	5525	3999	74	8771	7178
13 +	9,005	18	9209	7314	82	12357	10382
Number of dependent children (under 18):							
0	47,770	19	4211	1588	81	7679	5675
1	5,553	33	5506	4341	67	8579	6513
2	3,234	29	5816	5510	72	7140	5619
3	1,879	43	5905	6089	57	8222	5982
4 +	1,908	56	7441	4442	44	9279	8881
Beneficiary status:							
Mother w/dep. child	13,793	32	5322	3701	68	8139	5838
Retirement widow	36,404	16	3292	1180	84	7420	5543
Lump sum beneficiary	2,588	13	2804	996	87	9250	7240
Remarried widows	2,088	58	8837	7320	42	9558	7411
Mother w/adult child	5,472	33	6454	3936	68	8349	6493

[a]SOURCE: Gertrud Kim and Henry P. Brehm, "Income as a resource in the lives of widows," in *Support Systems Involving Widows in a Metropolitan Area of the United States* (Helena Z. Lopata et al., eds.). Report to the Social Security Administration, 1977. Table 4-22.

When we compare the total aggregated family incomes of the Chicago area widows represented by our sample to those of women in the United States, we find that the national mean falls between our computed and precoded average, but that the national median is higher than that computed for the Chicago area widows (again Table 24). The reason for this is the presence on the national scene of more divorced and single younger women who earn more than do widows dependent on social security and limited other sources. Female household heads in America in general report higher levels of income than our widows. On the other hand, the many very poor women without a male household head pull the average income down, despite the presence of the wealthier women.

Approximately 44 percent of the Chicago area widows who answered the income questions are living in poverty, as determined by the Social Security Administration's low-income index even when the earnings of the widows are included. The index is adjusted to the size of the family and recomputed for each year in response to the cost-of-living index. When the poverty index is set at 1.00, then we know that any family whose income (adjusted to family size) falls below 1.00 can be considered to be living in relative poverty. By that measure, 12 percent of the Chicago area widows are living on only a .24 or less on the index; six percent between .25 and .49; 11 percent between .50 and .74, and 16 percent between .75 and .99. This leaves 66 percent of the women at or above the poverty-line cutoff, including 24 percent who are very close to it, with an annual income ranging between 1.00 and 1.49; 10 percent who are between 1.50 and 1.99; 15 percent between 2.00 and 2.99; and 17 percent on 3.00 or above.

Another way of presenting this significant data is contained in Table 27, which breaks down the percentages of widows living below the 1970 Census poverty cutoff by age and education and compares these figures to those for Americans of both sexes and for American women alone. A number of facts emerge from this presentation. In the first place, it is evident

338

that education strongly affects the percentages of Americans in general, and of American women in particular, living in poverty. This influence is particularly strong for black women and men, since both the general population and the female population in the country show the same pattern. With some exception the probability that black women will live in poverty is dramatically influenced by education and it diminishes with an increase in years of schooling. Throughout the nation the most likely to be poor are the very young and the very old, uneducated black women. Among the Chicago area widows the same holds true for the nonwhites. That is, the most uneducated black women of the youngest and the oldest age groups are apt to be living in poverty. (The unexpectedly high proportion of old and poor high-school graduates is a result of a small cell size.)

The nonwhite widows in the youngest age group are more disadvantaged than their white counterparts in all marital situations. They tend to have more children at home and lack the husband's income that brings in the money available to other black women of their age. It is difficult to say why the association between education and probability of poverty does not hold as strongly for the white widows as it generally does for the nonwhites. The table indicates that both the youngest most uneducated and the oldest most educated white women are the most apt to be in poverty, although those not listing any income are not included.

It is possible to compress the categories of women in their relation to the low-income cutoff index into four groups, labeled, in Table 28, "destitute," because they are living on less than .5 of the index; "poor," because they are living on between .5 and 1.0; "comfortable," or those who have incomes between 1.0 and 2.0 on the index; and "rich," whose incomes are more than twice the figure used as the cutoff for poverty. It then becomes possible to look more closely at those characteristics of women at these levels of income which show significant differences. One of the background characteristics

TABLE 27

Percentages of U.S. Population and Female Headed Households and of Chicago Area Widows with Incomes Below the 1970 Census Poverty Cutoffs, by Age, Education and Sex

	PERCENT BELOW POVERTY CUTOFF								
	U.S.[a]						CHICAGO AREA WIDOWS[b]		
	BOTH SEXES			FEMALE					
Age by Education	Total	White	Negro	Total	White	Negro	Total	White	Nonwhite
22–44[c]									
1–8	21	18	37	28	23	47	54	43	60
9–11	14	10	31	18	12	41	26	8	45
12	5	4	16	7	5	23	21	13	44
13+	4	4	8	4	4	15	17	16	22
45–54									
1–8	16	12	30	19	15	37	19	10	30
9–11	8	6	21	10	7	27	20	13	39
12	4	4	15	5	4	13	19	18	30
13+	3	3	9	4	4	14	17	18	15

TABLE 27 *(cont.)*

	1	2	3	4	5	6	7	8	9
55–64									
1–8	16	13	33	20	16	40	27	19	49
9–11	9	7	20	12	10	26	35	37	18
12	5	5	13	6	6	14	21	21	20
13+	5	5	19	6	6	17	26	27	0
65+									
1–8	21	19	38	25	23	42	35	33	52
9–11	13	12	32	17	15	39	27	31	0
12	10	9	33	12	11	36	44	42	85
13+	8	8	18	11	11	17[d]	39	41	4

SOURCE: CPR: "Characteristics of the low-income population, 1973." Table 6: "Age—persons by low-income status in 1973, sex and race"; Table 11: "Educational attainment—persons 14 years old and over by low-income, status in 1973, age, sex and race."

[b]SOURCE: Gertrud Kim and Henry P. Brehm. "Income as a resource in the lives of widows," in *Support Systems Involving Widows in a Metropolitan Area of the United States* (Helena Z. Lopata et al., eds.). Report to the Social Security Administration, 1977. Table 4-27.

[c]Data from Table 6 of CPR differ from others (e.g., Table cp88 at the present) because of its cross-classification on the basis of race of persons rather than race of the family head (c.f. Note 1 of Table 6 in CPR).

[d]The original table (Table 11 of CPR) does not provide his percentage because the base Ns are less than 75,000. Therefore this percentage is computed from numbers reported in CPR.

341

TABLE 28

Selected Characteristics of Chicago Area Widows in
Relative Income Categories[a,b]

	Base		Destitude 0–.5		Poor .5–1.0		Comfortable 1.0–2.0		Rich 2.0+	
	N	%	R%	C%	R%	C%	R%	C%	R%	C%
Place: M[c]										
Large city	10,304	15	4	6	21	13	28	12	47	22
Middle size city	6,715	10	13	15	29	12	38	11	20	6
Small city, town	36,894	54	8	27	26	20	37	19	30	22
Rural, farm	14,588	21	11	52	24	55	31	58	34	49
Income										
Less than $1,000	2,686	4	100	43	0	0	0	0	0	0
$1,000–$2,499	14,281	20	19	44	81	62	0	0	0	0
$2,500–$3,999	17,566	25	4	10	28	26	68	50	0	0
$4,000–$6,999	15,063	21	1	1	12	10	57	36	30	20
$7,000–$9,999	6,917	10	0	0	4	2	33	10	63	19
$10,000+	15,306	21	0	0	1	0	8	5	91	61
Marital status										
Remarried	4,059	6	7	5	8	2	14	2	70	13
Widowed	67,490	94	9	95	27	98	35	98	29	87
New friends[d]										
Yes	32,134	45	5	27	29	49	31	41	35	50
No	39,415	55	11	73	24	51	36	59	29	50
Organization[e]										
None	37,091	52	10	59	28	56	36	56	25	42
1	16,432	23	9	25	29	26	25	17	35	26
2	9,425	13	2	4	23	12	47	18	27	12
3+	8,590	12	9	12	14	6	24	9	54	20
Total	71,538		9		26		34		32	

[a]Source: Gertrud Kim and Henry P. Brehm, "Income as a resource in the lives of widows," in *Support Systems Involving Widows in a Metropolitan Area of the United States* (Helena Z. Lopata et al., eds.). Report to the Social Security Administration, 1977. Table 4-9, modified.
[b]Respondents who have no income are excluded. R%=row percent; C%=column percent.
[c]Size of place where mother was born.
[d]New friends made since husband's death.
[e]Number of organizations to which the respondent belongs.

is the size of the community in which the parents were born. The length of family urbanization, as has been pointed out, influences the life chances (i.e., the foundation upon which people build their lives) of the widows. Mothers born in cities are more apt to provide a home background leading to greater utilization of urban resources, such as education, and to marriage to men—with better life chances. Rich widows are much more likely to have been reared by city-born rather than small town mothers. Interestingly enough, a disproportionate number, other than those of urban parentage, come of parents born in rural areas rather than in middle-sized cities. The pattern is similar with the place of birth of the father. Women now living on an income above the poverty line, but not affluent enough to be labeled rich, are disproportionately likely to have mothers who were born in rural areas or farms. This distribution is unexpected, since the hypothesis led to the expectation that only the destitute and poor widows would be the offspring of country-born parents. The poor are disproportionately the daughters of city-born parents and the destitute are overrepresented among widows whose mother and father were born in small cities or towns. Thus, the urbanization hypothesis is a good predictor for the rich only.

There is, not surprisingly, a close association between actual income and the probability of location under the appropriate rubric, although the index uses family size to estimate the income level. This means that the few women defined as destitute or poor with incomes above $4,000 must have large families.

As far as social integration is concerned, we find that the remarried widows are much more apt to be listed in the rich category, while those who remained widows are more concentrated in the comfortable level. The rich are disproportionately likely to have made new friends; the destitute only half as often list friendships made since widowhood. Finally, we see that the rich are more likely to belong to one or more voluntary associations than the destitute widows. All in all, women with higher incomes, particularly those with double the poverty cutoff figure or more are more socially integrated than are their poorer sisters. Quite interesting differences exist among the widows in their involvement in the support systems in terms of income. Not too surprisingly, as income increases there is a decrease in the probability of an inflow and increase in the probability of an outflow of economic supports. Poor women need more help paying bills or meeting living expenses than the wealthy. However, being destitute or poor does not guarantee financial aid, since, almost seven out of 10 widows living on an income of less than half the established poverty cutoff are not receiving *any* financial aid. On the other hand, the destitute widows are unlikely to be giving money or helping other people financially, while over a quarter of the rich widows help others. Still, 26 percent is not a high figure for the affluent, considering that they have double the income needed for survival in the metropolis.

The poor and the destitute widows are not much better off than the comfortable or rich with regard to receiving services from others. Economic need does not necessarily translate itself into service supports. The four groups are really quite similar, except that the destitute women are apt to be at the extreme of receiving only one service or of listing only six persons in two or more supports, since each service can have up to three contributors. There is a difference between the four groups, however, in the outflow of services. Rich widows definitely do more things for others, or provide services to more people than do the poor, or even the comfortable ones. Interestingly enough, these two categories, the poor and the comfortable, are the least likely to be doing anything for anybody out of our list of ten services. Of course, they may be close to poverty as to be restricted in what they can do. Also, quite possibly these may be older women living on social security and unable to provide unrequested services. The rich widows not only provide services but also give more than one

344

service to more than one person more frequently than the less affluent women.

Income is a vital aspect of an active social life. Also, a high proportion of these women had a higher income in the past than they now have. The social life-style of people tends to stabilize in adulthood, especially after the children are grown, and only extraordinary circumstances, such as health problems or the total absence of discretionary income, tend to change it, with one exception: the effect of widowhood. Traditionally socialized women often decrease their level or forms of social engagement with the death of the husband because they are deprived of a masculine escort of a partner in various activities. Notwithstanding that, we find that women with high incomes tend to engage in the social activities about which we inquired in the interview, to be involved in several such events, and to interact with several different kinds of people. The associations are clear and strong. Some destitute women do not even spend holidays with anyone, but most list some person, usually an offspring, with whom they celebrate. Few score more than nine points, each point being a person in any of the eight activities we listed, or the ninth one they could add. On the other hand, over a quarter of the rich widows share these activities more than a dozen ways in a variety of combinations.

The importance of social integration, evident in the lives of the more affluent women, translates itself into the emotional support systems. Poverty impoverishes all of life including the emotional level. The financially destitute and poor women tend to list fewer people in their emotional supports, especially in the relational sentiments segment. They average fewer supports and they are less apt to have a full system. On the other hand, the rich women are involved in more emotional supports and list more people than do any other of the other income groups. However, an interesting shift is evident in the feeling-states segment of the emotional system: the contrast between the rich and the destitute remains great, but the poor and the comfortable widows are slightly reversed in that the women with a higher income than the index level tend to list fewer contributors to their feelings states than the poorer women. This is the only one of the seven support systems showing this reversal.

Summary

This study focused on widows living in metropolitan Chicago, a highly urbanized and industrialized center of a highly urbanized and industrialized society. Most of these women were traditionally socialized to depend on the wages or salary of a husband for their economic support. The schooling of most did not prepare them for highly paid occupations, and most did not gain job training early in life, even though they entered the labor market temporarily as young women. Their work history is spotty; very few worked steadily for pay or followed a prestige-increasing career path. In fact, few were employed for long periods during marriage. Although many were below retirement age when they became widowed, finding work was not a realistic possibility either because of the rustiness or lack of skills for jobs outside the home. On the other hand, one-third of all the wives were working the year before the late husband's fatal illness or accident and almost a half have held paying jobs since widowhood. In all Social Security beneficiary situations this proportion has dropped to just over one-quarter, because many have left the labor force and others have been unable to find new jobs.

Those women who were not in paid employment while their husband was alive offered traditional reasons for not doing so, such as the unwillingness of the husband to have them work or the absence of compelling economic need. Age-associated reasons predominate for women not now employed, although the lack of financial motivation is still cited. Women who were employed when the husband was alive also mention financial reasons, but most of them do not consider themselves the main or even an equal contributor to the family's economic maintenance. Women who have held jobs since widowhood definitely list economic factors, they need to support themselves and/or their children, in spite of inadequate preparation. Interestingly enough, after the financial factor, personal reasons for working in jobs are listed by one-third of the women for both the time before and since widowhood.

Background factors such as race, education, prior work experience and occupational training as well as current circumstances such as age, income adequacy, children at home, and marital status all influence whether a woman is employed for pay, but in different ways and to different degrees. Women whose children are grown before they themselves are of retirement age and who therefore are not eligible for social security benefits, or lump-sum beneficiaries who were recently widowed and do not have dependent children, are apt to be in the labor force. The most frequently employed are women between the ages of 45 and 54 with more than a high-school education; the least apt to be employed are the uneducated very young and very old widows. In spite of a concentration in low-paying, nonprestigeful jobs most widows are very satisfied with their work conditions and employment seems to have positive effects on social engagement.

Social involvement and the development of a full support system are also facilitated by relatively high personal or family income. Good income in marriage frequently depended on the women's ability to marry a man with good job prospects. At least, this has been the traditional way women established economic security, assisting the man by creating an appropriate life-style and sometimes, but not often, directly through their own earnings. The prospect of affluence in marriage is contingent on race; whites have a definite advantage in the economic marketplace over nonwhites. The background of the woman, including the place of birth of her parents, her education, her training or retraining in widowhood are also important variables. So are her age, the ages of her children, the number of sources from which she draws her income, particularly the number of earners who contribute, her earnings and especially those of a male household head, all bear on the amount of income she had in 1973. Even though white women lost more income than did the nonwhites in widowhood because of the wage differential among men by race, they still had more income. The influence of education and training or retraining and of several other factors is greater on the income of younger than of older women. In other words, more variables affect the income of widows under age 46 than affect the older and especially the elderly widows. Approximately 44 percent of the Chicago area widows who answered the income questions are living below the poverty index cutoff for size of family. About 11 percent of these women have incomes close to the cutoff, so that only nine percent are destitute in that they need to manage on half of the cutoff amount, and another 24 percent are also below the index in that they are living on between .5 and less than 1.0 of the index.

"Rich" widows, that is, ones who are living on twice the income used for the poverty cutoff for her size family have many advantages, carried through from marriage and their own background. They are most apt to be involved in social activities with others and to have a broader support network than do the poor and especially the destitute women. The whole combination of background, life-style of the past and the ability of the widow to utilize personal and societal resources for social engagement is consistent with very few exceptions.

N O T E S

1. A new study of the changing commitment of women aged 25 to 54 in metropolitan Chicago (Lopata and Norr, 1974) indicates that things are changing. Forty-four percent of the over 1,800 women returned to school

after having stopped their education earlier in life. Succeeding returns to school usually produced diplomas or degrees for the prior dropouts, or higher degrees for those who had graduated from a lower level school. These women are also more apt to have trained for a specific occupation and/or to be planning on returning to school in the future than had been the widows.

2. See Steinhart's chapter for the report to the Social Security Administration, "Labor Force Participation as a Resource," focusing on this subject. The discussion in this section is dependent on his analysis.

3. This section is dependent on the analyses of Gertrud Kim and the chapter in the final report to the Social Security Administration prepared by her and Dr. Henry P. Brehm.

TEN

Summaries, Profiles and Implications

This chapter will summarize the life-styles and support systems of the Chicago area widows represented by our sample to illustrate how these are woven into patterns for different kinds of women and to indicate some of the implications for action on the part of the women, their associates, the community and society in general.

Summaries

There were 379,390 women in 1970 in the Chicago Standard Metropolitan Area who have been widowed and 324,925 were still in this marital situation, the others having remarried. Our sample of 1,169 respondents, when weighted by sampling ratios, represents 82,085 women of our population of 195,789. The numerical gap between our population and all the widows and ex-widows in the Chicago area is due to the presence of many women who were not eligible for any but lump-sum benefits when they become widowed before 1970 or who left the rolls before our cutoff date. There are also widows who are not on the SSA rolls because their husbands were not covered by social security. The gap between our population and our sample is due to the difficulty of locating widows and ex-widows who had moved, as well as to the refusal of some, mainly older women, to be interviewed, or the interference of well-meaning associates.

CHARACTERISTICS OF CHICAGO AREA WIDOWS

The Chicago area widows about whom we can generalize are not likely to have grown up in households of Chicago-born and -reared parents. Only 11 percent of the mothers and 8 percent of the fathers were born in this metropolitan area, and 47 percent of the mothers and 53 percent of the fathers were born in another country. An additional third of both mothers and fathers were born in another state, in the case of the blacks almost always in the South. Forty-two percent of the mothers and 44 percent of the fathers were born in villages, farm towns or on farms. Not surprisingly, the parents of the women who knew the extent of their schooling had an average of less than eight years of education in probably inferior schools.

The women themselves are more likely to be Chicago-born (44 percent) while only 17 percent are foreign-born. A third came from a state other than Illinois. Therefore, in consequence and also because they attended school at a different historical time than their parents, the women attained just over 10 years of schooling. The backgrounds of the husbands were similar to those of the wives, except that more had immigrated from another country. There is a significant statistical association between the education of the widow and that of her late husband. These two sets of background characteristics, place of birth and education, have heavily influenced the lifestyles and support systems of the women in wifehood and in widowhood. This applies especially to the two historical generations of older women whose social engagement is heavily dependent upon their educational achievement.

Married at a median age of 23 to the man who left them widowed, all but 8.6 percent of the women had children and withdrew from the labor force, becoming economically dependent upon the husband's income contributing to a two-person career or job. Ninety percent of the first marriages ended in widowhood at the woman's median age of 58 years. Half of the husbands were 60 years of age or younger, three-fourths of them being under age 65 at the time of death. Most had been working at their usual job when suffering the fatal illness or accident. Most of the widows, especially the whites, suffered a large drop in income between the year before this event and the present time. More than 40 percent of those women who answered the income questions are now living on incomes on or below the poverty cutoff level established by the Social Security Administration or the U.S. Census. Some widows gained in income with the death of the husband, but not as many as those who lost income, and the mean and median gains are considerably smaller than the sums obtained by the same indeces for the loss. The probability of having to live below the poverty line increases significantly in the case of nonwhites. The most financially advantaged women are aged 41 to 54, mainly because they have several sources of income, including social security for dependent children or earnings, or both. Family income is influenced by the number of income sources, the number of earners, the widow's presence in the labor force, the number of children, the widow's age, education, and social security beneficiary status. Several of these factors are interdependent.

Other resources available to the widow besides education, urbanization and income background, as well as current income, include parents and siblings, children and other relatives, friends, membership in church and other voluntary associations, a new husband and a job. A husband in memory can also provide a form of support in that widows who feel that he was active in the wife's emotional system whem still alive and well, and those who identify him positively on the sanctification scale, appear to be more satisfied with their current situation than women who have negative memories of the man and the marriage. Even idealization to the point of sanctification appears to have positive functions, helping with grief work through the cutting of ties, even if it tends to antagonize associates who remember the man in more realistic terms. Of course, relative deprivation may make sanctification easier. There are women who do not feel obligated to sanctify the husband, evaluating him in more realistic terms and selectively by area of life and behavior. These tend to be the more educated women with a more complex support network, while the high-school graduates tend to be the most sanctifying. There are also widows who are unable to sanctify their late husband, and some even go to the other extreme because of their harsh life in the years of marriage.

As stated above, all but 8.6 percent of the women have had children, and almost half have at least one child in the home, usually a still unmarried or no longer married offspring. Eighty percent of the widows consider themselves heads of households, and because 58 percent have at least one unmarried child, it is not surprising that so many share their residence with a child. However, most of these children are no longer very young. Reflecting a national trend, the remaining widows tend to live alone. Involvement with an offspring living away from the home is asymmetrical, with one child, usually a daughter, being seen more often than others, so that the mean frequency of contact with all offspring living away from home does not exceed several times a month. Few widows are able or willing to devote their whole lives to interaction with children living away from home; having tasted independence, they are reluctant to return to heavy housework or child rearing. Frequency and form of contact varies by education, race, income and past life-style. Daughters contribute much more than sons to the various support systems of the widows.

Most widows do not have living parents, and those who do are not in easy contact with them, so that only the very young widows can depend on help from the older generation. Some widows are able to help a surviving mother or father, but these cases are rare because of distances between their residences. All but 19 percent of the women have living siblings, but these tend to be dispersed and do not form a viable part of the support network. Average frequency of contact tends to be low, limited to holidays or family events such as weddings or funerals. Other relatives are even less involved.

Three-quarters of the widows represented by our sample had close personal friends the year before the husband's fatal illness or accident, and 43 percent made new friends since his death. The vast majority of these friends are women; men enter into the listing as the husbands of couple companionate associates. The most isolated are the 16 percent of the women who have neither old nor new friends. The most engaged are the 40 percent who list people in both categories. Friends made in widowhood are seen more often on the average than any other associates. Friends are usually first met in the neighborhood, at work, through organizations such as churches or through other friends, and they tend to be of long standing. Married old friends are, however, rarely seen, mainly because of the strain created in couple companionate interaction by the death of the husband. Old friends are considered to still be friends, in spite of their noninvolvement in the widow's social support system.

Only 22 percent have had a "close male friendship" since becoming widowed, and almost all of these women understood the question the way we mean it, in dating terms. Boyfriends like other friends are met through work and voluntary associations, but contact is frequently made in public places like bars. Boyfriends are mainly involved with the women only socially, rather than in other supports, unless they live in the same house or become husbands. The remarried women are younger with small children, and have been working or socially active in other ways. Future husbands are often met through friends and past associations. Most of the remarried women report life satisfaction, companionship and assuagement of loneliness as advantages of their new marriage and the loss of independence as a disadvantage. Some of the remarried women are much happier than they had been in their prior marriage, but most are positive about both unions. The most unhappy are those whose remarriage broke up.

Just over a fourth of the widows are presently employed, although many more have held jobs since the death of the husband, and a third were already employed prior to the onset of his illness. The nonworkers give very traditional reasons for having been full-time homemakers during marriage or for being only on-and-off employees. The wife and the husband expected her to be economically dependent on him, at least the former wife reports that there was no need for her to work, that she did not want a paid job and that her husband did not want her to have one. Main factors affecting whether the woman is now working are age, income adequacy, the presence of children in the home, marital status, occupational training, work experience, race and education.

Although over three-quarters of the women belong to a religious congregation, almost half do claim not to have a membership in any voluntary association. Some obviously do not consider a church as a "social organization or group." As evident also in other studies, women with personal resources of an educated, urban background, and those with incomes way above the poverty line are the socially most engaged women, belonging to voluntary associations, having friends and using a complex network for their support exchanges. The poor are impoverished in many ways.

SUPPORT SYSTEMS

The independence of the Chicago area widows, many of whom are living very restricted lives, is evidenced by their failure to use many of the supports deemed beneficial in modern urban environments and identified in pretests as helpful in the maintenance of life styles. Even though four out of 10 widows are below the poverty line for their size families, only 11 percent receive food or payment for food, and between eight and nine percent receive money gifts or help with payment of rent, mortgage or other bills, such as medical or vacation expenses. The poor are not necessarily the recipients of such help; most, in fact, are not. The more affluent widows report themselves as giving gifts of money, mainly to grandchildren, but only 13 percent are involved in such an outflow of economic supports. In all, only about 5 percent of the widows help anyone financially. Some of the recipients are charitable organizations.

Ninety-seven percent of the widows do not receive any help with child care, mostly because they don't need it. Eighty-seven percent do not have a car so do not need that service. Legal aid is also not needed by 81 percent of the women, or at least is not supplied by anyone. Such services as yard work may also not be needed. Service supports are generally sex-segregated. However, it is somewhat surprising that relatively so few are helped with transportation or household repairs since these are common needs in urban America. Still, those are the most frequent areas of inflow or supports except for care during illness. The widows themselves are the most apt to give help in illness, although only about a third do so, either because the help is not asked for, or because they feel unable to meet the request. The women see themselves as recipients more often than as givers of services, but the combination reinforces our conclusions about the relative independence of these women. Most service exchanges are with adult children, though transportation and shopping are also shared with friends or co-workers. The widow does not count regular work as homemaker as a service to people living in the home. Help across household thresholds to siblings or other relatives is very rare, in spite of assumptions of a viable modified extended family.

Many of these widows are not involved in the social activities selected as part of a possible social support system, either because of past restrictive habits or current problems with time, money, health, or lack of escort, self-confidence or desire. Over half claim never to go to public places or to engage in sports, cards or other games. Four in 10 do not entertain, possibly because they view this concept as a middle-class style. One-quarter of the women travel alone and 40 percent never go out of town, which leaves only a third who travel with other people. Of course, they may visit people in the course of their trip or at their destination. The same is probably true of the women who go to church alone. Friends frequently enter the social support system of middle-class, relatively more highly educated and affluent women. However, they are not apt to be involved in the sharing of holiday celebrations, which are almost always spent with relatives. Nieces and nephews sometimes substitute for adult children in the case of childless women or women whose children are not available. This is one of the few places in which the extended family appears in the widow's support systems.

The late husband, children and the self appear in the emotional systems of the wives the year prior to the husband's fatal illness or accident. The husband dominates, with some variations. A number of widows feel that they did not confide their problems to anyone; few admit feeling anger with anyone. Friends tend to supply self-feelings of importance, usefulness and so forth, but they were not as deeply involved in the emotional support system of the past as might be expected from the social life of many of the couples. Friends also do not take over the late husband's role as a major supplier of emotional supports, although some of the widows retain important friends throughout. It is the children, especially the daughters, who take over the emotional support system. Their importance to the support systems of their mothers cannot be overemphasized.

One of the more dramatic findings of this study is the absence of the "helping professions and groups" during the period of the husband's illness, immediately after his death, when the widow was trying to establish a new life, and now. Even ministers, priests or rabbis are mentioned rarely; if they appear at all, it is often as persons who failed to provide expected and needed help. Voluntary associations, including church groups, contribute to the support systems of only a few widows, to proportionately more blacks than whites. Religion itself, in the form of "faith" or "God" appeared in the emotional supports of some of the older women, who also more often relied on themselves, especially as suppliers of self-feelings. The older the woman, up to the very aged level, the more apt is she to draw feelings of independence and self-sufficiency from herself. Many of the Chicago area widows, however, have no one to provide them with positive self-feelings or to serve as confidant, comforter or source of pleasure. Community resources are used very seldom to help solve acute or chronic problems or to help in the re-engagement after the dissolution of prior support systems and networks. Only the more cosmopolitan widows are able to draw on any of the vast sets of resources metropolitan Chicago offers to its residents. This finding supports other studies, such as Chicago's Needs Assessment Survey (Fewer, 1973; Lopata, 1975), documenting underutilization of resources on the part of Chicago area elderly. The women included in that study were even more ignorant of the resources and reluctant to use the ones they knew about than were the men.

Profiles

The profiles of some of the women, based on the interviews, can give a fuller picture of how the background characteristics and support systems combine into a life-style.

THE NORM-HUGGING WIDOW

The majority of the widows are older, not highly educated, with spasmodic participation in the labor force, and now mainly dependent on social security survivors' benefits. But even this group is not homogenous; size and complexity of their social life space vary by area of its focus.

A highly *family-oriented* widow emigrated to America from Greece in 1912 with three brothers. She was born in 1893 and on her arrival here, she married a restaurant owner, a man 12 years her senior. She helped her husband in the restaurant until his death in 1950. She never learned to speak English; her daughter acted as translator in the interview. However, she has a full social life centered on her family. Two of her children, born in 1925 and 1929, never married and are living with her; a third child lives in the neighborhood and is seen weekly. One brother also lives in the area and they get together several times a month. She stopped wearing deep mourning for her husband after 12 months and started visiting and entertaining at home with the help of the brother and sister-in-law. Her support network consists of the children, kin and many friends "from the old country."

Another *family-oriented* respondent moved to Chicago from Mexico with her husband, who subsequently developed heart trouble and went back to Mexico alone, where he died in 1961.

He had a bad heart, wasn't feeling good for the past couple of years before he died. He didn't like the cold weather in Chicago, so he went back to Mexico. He had this heart attack in Mexico, died instantly. He was buried in his home town.

She, however, remained in the neighborhood with her eldest son and some other of her 12 children. Two of her children are dead and she, a 90-year-old woman who had had a difficult life, is not well. Her children care for her and have all "stuck together through all our troubles." She enjoys the children and feels close to them, especially her daughters. Unlike the Greek woman, she is heavily dependent on her children because she neither made friends before her husband's death nor since. She had never belonged to any voluntary associations and still does not. She also never worked during her marriage or since. She seems to be the hub of the family life, never going out but having all her children visit her. She used to be more mobile but is now unable to walk. Her main complaint is society's failure to provide medical care. When asked to comment on the interview, she stated:

> I would like to see some type of home service, doctor calls for people like me. I can't walk and it takes two people to get me in the car to go to the doctor's office. I can't walk and it's hard for me to wait in a doctor's office. To have Medicare take care and pay for my pills and medicines. I had to pay for my ambulance when I was rushed to the hospital. I had to pay $37. I think they should find some way to help pay for these things.

Most widows' state of health is not as poor, but then most are not as old. Many other older widows, however, lead restricted lives.

THE DISADVANTAGED WIDOW

When looking over the interviews it is easy to pick out the disadvantaged widows. After all, so many are living on incomes below the poverty line, and they reached this position after a decline in income since widowhood. Some are very angry and *depressed*, although sometimes this fact does not appear in the beginning of the interview because they are able to list many resources. One woman is now going through a difficult period, although she had been widowed three years ago and reports many supports early in widowhood:

> It seems that I was better able to cope with the first two years. It seems now, I'm very depressed and think I'm making myself sick over it. It seems at first the friends flock around you, but now little by little they drop away. They don't call or talk. I guess they thought I was a rich widow, because I'm able to live in this apartment. I was much stronger then than I'm now and was able to cope.

The whole tenor is one of passivity. She expected a one-way flow of attention and now that it has dried up, she uses her poverty as the explanation. She has little awareness of the importance of reciprocal flow of supports, and many interviews testify to a similar attitude and lack of initiative.

Another *depressed* widow had only her niece to call on when she got desperate, and her doctor appears to be one of her few links to the world.

I wanted to take my life, end it all. It was a Saturday morning two weeks ago. I got up, I was so depressed. If I'd had sleeping pills I would have taken them, cause I was so low. I felt "What's the sense of me waking up? What's there for me to wake up to?" That's the day I called up my niece long distance and I told her. I told her how depressed I was. She asked "Is there anyone there to give you sleeping pills?" I said "No." She said "If you have any, throw them in the toilet." I didn't have any. She told me she'd come over. Late that afternoon she and her husband came over. They live far south on the Indiana border. They live in farm country. She tried to talk me out of it and promised to keep in touch. She called several times, but I haven't heard from her in a week.

I still feel that way. Several times I think "What's the use? What's there to live for? It's two weeks since I felt that way. I can eat very little. I saw a doctor a month ago. He didn't pinpoint it. He wants to put me in the hospital but I can't go cause Medicare won't pay for one year. He wants to x-ray my stomach. I got out my crocheting. I'm making a scarf for a little boy.

It isn't just a matter of health but attitudes toward life which create problems that impose restrictions on people. A perfect example is a very *unhappy and angry woman* who has not been able to voluntaristically solve her problems. Her anger stems mainly from a hearing loss suffered in 1943, when she was 26 years of age. The events which stand out in her mind, in the order of importance, are her marriage, the loss of hearing eight years later, the death of her husband in 1972, the birth of her only child, a daughter, in 1952, and the purchase of a car in 1950. She has no living siblings and both of her parents died many years ago, her father when she was only 12 years of age. One of the sources of her anger is the doctor who took care of her husband:

> He waited too long—three years—for his first operation. Then he had a second operation in November [the first one was in June]. Then he went back to work. About nine or 10 months later he had to quit and stayed home. He went into a coma the last few days before he died. He died here at home. The doctor was very unhelpful. He wouldn't tell me that my husband would die. He told me three times that my husband would live a long time. Then 10 days before he died, he told me not to bother with a hospital because he wouldn't live much longer anyway, and walked out of the office.

Although the undertaker helped her with the funeral arrangements and in filing for social security, no one helped her with loneliness and the emotional problems connected with her loss of hearing. She feels it is impossible for her to establish a new life because she is "cut off because of my deafness." She wants her hearing back but seems not to have done anything about it. The daughter was present during the first part of the interview but the minute she left the respondent complained about *her* "lack of interest and concern." She feels closest to her godmother, not her daughter, tells her problems to no one, is comforted by no one, and has no one to turn to in times of crisis. Both her daughter and her husband were the persons who most often made her angry in the past, and her daughter still does. She had one couple with whom she was friends when her husband was living but now she sees them only rarely. She has made no new friends since widowhood and had

> hoped to join an organization for the deaf, but couldn't because I don't know sign language and I'm too old to learn. I considered studying it before, but didn't because I thought my husband wouldn't learn it and therefore we would drift apart. [She is now 57 years old.]

She did not train for any job and thinks that her hearing defect would disqualify her for any job involving machines, so she has not even bothered to look. She does not go to public places or entertain because of her hearing problem, is not interested in sports or other games, and is afraid to travel out of town. The whole interview is negative, and it is not surprising that she strongly disagrees with the statement, "I am very satisfied with the way my life is going now."

One widow tried various methods to cope with the disengagement caused by several events in her life course but reports frequent failure and sounds *angry*. Born in 1924, and thus only 50 years old at the time of the interview, she was married in 1949; the marriage, which was childless, ended in 1972 with the death of her husband. She had quit working two years before her husband's death, losing her seniority.

> If I had continued working at this place I would have a pension now and not have to break my back working now. I would have had 30 years by now. I quit because the company moved—would have to travel far. Had no time for training, needed money when he died. I took in foster children to keep me company because it was lonely living alone. That didn't work out too good so I went to work. Had less time to think about myself.

Her sisters are reported as having failed her socially and emotionally and she feels that she made a mistake just after becoming widowed: "That I didn't sell my house; if I had sold it then I wouldn't have to take my father in. I'm busy keeping after him and it's more work."

THE OFF-TIME WIDOW

One of the respondents pointed out in the self-administered questionnaire that special attention should be paid to the problems of the younger widow, especially one who has small children.

One such widow had a complicated history. She had only 8 years of schooling because her mother died in 1925, when she was only 13 years of age. She took care of her younger brothers and sisters and then married in 1936. The marriage lasted only 10 years and was not satisfactory. Her husband "changed jobs a great deal," and she can't remember "that he worked at one occupation for a long time." She had 6 small children when her husband died of a fractured skull while in the custody of the police. She blames herself for some of her problems, "I should have been more friendly and outgoing." She wanted many things changed in her life after the husband's death, including a better house to live in and more modern equipment to make housework easier.

> Welfare wanted me to work. I am very attached to my children. I didn't want to leave my children alone and I had no friends to come in and look in on them. I was afraid they would get hurt because we lived on a busy street. Welfare also wanted me to be more strict and teach the children to help me. But I don't like to argue, I'd rather do it myself. When they got older they did help. [Mistake early in widowhood.] I did not go out with the opposite sex because I was afraid to have problems with my children.

One of the problems with being a young widow with children is the ease with which she can become dependent upon others who then feel they have a right to give advice and even to dictate her behavior. One 29 year-old woman continues to see the parents of her first husband in spite of their disapproval of things she does. Born in the Chicago area of German and Polish, relatively uneducated parents, she "never sees them" although they live in the same city. Her husband died in an automobile accident after suffering a cerebral hemorrhage due to a brain tumor. She was a passenger in the car but recovered. Her parents-in-law had her move in with them and helped her take care of her two children while she took a modeling job. They convinced her to sell her late husband's gun shop— a decision she now regrets. There must have been some tension in her relations with the in-laws, because they strongly disapproved of her marriage; however, that marriage ended in divorce and the relation with her former in-laws has been renewed. In fact, she sees them about once a week. Her mother-in-law remains the only person to whom she would turn in times of crisis, both parents-in-law made her feel accepted when their son was alive and they are the ones with whom she and her children celebrate holidays. The interviewer noted that she is a beautiful woman, and she has no problems meeting men because she models at conventions.

The third example of the problems of young widows is really a case of failure rather than an absence of resources. This woman was born in 1935 of immigrant parents. In addition to her three children living at home, she has seven siblings in the Chicago area whom she sees several times a month. The "family as a group" helped her right after the sudden death of her husband by taking care of the children and helping her pay bills. she defines her life as a rough one, having to take over the responsibility of being both father and mother to the children in addition to holding a job. In spite of all the recognized early assistance from her family, this woman is bitter about an alleged lack of supports from her associates, finding neighbors and in-laws "never helpful," and friends helpful only in special situations while she was trying to build a new life. She is emphatic about the failure of associates to meet expectations in answer to the questions: "Now I would like to know if there is any kind of help or advice you wish people had offered you, but which they did not." She wished her friends had provided services, invited her out or visited her. Two of her sisters are singled out as having failed to provide emotional supports. She wanted "people visiting me. Anyone, just to have someone to talk to." This young widow lists only one of her sons and one friend now and then in the relational segment of her current emotional support system, stating that she tells no one her problems and has no one comforting her when she becomes depressed, although she would turn to her sisters in times of crisis. No one makes her feel secure, and her emotional support system is relatively empty, the son and friend being the only ones mentioned in the feeling states, and not all that often. One brother helps her with household repairs and care of the car several times a year and one sister takes care of her when she is ill, otherwise the economic and service support systems are also empty, both in the in- and the outflow. She does not entertain at home because of lack of money, has never cared for sports or other games and has never traveled because she has "no place to go." She had made no friends since becoming widowed, which happened five years ago, and sees only two women friends, whom she met in school many years ago, perhaps once a week or a little less often. She has made no close male friends since becoming a widow and belongs to no voluntary associations.

She is one of the few women to place the role of wife in fifth rank out of nine in order of importance and to define her late husband in sixth place out of seven in the superior–inferior and in the kind–cruel ends of these continuums. That is a very strong rejection of the man. He is also defined on the cold rather than the warm side of that semantic-differential statement. The only two items in which the widow gives her late husband a "1" score, used so overwhelmingly by so many other women, is in the good and friendly traits. The combination is certainly unusual since it would seem impossible for someone who is defined as cold and cruel also to be good and friendly. A similar pattern emerges when we look at her judgements in the relational segment of the sanctification scale. The only statement this widow strongly agrees with is that her late husband had been a good father. She mildly agrees that he had been an unusually good man, that the marriage was above average, that she and her husband felt the same way about almost everything and that he had no irritating habits. Simultaneously, she strongly disagrees that they were always together except in working hours and she disagrees that theirs had been an unusually happy home. Finally, she defines herself as more lonely than most people and disagrees strongly with the statement, "I am very satisfied with the way my life is going now." All in all, she did not seem to have had positive expectations of marriage, accepting coldness and cruelty in the relation and an unhappy home, while having high and definitely unfulfilled expectations of a variety of supports in widowhood. The failure of the resources to provide desired supports have left her a dissatisfied woman, but she does not sound as if she had ever been very happy.

Another young widow with some of the same problems, mainly three small children, has a different approach of life, and has recently undertaken several actions to change the lifestyle forced on her by the death of the husband. She was widowed seven years ago, at the age of 29, and purposely limited her grieving to six months because of the children.

> I had such little kids. I didn't want to ruin their lives so I said to myself I better shape up. I had an aunt who was a widow for five years. She carried on and I remembered how she ruined one of her kid's life, and I did not want to do that to mine.

She faced the frequently reported problem with married friends. "Our couple friends just stopped inviting me, other than the afternoon visits by the wife." Her brother and a girlfriend encouraged her to go out more, rather than just staying home and taking of the children, but she could not. Her suggestions commenting on the interview in the self-administered segment suggest how difficult this early period of widowhood must have been for her.

> Maybe the why of things should have been asked more often. Circumstances can change the meaning to the answers of some of the questions. For instance, I think I probably came off rather dull, but for five of the seven years that I've been a widow my children were babies—(they were three and a half, two and a half,

367

and three months old when my husband died)—I didn't have much choice but stay home and care for them during these five years.

After a few years she decided to lose weight; she was very heavy when she became widowed. "I just lost 50 pounds of weight in the past four years. Men don't go for a 200-pounder. Maybe this will make a difference for me to meet a man." Her girlfriend wanted her to go to bars to meet men but she could not bring herself to go barhopping because "of the type of men I think you would meet in a bar. They'd be out for a one-night stand." She finally went back to college when the children started in primary school, working now for a two-year accounting degree. In the meantime, her family has been very supportive and she has become increasingly active. Her support systems include the father, and especially the mother, a sister and her husband, a brother and his wife, and girl-friends. Although her parents had advised her not to send the children to a Catholic school because of the expense, she insisted that they needed that kind of an education and the pastor of the church, who is also the school principal, appointed her to the school board. Other members of this board make her feel respected and important. She has had four boyfriends recently; two of them she met through the school. She did not "hit it off" with the blind date, a man whose name she does not remember, because "he was completely different than I am. He wasn't fun." Another man, met at a wedding and dated once, "got married right after that to someone else."

All in all, this young woman shows both the problems and the resources of becoming widowed "off time." She has taken the initiative to re-engage in a complex network, but it took several years before she could reach that stage of mobility in not just "grief work" but change in supports.

THE MINORITY WIDOW

Some of the problems faced by some of the minority widows, though by no means by all, can be illustrated by the lives of two women. One is Indian, now 65 years of age. She had married at age 14 in Alabama where she and her husband worked a rented farm. She had her first of seven children at 15, although she claims that:

> My husband never really lived with me and never contributed nothing to the security of the children. I worked in cotton fields and cleaned houses to bring them up. Funny, though, he came back long enough to give me seven children.

Once her husband died she turned the farm back to the people they rented from and moved to Gary, Indiana, where she lives with one of the children, and all but one of the offspring are around in the neighborhood. She does not know the occupation of any of her six boys but says the daughter is a housewife. She is very satisfied with the way her life is going now, never feels lonely and finds membership in church and participation in its activities a main source of pleasure. The relative ease of life is due to a diminution of work and an increase in income thanks to social security and old-age assistance. Her husband had been more of a burden than an asset and is identified as extremely cruel, bad and useless. The marriage had been a bad one and the home had not been happy. He was not even a good father.

Interestingly, her six children, who are in the area, do not appear often in her economic, service, social or emotional support systems. They do help her celebrate holidays "if they are around." She has a good friend and draws on herself for most self-feelings, except that one grandson makes her feel useful.

The subject of the following profile has a very restricted social life space, mainly because of a history of bad health, which affects black women more than the whites. The widow was born in 1912 in the South and did not obtain much education because, "My head hurt me so bad from an old bullet wound that I could not study." Her first marriage ended in divorce after four years; the second lasted nine years and ended in separation in 1962; then came widowhood. She had no children and sees her two siblings only occasionally. Aside from these contacts and a niece, the only person close to her, she lives in isolation. She attributes her inability to develop a new life and friends in widowhood to her arthritis; one of her legs is now bandaged because of it. She has no one she enjoys being with, telling problems to, being comforted by or to whom she could turn in times of crisis. She depends entirely on herself for all self-feelings, yet hers is a picture of isolation, not of satisfactory independence.

THE WORKING CLASS SOCIALITE: SATISFIED

The importance of the person herself as a major resource for both independence and the buildup of a complex support system is evident in the life of a widow who is "never lonely" and very satisfied with the way her life is going now, in spite of traumatic events of the past and a marginal economic existence. This widow is second-generation on her father's side and her parents did not go beyond grade school, although she finished high school. Her mother died when she was very young and she did not get along with her stepmother:

> I tried to get along with her but she just doesn't get along with me. When I was about four years old, she used to lock me in the clothes closet. She knocked all my teeth out when I was four years old. I ran to my grandmother's without clothes on in sleet and snow. I used to tell her "I'll tell my father," and she said "I'll lock you up more in the closet."

In addition to the death of the mother, she lost two children: one was stillborn, the other lived five days. Born in 1923, she had a stroke in 1968, the result of hypertension, which for awhile made it impossible for her to find a job. Her husband had been "sickly" most of their married life, so they sold all their furniture after her stroke and moved in with her daughter, whose husband had left her. She improved and went to work to help out her daughter. Her husband, who had bleeding ulcers, became progressively worse, and she reports the following circumstances surrounding his death.

I was working and I told him, I always called him Pa, "You are sick, aren't you?" He was very stubborn, he wouldn't give in that he was sick. He said to me, "Go to work today or you won't be paid for Memorial Day." Half an hour later after I got to work, my daughter called and said that my husband was sick. I ran home, it took me five minutes to get home. I called the V.A. hospital and told them my husband was sick. They said they had no ambulance and I should call somebody to take him there. So I called my sister-in-law who lived in _____ . She drove us to the V.A. hospital. He couldn't walk. I held him under the arm and then he told me, "Mary, I can't make it into admitting." So I went and got a mobile chair. Then I took him in there. I waited one hour for the doctor in intensive care. He was bleeding from the mouth and from the rectum. They put him in restraints. He was going out of sense. He died three days later.

She had let her husband's insurance lapse and so did not get any money from that source; her mother-in-law and her daughter paid for the burial with the help of some money from social security. The daughter remarried about that time and life for the mother does not sound very good.

Three months later, I asked my daughter, "Where's Dad?" and she said, "What's the matter, Mom, Dad's dead." At first I was pushed around by my daughter. She said I had friends and relatives who should take care of me. My relatives did help, but they couldn't do for long. I went to live with my cousin, that is, my Uncle John's daughter, for a month. My cousin's mother wanted the place so I had to get out. Then I went to Uncle John's for two months, but somebody squealed that I was there and I had to get out. Then I went to my Aunt Helen's for two months. They had a home where I had to sleep in the basement. I did not like that. Then I went to live with Susan, my daughter's friend, for one month. After all, I felt I was imposing sleeping on a couch when they were a young couple. I lived in a furnished apartment on 51st and

Aberdeen, maybe three months—it was a hole in the wall, I couldn't stand it. Then I lived with my best friend for one month, but I was afraid her landlady would object, because no one extra was allowed to live there. Then I moved to 52nd and near Justine in a furnished apartment for two months. They had roaches, so I went back to my best friend for about four months. I was sleeping in her son's bedroom and I didn't want to take it away from him. I finally decided I had to get on my own feet and this is when I found this apartment six months ago.

The interviewer notes that she is very proud of her small, immaculate apartment. In spite of all these problems she obviously had at least temporary help from a variety of people. In fact, she now feels very satisfied and, in spite of gnarled fingers, she loves to have a good time and has many friends. She meets most of her women and men friends in taverns or lounges, although she met two of her friends at the launder-mat. She visits taverns daily, one of these places being a "lonely-hearts" hangout; several marriages resulted from meetings there. She herself does not care to remarry because of her late husband's chronic health problems, but she loves to dance, drink and swim, and sees about five boyfriends at least once a week. Her social and emotional support systems include her friends, although she depends on her daughter for the few service supports she exchanges and she celebrates holidays with her. She goes to public places with a variety of friends, visits and entertains with them at least once a week, and engages in sports and games. She does not eat lunch with others simply because she eats only once a day and she never travels out of town. She goes to church only on holidays.

Her active support systems are paralleled by a consistent strain of independence. "That's what's wrong with me. I'm too independent," she states, and her actions prove that type of behavior, though it is hard to judge whether it is dysfunctional. Whe she fell behind in her rent, she went to the welfare people, and, "They sent me to SSI," so she has financial help.

She is the one who worked after the stroke as long as she was able to. Her behavior when the husband became fatally ill shows strength in spite of the powerlessness of the poor in the face of bureaucracies. Despite all the circumstances of her life that could push a woman into disengagement and social isolation, she has always pulled herself together and formed new close associates, found places to live and enjoyed herself. Her emotional support system reflects this. Most of her individual supports are filled with several people. She lists herself in the others, explaining for example, when asked who comforted her while her husband was living and who comforts her now, "I don't carry my problems to nobody," and, "No one, I grin and bear it." She has no one to whom to turn now in times of crisis, but at the same time, no one makes her angry. She provided herself with feelings of independence and security when the husband lived and continues to do so. Her late husband made her feel useful and self-sufficient the year before his fatal illness, and she now draws on herself for these feeling states.

Although her husband and she did not feel the same way about everything and their home was really not a very happy one, she defines him as not having had irritating habits and as having been a good man and father, and she describes the marriage as good. These seem to be contradictory judgements. Her various problems and past tragedies have not decreased her willingness to see life now as very satisfactory.

THE WORKING-CLASS SOCIALITE: MIXED FEELINGS

This widow, born in 1906, lists birth, graduation and marriage of children as major events and fails to mention her two marriages, including one in which she is still involved. She has eight living children and one who died. Four of the children live in either Texas and California and are not seen very often, but she lives with a 37-year-old unmarried daughter. The children's occupations vary in prestige, from social worker to a maintenance worker at a church. Seven siblings are seen several times a year. Her new life started after two years of widowhood, when she "began to go out to meet people again. I had gotten over loneliness. I always liked people and I wanted to be with my friends again." She has a very good friend who is active in her emotional support system, as is a sister, one daughter and the new husband. However, she does not always feel useful and self-sufficiency comes mainly from her work around the home. The late husband does not seem to have been very active in providing her with important self-feelings. She has active service and social support systems, with her husband, daughter, and a sister as the main contributors. She is active in voluntary associations. Most of her life was spent in domestic work in private homes, but she wishes that she would have done sewing at home to make money. She does not need to work now because her new husband is earning a good salary and she believes that she has worked enough in the past. The husband had been a longtime friend of theirs, and they married after both their spouses died. She is black and he is Chinese. He is not as sociable as her late husband, and she answered the question as to differences in marriages as follows:

> A difference in personalities. My present husband isn't as outgoing as my first husband. Also, my first husband would help more and help me with cooking. This husband just wants me to spend my time with him and he is jealous when the kids come in. He doesn't want to mingle with friends as much.

The advantages of not remarrying are apparent and she would advise a new widow not to remarry and to enjoy her freedom: "In my case she would be a lot freer and be able to do what she wants more and be able to go more places."

Born in 1917, this upper-middle-class widow was married in 1942 and widowed in 1969. Her father was a highly educated professional man, although the daughter only finished high school and then obtained training in the health-service industry. Her husband was a vice president of a large organization, and she has two sons who are currently away from home working and in the armed services, although neither is married. Two brothers live far away and are seen less than once a year. The mother is dead and the father lives in Florida. Her support systems have been varied and not continuous or sustaining, in that her husband's army buddies visited her and called her after the husband died but have not kept up the contact and financial matters have been handled by bank officers and lawyers. Yet, she defines neighbors, adult children, friends and club members as generally very helpful when she was building a new life in widowhood. There were no needs or kinds of help she wishes people had offered but did not receive, and the main aspect of her life that she wanted to change was to get rid of the big house she had in one of the "exurbanite" areas of Chicago. The house simply did not sell, possibly because of its high price, but she has retained or developed a social life in the community, which is much couple oriented.

Her late husband was a major contributor to her emotional supports before his death, yet she told her problems to no one, and her friends are listed as the only persons who comforted her even when he was alive. When asked who made her feel like an especially important person when the husband was alive, she responded, "I don't know," and she still states that, "I never thought I was that important." Nobody made her angry before and no one does now. Friends provided a refuge in times of crises before as well as now. The husband

375

was one of the two persons closest to her (one of the two sons was the other person) and was the person she most enjoyed being with. He is now replaced by three women friends and the children do not appear in either segment of the emotional support system at all. In fact, this respondent lists herself as the only provider of all her positive self-feelings. At least, she does not answer with "no one."

She belongs to a country club, a tennis club and a drama league. She met three of her closest women friends through the country club. There are no friends listed since widowhood, although she goes to both clubs several times a week. She has neither wanted nor needed to work outside of the home; her husband's earnings and the family investments since his death have enabled her to stay out of the labor force. Her only employment experience has been as a technician in her father's practice. She has not worked since. She calls on a lawyer to help her make important decisions and is not involved in any other service supports or in any economic exchanges defined as "help."

Basically, this woman has two women friends with whom she shares social activities and no relatives, even the sons, appear frequently in the various support systems. This dearth of contributors may be partly due to her disinclination to discuss her personal life, but the whole interview indicates a very formalized use of resources centered on the country and tennis clubs. Although she is extreme in the semantic differential segment of the sanctification scale, she disagrees with the statements that she and her husband shared their time except for working hours, that her husband had no irritating habits and that she is satisfied with the way her life is going now.

THE MIDDLE-CLASS SOCIALITE: SATISFIED

This 40-year-old former widow has a complex set of resources available for use in the support systems. She was prematurely widowed after 17 years of marriage, when her four children were all relatively young. She married a previously married man four years later, who probably was also a widower, because he had full custody of his three children. She thus considers herself as having mothered seven children, all of whom are still in the household. She has had 14 years of schooling, plus an art course, and currently teaches an adult art class five hours a week. She does not report any major problems after the death of her husband, and she remarried after having dated one other man prior to meeting her current husband. Each of her husbands has major contributions to her emotional support systems at both time periods we covered, and her present husband is very active in the social system as well as in selected service supports. This woman is one of the respondents who refused to discuss the amount of income the family derived from various sources, feeling that such information is no one's business, and she lists no one as contributing to her economic system, which reflects a view of the marriage as a shared relationship. (This is an interesting finding in many interviews: that women who are mainly housewives do not consider the money they spend on clothing, food, hospital or vacation bills as "help" from the income-earning husband.) Married first to a lawyer and now to a self-employed manufacturer's representative, she obviously defines herself as part of a team involved in a "two-person career." Her lack of dependency feelings emerges in the emotional system in that the supports in which the husbands do not appear are consistently filled with the self. She obtained her feelings of being respected, independent and self-sufficient from herself the year prior to her first husband's sudden death as well as in her present marriage.

Four friends are listed in this woman's past and three have been made since widowhood. She met two of the closest new friends in the class she teaches; the third is a neighbor. Not active in voluntary associations and limited in the time she can devote to her occupation, her social life does not include sports, cards or other games. Her husband as well as her parents and parents-in-law are co-celebrants of holidays; the nuclear family goes to church together; attendance at public functions and visits are shared with friends, and business associates of the husband are also entertained at home.

Although of a different social class than the woman portrayed in *Alice Does Not Live Here Anymore*, this respondent states openly that she wants to be married; "I am a complete person married." Her advice to widows about remarriage may be a major factor in the success of this relation: "Stay out of the past and stay in the present and future in any relationship with a man." She strongly disagrees with the statement, "Many widows who remarry are very unhappy in this marriage." She feels that she is less lonely than most people and recommends that our interview be restructured to "keep all past questions together and keep all present questions together."

Implications

Our study of widows in metropolitan Chicago documents the heterogeneity of these women in background, forms and degree of disorganization brought about by the circumstances of the husband's death and by the death itself, and the support systems and networks they have developed since that time. More than 10 million living women have gone through all these experiences and most of them have been able to reorganize themselves and their lives into a rather independent existence with varying amounts of assistance from the society, the community and their personal resources. They are not politically organized to protest lack of services or push for better living conditions. Despite their numbers they have been rather invisible in our society. One of the reasons is their age, but a major reason is the fact that they are women, many of them traditionally socialized to be passive vis-à-vis the world outside their immediate home environment. Such women were trained (1) to expect automatically available support systems in the form of a constantly present family and an unchanging neighborhood, (2) to be supported economically and in a division of labor by a husband, sons and the patrilineal line, (3) to have their children "fathered" by men replacing the deceased father, and so forth. However, society has changed, has become highly urbanized, mobile geographically and socially individuated, requiring voluntaristic engagement by members in a complex of available social roles. This society has not neglected its members, having built vast networks of resources, jobs providing income and social intergration, innumerable voluntary associations, friendships with non-kin-related people, "helping" groups, and specially trained personnel to solve acute and chronic problems and self-help groups or courses training people to use these resources.

So here we are in the last quarter of the 20th century, with this vast network on one side of the societal fence and a relatively large number of its members unable to utilize these resources on the other side of the fence. There are many who use the resources, or most of these agencies (at least some of them) would go out of business or lose support. However, the users tend to be people who were born and socialized into this type of society, who step-by-step learned to map out the resources and prepare themselves for multidimensional lives, utilizing them and modifying support networks as self-defined needs change. Those able to utilize the various resources are not hampered by the lack of self-confidence or by ideologies that negatively define as aggressive any attempt to change the script written for one's life by other people or groups.

There is no actual count of people who have the abilities to function in the modern urban world through a flexible use of resources and supports. It is apparent from the study of the Chicago area widows that not many are functioning in the fullest possible life space. Some do not wish to change what is happening or what they are causing to happen. Some have rebuilt their support networks after completing their grief work

379

following the death of their husband. There are widows who are simply relieved by the death and gratified over the decrease in work that time has brought. There are also women who live very restricted lives who wish for contact with others but do not have any connecting links to the world outside of their home.

Thus, most of the older urban widows—and most American widows are older and live in urban surroundings—have been caught between two styles of life: the one in which they were socialized and educated and the one in which they now live. Obviously, this can be said of many groups of people who live in a changing society for an extended period of time. However, the rate of change during the past six decades in America has been so rapid, life has become so different, and the opportunities for flexible and complex social engagement by women so dramatically expanded, and pre-World War II traditional socialization and limited education have failed to equip many women for living competently in the world we have created. Traditional support systems have disappeared and none has automatically replaced them, or they are gradually being stripped away, while these women do not have the personal resources to voluntaristically build their own new support systems. Newer generations of women will not be facing many of the problems and restrictions typical of today's older widow. The 60 and above cohort of American women, comprising more than one generation, is unique in many ways, and because of the pace of change in the lives of American women, future generations will not have to cope with as many of the problems and needs, and not as frequently, as their predecessors. Whatever society does to help solve some of the problems and restrictions that confronted the Chicago area women represented in this study will not necessarily burden its future, because as newer types of women with different stances vis-à-vis the world and role complexes become widowed, the need will diminish. Even the women in this study are a heterogeneous aggregate, reflecting age, racial, ethnic, education and urbanization differences, and private or public policies designed to alleviate the needs of one segment may be irrelevant or unhelpful to other segments.

What remains in this analysis is the presentation of some recommendations of how different segments of the society can now alleviate the problems of different categories of widows. These recommendations depend on the problems.

COMMON PROBLEMS

1. Lack of opportunity to grieve. There is an increasing literature about death and grief which will, we hope, make for healthier ways of dealing with the major losses. I am firmly convinced from the studies and the scientific literature that dying patients and their families must be told of the impending death and must cooperate with the medical staff and anyone else involved in the care of the patient and the other grievers throughout the process. Grief work is a necessary process and involves emotional responses, life review, probably some sanctification, but, at a minimum, the opportunity to talk and have someone listen. The need to talk, sometimes over and over again, and not to be burdened with other people's problems and situations is recognized—well institutionalized in the Jewish practice of the shiva.

2. The need for a return to traditional or the development of new rituals surrounding the death.

3. Lack of emotional supports after the short official mourning period and probably well into the second year.

4. Lack of daily services extending beyond the funeral, while the widow tries to deal with the shock and grief work.

5. Bad advice from people who do not understand the widow's situation and who force decisions on her which she later regrets. The need is for action on the part of significant others which builds the widow's feelings of

competence, self-confidence, importance, and other self-feelings, not for advice that makes her feel incompetent.

6. Lack of supports for the children, whose need for knowledge and for grief is largely unrecognized. The mother is usually incapable of providing the kind of help children need, often because she has very mixed emotions, so children are basically ignored unless they cause trouble by attention-getting behavior.

7. Lack of companionship, alleviation of loneliness, lack of escorts and exclusion from couple companionate interaction and of family events that include children.

8. Lack of self-help groups concerned with the solution of some of the above-mentioned problems, such as the widow-to-widow program (see Silverman in Bibliography), or branches of Parents without Partners devoted to the widowed. (The feelings of widowed and divorced persons are initially so mutually hostile that the newly widowed withdraw from membership or do not even attempt to join.)

9. Lack of job training and job search information resulting in inefficient job-hunting methods and poorly paying jobs.

10. Financial problems early in widowhood resulting in some long-range dysfunctional decisions.

PROBLEMS OF YOUNGER WIDOWS

1. Isolation at home with small children, needs for opportunities to get together with other mothers and children.

2. Lack of adequate, inexpensive day-care centers and of information about them and the presence of outdated attitudes that fail to recognize the extreme importance for both the mother and the children to get away from each other and to relate to other people. Children who

have lost their father need other people besides the mother to care for them, to show interest in them and to allow them to grieve.

3. Lack of opportunities for contact with men, for companionate interaction and, often in different relationships, for sexual interaction.
4. Lack of money, sources, limits and methods of budgeting.
5. Lack of a whole variety of services as giver, not just receiver, that also provide companionship and opportunity to move in a wider network.
6. Need for continued friendship with prior friends and inclusion in their activities, as well as opportunity to meet new friends who are not bound to the image of the woman as "Tom's widow."

PROBLEMS PECULIAR TO OLDER WIDOWS

1. Inability to earn an income and high probability of poverty, as well as inadequate development and information about part-time jobs.
2. Agism, or stereotyping people by age.
3. Inadequate background due to the traditional liminations imposed on women.
4. Inadequate facilities in many communities for social contact with peers.
5. Fear of rejection, which decreases the probability of using existing resources.
6. Sexual imbalance making male companionship very rare; the older the woman, the fewer men are available for egalitarian interaction. Assumption of absence of sexual and other intimacy desires.
7. Inadequate, often dangerous, housing—a barrier to social contact.
8. Lack of contacts to prevent or handle emergencies, such as daily calls or a "hot line."
9. If relatively house-bound, lack of social contact; lack of medical and dental care; and lack of adequate nutrition.

In addition, of course, individual life-styles and circumstances bring needs or problems specific for each widow. The main problem is that these women often do not have sufficient contact with people who will listen to them and try to meet their needs as they define them, not as the observer defines them. Over and over in the interviews the women complain that people will not let them express themselves or will not listen to what they are trying to say. Associates are impatient or simply withdraw while the widows need to work out their grief and feelings of loneliness. Although often living independently, many of the women enjoy *freedom from* work, from control by the husband's family, from control by welfare or other agencies, from imposition by others, including their children, etc., but have not yet gained *freedom to* pull together their resources and develop satisfactory new lives (Fromm, 1947).

The report to the Social Security Administration included numerous recommendations for improving the financial situation of the women who do not qualify for benefits and those whose benefits are limited for a variety of outdated reasons. Also included was the recommendation that much more be done to contact new widows or women whose children have grown to provide job training and better employment information so that they can re-enter the labor market or upgrade their jobs now that they are the primary earners in the family or their own sole supporter. The society also needs to be much more flexible concerning work schedules, with flextime being only one of the alternatives. There is actually little logic to much of the way work is organized in America, except that that's how it was done in the past. Many organizations are only now beginning to experiment with alternate schedules. The whole relation between the home and the society is undergoing reexamination, and we can expect these changes to affect the lives of women as they move through various stages of their life course. It is to be hoped that future widows will not face what widows today are going through if the home ceases to be a unit isolated from societal life and if the woman once she marries ceases to be looked on as a dependent and limited human being, so that widowhood leaves her with few personal resources. Not all of today's widows are limited, but in a world with so many resources, the number encumbered by numerous societally and personally imposed restrictions is frightening.

NEIGHBORHOOD NETWORKS

The ideal solution to the multiple problems of the different types of widows would be the creation of neighborhood networks in congested cities and community networks in smaller locations. These can be developed and maintained by a paid volunteer working out of a federal agency (such as a Social Security Administration branch office or an ACTION group), community mental health center, school, church, or even a private agency. The function of the paid volunteer or regular employee would be to serve as a link between the new widow, or the widow whose life is being shifted through other events, and societal resources. It would be particularly important for the linking person to bring together already existing volunteer services in the area that ignore the nonvisible neighborhood women who become widows or widows who move there. The coordinator and her network drawn from local voluntary associations would combine a widow information service, a method of dealing with acute problems of widowhood such as a "hot line" for heavily grieving women, with consistent and repeated contact by trained volunteers who can help the widow solve her problems. The duties of such a coordinator would be to:

A. Become a resource expert:
1. Investigate all the resources of the neighborhood that could be of use in reengagement by older women: governmental agencies and their functions, voluntary or-

ganizations, churches, occupational, educational, social facilities, etc.
2. Investigate the major resources of the larger community employment agencies and the kinds of jobs they have for women, transportation routes, organized activities and how reached, etc.
3. Learn lines of connection to special problem-solving agencies, legal, financial, health, etc.
B. Develop neighborhood networks:
1. Contact local organizations and help them form committees of volunteers to work with the network coordinator to provide contact points and services for newly disengaged older women.
2. Coordinate the volunteer committees of the different organizations in the neighborhood.
C. Bring widowed women into the neighborhood networks:
1. Keep an active file of all women who may need acute problem help because they are recently widowed, divorced or deserted; are ill or caring for a sick husband or other person, moved into the area, retired, etc.
2. Keep an active file of women with chronic problems.
3. Assign members of committees from the organizations who form the network to each new acute problem case to ensure continued, regular contact with both acute and chronic cases; make sure that anyone dropping from the help segment of the network is replaced so that no one becomes neglected.

Such neighborhood networks utilizing local resources to help widows re-engage in society after their prior engagement and support systems have been disorganized through the death of the husband or subsequent events must clearly define their values without resorting to the so useful philosophy of voluntary disengagement of older people and society from each other. One of the findings of our study is that many of the widows have adjusted, slowly although often painfully, to circumstances which may appear appalling to modern observers. There are many ill, hungry, isolated, limited, non-involved widows who do not seek help, and to say that they are in that state voluntarily is no excuse for inadequate societal services, particularly those linking the person to existing resources. Whether temporarily disorganized by life events or chronically peripheral to the society, many widows are not living "dignified lives" because they do not have personal resources for re-engagement, depend heavily on their children and lack skills to function as "urbanized" residents of our multi-resource-filled cites. Those who have complex support networks are able to build them voluntaristically because ascribed support systems are vanishing or scattered in modern society. There are many widows who, socialized to be surrounded by decision-making and automatically engaging social networks, cannot initiate a support system through their own efforts. It is these women who need to be helped by linking persons and groups, with the awareness that their numbers are decreasing rapidly *and* will continue to do so as modern America helps women develop greater competence in living in modern America.

APPENDIX

1/74

UNIVERSITY OF ILLINOIS
SURVEY RESEARCH LABORATORY

Acting as Collecting Agent

for LOYOLA UNIVERSITY OF CHICAGO
CENTER FOR THE COMPARATIVE STUDY OF SOCIAL ROLES

Support Systems Involving Widows: USA

O.M.B. No. 72-S-73013
Approval Expires December, 1974

391

Time interview began: _____ AM
PM

A. Overview

1. The first set of questions deals with the major events of your life.
First of all, in what year were you born? . . . . _____   13-15

2a. My second question is a very broad one. Please look back over your
entire life and tell me what you think of as the most important <u>events</u>
of your life. First, what is the most important event? What is the
second most important event, and the next? *(Beginning with the most
important event, record in the table the number of each event from the
codes below. Repeat for five events, and record an answer code for each;
then ask Q.2b, c, and d for each event. Record responses in the table.)*

Event

```
Marriage . . . . . . . . . . . . . . . . . . . . . . . . . . . . . . . . 01
Birth . . . . . . . . . . . . . . . . . . . . . . . . . . . . . . . . . 02
Illness, death . . . . . . . . . . . . . . . . . . . . . . . . . . . . . 03
Personality, growth, rearing, life cycle changes . . . . . . . . . . . 04
Tragedy (not 03), war, depression, alcoholism, retardation of child . . 05
Buying, selling, finances, material things . . . . . . . . . . . . . . 06
Moving . . . . . . . . . . . . . . . . . . . . . . . . . . . . . . . . . 07
Holiday, vacation, celebration, special event . . . . . . . . . . . . . 08
Work . . . . . . . . . . . . . . . . . . . . . . . . . . . . . . . . . . 09
School . . . . . . . . . . . . . . . . . . . . . . . . . . . . . . . . . 10
Other (Specify in table). . . . . . . . . . . . . . . . . . . . . . . . 11
(Don't know) . . . . . . . . . . . . . . . . . . . . . . . . . . . . . . 88
```

2b. Who was involved in this event? *(List persons involved in each
event. If the event involves only the respondent, record "self"
on the appropriate blank in table. If the event involves someone
else, such as husband in marriage or child in birth, record each
person's first name and relationship to R.)*

2c. *(Ask if not obvious.)* Is this person male or female?

2d. In what year or years did this event take place?

392

-3-

	a. Event	b. Person(s)	c. Sex				d. Year(s)
			M	F	C		

(1) _____ 16-17 _____ 18-19 1 2 3 20 _____ 21-23

_____ 24-25 4 5 6 26 _____ 27-29

_____ 30-31 1 2 3 32 _____ 33-35

(2) _____ 36-37 _____ 38-39 4 5 6 40 _____ 41-43

_____ 44-45 1 2 3 46 _____ 47-49

_____ 50-51 4 5 6 52 _____ 53-55

(3) _____ 56-57 _____ 58-59 1 2 3 60 _____ 61-63

_____ 64-65 4 5 6 66 _____ 67-69

_____ 70-71 1 2 3 72 _____ 73-75
76-78/BK
79-80/01
1-9/DUP

(4) _____ 10-11 _____ 12-13 4 5 6 14 _____ 15-17

_____ 18-19 1 2 3 20 _____ 21-23

_____ 24-25 4 5 6 26 _____ 27-29

(5) _____ 30-31 _____ 32-33 1 2 3 34 _____ 35-37

_____ 38-39 4 5 6 40 _____ 41-43

_____ 44-45 1 2 3 46 _____ 47-49

393

B. Resources

3. How many times have you been married? . . . . _____ 50

4a. What was your (first, second, etc.) husband's first name? *(Beginning with the first husband, record the first name of each husband in the table below. Then ask Q.4b through e for each. Use the first name of each husband when asking these questions. Record responses in table below.)*

    4b. In what year was _____ born?
                      (husband)

    4c. In what year were you married to _____ ?
                               (husband)

    4d. In what year did that marriage end?

    4e. How did that marriage end? Did it end in. . . *(Read categories; record one answer code for each marriage.)*

                          Separation 1
                          Divorce 2
                          Separation and then widowhood 3
                          Divorce and then widowhood 4
                          Widowhood 5
                          Still married 6

	a. Name	b. Year born	c. Year married	d. Year ended	e. How ended
(1)	_____	_____ 51-53	_____ 54-56	_____ 57-59	_____ 60
(2)	_____	_____ 61-63	_____ 64-66	_____ 67-69	_____ 70
(3)	_____	_____ 10-12	_____ 13-15	_____ 16-18	_____ 19
(4)	_____	_____ 20-22	_____ 23-25	_____ 26-28	_____ 29
(5)	_____	_____ 30-32	_____ 33-35	_____ 36-38	_____ 39

79-80/02
1-9/DUP

71-72/
73-74/
75-76/
77-78/

We are interested in learning more about your late husband, _____.
(husband)

(Use name of husband who left her a widow last time. Ask Q.5a through Q.6b for late husband as appropriate; then, IF REMARRIED, go back and ask these questions for present husband.)

	Late Husband	Present Husband

5a. Where was _____ born?
       (husband)

	Late Husband		Present Husband	
This neighborhood	1		1	
Chicago metropolitan area	2	40	2	58
State of Illinois	3	41-42	3	59-60
Another state *(Specify)*	4 _____		4 _____	
Another country *(Specify)*	5 _____		5 _____	

5b. Was that a . . . *(Show Card #1 and read categories.)*

	Late Husband		Present Husband	
Large city (1 million or more). .	1		1	
Middle-sized city (250,000-999,999)	2	43	2	61
Small city (50,000-249,999) . . .	3		3	
Small town (10,000-49,999) . . .	4		4	
Village or farm town (2,500-9,999)	5		5	
Rural or farm	6		6	

5c. What was the last year of school _____ completed? *(Record on blank (husband) provided.)*

	Late Husband	Present Husband
	44-46	62-64
	_____	_____

5d. What degree did your husband receive as his last degree, if any?

	Late Husband		Present Husband	
Grade school diploma	1		1	
High school diploma	2	47	2	65
Special diploma *(Specify)* . . .	3 _____	48	3 _____	66
B.A. or B.S.	4		4	
M.A. or M.S.	5		5	
Ph.D or other professional . . .	6		6	
None	7		7	

5e. What was (is) his usual occupation and job title? *(Record on blank provided.)*

	Late Husband	Present Husband
	49-51	67-69
	_____	_____

	Late Husband	Present Husband

5f. What kind of work did (does) he do; that is what were (are) his duties on the job?　　52-54　　　70-72

5g. What kind of company or industry is that? What product is produced or service given?

6a. Are the parents of _____ still living? (husband)

	Late Husband	Present Husband
Yes, both parents	1　　55	1　　73
Yes, mother only	2	2
Yes, father only	3	3
No, neither parent	4 *(Skip to Q.5a if remarried, Q.7a if not)*	4 *(Skip to Q.7a)*

6b. How often do you see the parent(s) _____? *(Show Card #2.)* (husband)

	Late Husband	Present Husband
Daily	01	01
Several times a week	02　　56-57	02　　74-75
About once a week	03	03　　76-78 BK 79-80/03
Several times a month	04	04　　1-9 DUP
About once a month	05	05
Several times a year	06	06
About once a year	07	07
Less than once a year	08	08
Never	09	09

(Skip to Q.5a if remarried)

7a. Have you ever had any children or stepchildren to whom you have been a mother, including those who are no longer living?

Yes 1
No *(Skip to Q.9)* . . . 2　　10

(If Yes)

7b. How many children have you been mother to altogether? . . . _____ 11-12

7c. How many of these children are still living? . . . . _____ 13-14

(If none, skip to Q.9)

-8-

8a. Please tell me a few things about your <u>living</u> children. Beginning with
the oldest, what are the first names of each of your living children?
*(Beginning with the oldest living child, record the first names of all
children; then go back and ask Q.8b through m for each child as appropriate.
Record responses in table below.)*

8b. *(Ask if not obvious.)* Is _____ male or female?
(child)

8c. In what year was _____ born?
(child)

<u>FOR CHILDREN BORN BEFORE 1958, ASK:</u>

8d. What is his/her marital status? Is he/she . . . *(Show Card #3.
Read categories and record answer code in table.)*

Married 1
Separated 2
Divorced 3
Widowed 4
Never married 5

<u>ASK FOR ALL CHILDREN:</u>

8e. Where does _____ live now? *(Show Card #4. Read categories
(child)
and record answer code in table.)*

This housing unit 01
Elsewhere in this building 02
Elsewhere in this block 03
Elsehwere in same neighborhood 04
Chicago area 05
Illinois 06
Another state *(Specify in table)* 07
Another country *(Specify in table)* . . . 08

	a. Name	b. Sex M F	c. Year born	d. Marital status	e. Where living	f. Lived away from home No Yes	*(If Yes)* g. Year first moved away
(1)	_____ 15, 16	1 2 17	18-20	____ 21	22-23	2 1 →24	25-27
(2)	_____ 15, 16	1 2 17	18-20	____ 21	22-23	2 1 →24	25-27
(3)	_____ 15, 16	1 2 17	18-20	____ 21	22-23	2 1 →24	25-27
(4)	_____ 15, 16	1 2 17	18-20	____ 21	22-23	2 1 →24	25-27
(5)	_____ 15, 16	1 2 17	18-20	____ 21	22-23	2 1 →24	25-27
(6)	_____ 15, 16	1 2 17	18-20	____ 21	22-23	2 1 →24	25-27
(7)	_____ 15, 16	1 2 17	18-20	____ 21	22-23	2 1 →24	25-27
(8)	_____ 15, 16	1 2 17	18-20	____ 21	22-23	2 1 →24	25-27

398

IF LIVING AT HOME (CODE 01), ASK:

8f. Has_____ever lived away from home other than going away to
     (child)
    school?

       (If no, skip to Q.8l.)

       (If Yes)

       8g. In what year did he/she move away?

       8h. In what year did he/she move back home?
                                 (Skip to Q.8l)

IF NOT LIVING AT HOME IN Q.8e, ASK:

8i. In what year did he/she first move away from home?

8j. Did he/she ever move back home at any time?

8k. How often do you see_____? Would you say . . . *(Show Card #2.*
                  (child)
    Read categories and record answer code in table.)

                    Daily 01
                    Several times a week 02
                    About once a week 03
                    Several times a month 04
                    About once a month 05
                    Several times a year 06
                    About once a year 07
                    Less than once a year 08
                    Never 09

ASK FOR ALL CHILDREN:

8l. What was the last year of school_____completed? *(Record number*
                               (child)
    of completed years.)

8m. What is_____usual occupation or job title? In what business
          (child's)
    or industry is this? What product is produced or service given?

(If Yes) h. Year moved back home	i. Year first moved away	j. Moved back home Yes	No	k. How often seen	l. Year of school	m. Occupation/ Industry
_____ 28-30	_____ 31-33	1	2 34	_____ 35-36	_____ 37-38	_____ 39-44 A4
_____ 28-30	_____ 31-33	1	2 34	_____ 35-36	_____ 37-38	_____ 39-44 B4
_____ 28-30	_____ 31-33	1	2 34	_____ 35-36	_____ 37-38	_____ 39-44 C4
_____ 28-30	_____ 31-33	1	2 34	_____ 35-36	_____ 37-38	_____ 39-44 D4
_____ 28-30	_____ 31-33	1	2 34	_____ 35-36	_____ 37-38	_____ 39-44 E4
_____ 28-30	_____ 31-33	1	2 34	_____ 35-36	_____ 37-38	_____ 39-44 F4
_____ 28-30	_____ 31-33	1	2 34	_____ 35-36	_____ 37-38	_____ 39-44 G4
_____ 28-30	_____ 31-33	1	2 34	_____ 35-36	_____ 37-38	_____ 39-44 H4

9a. Do you have any brothers or sisters?

Yes 1

No *(Skip to Q.11)* 2

44

(If Yes)

9b. How many brothers and/or sisters do you have? . . . . _____   45-46

10a. Now I would like to know something more about your brothers and sisters. Beginning with the oldest brother or sister, what is the first name of each? *(Beginning with the oldest sibling, record the first name of each brother and/or sister; then ask Q.10b through f for each. Record responses in table below.)*

> 10b. *(Ask if not obvious.)* Is _____ male or female?
>   (sibling)
>
> 10c. How old is _____ in relation to you? Is he/she . . . *(Read*
>   (sibling)
>   *categories.)*

Older 1
Younger 2
Same age 3

	a. Name		b. Sex M F		c. Age in rela- tion to R	
(1)	_____	13, 14	1 2	15	_____	16
(2)	_____	22, 23	3 4	24	_____	25
(3)	_____	31, 32	1 2	33	_____	34
(4)	_____	40, 41	3 4	42	_____	43
(5)	_____	49, 50	1 2	51	_____	52
(6)	_____	58, 59	3 4	60	_____	61
(7)	_____	67, 68	1 2	69	_____	70
(8)	_____	10, 11	3 4	12	_____	13
(9)	_____	19, 20	1 2	21	_____	22
(10)	_____	28, 29	3 4	30	_____	31

400

10d. What is_____marital status? *(Show Card #3. Read categories*
     (sibling's)
     and record answer code in table.)

                                        Married 1
                                        Separated 2
                                        Divorced 3
                                        Widowed 4
                                        Never married 5

10e. Where does_____live? *(Show Card #4. Read categories and*
     (sibling)
     record answer code in table.)

                                        This housing unit 01
                                        Elsewhere in this building 02
                                        Elsewhere in this block 03
                                        Elsewhere in same neighborhood . . 04
                                        Chicago area 05
                                        Illinois 06
                                        Another state *(Specify in table)*· · 07
                                        Another country *(Specify in table)*. 08

10f. How often do you see_____? Would you say . . . *(Show Card #2.*
     (sibling)
     Read categories and record answer code in table.)

                                        Daily 01
                                        Several times a week 02
                                        About once a week 03
                                        Several times a month 04
                                        About once a month 05
                                        Several times a year 06
                                        About once a year 07
                                        Less than once a year 08
                                        Never 09

d. Marital status		e. Where lives		f. How often seen	
_____	17	_____	18-19	_____	20-21
_____	26	_____	27-28	_____	29-30
_____	35	_____	36-37	_____	38-39
_____	44	_____	45-46	_____	47-48
_____	53	_____	54-55	_____	56-57
_____	62	_____	63-64	_____	65-66
_____	71	_____	72-73	_____	74-75 76-78/BK 79 80/07
_____	14	_____	15-16	_____	17-18
_____	23	_____	24-25	_____	26-27
_____	32	_____	33-34	_____	35-36 37-48/BK

Now I would like to find out more about your parents. *(Ask Q.11a through e for mother as appropriate; then go back and repeat for father.)*

	Mother	Father
11a. What year was your mother (father) born?	_____ 49-51	_____ 60-62

11b. Is she (he) still living?

	Mother	Father
Yes	1 52	1 63
No	2 *(Skip to Q.11e)*	2 *(Skip to Q.11e)*

(If Yes)

11c. Where is she (he) living now? *(Show Card #4.)*

	Mother	Father
This housing unit	01 53,54	01 64,65
Elswhere in this building . .	02	02
Elsewhere in this block . . .	03	03
Elsewhere in this neigh- borhood	04	04
Chicago area	05	05
Illinois	06	06
Another state *(Specify)* . . .	07 _____	07 _____
Another country *(Specify)*. . .	08 _____	08 _____

11d. How often do you see her (him)? *(Show Card #2.)*

	Mother	Father
Daily	01 55,56	01 66,67
Several times a week	02	02
About once a week	03	03
Several times a month	04	04
About once a month	05	05
Several times a year	06	06
About once a year	07	07
Less than once a year	08	08
Never	09	09
	(Skip to Q.11a)	*(Skip to Q.12)*

IF NO LONGER LIVING:

	Mother	Father
11e. In what year did she (he) die? . .	_____ 57-59	_____ 68-70
	(Skip to Q.11a)	

12a. Since your first marriage, have you ever had anyone living with you besides your husband(s) and your child(ren)?

Yes 1

No *(Skip to Q.13)* 2

71
72-78/BK
79-80/08
1-9/DUP

(If Yes)

12b. Who has lived with you since your first marriage? How are you related to this person? *(List each person by recording his or her first name and relationship to R; then ask Q.12c through e for each. Record responses in table below.)*

12c. *(Ask if not obvious.)* Is this person male or female?

12d. What year did this person begin living with you?

12e. What year did this person stop living with you?

b. Person	c. Sex M F	d. Year came	e. Year moved
(1) _____ 10-11	1 2 12	_____ 13-15	_____ 16-18
(2) _____ 19-20	1 2 21	_____ 22-24	_____ 25-27
(3) _____ 28-29	1 2 30	_____ 31-33	_____ 34-36
(4) _____ 37-38	1 2 39	_____ 40-42	_____ 43-45
(5) _____ 46-47	1 2 48	_____ 49-50	_____ 51-53

13a. Do you have any relatives who are living with you now including husband or children?

Yes 1

No *(Skip to Q.14)*. . . . 2

54

(If Yes)

13b. How many of these relatives are living with you now? . . _____   55

14a. Do you have any relatives who presently live within a four block radius of your residence? *(IF RELATIVES LIVE WITH HER NOW, ADD:* other than those living with you now?*)*

Yes 1

No *(Skip to Q.15)* . . 2

56

(If Yes)

14b. How many of your relatives presently live within a four block radius of your residence? . . . . _____   57-58

403

C. Widowhood Period

Now that I know some things about your family, I would like you to think back to
the time of your late husband's death. *(If widowed more than once, explain that
we are interested in the husband who left her a widow last. If remarried, explain
again that we are interested in her widowhood period.)*

15a. What was the cause of your late husband's death? *(Be sure you understand
the nature of the final diagnosis.)*

Accident *(Specify)* _____

_____ . . 1   59

War, suicide, homocide 2   60

Heart, stroke, vascular 3

Cancer 4

Other chronic infections . . . 5

Combination of illnesses . . . 6

Other *(Specify)* _____   61

_____ . . 7

(Don't know) 8

IF ACCIDENT, ASK Q.15b, OTHERWISE SKIP TO Q.16.

15b. Did this accident happen on the job?

Yes 1   62

No 2

ASK EVERYONE:

16. Which one of the following best describes your late husband's employment
status before his last illness (accident)? Was he . . . *(Read categories.)*

Working full-time at his usual job? 1   63

Working full-time, but at a job other than his
usual job? 2

Working part-time? 3

Retired? 4

Not working? *(Specify reason)* _____ . . 5   64

Something else? *(Specify)* _____ . . 6   65

17. How long was your husband ill or incapacitated before he died?

Immediate death *(Skip to Q. 19)* 01

Less than a week 02

A week or more but less than a month . . 03

A month or more but less than six
   months 04

Six months or more but less than a
   year 05

A year or more but less than six
   years 06

Six years or more but less than ten
   years 07

Ten years or more 08

66-67

18. During his last illness (After his accident), was he able to remain in the same work situation, did he have to change his work situation, was he unable to work at all because of the illness (accident), or was he not working prior to his illness (accident)? *(Show Card #5.)*

Remained in same work situation . . 1   **68**

Changed work situation *(Specify)*

_____ . . 2   **69**

Unable to work at all 3

Unemployed before illness
   (accident) 4

19. What were the circumstances surrounding your husband's death? *(Record verbatim response.)*

_____

_____

_____

_____

70-71

72-78/BK

79-80/09

1-9/DUP

20a. *IF DEATH WAS IMMEDIATE:* Right after your late husband's death, what were the three main problems you faced or for which you needed help? *(Beginning with the first problem mentioned, record in the table the number of each problem from the code below; then ask Q.20b through d for each as appropriate.)*

IF DEATH WAS NOT IMMEDIATE: During your late husband's illness and right after his death, what were the three main problems you faced or for which you needed help? *(Beginning with the first problem mentioned, record in the table the number of each problem from the code below; then ask Q.20b through d for each as appropriate.)*

Problem

Needed money to pay bills, expenses 01
Financial problems in settling business, house insurance advice or
   arrangements 02
Help with funeral arrangements 03
Other services, transportation, food 04
Help with children, care of dependents 05
Loneliness, contact with people, social activities 06
Emotional problems other than loneliness 07
Health 08
Other *(Specify in table)*_____ 09

    20b. Who helped you with this problem? *(Record name of group or, if person, the first name and relationship to R in the table.)*

       IF PERSON:

       20c. *(Ask if not obvious.)* Is_____male or female?
                   (person)

    20d. How was this problem solved? *(Record verbatim response.)*

a. Problem	b. Who helped	c. Sex M F Grp		d. Solution	
(1) ____ 10-11	_____	12-13 1 2 3	14	_____	15-16
	_____	17-18 1 2 3	19	_____	20-21
	_____	22-23 1 2 3	24	_____	25-26
(2) ____ 27-28	_____	29-30 1 2 3	31	_____	32-33
	_____	34-35 1 2 3	36	_____	37-38
	_____	39-40 1 2 3	41	_____	42-43
(3) ____ 44-45	_____	46-47 1 2 3	48	_____	49-50
	_____	51-52 1 2 3	53	_____	54-55
	_____	56-57 1 2 3	58	_____	59-60

406

21. In reviewing your life since you became a widow, how helpful have each of the following persons or groups been in your building a new life? *(Show Card #6. Read each lettered category and circle one answer code for each.)*

	Generally very helpful	Helpful in special situations	Rarely helpful	Never helpful	Not appropriate	
a. Neighbors	1	2	3	4	0	61
b. Adult children . . .	5	6	7	8	0	62
c. Parents, siblings . .	1	2	3	4	0	63
d. In-laws	5	6	7	8	0	64
e. Other relatives . . .	1	2	3	4	0	65
f. Friends	5	6	7	8	0	66
g. Work associates . . .	1	2	3	4	0	67
h. Club members	5	6	7	8	0	68
i. A woman not yet mentioned *(Specify)* _____	1	2	3	4	0	69
j. A man not yet mentioned *(Specify)* _____	5	6	7	8	0	70
k. The go rnment . . .	1	2	3	4	0	71
l. Social Security Administration . . .	5	6	7	8	0	72

22a. How long did it take you to establish a new life? *(Record answer in months.)*.

73-74 _____

22b. In what ways do you feel this was a new life? *(Record verbatim response.)*

_____ 75-76

_____ 77-78/BK

_____ 79-80/10

_____ 1-9/DUP

23a. Now I would like to know if there is any kind of help or advice you wish
people had offered you, but which they did not. Do you wish you had received
any of the following kinds of help or advice? *(Read each numbered category.
Record one answer code for each; then ask Q. 23b for all "Yes" responses.)*

(If Yes)

23b. From what persons or groups
did you wish this help?
*(For persons, record first
name and relationship to R.
Record sex if not obvious.)*

		a. Wished help/advice			b. Person(s)/group(s)	
		Yes	No			
(1)	Financial	1	2	10	_____	11-13
					_____	14-16
(2)	Services, such as driving you places, housekeeping, legal aid	1	2	17	_____	18-20
					_____	21-23
(3)	Social, such as visits, social contacts, invitations . .	1	2	24	_____	25-27
					_____	28-30
(4)	Emotional, such as comfort, a good listener, a problem solver	1	2	31	_____	32-34
					_____	35-37
(5)	Something else *(Specify)* _____ . .	1	2	38 39	_____	40-42
					_____	43-45
	_____ . .	1	2	46 47	_____	48-50
					_____	51-53
	_____ . .	1	2	54 55	_____	56-58
					_____	59-61

*IF ALL "NO" ABOVE, SKIP TO
Q. 25a.*

24. Why do you think you did not get this help? *(Circle as many as apply.)*

Did not ask or apply 1	62
Others had their own problems 2	63
Regulations, not eligible 3	64
Mistake or confusion 4	65
Not part of duties or jurisdiction . . . 5	66
Unwilling to help 6	67
Other *(Specify)* _____ . . 7	68

25a. During the time you were trying to establish a new life, were there any major things about your life that you wanted to change?

Yes 1

No *(Skip to Q.26)* 2   69

(If Yes)

25b. What did you want to change? *(Record verbatim response.)*

_____   70-71

_____

_____

25c. In general, how successful do you feel you were in changing these things? Would you say . . . *(Read categories.)*

Very successful *(Skip to Q.26)* 1

Moderately successful *(Skip to Q.26)* . . 2   72

Not too successful 3

Not successful at all 4

25d. Why do you feel you had difficulty or were unable to change these things? *(Circle as many as apply.)*

Did not know how 1	73
Could not, had no means 2	74
Received bad advice 3	75
Others prevented, discouraged 4	76
Feelings about late husband 5	77
Other *(Specify)* _____	
_____ 6	78

79-80/11
1-9/DUP

409

26a. During the time you were trying to establish a new life, were there any changes that others expected you to make?

$$Yes \ldots \ldots \ldots \ldots \ldots 1$$
$$No \ (Skip \ to \ Q. \ 27) \ldots \ldots \ldots 2 \qquad 10$$

(If Yes)

26b. What was the major change expected of you? (Record verbatim response.)

_____   11-12

_____

_____

26c. What persons or groups expected you to make this change? (For persons, record first name and relationship to R. Record sex if not obvious.)

_____   13-14

_____   15-16

_____   17-18

26d. Did you or did you not make this change?

$$Yes \ (Skip \ to \ Q.26f) \ \ldots \ldots 1$$
$$No \ldots \ldots \ldots \ldots \ldots 2 \qquad 19$$

(If No)

26e. Why didn't you make this change? (Record verbatim response.)

_____   20-21

_____

_____

410

26f. Was there any other change that was expected of you?

Yes 1   22

No *(Skip to Q.27)* 2

26g. What other change was expected of you? *(Record verbatim response.)*

_____   23—24

_____

_____

26h. What persons or groups expected you to make this change? *(For persons, record first name and relationship to R. Record sex if not obvious.)*

_____   25—27

_____   28—30

_____   31—33

26i. Did you or did you not make this change?

Yes *(Skip to Q.27)* 1   34

No 2

(If No)

26j. Why didn't you make this change? *(Record verbatim response.)*

_____   35—36

_____

_____

411

-22-

7a. After you became a widow did you make any major change or decision in your life which you now regret?

Yes 1   37

No *(Skip to Q.28)* · · · · · 2

(If Yes)

27b. What was the one major change or decision you made which you now regret? *(Record verbatim response.)*

_____   38-39

_____

_____

27c. Would you say this change or decision was primarily related to . . . *(Read categories.)*

Health 01   40-41

Finances 02

Housing 03

Work 04

Family 05

Remarriage 06

Social life 07

Something else *(Specify)* _____   42

_____ 08

28. Have you ever had any children or stepchildren to whom your late husband was a father?

Yes 1   43

No *(Skip to Q.34)* · · · · 2

412

29a. Generally speaking, do you think this child was (any of these children were) strongly affected by the death of their father (your late husband)?

Yes 1   44

No *(Skip to Q.30)* 2

(If Yes)

    29b. What is the name of this child who was (these children who were) strongly affected by the father's death? *(Record first name of each child in table below; then ask Q.29c through f for each as appropriate.)*

        29c. How was_____affected by his/her father's death? *(Record*
            (child)
        verbatim response.)

        29d. Were you able to help_____recover from this?
                     (child)

            (If Yes)

            29e. How were you able to help_____? *(Record verbatim*
                          (child)
            response.)

            (If No)

            29f. Why do you feel you were not able to help? *(Record verbatim response.)*

b. Name	c. How affected	d. Helped child Yes	No	*(If Yes)* e. How helped	*(If No)* f. Why unable to help
(1) _____	_____ 45‾46	1	2 47	48‾49 _____	_____ 50‾51
	_____			_____	_____
	_____			_____	_____
(2) _____	_____ 52‾53	1	2 54	55‾56 _____	_____ 57‾58
	_____			_____	_____
	_____			_____	_____
(3) _____	_____	1	2	_____	_____
	_____			_____	_____ 59-61
	_____			_____	62-64
					65/BK

413

30. Generally speaking, do you think any of your children were n̲o̲t̲ strongly affected by the death of their father?

                                  Yes 1   66
                                  No *(Skip to Q.32)* 2

IF ANY CHILD NOT STRONGLY AFFECTED:

31. What do you think is the main reason that this child or these children were not strongly affected by the death of their father? *(Record verbatim response.)*

_____   67-68

_____

_____

32a. Do you think any of your children had problems in school or in their relations with others as a result of being without a father *(IF REMARRIED,* during the time they were without a father)?

                                  Yes 1   69
                                  No *(Skip to Q.33)* 2
                                                                   79-80/12
                                                                   1-9/DUP
    (If Yes)

    32b. Which child (Which children) had these problems?   *(Record first name of each child in table below; then ask Q.32c and d for each as appropriate.)*

    32c. What kind of problems did this child have as a result of being without a father *(IF REMARRIED,* during the time he/she was without a father)? Do you think he/she . . . *(Read each category. For each child, record in the table as many answer codes as apply.)*

                              Got into trouble at school . . . 1
                              Got into trouble with police . . 2
                              Had problems with you. 3
                              Made some wrong decisions . . . 4
                              Something else *(Specify in table)* 5

    IF WRONG DECISIONS (CODE 4), ASK:

    32d. What decisions did this child make which you think were wrong? *(Record verbatim response.)*

	b. __Name__	c. __Problems__		IF WRONG DECISIONS: d. __Wrong decisions__	
(1)	_____	_____	10 11	_____	12⌐13
(2)	_____	_____	14 15	_____	16⌐17
(3)	_____	_____	18 19	_____	20⌐21

414

33a. Do you think the child's (children's) future was affected by being without
a father *(IF REMARRIED,* during the time he/she was (they were) without a
father)?

Yes 1   22

No *(Skip to Q.34)* . . . 2

(If Yes)

33b. How was your child's (children's) future affected by being without
a father? Did he/she (they) receive more, less, or about the
same amount of . . . *(Read each lettered category. Circle one answer
code for each.)*

	More	Less	About the same	
(1) Schooling	1	2	3	23
(2) Work, employment	4	5	6	24
(3) Money, insurance, Social Security	1	2	3	25
(4) Help from other people	4	5	6	26
(5) Responsibility for you	1	2	3	27
(6) Freedom, independence	4	5	6	28
(7) Peace and quiet	1	2	3	29
(8) Something else *(Specify)*				
_____				
_____ . .	4	5	6	30

70-72/
73-75/
76-78/

415

D. Before Widowhood and Now

Now I would like to go back to the year <u>before</u> your late husband's illness (accident) which finally caused his death.

34a. What year was that? . . . . _____

(Use this year for every question referring to before death.)

34b. Where were you living in 19__?   *(Show Card #4 and read categories.)*

This housing unit	01
Elsewhere in this building	02
Elsewhere in this block	03
Elsewhere in same neighborhood	04
Chicago area	05
Illinois	06
Another state *(Specify)* _____ . .	07
Another country *(Specify)* _____ . .	08

Let us compare some things about your life in 19__to your situation now.
(Ask each question for before; then repeat same question for now.)

	Before	Now
35. In what kind of housing did (do) you live in 19__(now)? Was (Is) it a . . . *(Read categories.)*		
House	1	1
Apartment	2	2
Hotel	3 36	3 *(Skip to Q.39)*
Retirement hotel	4	4 *(Skip to Q.39)*
Nursing home	5	5 *(Skip to Q.39)*
Other long-term hospital or institution	6	6 *(Skip to Q.39)*
Something else *(Specify)*	7 _____	7 _____

37

416

	Before	Now
36. Did (Do) you own, share ownership, rent, or something else in 19__ (now)?		
Own . . . . ,	1 38-39	1 62-63
Share ownership *(Specify)*	2 _____	2 _____
Rent	3 _____	3 _____
Other *(Specify)*	4 _____	4 _____
37. How many rooms were (are) in this household in 19__ (now)?	_____ 40-41	_____ 64-65
38. Who was (is) the head of this household in 19__ (now)? *(Record first name, relationship to R, and sex if not obvious.)*	_____ 42-44	_____ 66-68

ASK EVERYONE:

	Before	Now
39. In 19__ before your husband's last illness (accident), what persons were closest to you? (What persons are closest to you now?) *(Record each person's first name, relationship to R, and sex if not obvious.)*	_____ 45-47	_____ 69-71
	_____ 48-50	_____ 72-74
	_____ 51-53	_____ 75-77 / 78 79-80/14 1-9
40. Whom did (do) you most enjoy being with in 19__ (now)? *(Record each person's first name, relationship to R, and sex if not obvious.)*	_____ 54-56	_____ 10-12
	_____ 57-59	_____ 13-15
	_____ 60-62	_____ 16-18
41. To whom did (do) you tell your problems in 19__ (now)? *(Record each person's first name, relationship to R, and sex if not obvious.)*	_____ 63-65	_____ 19-21
	_____ 66-68	_____ 22-24
	_____ 69-71	_____ 25-27
42. Who comforted (comforts) you when you were (are) depressed in 19__ (now)? *(Record each person's first name, relationship to R, and sex if not obvious.)*	_____ 72-74	_____ 28-30
	_____ 75-77 / 78 79-80/13 1-9	_____ 31-33
	_____ 10-12	_____ 34-36

	Before	Now

43. How many people, including yourself, were (are) living in your household in 19__ (now)?

Before: _____ 13-14   Now: _____ 37-38

44. Did (do) you share household management with anyone outside your immediate family in 19__ (now)?

       Yes (Specify who) . . . . . 1 _____ 15   1 _____ 39

       No 2 16-17   2   40-41

45. Did (Do) you share any of the following facilities inside your apartment or house with anyone not a member of your immediate family in 19__ (now)? (Read each category. Circle one answer code for each.)

	Yes	No		Yes	No	
a. Meals	1	2	18	1	2	42
b. Bathroom	1	2	19	1	2	43
c. Kitchen	1	2	20	1	2	44
d. Telephone	1	2	21	1	2	45
e. Television	1	2	22	1	2	46
f. Porch	1	2	23	1	2	47
g. Something else (Specify)	1____	2	24	1____	2	48
			25			49

46. Did (Do) you share any of the following facilities in the building or yard with anyone other than your immediate family in 19__ (now)? (Read each category. Circle one answer code for each.)

	Yes	No		Yes	No	
a. Entry, vestibule . .	1	2	26	1	2	50
b. Garden or playground	1	2	27	1	2	51
c. Laundry room	1	2	28	1	2	52
d. Garage	1	2	29	1	2	53
e. Recreational area .	1	2	30	1	2	54
f. Something else (Specify)	1____	2	31	1____	2	55
			32			56

418

	Before	Now

47. What persons made (make) you feel like
an especially important person in 19___
(now)? *(Record each person's first
name, relationship to R, and sex if
not obvious.)*

    _____ 33-35   _____ 57-59

    _____ 36-38   _____ 60-62

    _____ 39-41   _____ 63-65

48. What persons made (make) you angry
most often in 19___ (now)? *(Record
each person's first name, relationship
to R, and sex if not obvious.)*

    _____ 42-44   _____ 66-68

    _____ 45-47   _____ 69-71

    _____ 48-50   _____ 72-74

49. To whom did you turn (do you turn)
in a crisis in 19___ (now)? *(Record
each person's first name, relationship
to R, and sex if not obvious.)*

    _____ 51-53   _____ 75-77

                              79-80/15

    _____ 54-56   _____ 10-12

    _____ 57-59   _____ 13-15

50. Considering all of the income of
everyone in your household from
employment and from all other
sources, which letter category on
this card best describes your total
family income before taxes in 19___
before your husband's illness (accident)?
(Show Card #7.) If you are uncertain,
please give your best estimate. (Which
letter category best describes your total
family income before taxes in 1973?)

	Before	Now
a. Under $1,000	01	01
b. $1,000-1,999	02	02
c. $2,000-2,999	03	03
d. $3,000-3,999	04 60-61	04 16-17
e. $4,000-4,999	05	05
f. $5,000-5,999	06	06
g. $6,000-6,999	07	07
h. $7,000-7,999	08	08
i. $8,000-8,999	09	09
j. $9,000-9,999	10	10
k. $10,000-14,999	11	11
l. $15,000-19,999	12	12
m. $20,000 and over	13	13
n. *(Don't know)*	*88*	*88*

FOR BEFORE INCOME ONLY:

51. Now I would like to know the major sources of your family income in 19__.
About how much of the total income came from these sources in 19__? *(Show Card #8. Read each category. Circle one answer code for each.)*

	All	Most	About half	1/3 to 1/4	Less than 1/4	None	*(Don't know)*	
a. Your wages	1	2	3	4	5	6	8	18
b. Husband's wages	1	2	3	4	5	6	8	19
c. Children's wages	1	2	3	4	5	6	8	20
d. Your pension	1	2	3	4	5	6	8	21
e. Husband's pension . . .	1	2	3	4	5	6	8	22
f. Your Social Security . .	1	2	3	4	5	6	8	23
g. Husband's Social Security	1	2	3	4	5	6	8	24
h. Welfare payments *(Specify)* _____ . .	1	2	3	4	5	6	8	25—26
i. Investments (including property rental)	1	2	3	4	5	6	8	27
j. Rent from roomers/boarders in your household . . .	1	2	3	4	5	6	8	28
k. Other *(Specify)* _____	1	2	3	4	5	6	8	29—30

FOR 1973 INCOME ONLY:

52. Now I would like to know the major sources of your family income in 1973. About how much of the total income came from these sources in 1973? *(Show Card #8. Read each category. Circle one answer code for each.)*

	All	Most	About half	1/3 to 1/4	Less than 1/4	None	*(Don't know)*	
a. Your wages	1	2	3	4	5	6	8	31
b. Husband's wages	1	2	3	4	5	6	8	32
c. Children's wages	1	2	3	4	5	6	8	33
d. Your pension	1	2	3	4	5	6	8	34
e. Husband's pension . . .	1	2	3	4	5	6	8	35
f. Your Social Security . .	1	2	3	4	5	6	8	36
g. Husband's Social Security	1	2	3	4	5	6	8	37
h. Welfare payments *(Specify)* _____	1	2	3	4	5	6	8	38—39
i. Investments (including property rental)	1	2	3	4	5	6	8	40
j. Rent from roomers/ boarders in your household	1	2	3	4	5	6	3	41
k. Other *(Specify)* _____	1	2	3	4	5	6	8	42—43

420

53. Now I am going to read some "feeling states" which many people think are important for a full life. What persons or groups made (make) you feel this way in 19__(now)? *(Ask "before" and "now" for each lettered category. For persons, record first name and relationship to R. Record sex if not obvious.)*

		Before		Now
a.	Respected		44-46	31-33
			47-49	34-36
			50-52	37-39
b.	Useful		53-55	40-42
			56-58	43-45
			59-61	46-48
c.	Independent		62-64	49-51
			65-67	52-54
			68-70	55-57
d.	Accepted		71-73	58-60
			74-76 77-78 79-80/16 1-9 10-12	61-63 64-66
e.	Self-sufficient		13-15	67-69
			16-18	70-72
			19-21	73-75
f.	Secure		22-24	76-78 79-80/17 1-9
			25-27	10-12
			28-30	13-15

421

54a. Did you have any close, personal friends in 19__?

Yes 1   16

No *(Skip to Q.56)* . . . 2

(If Yes)

54b. What is the first name of each of these friends? *(Obtain five names if possible; then ask Q.54c through l for each of individuals or couples as appropriate. Record responses in table below.)*

54c. *(Ask if not obvious.)* Is _____male or female? *(Circle answer code 3 for couple.)* (friend)

54d. How long had you known_____in 19__? *(Record answer in years.)* (friend)

54e. How and where did you first meet_____? (friend)

54f. Was_____a friend of your late husband's? (friend)

54g. In 19__, what was_____marital status? Was he/she . . . *(Show Card #3. Read categories and record answer code in table.)* (friend's)

Married 1

Separated 2

Divorced 3

Widowed 4

Never married 5

54h. How often did you see _____in 19__? Would you say . . . *(Show Card #2. Read categories and record answer code in table.)* (friend)

Daily 01

Several times a week 02

About once a week 03

Several times a month 04

About once a month 05

Several times a year 06

About once a year 07

Less than once a year 08

Never 09

b. Name	c. Sex M F C	d. Years known	e. How and where met	f. Husband's friend Yes No
(1) _____11,12	1 2 3 ¹³	14-15	16-17	1 2 ¹⁸
(2) _____11,12	1 2 3 13	14-15	16-17	1 2 ¹⁸
(3) _____11,12	1 2 3 13	14-15	16-17	1 2 ¹⁸
(4) _____11,12	1 2 3 13	14-15	16-17	1 2 18
(5) _____11,12	1 2 3 13	14-15	16-17	1 2 18

54i. Is_____still living?
    (friend)

IF NOT LIVING, Skip to Q.56a.

IF STILL LIVING ASK:

54j. What is his/her marital status now? Is he/she . . . *(Show Card #3.*
Read categories and record answer code in table.)

                       Married 1
                       Separated 2
                       Divorced 3
                       Widowed 4
                       Never married 5

54k. How often do you see_____now? *(Show Card #2. Read categories*
                    (friend)
    and record answer code in table.)

                       Daily 01
                       Several times a week 02
                       About once a week 03
                       Several times a month 04
                       About once a month 05
                       Several times a year 06
                       About once a year 07
                       Less than once a year 08
                       Never 09

54l. Is_____still a close personal friend?
    (friend)

IF LIVING:

g. Marital status	h. How often seen in 19	i. Still living No Yes	j. Present marital status	k. How often seen now	l. Still friends Yes No	
_____ 19	_____ 20-21	2 1 →22	23	_____ 24-25 1 2 26	27/2A
_____ 19	_____ 20-21	2 1 →22	23	_____ 24-25 1 2 26	27/2B
_____ 19	_____ 20-21	2 1 →22	23	_____ 24-25 1 2 26	27/2C
_____ 19	_____ 20-21	2 1 →22	23	_____ 24-25 1 2 26	27/2D
_____ 19	_____ 20-21	2 1 →22	23	_____ 24-25 1 2 26	27/2E

IF LESS THAN ONCE A YEAR OR NEVER IN Q.54k (CODE 08-09), ASK:

55a. Why don't you see this friend (these friends) more often? Is it mostly
because of . . . (Read categories.)

Changes in the lives of your friends (Skip to Q.56) . . . 1

Your husband's death (Skip to Q.56) 2   28

Other changes in your life 3

IF OTHER CHANGES IN HER LIFE, ASK:

55b. What kind of changes were they? Were they related to . . . (Read
categories. Circle as many as apply.)

Health 1   29

Lack of partner 2   30

Transportation 3   31

Moving away 4   32

Not being invited 5   33

Persons being husband's friends 6   34

Something else (Specify) _____

_____ 7   35
36-78/BK
79, 80/2^

ASK EVERYONE:

56a. Have you made any new, close personal friends since your late husband's death?

Yes 1   10

No Skip to Q.57) . . 2

(If Yes)

56b. Who are these friends? Please give me the first name of each friend.
(Obtain five names if possible, then ask Q.56c through h for each
as appropriate; record responses in the table below.)

56c. (Ask if not obvious.) Is_____male or female? (Circle answer
                          (friend)
code 3 for couple.)

56d. How long have you known_____? (Record number of years.)
                                  (friend)

	b. Name	c. Sex M F C	d. Years known
(1)	_____ 11 12	1 2 3 13	_____ 14-15
(2)	_____ 11,12	1 2 3 13	_____ 14-15
(3)	_____ 11,12	1 2 3 13	_____ 14-15
(4)	_____ 11,12	1 2 3 13	_____ 14-15
(5)	_____ 11,12	1 2 3 13	_____ 14-15

(If Yes cont.)

56e. How and where did you first meet_____?
                                    (friend)

56f. What is _____ marital status? Is he/she . . .
              (friend's)
     (Show Card #3. Read categories and record answer code in table.)

                              Married 1
                              Separated 2
                              Divorced 3
                              Widowed 4
                              Never married 5

56g. How often do you see _____ ? Would you say . . . *(Show Card*
                            (friend)
     #2. Read categories and record answer code in table.)

                              Daily 01
                              Several times a week 02
                              About once a week 03
                              Several times a month 04
                              About once a month 05
                              Several times a year 06
                              About once a year 07
                              Less than once a year 08
                              Never 09

IF LESS THAN ONCE A YEAR OR NEVER (CODE 08-09), ASK:

56h. Why don't you see this friend more often? *(Record verbatim*
     response.)

e. How and where met	f. Marital status	g. How often seen	IF LESS THAN ONCE A YEAR OR NEVER: h. Why not seen more		
_____ 16-17	___ 18	_____ 19-20	_____	21-22	27/2 2K
_____ 16-17	___ 18	_____ 19-20	_____	21-22	27/2 2L
_____ 16-17	___ 18	_____ 19-20	_____	21-22	27/2 2M
_____ 16-17	___ 18	_____ 19-20	_____	21-22	27/2 2N
_____ 16_17	___ 18	_____ 19-20	_____	21-22	27/2 20

57a. Do you belong to any social organizations or groups now?

$$\text{Yes} \ldots \ldots \ldots \ldots \ldots 1 \qquad 77$$
$$\text{No } (Skip\ to\ Q.59) \ldots \ldots 2 \qquad 7\text{8}/BK$$
$$79-80/\ 19$$

(If Yes) $\qquad\qquad\qquad\qquad\qquad\qquad\qquad\qquad\qquad\qquad$ 1-9/DUP

57b. To how many organizations or groups do you belong? . . . . _____ 10-11

58a. I would like to know more about these organizations and groups. What are the names of these organizations and groups? *(Record names of all organi- zations and groups in table below; then ask Q.58b through e for each. Record responses in table below.)*

58b. What kind of organization is_____? Is it mainly . . .
(name)
(Read categories and record answer code in table.)

    Religious, church related 01
    Ethnic 02
    Political, charitable, community 03
    Union, professional 04
    Sports, cards, social 05
    Auxiliary of man's 06
    Youth, school, scouts 07
    Other *(Specify in table)* 08

58c. In what year did you join this organization?

58d. Are you presently an office holder in_____?
(name)

58e. How often do you attend meetings? Would you say . . . *(Show Card #ε. Read categories and record answer code in table for each organization.)*

    Daily 01
    Several times a week 02
    About once a week 03
    Several times a month 04
    About once a month 05
    Several times a year 06
    About once a year 07
    Less than once a year 08
    Never 09

	a. Name	b. Type	c. Year joined	d. Office holder Yes No	e. How often attending	
(1)	_____	____	12-13 ____	14-15 1 2 16	_____	17-18
(2)	_____	____	19-20 ____	21-22 1 2 23	_____	24-25
(3)	_____	____	26-27 ____	28-29 1 2 30	_____	31-32
(4)	_____	____	33-34 ____	35-36 1 2 37	_____	38-39
(5)	_____	____	40-41 ____	42-43 1 2 44	_____	45-46
(6)	_____	____	47-48 ____	49-50 1 2 51	_____	52-53

426

59. Have you changed your membership in social organizations and groups by adding or dropping groups since your late husband's death?

Yes, added organizations 1

Yes, dropped organizations 2   54

Yes, both added and dropped . . . 3

No 4

60. Since your late husband's death, would you say you have become more active, less active or maintained about the same amount of activity in organizations and groups?

More active 1

Less active 2   55

About the same *(Skip to Q.62)* 3

IF MORE OR LESS ACTIVE (CODE 1-2), ASK:

61. Why did you change your participation in social organizations and groups? Was it because . . . *(Read each category; circle one answer code for each.)*

	Yes	No	
a. The groups were for couples only	1	2	56
b. You belonged through your late husband	1	2	57
c. Of transportation	1	2	58
d. Of health	1	2	59
e. Of money	1	2	60
f. Your interests changed	1	2	61
g. You moved	1	2	62
h. The group disbanded	1	2	63
i. Of time *(Specify more or less)_____* . .	1	2	64
j. Of eligibility	1	2	65
k. You wanted to expand your activities	1	2	66
l. Of something else *(Specify)* _____			67
_____ . .	1	2	

IF REMARRIED, ALSO ASK:

	Yes	No	
m. Your present husband discouraged you	1	2	68
n. Your present husband encouraged you	1	2	69
o. Your present husband belongs	1	2	70

427

Now I would like to know some things about your work history.

62. During your marriage to your late husband, what was your <u>usual</u> employment status? Did you work . . . *(Read categories.)*

All the years of your married life . . . 1

All the years until retirement 2   71

Most of the years 3

Some of the years 4

On-and-off 5

Never *(Skip to Q.69)* 6

63. Were you working in 19__before your late husband's illness (accident)?

Yes 1   72

No *(Skip to Q.69)* 2

64. What were your reasons for working during that time? I will show you a card listing answers most frequently given by women to this question. From the card, please tell me <u>your</u> most important reason for working then. What is your second most important reason? And your third? *(Show Card #9. Obtain three reasons for working and record answer codes for each on blanks below. Be sure to record the most important reason on blank 1.)*

a. I had to support myself; no one else supported me 01
b. I had to work; I was the only breadwinner in the family 02
c. My earnings helped to better meet the needs of the family 03
d. I worked so the children could have a better life 04
e. I had chosen an occupation, and I wanted to work in it 05
f. I like my work, my job 06
g. I worked for investments such as a house, apartment, car 07
h. I didn't like housework 08
i. I thought a healthy adult should work 09
j. Working gave me independence and self-sufficiency 10
k. I liked to work because it gave me contact with people 11
l. My job gave me a feeling of achievement 12
m. Work offered me the opportunity for self-development 13
n. My husband's earnings were not enough to support the family 14

(1) _____ (2) _____ (3) _____
      73-74   75-76   77-78/BK
                                                       79-80/20
                                                       1-9/DUP

65a. What was your usual occupation or job title in 19__?

10⁻12
13⁻15

_____

65b. What were your duties on the job; that is, what kind of work
did you do?

_____

65c. In what company or industry was this? What product was produced
or service given?

_____

66. About how many hours a week were you working in 19__? . . . . _____   16-17

67. Were you usually working . . . *(Read categories.)*

Regularly 1

Seasonally 2   18

Irregularly 3

Something else *(Specify)* . . 4   19

_____

68. Did you usually work . . . *(Read categories.)*

Daytime hours 1

Evening hours 2   20

Nighttime hours 3

Rotating shifts or combinations . . 4

(Skip to Q.70)

IF NOT WORKING DURING MARRIAGE OR IN 19 — ; ASK:

69. What were your reasons for <u>not</u> working during that time? I will show you a
card listing answers most frequently given by women to this question. From
the card, please tell me <u>your</u> most important reason for not working then.
What is your second most important reason? And your third? *(Show Card # 10.*
Obtain three reasons for not working and record answer codes for each on
blanks below. Be sure to record the most important reason on blank 1.)

a. I had to take care of the children 01
b. I had to take care of other dependents 02
c. I had difficulty finding work 03
d. My health did not permit me to work 04
e. I was in school, studying 05
f. I was retired, laid off, company folded 06
g. I did not want to work 07
h. I did not like my last job, got tired of working 08
i. There was no need; my husband's earnings were sufficient 09
j. My husband did not want me to work 10
k. My husband's health kept me from working 11
l. Other *(Specify)* _____ . . . 12

(1)_____   (2)_____   (3)_____
  21-22   23-24   25-26

429

70. Have you worked at any time since your late husband's death *(IF REMARRIED:* Did you work during the time you were a widow)?

Yes *(Skip to Q.72)* 1   27

No 2

71. What were your reasons for not working during that time? From the card, please tell me your most important reason why you were not working. What is your second most important reason? And your third? *(Show Card #11. Obtain three reasons for not working and record answer codes for each on blanks below. Be sure to record the most important reason on blank 1.)*

a. I had to take care of the children 01
b. I had to take care of other dependents 02
c. I had difficulty finding work 03
d. My health did not permit me to work 04
e. I was in school, stud,ing 05
f. I was retired, laid off, company folded 06
g. I did not want to work 07
h. I did not like my last job, got tired of working 08
i. There was no need; my late husband's earnings were sufficient . . 09
j. Other *(Specify)*_____ . . . 10

(1) _____   (2)_____   (3) _____
       28-29   30-31   32-33

72a. Are you presently employed (working)?

Yes *(Skip to Q.73)* 1   34

No 2

(IF No)

72b. What are your reasons for <u>not</u> working now? From the card, what is your most important reason? What is your second most important reason? And your third? *(Show Card #12. Obtain three reasons for not working and record answer codes for each on blanks below. Be sure to record the most important reason on blank 1.)*

a. I have to take care of the children 01
b. I have to take care of other dependents 02
c. I have difficulty finding work 03
d. My health does not permit me to work 04
e. I am in school, studying 05
f. I am retired, laid off, company folded 06
g. I do not want to work 07
h. I did not like my last job, got tired of working 08
i. There is no need; my late husband's earnings are
sufficient 09
j. Other *(Specify)*_____ . . 10

IF REMARRIED, ALSO CONSIDER:

k. There is no need, my present husband's earnings are
sufficient 11
l. My present husband does not want me to work 12
m. My present husband's health keeps me from working 13

(1) _____   (2) _____   (3) _____
       35-36   37-38   39-40

430

(*If No cont.*)

72c. In what year did you leave your last job? . . . . _____   41-42

IF WORKING NOW OR WORKED SINCE WIDOWHOOD, ASK:

73. What were (are) your reasons for working(now)? From the card what is your
     most important reason? What is your second most important reason? And
     your third? *(Show Card #13. Obtain three reasons for working and record
     answer codes for each on blanks below. Be sure to record the most important
     reason on blank 1.)*

     a. I have to work to support myself, no one else supports me 01
     b. I have to work, I am the only breadwinner in the family 02
     c. My earnings help to better meet the needs of the family 03
     d. I work so that the children can have a better life 04
     e. I chose an occupation and I want to work at it 05
     f. I like my work, my job 06
     g. I work for investments such as a house, apartment, car 07
     h. I do not like housework 08
     i. I think that a healthy adult should work 09
     j. Working gives me independence and self-sufficiency 10
     k. I like to work because it gives me contact with people 11
     l. My job gives me a feeling of achievement 12
     m. Work offers me the opportunity for self-development 13

     IF REMARRIED, ALSO CONSIDER:

     n. My present husband's earnings are not enough to support the family . 14

     (1) _____   (2) _____   (3) _____
           43-44   45-46   47-48
74a. What is (was) your present (last) occupation or job title?

                                                                              49-51
     _____
                                                                              52-54

          74b. What are (were) your duties on the job; that is, what kind of
                work do (did) you do?

                _____

          74c. In what company or industry is (was) this? What product is (was)
                produced or service given?

                _____

75. How did you find this job? *(Circle as many as apply.)*
                          Employment agencies 01   55-56
                          Advertisements 02   57-58
                          A help wanted sign 03   59-60
                          A friend 04   61-62
                          A work friend of my husband 05   63-64
                          Politician 06   65-66
                          A relative 07   67-68
                          Other *(Specify)*_____ . . 08   69-70

76. About how many hours a week do (did) you work? . . . . _____   71-72

431

77. Do (Did) you usually work . . . *(Read categories.)*

7 3

Regularly 1	
Seasonally 2	
Irregularly 3	
Something else *(Specify)*	
_____ . . 4	

78. Do (Did) you usually work . . . *(Read categories.)*

Daytime hours 1	7 4
Evening hours 2	
Nighttime hours 3	
Rotating shifts or combinations . . 4	

IF NOT WORKING NOW, SKIP TO Q.80)

IF PRESENTLY EMPLOYED, ASK:

79. Now I would like to read you some statements made by many people about their work situations. Please tell me if you strongly agree, agree, disagree, or strongly disagree with each statement. *(Show Card #14. Read each statement and circle one answer code for each.)*

	Strongly agree	Agree	Disagree	Strongly disagree	*(Don't know)*	
a. Commuting to work is hard on me	1	2	3	4	8	7 5
b. My work is tiring and exhausting	1	2	3	4	8	7 6
c. My working conditions are good and pleasant	1	2	3	4	8	7 7
d. I have conflicts and misunderstandings with co-workers . .	1	2	3	4	8	7 8 79=80/21 1-9
e. My work supervisors are good	1	2	3	4	8	1 0
f. My work is properly appreciated	1	2	3	4	8	1 1
g. The place where I work is poorly organized	1	2	3	4	8	1 2
h. The people I know find my job interesting and they respect my position in it	1	2	3	4	8	1 3
i. My work brings a good and fair wage	1	2	3	4	8	1 4
j. I like my work	1	2	3	4	8	1 5
k. My work is interesting and varied	1	2	3	4	8	1 6
l. My work gives me opportunities for self-development	1	2	3	4	8	1 7

432

80a. Since becoming a widow, have you received any training or retraining to enable you to earn enough money to support a family?

$$\text{Yes} \ldots \ldots \ldots \ldots 1$$
$$\text{No } (Skip\ to\ Q.81) \ldots \ldots 2 \qquad 18$$

(If Yes)

    80b. What training or retraining did you receive? *(Record verbatim response.)*

19-20

_____

_____

_____

81a. Is there any kind of training or retraining that you <u>wish</u> you had received?

$$\text{Yes} \ldots \ldots \ldots \ldots 1$$
$$\text{No } (Skip\ to\ Q.82) \ldots \ldots 2 \qquad 21$$

(If Yes)

    81b. What training or retraining do you wish you had received? *(Record verbatim response.)*

22-23

_____

_____

_____

    81c. Why were you not able to receive this training or retraining? *(Record verbatim response.)*

24-25

_____

_____

_____

E. Present Sources of Support

82a. During the past year, 1973, did you or any members of your family living
with you receive income from any of the following sources? *(Read each
category. Circle response in table below; then go back and ask Q.82b through
d for each "Yes" answer. Record responses in table below.)*

 82b. Who received this income? Was it . . . *(Read all categories and
 record answer code(s) in table.)*

 Yourself 1
 Your children 2
 Your late husband 3
 Received jointly *(Specify with whom
 in table)* 4
 Received by someone else *(Specify who
 in table)* 5
 IF REMARRIED:
 Your present husband 6

 82c. How much has this person received during the past year? *(Record
 separately for each person specified in Q.82b.)*

 82d. How often does (did) this person receive income from this source? Would
 you say . . . *(Read categories and record answer code in table.)*

 Weekly 1
 Bi-weekly 2
 Monthly 3
 Quarterly 4
 Yearly 5
 Less than yearly 6

(If Yes)

	a. Received income No Yes	b. Person(s) receiving	c. Amount Received	d. How often received
(1) Wages and salaries	2 1 → 26	27-28	29-33	34
		35-36	37-41	42
		42-44	45-49	50
		51-52	53-57	58
(2) Rent from property, sales, special money making projects .	2 1 → 59	60-61	62-66	67
		68-69	70-74	75
		76-77 78 79-80/22	10-14	15
		1-9 16-17	18-22	23

434

	a. Received income No Yes	*(If Yes)* b. Person(s) receiving	c. Amount received	d. How often received

(3) Interest on savings, dividends, stocks, bonds . . . . 2 1→24

	25-26	27-31	32
	33-34	35-39	40
	41-42	43-47	48
	49-50	51-55	56

(4) Social security benefits such as . . .

a. Old age . . . . . . 2 1→57

	58-59	60-64	65

b. Disability . . . . . 2 1→66

	67-68	69-73	74

c. Survivor . . . . . . 2 1→75

	76-77 78	10-14	15

79-80 /23
1-9

d. Supplementary security income . . 2 1→16

	17-18	19-23	24

(5) Veteran widow's pension . . . . 2 1→25

	26-27	28-32	33
	34-35	36-40	41
	42-43	44-48	49

(6) Employee pensions *(Specify)* 2 1→50

51-53

	54-55	56-60	61

62-64

	65-66	67-71	72

73-75

	76-77	10-14	15

78
79-80 /24
1-9

(7) Private insurance . . 2 1→16

	17-18	19-23	24
	25-26	27-31	32
	33-34	35-39	40
	41-42	43-47	48

(8) Assistance or welfare, public or private *(Specify)* 2 1→49

50-52

	53-54	55-59	60

61-63

	64-65	66-70	71

72-74

	75-76 77-78	10-14	15

79-80 /25
1-9/DUP

(9) Other sources, public or private *(Specify)* 2 1→16

17-19

	20-21	22-26	27

28-30

	31-32	33-37	38

435

83a. Since the death of your late husband, have you or your children requested any Social Security Benefits?

Yes 1   39

No *(Skip to Q.84)* 2

(If Yes)

83b. What happened to this request? Was it . . . *(Read categories.)*

Approved and you are receiving benefits now 1

Approved, but you have not received benefits yet 2   40

Not approved and no further action has been taken 3

You have not been informed of a decision 4

                                41-42

You stopped receiving benefits *(Specify reason)*_____

_____ . . . 5

Something else *(Specify)*_____ . . . 6

(Don't know) 8

(Skip to Q.85)

IF NO BENEFITS REQUESTED, ASK:

84. Why haven't you requested any Social Security Benefits since the death of your late husband? Is it <u>mainly</u> because you . . . *(Read categories.)*

Have not needed benefits 1   43

Were not eligible for benefits 2

Were already receiving benefits
  before husband's death 3

Did not want to request benefits . . . 4

Something else *(Specify)*_____   44

_____ . . 5

85a. Do you know about the earnings test which determines how much money a
Social Security beneficiary can earn in wages or salaries without affecting
the amount he or she receives in Social Security benefits?

$$\text{Yes} \ldots \ldots \ldots \ldots 1$$
$$\text{No } (Skip \ to \ Q.86) \ldots \ldots 2$$

45

(If Yes)

85b. What is the yearly amount a woman of your age and family situation can earn in wages or salaries without affecting the amount of
her Social Security benefits? . . . . _____

46-50

(Don't know) 8

85c. What additional income, other than wages and salaries, affects the
amount a beneficiary can receive from Social Security? (Record
verbatim response.)

51-52

_____

(Don't know) 8

85d. How has this earnings test affected your job decisions?
(Record verbatim response.)

53-54

_____

_____

_____

(Don't know) 8

85e. How does a widow report a change in her life or the taking over
care of a child which might affect her earnings test? (Record
verbatim response.)

55-56

_____

_____

_____

(Don't know) 8

86a. Since the death of your late husband, have you or your children requested any public welfare assistance?

$$\text{Yes . . . . 1} \qquad {}_{57}$$
$$\text{No } (Skip\ to\ Q.87) \text{ . . . . . 2}$$

(If Yes)

86b. Which public welfare assistance did you request? Was it . . .
(Read each category. Circle one answer code for each.)

	Yes	No	
a. Aid to the blind or disabled	1	2	58
b. Old age assistance	1	2	59
c. Aid to families with dependent children	1	2	60
d. Something else *(Specify)* _____			
_____	1	2	61 / 62,63

86c. What happened to this request? Was it . . . *(Read categories.)*

Approved and you are receiving assistance now 1   64
Approved, but you have not received assistance yet 2
Not approved and no further action has been taken 3
You have not been informed of a decision 4
You stopped receiving benefits *(Specify reason)* _____
_____ 5   65-66
Something else *(Specify)*_____ 6
(Don't know) 8

(Skip to Q.88)

<u>IF NO ASSISTANCE REQUESTED, ASK:</u>

87. Why haven't you requested any public welfare assistance? Is it <u>mainly</u> because you . . . *(Read categories.)*

Have not needed assistance 1   67
Were not eligible for assistance 2
Were already receiving assistance before
    husband's death. 3
Did not want to request assistance 4
Something else *(Specify)* _____   68
_____ 5

438

ASK EVERYONE:

88a. Since the death of your late husband, have you or your children requested
any other kind of public or private aid?

$$Yes \ldots \ldots \ldots \ldots 1 \quad {}_{69}$$
$$No \ (Skip\ to\ Q.89) \ldots \ldots 2$$

(If Yes)

88b. What kind of aid did you or your children request? Was it . . .
(Read each category. Circle one answer code for each.)

	Yes	No	
a. Food stamps	1	2	70
b. Medicare, medicaid	1	2	71
c. Something else (Specify) ____			
_____	1	2	72/73

88c. What happened to this request? Was it . . . (Read categories.)

Approved and you are receiving aid now 1
Approved, but you have not received aid yet 2   74
Not approved and no further action has been taken . . . 3   75-76
You have not been informed of a decision . . . . . . •. . 4   77-78/BK
                                                                 79-80/26
You stopped receiving aid (Specify reason) _____   1-9/DUP
_____ 5

Something else (Specify)_____ 6
(Don't know) 8

(Skip to Q.90)

IF NO AID REQUESTED, ASK:

89. Why haven't you requested aid? Is it mainly because you . . . (Read categories.)

Have not needed aid 1
Were not eligible for aid 2   10
Were already receiving aid before
  husband's death 3
Did not want to request aid 4
Something else (Specify) _____   11
_____ 5

ASK EVERYONE:

90a. In addition to your regular income, are you presently <u>receiving</u> any of the following kinds of financial help? *(Read each category and circle responses; then go back and ask Q.90b and c for each "Yes" response obtained. Record responses in table below.)*

    (If Yes)

       90b. Who helps you? *(For person, record first name, relationship to R, and sex if not obvious.)*

       90c. How often do you get this help? Would you say . . . *(Show Card #2. Read categories and record answer code in table.)*

Daily	01
Several times a week	02
About once a week	03
Several times a month	04
About once a month	05
Several times a year	06
About once a year	07
Less than once a year	08
Never	09

	a. Received help		*(If Yes)* b. Who helped	c. How often
	No	Yes		
(1) Gifts	2	1→12	_____ 13-15 _____	16-17
			_____ 18-20 _____	21-22
			_____ 23-25 _____	26-27
(2) Payment or help on payment of your rent or mortgage	2	1→28	_____ 29-31 _____	32-33
			_____ 34-36 _____	37-38
			_____ 39-41 _____	42-43
(3) Food or payment for food . . .	2	1→44	_____ 45-47 _____	48-49
			_____ 50-52 _____	53-54
			_____ 55-57 _____	58-59
(4) Clothing or payment for clothing	2	1→60	_____ 61-63 _____	64-65
			_____ 66-68 _____	69-70
			_____ 71=73 _____	74-75 76-78
(5) Payment or help in payment of other bills such as medical or vacation expenses	2	1→10	_____ 11-13 _____	79-80/27 1-9 14-15
			_____ 16-18 _____	19-20
			_____ 21-23 _____	24-25
(6) Any other financial help (Specify) _____	2	1→26	_____ 28-30 _____	31-32
_____		27	_____ 33-35 _____	36-37
			_____ 38-40 _____	41-42

440

91a. Are you presently <u>giving</u> any of the following kinds of financial help to anyone? *(Read each category and record responses; then go back and ask Q.91b and c for each "Yes" response obtained. Record response in table below.)*

(If Yes)

> **91b.** Who are you helping? *(For persons, record first name, relationship to R, and sex if not obvious.)*

> **91c.** How often do you give this help? *(Show Card #2. Read categories and record answer code in table.)*

> Daily 01
> Several times a week 02
> About once a week 03
> Several times a month 04
> About once a month 05
> Several times a year 06
> About once a year 07
> Less than once a year 08
> Never 09

	a. Give help No / Yes	(If Yes) b. Who helped	c. How often
(1) Gifts	2 1→ ⁴³	_____ 44-46	_____ 47-48
		_____ 49-51	_____ 52-53
		_____ 54-56	_____ 57-58
(2) Payment or help in payment of your rent or mortgage . .	2 1→ ⁵⁹	_____ 60-62	_____ 63-64
		_____ 65-67	_____ 68-69
		_____ 70-72	_____ 73-74
(3) Food or payment for food . .	2 1→ ⁷⁵	_____ 76-78 79-80 /28 1-9	10-11
		_____ 12-14	_____ 15-16
		_____ 17-19	_____ 20-21
(4) Clothing or payment for clothing	2 1→ ²²	_____ 23-25	_____ 26-27
		_____ 28-30	_____ 31-32
		_____ 33-35	_____ 36-37
(5) Payment or help in payment of other bills such as medical or vacation expenses	2 1→ ³⁸	_____ 39-41	_____ 42-43
		_____ 44-46	_____ 47-48
		_____ 49-51	_____ 52-53
(6) Any other financial help (Specify)_____, _____	2 1→ ⁵⁴ 55	_____ 56-58	_____ 59-60
		_____ 61-63	_____ 64-65
		_____ 66-68	_____ 69-70

441

92a. Now I will read you a list of things people often do for each other in
daily life or in solving special problems. Does anyone do any of these
things for you? Does anyone . . . *(Read each category; circle responses; then
go ask Q.92b and c for each "Yes" response obtained. Record responses in table
below.)*

   (If Yes)

   92b. Who does this for you? *(For persons, record first name, relationship to R, and sex if not obvious.)*

   92c. How often is this done for you? Would you say . . . *(Show Card #2.
   Read categories and record answer code in table.)*

Daily	01
Several times a week	02
About once a week	03
Several times a month	04
About once a month	05
Several times a year	06
About once a year	07
Less than once a year	08
Never	09

	a. Receives this		b. Who *(If Yes)* provides	c. How often
	No	Yes		
(1) Provide transportation or drive you places	2	1→ 71	_____ 72-74	75-76 77-78 79-80/29 1-9
(2) Make minor household repairs for you	2	1→ 10	_____ 11-13	14-15
(3) Help you with housekeeping . . .	2	1→ 16	_____ 17-19	20-21
(4) Help you with shopping	2	1→ 22	_____ 23-25	26-27
(5) Help you with yard work	2	1→ 28	_____ 29-31	32-33
(6) Help you with child care	2	1→ 34	_____ 35-37	38-39
(7) Help you take care of your car	2	1→ 40	_____ 41-43	44-45
(8) Care for you when you are ill . .	2	1→ 46	_____ 47-49	50-51
(9) Help you make important decisions	2	1→ 52	_____ 53-55	56-57
(10) Provide you with legal aid . . .	2	1→ 58	_____ 59-61	62-63

442

93a. Do you do any of these things for others? Do you . . . *(Read each category and circle responses; then go back and ask Q.93b and c for each "Yes" response obtained. Record responses in table below.)*

    (If Yes)

        93b. For whom do you do these things? *(For persons; record first name, relationship to R, and sex if not obvious.)*

        93c. How often do you do this? Would you say . . . *(Show Card #2. Read categories and record answer code in table.)*

Daily	01
Several times a week	02
About once a week	03
Several times a month	04
About once a month	05
Several times a year	06
About once a year	07
Less than once a year	08
Never	09

	a. Provide this		*(If Yes)* b. For	c. How
	No	Yes	whom	often
(1) Provide transportation or drive others places	2	1→64	_____ 65-67 _____	68-69
(2) Make minor household repairs for others	2	1→70	_____ 71-73 _____	74-75 76-78 79-80 /30
(3) Help others with housekeeping	2	1→10	_____ 11-13 _____	14-15
(4) Help others with shopping	2	1→16	_____ 17-19 _____	20-21
(5) Help others with yard work	2	1→22	_____ 23-25 _____	26-27
(6) Help others with child care	2	1→28	_____ 29-31 _____	32-33
(7) Help others take care of their car . . .	2	1→34	_____ 35-37 _____	38-39
(8) Care for others when they are ill	2	1→40	_____ 41-43 _____	44-45
(9) Help others make important decisions . .	2	1→46	_____ 47-49 _____	50-51
(10) Provide others with legal aid	2	1→52	_____ 53-55 _____	56-57

443

Now I would like to know some things about your social acitivities.

94a. I will read you a list of social activities that people can do with others. Please tell me which of these activities you do. *(Read each category and circle responses; then ask Q.94b through d for each as appropriate. Record responses in table.)*

    (If Yes)

        94b. With whom do you do this? *(Record first name, relationship to R, and sex if not obvious.)*

        94c. How often do you do these things? *(Show Card #2. Record answer code in table.)*

Daily	01
Several times a week	02
About once a week	03
Several times a month	04
About once a month	05
Several times a year	06
About once a year	07
Less than once a year	08
Never	09

    (If No)

        94d. Why aren't you doing these things now? Is it mainly because of your . . . *(Read categories. Record answer code in table.)*

a. Health	1
b. Lack of money	2
c. Transportation difficulties	3
d. Lack of male escort	4
e. Lack of time or energy	5
f. Feelings and emotions	6
g. Something else *(Specify in table)*	7

	a. Does activity		(If Yes) b. With Whom	c. How often	(If No) d. Why Not
	Yes	No			
(1) Go to public places, movies theater	1	2 ⁵⁸	_____ 59-61	65	_____ 66
			_____ 62-64		_____
(2) Visit	1	2 ⁶⁷	_____ 68-70	74	_____ 75
			_____ 71-73		76-78/BK 79-80/³¹ 1-9/DUP
(3) Entertain in your home	1	2 ¹⁰	_____ 11-13	17	_____ 18
			_____ 14-16		_____
(4) Go out to lunch or eat lunch with some- one	1	2 ¹⁹	_____ 20-22	26	_____ 27
			_____ 23-25		_____
(5) Go to church. . .	1	2 ²⁸	_____ 29-31	35	_____ 36
			_____ 32-34		_____
(6) Engage in sports, cards, games . .	1	2 ³⁷	_____ 38-40	44	_____ 45
			_____ 41-43		_____
(7) Travel out of town	1	2 ⁴⁶	_____ 47-49	53	_____ 54
			_____ 50-52		_____
(8) Celebrate holidays	1	2 ⁵⁵	_____ 56-58	62	_____ 63
			_____ 59-61		_____
(9) Something else (Specify)					
_____	1	2 ⁶⁴	_____ 66-68	72	_____ 73
_____		⁶⁵	_____ 69-71		_____

445

95a. Since your late husband's death, have you had any close male friendships or relationships?

$$\text{Yes} \dots \dots \dots 1 \quad _{74}$$
$$\text{No } (Skip \text{ to } Q.100) \dots 2$$

(If Yes)

95b. How many close male friendships or relationships have you had? . . . . _____

75_76
77-78/BK
79-80/32
1-9 /DUP

96a. I would like to know some things about this friendship or relationship (these friendships or relationships). What is the first name of your (first, second, third, etc.) male friend since the death of your late husband? *(Record all names in table below; then go back and ask Q.96b through h for each as appropriate. Record responses in table below.)*

96b. In what year did you meet?

96c. Where or how did you meet? *(Record answer code in table for each friend.)*

Your past life	01
Late husband's friend or past life	02
Public place	03
Relatives or in-laws	04
Friends, neighbors	05
Children	06
Work	07
Club, church or organization	08
Other *(Specify in table)*	09

	a. Name	b. Year met	c. Where and how met	
(1)	_____ 10,11	_____ 12-14	_____	15,16
(2)	_____ 29,30	_____ 31,33	_____	34,35
(3)	_____ 48,49	_____ 50-52	_____	53,54
(4)	_____ 67,68	_____ 69-71	_____	72,73
(5)	_____	_____	_____	73,74

96d. What activities have you shared with _____?
                                            (male friend)

96e. Is this friendship or relationship a past or current one?
     (Record answer code in table.)

                                Past 1

                                Current 2

96f. How often do (did) you see _____? Would you say . . .
                                (male friend)
     (Show Card #2. Read categories and record answer code in table.)

                                Daily 01
                                Several times a week 02
                                About once a week 03
                                Several times a month 04
                                About once a month 05
                                Several times a year 06
                                About once a year 07
                                Less than once a year 08
                                Never 09

IF CURRENT RELATIONSHIP, SKIP TO Q.97.

IF PAST RELATIONSHIP, ASK:

        96g. In what year did this friendship or relationship end?

        96h. Why did this relationship end? *(Record verbatim response.)*

d. Activities shared	e. Past or current		f. How often seen	g. Year ended	h. Why ended
	17-18 19-20	21	22-23	24-26	27-28
	36-37 38-39	40	41-42	43-45	46-47
	55, 56 57, 58	59	60-61	62-64	65-66
	74, 75 76-77	78	10, 11	12-14	15-16
		79 80 33			

447

97a. Since your late husband's death, have you had the opportunity to remarry, but did <u>not</u> choose to do so?

$$\text{Yes} \ldots \ldots \ldots \ldots \ldots 1$$

$$\text{No } (Skip \ to \ Q.98) \ldots \ldots 2 \qquad 1\ 7$$

<u>(If Yes)</u>

97b. Where did you meet the last man you had the opportunity to marry?

```
Your past life . . . . . . . . . . . . 01
Husband's friend or past life  . . . . 02
Public place . . . . . . . . . . . . . 03      1 8 - 1 9
Relatives or in-laws . . . . . . . . . 04
Friends, neighbors . . . . . . . . . . 05
Children . . . . . . . . . . . . . . . 06
Work . . . . . . . . . . . . . . . . . 07
Club, church, or organization  . . . . 08
Other (Specify) _____          2 0
_____ . . 09
```

97c. Why didn't you marry this man?

```
I did not want to marry . . . . . . . . 01
He did not want to marry  . . . . . . . 02      2 1 - 2 2
I did not like some things about
   him . . . . . . . . . . . . . . . . 03
Children objected . . . . . . . . . . . 04
I didn't want to give up Social
   Security  . . . . . . . . . . . . . 05
Money . . . . . . . . . . . . . . . . . 06
Health, death . . . . . . . . . . . . . 07
Other (Specify) _____          2 3
_____ . . 08

(Don't know)  . . . . . . . . . . . . . 88
```

98. In general, how have your children felt about your male friendship(s)?
(Record verbatim response.)

_____   2 4 - 2 5

_____

_____

_____

(Not appropriate, no children) . . . 0

448

99a. At any time, have you felt it was necessary to keep your child from knowing how close a male friendship had become?

Yes 1

No 2

(Not appropriate - Skip to Q.100) 0   26

99b. Why did you feel this way? *(Record verbatim response.)*

27-28

_____

_____

_____

IF NOT REMARRIED, SKIP TO Q.104.

IF REMARRIED, ASK:

100a. Some women who have remarried feel their present marriage is different from their past marriage; others feel there is not much difference between these marriages. Would you say uour present marriage is different or not different from your past marriage?

Different 1   29

Not different *(Skip to Q.101)* . . . 2

(If Different)

100b. What do you think makes your present marriage different from your past marriage? *(Record verbatim response.)*

30-31

_____

_____

_____

(Don't know) 8

449

Now I would like to ask you about the possible advantages of a widow remarrying and the possible advantages of a widow remaining unmarried.

101a. Do you think a <u>remarried</u> widow has any advantages over a widow who does not remarry?

Yes 1

No *(Skip to Q.102)* 2

32

(If Yes)

101b. What are these advantages? *(Record verbatim response.)*

_____ 33-34

_____

_____

102a. Do you think a widow <u>who does not</u> remarry has any advantages over a remarried widow?

Yes 1

No *(Skip to Q.103)* 2

35

(If Yes)

102b. What are these advantages? *(Record verbatim response.)*

_____ 36-37

_____

_____

103. What advice would you give to a widow about remarriage? *(Record verbatim response.)*

_____ 38-39

_____

_____

(Don't know) 8

F. Background Characteristics

Now I would like to know a few more things about your background. Lets begin
with your parents. *(Ask Q.104 through 107 for mother then go back and repeat
for father.)*

ASK EVERYONE:

		Mother		Father	
104.	Where was you mother (father) born? Was it in . . . *(Read categories.)*		40		49
	This neighborhood	1	41-42	1	50-51
	The Chicago metropolitan area	2		2	
	The State of Illinois	3		3	
	Another state *(Specify)*	4 _____		4 _____	
	Another country *(Specify)*	5 _____		5 _____	
105.	Was your mother (father) born in a . . . *(Show Card #1 and read categories.)*				
	Large city (1 million or more) . . .	1		1	
	Middle-size city (250,000 – 999,999)	2	43	2	52
	Small city (50,000-249,999)	3		3	
	Small town (10,000-49,999)	4		4	
	Village or farm town (2,500-9,999). .	5		5	
	Rural or farm	6		6	
106a.	What was the last year of school your mother (father) completed?	_____	44-45	_____	53-54
106b.	What degree did she (he) receive as her (his) last degree, if any?				
	Grade school diploma	1		1	
	High school diploma	2	46	2	55
	Special diploma *(Specify)*	3 _____	47	3 _____	56
	B.A. or B.S.	4		4	
	M.A. or M.S.	5		5	
	Ph.D or other professional	6		6	
	None	7		7	

	Mother	Father

107. What was your mother's (father's)
     religious preference?

	Mother	Father
Roman Catholic	1	1
Protestant	2 48	2 57
Jewish	3	3
Other *(Specify)*	4 _____	4 _____
No preference	5	5

(Skip to Q.104)

108a. What is your religious preference?

            Roman Catholic 1
                                    58
            Protestant 2
            Jewish 3
                                    59
            Other *(Specify)* _____ 4
            No preference *(Skip to Q.109)* . . 5

108b. Are you a member of a particular congregation or parish?

            Yes 1
                              60
            No 2

108c. Do you consider yourself a practicing _____?
                                        (religion)

            Yes 1   61
            No 2

108d. How often do you attend religious services? Would you say . . .
      (Show Card #2. Read categories.)

            Daily 01
                                      62-63
            Several times a week 02
            About once a week 03
            Several times a month 04
            About once a month 05
            Several times a year 06
            About once a year 07
            Less than once a year 08
            Never 09

109. What is your racial identification?

White 1	
Negro/Black 2	64
Spanish American 3	
Asian American 4	
American Indian 5	65
Other (Specify) _____ 6	

110. What is your nationality or ethnic background? (Circle as many as apply. Probe responses such as "American", "Mixed", or "Don't know".)

English, Scotch 01	
German 02	66-67
Irish 03	
Italian 04	
Polish, Russian 05	
Mexican, Puerto Rican, other Central or South American . . . 06	
Jewish 07	
African 08	
Mixed (3 or more) 09	
Other (Specify) _____ 10	68
(Don't know) 88	

111. What languages were mostly spoken in your home during your childhood? (Circle all that apply.)

English 1	
Polish 2	69
German 3	
Italian 4	
Yiddish 5	
Spanish 6	
Other (Specify) _____	70
_____ . . 7	

112a. What was the last year of school that you completed? *(Record on blank provided.)* . . . . _____ 71-72

      112b. What degree did you receive as your last degree, if any?

                                Grade school diploma 1

                                High school diploma 2   73

                                Special diploma *(Specify)* 3

                                _____   74

                                B.A. or B.S. 4

                                M.A. or M.S. 5

                                Ph.D or other professional 6

                                None 7

113. In what year did you complete your education? . . . . _____ 75-77

                                                           78/BK

                                                     79-80/34

                                                     1-9/DUP

114a. Did you interrupt your education at any time?

                                Yes 1

                                No *(Skip to Q.115)* 2   10

     (If Yes)

     114b. Why was your education interrupted? *(Record verbatim response.)*

          _____   11-12

          _____

          _____

115a. Did you obtain any additional training after you completed your education, but before you were widowed?

> Yes 1   13
>
> No *(Skip to Q.116)* 2

(If Yes)

> 115b. What kind of training was this? Was it mostly . . . *(Read categories.)*
>
> > Adult education courses, handicraft, sports, or hobby courses 1   14
> >
> > Academic, university courses 2
> >
> > Career-specific courses, such as business school, airlines school, modeling, etc. 3
> >
> > On-the-job training 4
> >
> > Refresher courses to retrain or update skills 5
> >
> > Other special training programs *(Specify)*   15-16
> >
> > _____ . . 6
>
> 115c. In what year did you begin this additional training? . . ._____ 17-19
>
> 115d. How many months did this training last? . . . . ._____ 20-21

116. Where were you born? Were you born in . . . *(Read categories.)*

> This neighborhood *(End interview)* 1
>
> The Chicago metropolitan area *(Skip to Q.118)* . . . 2   22
>
> The State of Illinois 3
>
> Another state *(Specify)* _____ . . . 4   23-24
>
> Another country *(Specify)*_____ . . . 5

117. How old were you when you first came to live in the Chicago area? . . _____ 25-26

118. Were you born in a . . . *(Show Card #1. Read categories.)*

             Large city (1 million or more) 1

             Middle-sized city (250,000-999,999) 2   27

             Small city (50,000-249,999) 3

             Small town (10,000-49,999) 4

             Village or farm town (2,500-9,999) 5

             Rural or farm 6

That was my last question. Now I would appreciate your completing this short form. *(Hand respondent Form 2.)*

             Phone number of respondent _____

Time interview ended _____ AM / PM

G. INTERVIEWER REPORT:

119. Total length of interview: . . . . _____minutes   2∎-30

120. Total length of editing . . . . _____minutes   31-33

121a. Were there any adults present during the interview other than R?

Yes 1   34
No *(Skip to Q.122)* 2

(If Yes)

121b. How many? . . . . Number _____ _____   35

121c. Who was this (were these) person(s)? *(Record relationship to R and sex if not obvious.)*

_____   36-37

_____   38-39

_____   40-41

121d. Did any of the others present take part in the interview or did respondent seek advice or opinion from any of them?

Yes 1   42
No 2

122. Is there anything unusual about the respondent, for example, physical defects or handicaps or serious emotional disorders?

_____   43-44

_____

_____

_____

_____

_____

_____

457

123a. Respondent's dwelling:

Single family, detached 01

Single family, attached (including
row or town houses) 02   45-46

Two family 03

Three units 04

Four to six units 05

Seven to nine units 06

Ten or more units 07

Other *(Specify)* _____ . . 08

    123b. Was this in a public housing project?

Yes 1   47

No 2

124. Is respondent's dwelling better kept, the same, or not as well kept as
surrounding dwellings on the block? (This means the outside appearance
of the dwelling and the yard.)

Better kept 1

Same 2   48

Not as well kept 3

*(Please use the word-pair technique to give the following ratings on the basis
of your observation of the respondent and her home and neighborhood. Circle
one answer code for each row.)*

125. Respondent in interview situation:

Not smart . . 1	2	3	4	5	6 . . Smart	49
Friendly . . 1	2	3	4	5	6 . . Hostile	50
Slow . . 1	2	3	4	5	6 . . Quick	51
Silent . . 1	2	3	4	5	6 . . Talkative	52
Grieving . . 1	2	3	4	5	6 . . Non-grieving	53

126. Respondent's speech:

Correct . . 1 grammar	2	3	4	5	6 . . Incorrect grammar	54
Heavy regional or foreign accent . . 1	2	3	4	5	6 . . No regional or or foreign accent	55
Difficult to understand . . 1	2	3	4	5	6 . . Easy to understand	56

127. Respondent's appearance:

Well dressed . . 1	2	3	4	5	6 . . Poorly dressed	57
Neat . . 1	2	3	4	5	6 . . Sloppy	58
Young looking (Well preserved) . . 1	2	3	4	5	6 . . Old looking (wrinkled, bad posture)	59
Healthy looking . . 1	2	3	4	5	6 . . Sick looking	60

128. Respondent's home:

Neat . . 1	2	3	4	5	6 . . Disorderly	61
Dirty . . 1	2	3	4	5	6 . . Clean	62
Rich . . 1	2	3	4	5	6 . . Poor	63
Relaxed . . 1	2	3	4	5	6 . . Tense	64

129. Respondent's block (surrounding dwellings):

Well-kept dwellings . . 1	2	3	4	5	6 . . Poorly-kept dwellings	65
Littered streets (refuse, glass, etc.) . . 1	2	3	4	5	6 . . Clean streets (no refuse, glass, etc.)	66
Very poor neighborhood . . 1	2	3	4	5	6 . . Very well-to-do neighborhood	67
Mainly apartments . . 1	2	3	4	5	6 . . Mainly single dwellings	68
Open spaces (lawns, yards, space between buildings) . . 1	2	3	4	5	6 . . Crowded (no lawns, yards, space between buildings)	69
Mainly commercial and/or industrial buildings . . 1	2	3	4	5	6 . . No commercial or industrial buildings	70

130. Interviewer's signature and ID #: _____

131. Date of interview: _____

71-75
76-78/BK
79-80/35

6/27/74

459

1/74

UNIVERSITY OF ILLINOIS
SURVEY RESEARCH LABORATORY

Acting as Collecting Agent

for LOYOLA UNIVERSITY OF CHICAGO
CENTER FOR THE COMPARATIVE STUDY OF SOCIAL ROLES

ASSURANCE OF CONFIDENTIALITY -- All information you give me will be held in strict confidence, will be used only by persons engaged in and for the purpose of the survey, and will not be disclosed or released to others for any purpose. The results will be used only when combined with those of many other people.

O.M.B. No. 72-S-73013
Approval Expires December, 1974

These questions refer to you, your late husband, and your widowhood period. Please answer them even if you have remarried.

1. In your opinion, which of these roles is the most important for a woman to perform? Which is the second most important and the next. *(Please number each role according to how important you feel it is. Number one should be the most important, number two the second most important and so forth.)*

Daughter . . . . • _____
Worker, career woman . . . . • _____ 13-30
Wife . . . . • _____
Housewife . . . . • _____
Mother . . . . • _____
Member of society . . . . • _____
Member of religious group . . . . . • _____
Friend . . . . • _____
Grandmother . . . . • _____

2. How would you describe your present feelings about yourself? *(Please circle the one answer code which best describes how you feel.)*

I am the most lonely person I know 1   31

I am more lonely than most people . . . 2

I am about as lonely as most people . . 3

I am less lonely than most people . . . 4

I rarely feel lonely 5

I never feel lonely 6

3. Here are some words which people often use to describe themselves or other persons. Which answer code number comes closest to how you think your late husband fits each pair of word contrasts? *(Circle one answer code for each pair of words.)*

a. Good 1   2   3   4   5   6   7 . . . . . Bad   32

b. Useful 1   2   3   4   5   6   7 . . . . . Useless   33

c. Honest 1   2   3   4   5   6   7 . . . . . Dishonest   34

d. Superior . . . 1   2   3   4   5   6   7 . . . . . Inferior   35

e. Kind 1   2   3   4   5   6   7 . . . . . Cruel   36

f. Friendly . . . 1   2   3   4   5   6   7 . . . . . Unfriendly   37

g. Warm 1   2   3   4   5   6   7 . . . . . Cold   38

461

4. Do you strongly agree, agree, disagree, or strongly disagree with these
statements? *(Circle one answer code for each statement.)*

		Strongly agree	Agree	Disagree	Strongly disagree	
a.	My husband was an unusually good man	1	2	3	4	39
b.	My marriage was above average . .	1	2	3	4	40
c.	My husband and I were always together except for working hours .	1	2	3	4	41
d.	My husband and I felt the same way about almost everything . . .	1	2	3	4	42
e.	My husband was a very good father to our children	1	2	3	4	43
f.	Our home was an unusually happy one	1	2	3	4	44
g.	My husband had no irritating habits	1	2	3	4	45
h.	Many widows who remarry are very unhappy in this marriage	1	2	3	4	46
i.	I wish I had more friends	1	2	3	4	47
j.	I am very satisfied with the way my life is going now	1	2	3	4	48

5. As you can imagine, it is very difficult to write an interview on such a
    complicated subject as widowhood. I am sure that we have missed important
    aspects. In thinking over this interview, what additional things do you
    think we should have asked, or what should we have asked differently?

49-52
53-78/BK
79-80/ 35

That was the last question.
Thank you for your cooperation.

BIBLIOGRAPHY

Adams, Bert
  1968   *Kinship in an Urban Setting*. Chicago: Markham Publishing Co.
Adams, David
  1969   "Adjustment to Widowhood." Columbia, Missouri: University of Missouri. (Mimeographed).
Aries, Philippe
  1965   *Centuries of Childhood*. New York: Random House, Vintage Books.
Atchley, Robert C.
  1975   *Sociology of Retirement*. Cambridge, Massachusetts: Schenkman Publishing Co.
Babchuk, Nicholas and Alan P. Bates
  1963   "Primary Relations of Middle-Class Couples: A Study of Male Dominance." *American Sociological Review* 28 (June), 374–384.
Bart, Pauline B.
  1973   "Portnoy's Mother's Complaint." In Helena Z. Lopata (ed.) *Marriages and Families*. New York: D. Van Nostrand and Co., pp. 222–228.
Berardo, Felix M.
  1967   "Social Adaptation to Widowhood Among a Rural-Urban Aged Population." Washington State University, College of Agriculture, Experiment Station Bulletin 689 (December).
  1968   "Widowhood Status in the United States: Perspective on a Neglected Aspect of the Family Life-Cycle." *The Family Coordinator* 17 (July), 191–203.
  1970   "Survivorship and Social Isolation: The Case of the Aged Widower." *The Family Coordinator* 1 (January): 11–25.
Berger, Peter and Hansfried Kellner
  1970   "Marriage and the Construction of Reality: An Excercise in the Microsociology of Knowledge." In Hans Dreitzel (ed.) *Patterns of Communicative Behavior*. London: Collier-Macmillan, pp. 50–73.
Berger, Peter and Thomas Luckman
  1966   *The Social Construction of Reality*. Garden City, New York: Anchor Books, Doubleday and Co.
Bernard, Jessie
  1956   *Remarriage*. New York: Holt, Rinehart and Winston.

1973   *The Future of Marriage*. New York: Bantam Books.

1975   *Women, Wives, Mothers: Values and Options*. Chicago: Aldine Publishing Co.

Billingsley, A.

1968   *Black Families in White America*. Englewood Cliffs, New Jersey: Prentice-Hall, Inc.

Blau, Zena

1961   "Structural Constraints of Friendship in Age." *American Sociological Review* 26 (June), 429–439.

1973   *Old Age in a Changing Society*. New York: Franklin Watts.

Blauner, Robert

1966   "Death and Social Structure." *Psychiatry* 29, 378–394.

Bohannan, Paul J.

1963   *Social Anthropology*. New York: Holt, Rinehart and Winston.

Boorstin, Daniel, J.

1958   *The Americans: The Colonial Experience*. New York: Random House.

1965   *The Americans: The National Experience*. New York: Random House.

1973   *The Americans: The Democratic Experience*. New York: Random House.

Bornstein, Philip E., Paula J. Clayton, James A. Halikas, William L. Maurice and Eli Robins

1973   "The Depression of Widowhood After Thirteen Months." *British Journal of Psychiatry* 122 (May), 561–566.

Bott, Elizabeth J.

1957   *Family and Social Network*. London: Tavistock Publications, Ltd.

Breton, Raymond

1964   "Institutional Completeness of Ethnic Communities and the Personal Relations of Immigrants." *American Journal of Sociology* 70 (September), 193–205.

Brunner, Edmund

1928   *Village Communities*. New York: Doubleday, Doran and Co., Inc.

Burgess, Ernest W.

1925   "The Growth of the City." In R. E. Park and E. W. Burgess (eds.) *The City*. Chicago: University of Chicago Press.

Caine, Lynn

1974   *Widow*. New York: William Morrow and Co., Inc.

Carnegie, Dale

1936   *How to Win Friends and Influence People*. New York: Simon and Schuster.

Chafe, William H.

1972   *The American Woman: Her Changing Social, Economic and Political Roles, 1920–70*. New York: Oxford University Press.

Chevan, Albert and Henry Korson

1972   "The Widowed Who Live Alone: An Examination of Social and Demographic Factors." *Social Forces* 51 (September), 45–53.

1975   "Living Arrangements of Widows in the United States and Israel, 1960 and 1961." *Demography* 12 (August), 505–518.

Chinoy, Ely

1965   *Automobile Workers and the American Dream*. Boston: Beacon Press.

Clayton, Paula J.

1973a   "Anticipatory Grief and Widowhood." *British Journal of Psychiatry* 122 (January), 47–51.

1973b   "The Clinical Morbidity of the First Year of Bereavement: A Review." *Comprehensive Psychiatry* 14 (March/April), 151–157.

466

1975   "Weight Loss and Sleep Disturbance in Bereavement." In Bernard Schoen-
        berg et al. (eds.) *Bereavement: Its Psychosocial Aspects*. New York: Columbia
        University Press, pp. 72–77.

Coleman, Emily
1976   "Infanticide in the Early Middle Ages." In Susan Mosher Stuard (ed.)
        Women in Medieval Society. Philadelphia, Pennsylvania: University of
        Pennsylvania Press, pp. 47–70.

Cooley, Charles H.
1922   *Human Nature and the Social Order*. New York: Charles Scribner's Sons.

Cosneck, Bernard
1970   "Family Patterns of Older Widowed Jewish People." *The Family Coordinator*
        19 (October), 368–373.

Cowgill, Donald and Lowell Holmes (eds.)
1972   *Aging and Modernization*. New York: Appleton-Century-Crofts.

DeHoyos, Arturo and G. DeHoyos
1966   "The Amigo System and Alienation of the Wife in the Conjugal Mexican
        Family." In Bernard Farber (ed.) *Kinship and Family Organization*. New York:
        John Wiley and Sons, Inc., pp. 102–115.

Deutsche, Helene
1944   *The Psychology of Women*. New York: Grune and Stratton.

Dube, S. C.
1963   "Men's and Women's Roles in India: A Sociological Review." In Barbara
        Ward (ed.) *Women in New Asia*. Paris: UNESCO, pp. 174–203.

Dubin, Robert
1956   "Industrial Workers' World: A Study of the Central Life Interests of
        Industrial Workers." *Social Problems* 3 (January), 131–142.

Dulles, Foster Rhea
1965   *A History of Recreation: America Learns to Play*. New York: Appleton-
        Century-Crofts.

Durham, Mary Edith
1928   *Some Tribal Origins, Laws and Customs of the Balkans*. London: George Allen
        and Unwin, Ltd.

Dyer, Everett D.
1963   "Parenthood as a Crisis: A Re-Study." *Marriage and Family Living* 25 (May),
        196–201.

Engels, Friedrich
1958   *The Condition of the Working Class in England*. Oxford: W. D. Henderson and
        W. H. Chaloner.

Etzioni, Amitai (ed.)
1964   *Complex Organizations*. New York: Holt, Rinehart and Winston.

Evans-Pritchard, Edward Evan
1956   *Nuer Religion*. Oxford: Clarendon Press.

Farr, Fenis
1973   *Chicago: A Personal History of America's Most American City*. New York:
        Arlington House.

Farrell, Warren
1975   *The Liberated Man*. New York: Bantam Books.

Felton, Monica
1966   *A Child Widow's Story*. New York: Harcourt, Brace and World, Inc.

Fewer, Clarence
1973   "Chicago's Black Elderly." Mayor's Office for Senior Citizens, June 15 (Mimeographed).

Fortune, Red Franklin
1935   *Manus Religion: An Ethnological Study of the Manus Natives of the Admiralty Islands*. Lincoln, Nebraska: University of Nebraska Press.

Freedman, Maurice
1965   *Lineage Organization in Southeastern China*. New York: The Humanities Press.

Freidan, Betty
1963   *The Feminine Mystique*. New York: W. W. Norton.

Fromm, Erich
1947   *Escape from Freedom*. New York: Rinehard and Co.

Gans, Herbert
1962   *The Urban Villagers*. New York: The Free Press of Macmillan.

Gist, Noel P. and Sylvia Fleis Fava
1964   *Urban Society*, fifth edition. New York: Thomas Y. Crowell Co.

Glazer-Malbin, Nona (ed.)
1975   *Old Family/New Family*. New York: D. Van Nostrand and Co.

Glazer-Malbin, Nona and Helen Younelson Waehrer (eds.)
1972   *Woman in a Man-Made World*. Chicago: Rand McNally and Co.

Glick, Ira, Robert Weiss and C. Murray Parkes
1974   *The First Years of Bereavement*. New York: John Wiley and Sons, Inc.

Goffman, Erving
1967   *Interaction Ritual*. Garden City, New York: Anchor Books, Doubleday and Co.

Goldstein, Rhoda (ed.)
1971   *Black Life and Culture in the United States*. New York: Thomas Y. Crowell, Co.

Goode, William
1956   *After Divorce*. New York: The Free Press of Macmillan.
1963   *World Revolution and Family Patterns*. New York: The Free Press of Macmillan.

Gorer, Geoffrey
1967   *Death, Grief and Mourning*. Garden City, New York: Anchor Books, Doubleday and Co.

Greeley, Andrew M.
1971   "Ethnicity as in Influence on Behavior." In Otto Feinstein (ed.) *Ethnic Groups in the City*. Lexington, Massachusetts: Heath Lexington Books.

Green, Betty and Donald P. Irish (ed.)
1971   *Death Education: Preparation for Living*. Cambridge, Massachusetts: Schenkman Publishing Co.

Grusky, Oscar and George A. Miller (eds.)
1970   *The Sociology of Organizations: Basic Studies*. New York: The Free Press.

Hall, Richard
1976   *Occupations and Social Structure*. Englewood Cliffs, New Jersey: Prentice-Hall, Inc.

Harvey, Carol D. and Howard M. Bahr
1974   "Widowhood, Morale and Affiliation." *Journal of Marriage and the Family* 36 (February), 95–106.

Heilbroner, Robert L.
1973   "Economic Problems of a 'Post-Industrial Society.'" *Dissent* 20 (Spring), 163–176.

Heinemann, Gloria
1977   "Methodology." Appendix A3 in Helena Z. Lopata (ed.) *Support Systems Involving Widows in a Metropolitan Area of the United States.* Report to the Social Security Administration.

Herlihy, David
1976   "Land, Family and Women in Continental Europe, 701–1200." In Susan Mosher Stuard (ed.) *Women in Medieval Society.* Philadelphia, Pennsylvania: University of Pennsylvania Press, pp. 13–45.

Hill, Reuben
1965   "Decision Making and the Family Life-Cycle." In Ethel Shanas and Gordon Streib (eds.) *Social Structure and the Family: Generational Relations.* Englewood Cliffs, New Jersey: Prentice-Hall, Inc., pp. 113–139.

Hobbs, Daniel F. Jr.
1965   "Parenthood as Crisis: A Third Study." *Marriage and Family Living* 27 (May), 367–372.

Hochschild, Arlie Russell
1973   *The Unexpected Community.* Englewood Cliffs, New Jersey: Prentice-Hall, Inc.

Homans, George
1961   *Social Behavior: Its Elementary Forms.* New York: Harcourt, Brace and World.

Hunt, Morton
1966   *The World of the Formerly Married.* New York: McGraw-Hill.

Huntington, Suellen
1975   "Issues in Women's Roles in Economic Development: Critique and Alternatives." *Journal of Marriage and the Family* 37 (November), 1001–1012.

Jackson, Jacquelyne Johnson
1973   "Family Organization and Technology." In Kent Miller and Ralph Dreger (eds.) *Comparative Studies of Blacks and Whites in the United States.* New York: Seminar, pp. 408–445.

James, William
1900   *Psychology.* New York: Henry Holt and Co.

Jencks, Christopher et al.
1972   *Inequality.* New York: Basic Books.

Kennedy, Robert
1976   Special Tabulations from the 1/1,000 Public Use Sample of the United States Census of Population. Department of Sociology, University of Minnesota.

Kerckhoff, Alan C.
1965   "Nuclear and Extended Family Life-Cycle." In Ethel Shanas and Gordon Streib (eds.) *Social Structure and the Family: Generational Relations.* Englewood Cliffs, New Jersey: Prentice-Hall, Inc., pp. 93–112.

Kim, Gertrud, Henry Brehm and Helena Z. Lopata
1977   "Income as a Resource in the Lives of Widows." In Helena Z. Lopata et al (ed.) *Support Systems Involving Widows in a Metropolitan Area of the United States.* Report to the Social Security Administration.

Kitson, Gay C. and Marvin Sussman
1977   "Marital Complaints, Demographic Characteristics and Symptoms of Men-

tal Distress among the Divorcing." Paper presented at Midwest Sociological Society meeting, Minneapolis, Minnesota.

Komarovsky, Mirra
1953   *Women in the Modern World: Their Education and Their Dilemmas.* Boston: Little, Brown and Co.
1967   *Blue-Collar Marriage.* New York: Random House.
1976   *Dilemmas in Masculinity: A Study of College Youth.* New York: W.W. Norton.

Kreis, Bernadine
1975   *To Love Again.* New York: The Seabury Press.

Kreis, Bernadine and Alice Pattie
1969   *Up From Grief.* New York: The Seabury Press.

Kubler-Ross, Elizabeth
1977   *Death: The Final Stage of Growth.* Englewood Cliffs, New Jersey: Prentice-Hall, Inc.

La Pierre, Richard
1959   *The Freudian Ethic.* New York: Duell, Sloan and Pierce.

Laslett, Peter
1973   *The World We Have Lost,* second edition. New York: Charles Scribner's Sons.

Laslett, Peter and Richard Wall
1972   *Household and Family in Past Time.* Cambridge, Massachusetts: University Press.

LeMasters, E. E.
1957   "Parenthood as Crisis." *Marriage and Family Living* 19 (November), 352–355.

Leslie, Gerald
1967   *The Family in Social Context.* New York: Oxford University Press.

Lindemann, Eric
1944   "Symptomology and Management of Acute Grief." *American Journal of Psychiatry* 101 (July), 141–148.

Little, Roger W.
1970   "Buddy Relations and Combat Performance." In Oscar Grusky and George A. Miller (eds.) *The Sociology of Organizations: Basic Studies.* New York: The Free Press of Macmillan, pp. 361–375.
forth- "Friendship in the Military Community." In Helena Z. Lopata (ed.)
coming *The Interweave of Social Roles: Friendship.* New York: JAI Press.

Litwak, Eugene
1959–   "The Use of Extended Family Groups in the Achievement of Social Goals:
1960   Some Policy Implications. *Social Problems* 7 (Winter), 177–187.
1960a   "Occupational Mobility and Extended Family Cohesion." *American Sociological Review* 25 (February), 9–21.
1960b   "Geographical Mobility and Extended Family Cohesion." *American Sociological Review* 25 (June), 385–394.
1965   "Extended Kin Relations in an Industrial Democratic Society." In Ethel Shanas and Gordon Streib (eds.) *Social Structure and the Family: Generational Relations.* Englewood Cliffs, New Jersey: Prentice-Hall, Inc., pp. 290–323.

Lobodzinska, Barbara
1970   *Malzenstwo w Miescie.* Warszawa, Pnastwowe: Wydawnictwo Naukowe.
1974   *Rodzina w Polsce.* Warszawa: Sydawnictwo Interpress.

Lopata, Helena Znaniecki
1966 "The Life Cycle of the Social Role of Housewife." *Sociology and Social Research* 51 (October), 6–22.
1969 "Social Psychological Aspects of Role Involvement." *Sociology and Social Research* 58 (April), 285–298.
1971a *Occupation: Housewife.* New York: Oxford University Press.
 "Living Arrangements of Urban Widows and their Married Children." *Sociological Focus* 5 (Autumn), 41–61.
1972 "Role Changes in Widowhood: A World Perspective." In Donald Cowgill and Lowell Holmes (eds.) *Aging and Modernization.* New York: Appleton-Century-Crofts, pp. 275–304.
1973a *Widowhood in an American City.* Cambridge, Massachusetts: Schenkman Publishing Co.
1973b "Loneliness: Forms and Components." In Robert S. Weiss (ed.) *Loneliness: The Experience of Emotional and Social Isolation.* Cambridge, Massachusetts: The MIT Press, pp. 102–115.
1973c "Self-Identity in Marriage and Widowhood." *Sociological Quarterly* 14 (Summer), 407–418.
1975a ""Couple-Companionate Relations: Wives and Widows." In Nona Glazer-Malbin (ed.) *Old Family/New Family.* New York: D. Van Nostrand and Co., pp. 119–149.
1975b "Grief Work and Identity Reconstruction." *Journal of Geriatric Psychiatry* 31 (November), 41–55.
1976a *Polish Americans: Status Competition in an Ethnic Community.* Englewood Cliffs, New Jersey: Prentice-Hall, Inc.
1976b "Polish American Family Life." In Charles Mindel and Robert Habenstein (eds.) *Ethnic Families in America.* New York: Elsevier Publishing Company, pp. 15–40.
1977a *Support Systems Involving Widows in a Metropolitan Area of the United States.* Report to the Social Security Administration.
1977b "The Meaning of Friendship in Widowhood." In Lillian Troll et al. (eds.) *Looking Ahead.* Englewood Cliffs, New Jersey: Prentice-Hall, Inc., pp. 93–105.
Lopata, Helena Z. and Joseph R. Noel
1967 "The Dance Studio: Style without Sex." *Transaction/Society* 5 (January–February), 35–42.
Lopata, Helena Z. and Kathleen Norr
1974 "Changing Commitments of Women to Work and Family Roles." Proposal for study, Social Security Administration.
Lopata, Helena Z. and Frank Steinhart
1971 "Work Histories of American Urban Women." *Gerontologist* 11 (Winter), 27–36.
Lowenthal, Marjorie and C. Haven
1968 "Interaction and Adaptation: Intimacy as a Critical Variable." *American Sociological Review* 33 (February), 20–30.
Lundberg, Ferdinand and Marynia F. Farnham
1947 *Modern Woman: The Lost Sex.* New York: Harper and Bros.
McKaine, Walter C.
1969 *Retirement Marriage.* Chicago: University of Chicago Press.

Maddison, David and Beverly Raphael
1973   "Conjugal Bereavement and the Social Network." Paper given at the meetings of the Foundation of Thanatology, New York.

Maddison, David and Wendy L. Walker
1967   "Factors Affecting the Outcome of Conjugal Bereavement." *British Journal of Psychiatry* 113 (October), 1057–1067.

Maines, David
forth-   "The Context of Friendship Among Postdoctoral Researchers."
coming   In Helena Z. Lopata (ed.) *The Interweave of Social Roles: Friendship.* New York: JAI Press.

Mallen, Lucy B.
1975   "Young Widows and Their Children: A Comparative Report." *Social Security Bulletin,* Publication No. (SSA) 75-11700 (May): 3–21.

Marris, Peter
1958   *Widows and Their Families.* London: Routledge and Kegan Paul, Ltd.

Masson, Margaret W.
1976   "The Typology of Female as Model for the Regenerate: Puritan Preaching, 1690–1930." *Signs* 2 (Winter), 304–315.

Mead, George Herbert
1934   *Mind, Self and Society.* Chicago: University of Chicago Press.

Mead, Margaret
1930   *Growing up in New Guinea: A Comparative Study of Primitive Education.* New York: William Morrow and Co., Inc.

Millet, Kate
1970   *Sexual Politics.* Garden City, New York: Doubleday and Co.

Mills, C. Wright
1956   *White Collar: The American Middle Class.* New York: Oxford University Press.

Mostwin, Danuta
1972   "The Transplanted Family, A Study of Social Adjustment of the Polish Immigrant Family to the United States After the Second World War." University Microfilms, Ann Arbor, Michigan.

Moynihan, Daniel P.
1965   *The Negro Family: The Case for National Action.* Washington, D.C.: Office of Policy Planning and Research, United States Department of Labor.

Murdock, George Peter
1949   *Social Structure.* New York: Macmillan.

Murstein, William I.
1974   *Love, Sex and Marriage Through the Ages.* New York: Springer Publishing Co.

Nelson, Catherine
forth-   "Friendship in the Prison Community." In Helena Z. Lopata (ed.) *The*
coming   *Interweave of Social Roles: Friendship.* New York: JAI Press.

Nelson, Joel J.
1966   "Clique Contacts and Family Orientation in the Nuclear Family." *American Sociological Review* 31 (October), 663–672.

Neugarten, Bernice
1968   *Middle Age and Aging.* Chicago: University of Chicago Press.

Newcomb, Theodore M.
1961   *The Acquaintance Process.* New York: Holt, Rinehart and Winston.

472

Novak, Michael
   1972   *The Rise of the Unmeltable Ethnics: Politics and Culture in the Seventies*. New York: Macmillan.

Nye, Ivan F. and Felix M. Berardo
   1973   *The Family*. New York: Macmillan.

Oakley, Ann
   1975   *Women's Work*. New York: Vintage Books.

Obidinski, Eugene Edward
   1968   "Ethnic to Status Group: A Study of Polish Americans in Buffalo." University Microfilms, Ann Arbor, Michigan.

Opperman, Paul
   1970   "Note to the Reader." *Suburban Factbook*, Northeastern Illinois Metropolitan Area Planning Commission, Chicago.

Orbach, Harold L. and Eugene A. Friedmann
   1974   "Adjustment to Retirement." In S. Arieti (ed.) *American Handbook of Psychiatry*, Vol. 1, second edition. New York: Basic Books, pp. 601–645.

Origo, Iris
   1957   *The Merchant of Prato: Francesco di Marco Datini*. New York: Alfred A. Knopf.

Oxford Universal Dictionary
   1955   Third edition, revised with addenda. New York: Oxford University Press.

Parkes, C. Murray
   1964   "Effects of Bereavement on Physical and Mental Health, A Study of the Medical Records of Widows." *British Medical Journal* 2 (August), 274–279.
   1965   "Bereavement and Mental Illness: A Clinical Study." *British Journal of Medical Psychology* 38 (March), 1–26.

Parsons, Talcott
   1943   "The Kinship System on the Contemporary United States." *American Anthropologist* 34 (January–March), 22–38.

Parsons, Talcott and R. Bales
   1955   *The Family and Socialization*. Glencoe, Illinois: The Free Press.

Peterson, James A. and Michael P. Briley
   1977   *Widows and Widowhood: A Creative Approach to Being Alone*. New York: Association Press.

Phares, E. J.
   1976   *Focus of Control in Personality*. Morristown, New Jersey: General Learning Press.

Philblad, Terence and Howard Rosencranz
   1968   *Old People in the Small Town*. Columbia, Missouri: University of Missouri.

Pleck, Joseph H.
   1975   "Man to Man: Is Brotherhood Possible?" In Nona Glazer-Malbin (ed.) *Old Family/New Family*. New York: D. Van Nostrand and Co., pp. 229–244.

Pleck, Joe and Jack Sawyer
   1974   *Men and Masculinity*. Englewood Cliffs, New York: Prentice-Hall, Inc.

Random House Dictionary of the English Language
   1966   New York: Random House.

Rees, W. Dewi
   1975   "The Bereaved and Their Hallucinations." In Bernard Schoenberg et al. (eds.) *Bereavement: Its Psychosocial Aspects*. New York: Columbia University Press, pp. 66–71.

Reeves, Nancy
1971   *Womankind: Beyond the Stereotypes.* Chicago: Aldine Publishing Co.
Riesman, David, Nathan Glazer and Vevel Denney
1955   *The Lonely Crowd.* New Haven, Connecticut: Yale University Press.
Ritzer, George
1976   *Working: Conflict and Change.* Englewood Cliffs, New Jersey: Prentice-Hall, Inc.
Rosenmeyer, Leopold and Eva Kockeis
1963   "Propositions for a Sociological Theory of Aging and the Family." *International Social Science Journal* 15 (Issue #3), 410–426.
Rosow, Irving
1967   *The Social Integration of the Aged.* New York: The Free Press of Macmillan.
Ross, Arlene
1961   *The Hindu Family in Its Urban Setting.* Toronto: The University of Toronto Press.
Rossi, Peter and Andrew M. Greeley
1968   *The Education of Catholic Americans.* New York: Anchor Books, Doubleday and Co.
Rubin, Lillian Breslow
1976   *Worlds of Pain: Life in the Working-Class Family.* New York: Basic Books.
Sandberg, Carl
1916   *Chicago Poems.* New York: H. Holt Publishing.
Sarasvati, Pundita Ramatai
1888   *The High-Caste Hindu Woman.* Philadelphia, Pennsylvania: The James B. Rodgers Printing Co.
Scanzoni, Letha and John Scanzoni
1976   *Men, Women and Change.* New York: McGraw-Hill.
Schoenberg, Bernard et al.
1970   *Bereavement: Its Psychosocial Aspects.* New York: Columbia University Press.
Schramm, Louis M. J.
1954   "The Mongours of the Kansu-Tibetan Frontier." *Transactions of the American Philosophical Society* 44 (April), 1–38.
Sennett, Richard
1970   *Families Against the City.* Cambridge, Massachusetts: Harvard University Press.
1973a   "Genteel Backlash: Chicago 1886." In Helena Z. Lopata (ed.) *Marriages and Families.* Cambridge, Massachusetts: D. Van Nostrand and Co., pp. 70–80.
1973b   "The Brutality of Modern Families." In Helena Z. Lopata (ed.) *Marriages and Families.* Cambridge, Massachusetts: D. Van Nostrand and Co., pp. 70–80.
Shanas, Ethel
1962   *The Health of Older People.* Cambridge, Massachusetts: Harvard University Press.
Shanas, Ethel and Gordon Streib (eds.)
1965   *Social Structure and the Family: Generational Relations.* Englewood Cliffs, New Jersey: Prentice-Hall, Inc.
Shanas, E hel et al.
1968   *Old People in Three Industrial Societies.* New York: Atherton Press.
Shorter, Edward
1975   *The Making of the Modern Family.* New York: Basic Books.

Sicherman, Barbara
1975   "Review Essay: American History." *Signs* 1 (Winter), 462–485.
Siedan, Anne M. and Pauline B. Bart
1975   "Woman to Woman: Is Sisterhood Possible?" In Nona Glazer-Malbin (ed.) *Old Family/New Family*. New York: D. Van Nostrand and Co., pp. 189–229.
Silverman, Phyllis
1972   "Widowhood and Preventative Intervention." *The Family Coordinator* 21 (January), 95–102.
Simmel, Georg
1950   *Sociology of Georg Simmel*. Glencoe, Illinois: The Free Press.
Smith, Adam
1953   *The Theory of Moral Sentiments*. London: Henry G. Bhon.
Smutz, Robert W.
1959   *Women and Work in America*. New York: Columbia University Press.
Spectorsky, A. C.
1955   *The Exurbanites*. Philadelphia: J. B. Lippincott Co.
Staples, Robert
1971   *The Black Family: Essays and Studies*. Belmont, California: Wadsworth Publishing Co.
Starr, Joyce R. and Donale E. Carnes
1973   "Singles in the City." In Helena Z. Lopata (ed.) *Marriages and Families*. Cambridge, Massachusetts: D. Van Nostrand and Co., pp. 154–161.
Stein, Maurice
1960   *The Eclipse of Community*. Princeton, New Jersey: Princeton University Press.
Steinhart, Frank
1975   The Social Correlates of Working Widows." Paper presented at the Midwest Sociological Society meeting, Chicago.
1977   "Labor Force Participation as a Resource." Chapter in Helena Z. Lopata *Support Systems Involving Widows in a Metropolitan Area of the United States*. Report to the Social Security Administration.
Streib, George F. and C. J. Schneider
1971   *Retirement in American Society: Impact and Process*. Ithaca, New York: Cornell University Press.
Stuard, Susan Mosher (ed.)
1976   *Women in Medieval Society*. Philadelphia, Pennsylvania: University of Pennyslvania Press.
Sussman, Marvin
1962   "The Isolated Nuclear Family: Fact or Fiction." In Robert Winch et al. (eds.) *Selected Studies in Marriage and the Family*. New York: Holt, Rinehart and Winston, pp. 49–57.
1965   "Relationships of Adult Children with Their Parents in the United States." In Ethel Shanas and Gordon Streib (eds.) *Social Structure and the Family: Generational Relations*. Englewood Cliffs, New Jersey: Prentice-Hall, Inc., pp. 62–92.
Sussman, Marvin and Lee Burchinal
1966   "Kin Family Network: Unheralded Structure in Current Conceptualization of Family Functioning." In Bernard Farber (ed.) *Kinship and Family Organization*. New York: John Wiley and Sons, Inc., pp. 123–133.

475

Sussman, Marvin, Judith N. Cates and David T. Smith
1970   *The Family and Inheritance*. New York: Russell Sage Foundation.
Thomas, P.
1964   *Indian Women Through the Ages*. New York: Asia Publishing House.
Thomas, W. I. and Florian Znaniecki
1918-   *The Polish Peasant in Europe and America*. New York: Alfred A. Knopf.
1920
Tocqueville, Alexis de
1835   *Democracy in America*.
Townsend, Peter
1957   *The Family Life of Old People*. London: Routledge and Kegan Paul, Ltd.
1968   "Isolation, Desolation and Loneliness." In Ethel Shanas et al. *Old People in Three Industrial Societies*. New York: Atherton Press, pp. 163–187.
Troll, Lillian, Joan Israel and Kenneth Israel (eds.)
1977   *Looking Ahead*. Englewood Cliffs, New Jersey: Prentice-Hall, Inc.
Turowski, Jan and Lili Maria Szwengrub (eds.)
1976   *Rural Social Change in Poland*. Warwaw: Ossolineum.
U. S. Bureau of the Census
1960   *Historical Statistics of the United States, Colonial Times to 1957*. Washington, D.C.: U.S. Government Printing Office.
1971   *Current Population Reports*. Series P-23. Washington, D.C.: U.S. Government Printing Office.
1971   *Detailed Characteristics*. Washington, D.C.: U.S. Government Printing Office.
1972   *Marital Statistics*. PC (2)-4C. Washington, D.C.: U.S. Government Printing Office.
1976   *Statistical Abstract of the United States*. Washington, D.C.: U.S. Government Printing Office.
U.S. Department of Health, Education and Welfare
1973   *Remarriages, United States*. DHEW Publication No. (HRA) 74-1903, Series 21, no. 25. Washington, D.C.: U.S. Government Printing Office.
U.S. Department of Labor, Women's Bureau
1975   *Handbook on Women Workers*. Bulletin 297. Washington, D.C.: U.S. Government Printing Office.
U.S. News and World Report
1974   "The Plight of America's Two Million Widowers." 15 (April), 59–60.
Veblen, Thorstein
1953   *The Theory of the Leisure Class*. New York: The New American Library.
Vernon, Glenn M.
1970   *The Sociology of Death*. New York: The Ronald Press Co.
Walter, Sue Sheridan
1976   "Widow and Ward: The Feudal Law of Child Custody in Medieval England." In Susan Mosher Stuard (ed.) *Women in Medieval Society*. Philadelphia, Pennsylvania: University of Pennsylvania Press, pp. 159–172.
Ward, Barbara (ed.)
1963   *Women in New Asia*. Paris: UNESCO.
Warshay, Leon
1962   "Breadth of Perspectives." In Arnold Rose (ed.) *Human Behavior and Social Processes*. Boston: Houghton Mifflin, pp. 148–176.

Weber, Max
    1930   *The Protestant Ethic and the Spirit of Capitalism*. London: George Allen and Unwin, Ltd.

Weiner, Alfred, Irwin Gerber, Delia Battin and Arthur Arkin
    1975   "The Process and Phenomenology of Bereavement." In Bernard Schoenberg et al. (eds.) *Bereavement: Its Psychosocial Aspects*. New York: Columbia University Press, pp. 53–65.

Weiss, Robert S.
    1973   *Loneliness: The Experience of Emotional and Social Isolation*. Cambridge, Massachusetts: The MIT Press.

Whyte, William H. Jr.
    1956   *The Organization Man*. New York: Simon and Schuster.

Wilmott, Peter and Michael Young
    1960   *Family and Class in a London Suburb*. London: Routledge and Kegan Paul, Ltd.

Winch, Robert
    1963   *Identification and the Modern Family*. New York: Holt, Rinehart and Winston.

Winch, Robert F. and Rae Lesser Blumberg
    1968   "Social Complexity and Family Organization." In Robert F. Winch and Louis Wold Goodman (eds.) *Selected Studies in Marriage and the Family*. New York: Holt, Rinehart and Winston, Inc., pp. 70–92.

Wirth, Louis
    1938   "Urbanism as a Way of Life." *American Journal of Sociology* 44: 1–25.

Wirth, Louis and Eleanor H. Bernert
    1949   *Local Community Fact Book of Chicago*. Chicago: University of Chicago Press.

Woodward, John and Harriette Woodward
    1972   "Loneliness Among the Elderly." Paper presented at the Ninth International Congress of Gerontology, Kiev, U.S.S.R.

Wylie, Phillip
    1955   *Generation of Vipers*. New York: Holt, Rinehart and Winston, Inc.

Young, Michael and Peter Wilmott
    1957   *Family and Kinship in East London*. New York: The Free Press of Macmillan.

Znaniecki, Florian
    1952   *Modern Nationalities*. Urbana, Illinois: University of Illinois Press.

    1965   *Social Relations and Social Roles*. San Francisco: Chandler Publishing Co.

Zorbaugh, Harvey
    1929   *The Gold Coast and the Slum: Chicago*. Chicago: University of Chicago Press.

Index

479

480